William Young Sellar

The Roman poets of the republic

William Young Sellar

The Roman poets of the republic

ISBN/EAN: 9783742862488

Manufactured in Europe, USA, Canada, Australia, Japa

Cover: Foto ©ninafisch / pixelio.de

Manufactured and distributed by brebook publishing software (www.brebook.com)

William Young Sellar

The Roman poets of the republic

CONTENTS.

CHAPTER I.

GENERAL CHARACTER OF ROMAN POETRY.

	PAGE
Recent change in the estimate of Roman Poetry	1
Want of originality	2
As compared with Greek Poetry	3
,, ,, with Roman Oratory and History	4
The most complete literary monument of Rome	5
Partly imitative, partly original	6
Imitative in forms	7
,, in metres	8
Imitative element in diction	9
,, ,, in matter	11
Original character, partly Roman, partly Italian	13
National spirit	14
Imaginative sentiment	15
Moral feeling	16
Italian element in Roman Poetry	17
Love of Nature	17
Passion of Love	19
Personal element in Roman Poetry	20
Four Periods of Roman Poetry	24
Character of each	24
Conclusion	26

CHAPTER II.

VESTIGES OF INDIGENOUS POETRY IN ROME AND ANCIENT ITALY.

Niebuhr's theory of a Ballad – Poetry	28
The Saturnian metre	29
Ritual Hymns	31
Prophetic verses	33
Fescennine verses	34

	PAGE
Saturae	35
Gnomic verses	36
Commemorative verses	37
Inferences as to their character	38
From early state of the language	39
No public recognition of Poetry	40
Roman story result of tradition and reflection	41
Inferences from the nature of Roman religion	43
From the character and pursuits of the people	44
Roman Poetry of Italian rather than Roman origin	45

FIRST PERIOD.

FROM LIVIUS ANDRONICUS TO LUCILIUS.

CHAPTER III.

BEGINNING OF ROMAN LITERATURE. LIVIUS ANDRONICUS, CN. NAEVIUS, 240–202 B.C.

Contact with Greece after capture of Tarentum	47
First period of Roman literature	49
Forms of Poetry during this period	50
Livius Andronicus	51
Cn. Naevius, his life	52
Dramas	55
Epic poem	57
Style	59
Conclusion	60

CHAPTER IV.

Q. ENNIUS, 239–170 B.C., LIFE, TIMES, AND PERSONAL TRAITS. VARIOUS WORKS. GENIUS AND INTELLECT.

Importance of Ennius	62
Notices of his life	63
Influences affecting his career	64
Italian birth-place	64
Greek education	65
Service in Roman army	66
Historical importance of his age	68
Intellectual character of his age	69
Personal traits	71
Description of himself in the Annals	72
Intimacy with Scipio	74
His enthusiastic temperament	75
Religious spirit and convictions	77

CONTENTS. xi

	PAGE
Miscellaneous works	78
Saturae	81
Dramas	83
Annals	87
Outline of the Poem	88
Idea by which it is animated	91
Artistic defects	93
Roman character of the work	94
Contrast with the Greek Epic	95
Contrast in its personages	95
Contrast in supernatural element	96
Oratory in the Annals	97
Description and imagery	99
Rhythm and diction	101
Chief literary characteristics of Ennius	105
Energy of conception	106
Patriotic and imaginative sentiment	109
Moral emotion	111
Practical understanding	113
Estimate in ancient times	115
Disparaging criticism of Niebuhr	117
Conclusion	118

CHAPTER V.

EARLY ROMAN TRAGEDY. M. PACUVIUS, 219–129 B.C.
L. ACCIUS, 170–ABOUT 90 B.C.

Popularity of early Roman Tragedy	120
Partial adaptation of Athenian drama	121
Inability to reproduce its pure Hellenic character	123
Nearer approach to the spirit of Euripides than of Sophocles	125
Grounds of popularity of Roman Tragedy	127
Moral tone and oratorical spirit	129
Causes of its decline	132
M. Pacuvius, notices of his life	134
Ancient testimonies	135
His dramas	136
Passages illustrative of his thought	137
Of his moral and oratorical spirit	139
Descriptive passages	141
Drama on a Roman subject	142
Character	142
L. Accius, notices of his life	143
His various works	145
Fragments illustrative of his oratorical spirit	147
,, ,, of his moral fervour	148
,, ,, of his sense of natural beauty	149
Conclusion as to character of Roman Tragedy	150

CHAPTER VI.

ROMAN COMEDY. T. MACCIUS PLAUTUS, ABOUT 254 TO 184 B.C.

	PAGE
Flourishing era of Roman Comedy	152
How far any claim to originality?	153
Disparaging judgment of later Roman critics	154
Connection with earlier Saturae	155
Naevius and Plautus popular poets	156
Facts in the life of Plautus	157
Attempt to fill up the outline from his works	159
Familiarity with town-life	160
Traces of maritime adventure	161
Life of the lower and middle classes represented in his plays	162
Love of good living	163
Love of money	164
Artistic indifference	165
Knowledge of Greek	165
Influence of the spirit of his age	166
Dramas adaptations of outward conditions of Athenian New Comedy	167
Manner and spirit, Roman and original	171
Indications of originality in his language	172
,, ,, in his Roman allusions and national characteristics	173
Favourite plots of his plays	176
Pseudolus, Bacchides, Miles Gloriosus, Mostellaria	177
Aulularia, Trinummus, Menaechmi, Rudens, Captivi, Ampitryo	180
Mode of dealing with his characters	188
Moral and political indifference of his plays	189
Value as a poetic artist	193
Power of expression by action, rhythm, diction	194

CHAPTER VII.

TERENCE AND THE COMIC POETS SUBSEQUENT TO PLAUTUS.

Comedy between the time of Plautus and Terence	201
Caecilius Statius	202
Scipionic Circle	203
Complete Hellenising of Roman Comedy	204
Conflicting accounts of life of Terence	205
Order in which his Plays were produced	206
His 'prologues' as indicative of his individuality	207
'Dimidiatus Menander'.	209
Epicurean 'humanity' chief characteristic	210
Sentimental motive of his pieces	211
Minute delineations of character	212
Diction and rhythm	214
Influence on the style and sentiment of Horace	215
Comoedia Togata, Atellanae, Mimus	216

CHAPTER VIII.

EARLY ROMAN SATIRE. C. LUCILIUS, DIED 102 B.C.

	PAGE
Independent origin of Roman satire	217
Essentially Roman in form and spirit	219
„ „ in its political and censorial function	220
Personal and miscellaneous character of early satire	222
Critical epoch at which Lucilius appeared	223
Question as to the date of his birth	224
Fragments chiefly preserved by grammarians	227
Miscellaneous character and desultory treatment of subjects	228
Traces of subjects treated in different books	229
Impression of the author's personality	230
Political character of Lucilian satire	232
Social vices satirised in it	233
Intellectual peculiarities	236
Literary criticism	238
His style	240
Grounds of his popularity	243

CHAPTER IX.

REVIEW OF THE FIRST PERIOD.

Common aspects in the lives of poets in the second century B.C.	247
Popular and national character of their works	250
Political condition of the time reflected in its literature	251
Defects of the poetic literature in form and style	253
Other forms of literature cultivated in that age	254
Oratory and history	255
Familiar letters	256
Critical and grammatical studies	257
Summary of character of the first period	258

SECOND PERIOD.

THE CLOSE OF THE REPUBLIC.

CHAPTER X.

TRANSITION FROM LUCILIUS TO LUCRETIUS.

Dearth of poetical works during the next half century	263
Literary taste confined to the upper classes	265
Great advance in Latin prose writing	266
Influence of this on the style of Lucretius and Catullus	267

Closer contact with the mind and art of Greece	268
Effects of the political unsettlement on the contemplative life and thought	270
„ on the life of pleasure, and the art founded on it	271
The two representatives of the thought and art of the time	272

CHAPTER XI.

LUCRETIUS. PERSONAL CHARACTERISTICS.

Little known of him from external sources	274
Examination of Jerome's statement	275
Inferences as to his national and social position	281
Relation to Memmius	282
Impression of the author to be traced in his poem	283
Influence produced by the action of his age	284
Minute familiarity with Nature and country life	286
Spirit in which he wrote his work	288
His consciousness of power and delight in his task	289
His polemical spirit	291
Reverence for Epicurus	292
Affinity to Empedocles	293
Influence of other Greek writers	295
„ of Ennius	297
His interests speculative, not national	298
His Roman temperament	299

CHAPTER XII.

THE PHILOSOPHY OF LUCRETIUS.

Three aspects of the poem	300
General scope of the argument	301
Analysis of the poem	303
Question as to its unfinished condition	313
What is the value of the argument?	316
Weakness of his science	317
Interest of the work as an exposition of ancient physical enquiry	325
„ from its bearing on modern questions	326
Power of scientific reasoning, observation, and expression	327
Connecting links between his philosophy and poetry	333
Idea of law	333
„ of change	336
„ of the infinite	339
„ of the individual	340
„ of the subtlety of Nature	341
„ of Nature as a living power	342

CHAPTER XIII.

THE RELIGIOUS ATTITUDE AND MORAL TEACHING OF LUCRETIUS.

	PAGE
General character of Greek epicureanism	348
Prevalence at Rome in the last age of the Republic	350
New type of epicureanism in Lucretius	352
Forms of evil against which his teaching was directed	355
Superstition	356
Fear of death	361
Ambition	366
Luxury	367
Passion of love	368
Limitation of his ethical views	370
His literary power as a moralist	374

CHAPTER XIV.

THE LITERARY ART AND GENIUS OF LUCRETIUS.

Artistic defects of the work	376
,, arising from the nature of the subject	377
,, from inequality in its execution	378
Intensity of feeling pervading the argument	380
Cumulative force in his rhythm	381
Qualities of his style	382
Freshness and sincerity of expression	383
Imaginative suggestiveness and creativeness	385
Use of analogies	387
Pictorial power	389
Poetical interpretation of Nature	390
Energy of movement in his descriptions	391
Poetic aspect of Nature influenced by his philosophy	393
Poetical interpretation of life	395
Modern interest of the poem	397

CHAPTER XV.

CATULLUS.

Contrast to the poetry of Lucretius	399
The poetry of youth	400
Accidental preservation of his poems	401
Principle of their arrangement	402
Vivid personal revelation afforded by them	404
Uncertainty as to the date of his birth	405

	PAGE
Birth-place and social standing	408
Influences of his native district	410
Identity of Lesbia and Clodia	412
Poems written between 61 and 57 B.C.	414
Poems connected with his Bithynian journey	418
Poems written between 56 and 54 B.C.	421
Character of his poems, founded on the passion of love	424
,, ,, ,, on friendship and affection	426
His short satirical pieces	430
Other poems expressive of personal feeling	437
Qualities of style in these poems	438
,, of rhythm	439
,, of form	440
The Hymn to Diana	441
His longer and more purely artistic pieces	442
His Epithalamia	443
His Attis	447
The Peleus and Thetis	448
The longer elegiac poems	455
Rank of Catullus among the poets of the world	457

CORRIGENDA ET ADDENDA.

Page xii, line 25 from top, *for* Ampitryo *read* Amphitryo.
,, 43, note, *for* Altus *read* Attus.
,, 90, line 26 from top, *for* Fos *read* Flos.
,, 157, note 2, add the words, 'Terence, who was by birth a foreigner, was probably brought to Rome as a child.'
,, 194, line 25 from top, *for* The Italian liveliness, &c., made them, *read* Their liveliness, &c., made the Italians.
,, 194, third line from bottom, *for* nisim *read* nisam.
,, 213, line 12 from top, *for* Æschylus *read* Æschinus.
,, 215, note, *for* debacehentur *read* debacchentur.
,, 230, foot of the page, *for* divitias *read* divitiis.
,, 287, line 12 from top, *for* arbonis *read* arboris.
,, 289, line 16 from top, *for* ardera *read* ardua.
,, 289, line 32 from top, *for* and *read* or.
,, 296, line 9 from bottom, *for* by *read* to.
,, 343, line 7 from bottom, *for* fungiferentis *read* frugiferentis.
,, 413, note 1, add the words, 'Cicero also, in his letters to Caelius, addresses him as mi Rufe,' Ep. II. 9. 3, 12. 2.

THE ROMAN POETS OF THE REPUBLIC.

CHAPTER I.

GENERAL CHARACTER OF ROMAN POETRY.

A GREAT fluctuation of opinion has taken place, among scholars and critics, in regard to the worth of Latin poetry. From the revival of learning till comparatively a recent period, the poets of ancient Rome, and especially those of the Augustan age, were esteemed the purest models of literary art, and were the most familiar exponents of the life and spirit of antiquity. Their works were the chief instruments of the higher education. They were studied imitated, and translated by some of the greatest poets of modern Europe; and they supplied their favourite text and illustrations to moralists and humourists, from Montaigne to the famous English essayists who flourished during the last century. Up to a still later period, their words were habitually used by statesmen to add weight to their arguments or point to their invectives. Perhaps no other writers have, for so long a period, exercised so powerful an influence, not only on literary style and taste, but on the character and understanding, of educated men in the leading nations of the modern world.

It was natural that this excessive deference to their authority should be impaired both by the ampler recognition of the claims of modern poetry, and by a more intimate familiarity with Greek literature. They have suffered, in the estimation of literary critics, from the change in poetical taste which commenced about the beginning of the present century, and, in that of scholars, from the superior attractions of the great epic, dramatic, and lyrical poets of Greece. They have thus, for some time, been exposed to undue disparagement rather than to undue admiration. The perception of the debt which they owed to their Greek masters, has led to some forgetfulness of their original merits. Their Roman character and Italian feeling have been partially obscured by the foreign forms and metres in which these are expressed. It is said, with some appearance of plausibility, that Roman poetry is not only much inferior in interest to the poetry of Greece, but that it is a work of cultivated imitation, not of creative art; that other forms of literature were the true expression of the genius of the Roman people; that their poets brought nothing new into the world; that they have enriched the life of after times with no pure vein of native feeling, nor any impressive record of national experience.

It is, indeed, impossible to claim for Roman poetry the unborrowed glory or the varied inspiration of the earlier art of Greece. To the genius of Greece alone can the words of the bard in the Odyssey be applied,

αὐτοδίδακτος δ' εἰμί, θεὸς δέ μοι ἐν φρεσὶν οἴμας
παντοίας ἐνέφυσεν.[1]

Besides possessing the charm of poetical feeling and artistic form in unequalled measure, Greek poetry is to modern readers the immediate revelation of a new world of thought and action, in all its lights and shadows and moving life. Like their politics, the poetry of the Greeks sprang from many independent centres, and renewed itself in every epoch of the national civilisation. Roman poetry, on the other hand, has neither the same novelty nor variety of matter; nor did it adapt itself to the changing phases of

[1] Hom. Od. xxii. 348.

human life in different generations and different States, like the epic, lyric, dramatic, and idyllic poetry of Greece. But it may still be answered that the poets of Rome have another kind of value. There is a charm in their language and sentiment different from that which is found in any other literature of the world. Certain deep and abiding impressions are stamped upon their works, which have penetrated into the cultivated sentiment of modern times. If, as we read them, the imagination is not so powerfully stimulated by the revelation of a new world, yet, in the elevated tones of Roman poetry, there is felt to be a permanent affinity with the strength and dignity of man's moral nature; and, in the finer and softer tones, a power to move the heart to sympathy with the beauty, the enjoyment, and the natural sorrows of a bygone life. If we are no longer moved by the eager hopes and buoyant fancies of the youthful prime of the ancient world, we seem to gather up, with a more sober sympathy, the fruits of its mature experience and mellowed reflexion.

While the literature and civilisation of Greece were still unknown to them, the Romans had produced certain rude kinds of metrical composition: they preserved some knowledge of their history in various kinds of chronicles or annals: they must have been trained to some skill in oratory by the contests of public life, and by the practice of delivering commemorative speeches at the funerals of famous men. But they cannot be said to have produced spontaneously any works of literary art. Their oratory, history, poetry, and philosophy owed their first impulse to their intellectual contact with Greece. But while the form and expression of all Roman literature were moulded by the teaching of Greek masters and the study of Greek writings, it may be urged, with some show of truth, that the debt incurred by the poetry and philosophy of Rome was much greater than that incurred by her oratory and history. The two latter assumed a more distinct type, and adapted themselves more naturally to the genius of the people and the circumstances of the

State. They were the work of men who took an active and prominent part in public affairs; and they bore directly on the practical wants of the times in which they were cultivated. Even the structure of the Latin language testifies to the oratorical force and ardour by which it was moulded into symmetry; as the language of Greece betrays the plastic and harmonising power of her early poetry. There is no improbability in the supposition that, if Greek literature had never existed, or had remained unknown to the Romans, the political passions and necessities of the Republic would have called forth a series of powerful orators; and that the national instinct, which clung with such strong tenacity to the past, would, with the advance of power and civilisation, have produced a type of history, capable of giving adequate expression to the traditions and continuous annals of the commonwealth.

But their poetry, on the other hand, came to the Romans after their habits were fully formed[1], as an ornamental addition to their power,—κηπίον καὶ ἐγκαλλώπισμα πλούτου. Unlike the poetry of Greece, it was not addressed to the popular ear, nor was it an immediate emanation from the popular heart. The poets who commemorated the greatness of Rome, or who sang of the passions and pursuits of private life, in the ages immediately before and after the establishment of the Empire, were, for the most part, men born in the provinces of Italy, neither trained in the formal discipline of Rome, nor taking any active part in practical affairs. Their tastes and feelings are, in some respects, rather Italian than purely Roman; their thoughts and convictions are rather of a cosmopolitan type than moulded on the national traditions. They drew the materials of their art as much from the stores of Greek poetry, as from the life and action of their own times. Their art is thus a composite structure, in which old forms are combined with altered conditions; in which the fancies of earlier

---

[1] Cf. Cic. Tusc. Disp. i. 2, 3. Sero igitur a nostris poetae vel cogniti vel recepti. At contra oratorem celeriter complexi sumus: nec eum primo eruditum, aptum tamen ad dicendum.

times reappear in a new language, and the spirit of Greece is seen interpenetrating the grave temperament of Rome, and the genial nature of Italy.

But, although oratory and history may have been more essential to the national life of the Romans, and more adapted to their genius, their poetry still remains their most complete literary monument. Of the many famous orators of the Republic one only has left his speeches to modern times. The works of the two greatest Roman historians have reached us in a mutilated shape; and the most important epochs in the later history of the Republic are not represented in what remains of the works of either writer. Tacitus records only the sombre and monotonous annals of the early Empire; and the extant books of Livy contain the account of times and events from which he himself was separated by many generations. Roman poetry, on the other hand, is the contemporary witness of several important eras in the history of the Republic and the Empire. It includes many authentic and characteristic fragments from the great times of the Scipios,—the complete works of the two poets of finest genius, who flourished in the last days of the Republic,—the masterpieces of the brilliant Augustan era;—and, of the works of the Empire, more than are needed to exemplify the decay of natural feeling and of poetical inspiration under the deadening pressure of Imperialism. And, besides illustrating different eras, the Roman poets throw light on the most various aspects of Roman life and character. They are the most authentic witnesses both of the national sentiment and ideas, and of the feelings and interests of private life. They stamp on the imagination the ideal of Roman majesty; and they bring home to modern sympathies the charm and the pathos of human life, under conditions widely different from our own.

Roman poetry was the living heir, not the lifeless reproduction of the genius of Greece. If it seems to have been a highly-trained accomplishment rather than the irrepressible outpouring of a natural faculty, still this accomplishment was based upon original gifts of feeling and character, and was marked by its own peculiar features. The creative energy of the Greeks died out with Theocritus; but their learning and taste, surviving the decay of their political existence, passed into the education of a kindred race, endowed, above all other races of antiquity, with the capacity of receiving and assimilating alien influences, and of producing, alike in action and in literature, great results through persistent purpose and concentrated industry. It was owing to their gifts of appreciation and their love of labour, that the Roman poets, in the era of the transition from the freedom and vigour of the Republic to the pomp and order of the Empire, succeeded in producing works which, in point of execution, are not much inferior to the masterpieces of Greece. It was due to the spirit of a new race,—speaking a new language, living among different scenes, acting their own part in the history of the world,—that the ancient inspiration survived the extinction of Greek liberty, and reappeared, under altered conditions, in a fresh succession of powerful works, which owe their long existence as much to the vivid feeling as to the artistic perfection by which they are characterised.

From one point of view, therefore, Roman poetry may be regarded as an imitative reproduction, from another, as a new revelation of the human spirit. For the form, and for some part of the substance, of their works, the Roman poets were indebted to Greece: the spirit and character, and much also of the substance of their poetry, are native in their origin. They betray their want of inventiveness chiefly in the forms of composition and the metres which they employed; occasionally also in the cast of their poetic diction, and in their conventional treatment of foreign materials. But, in even the least original aspects of their art, they are still national. Although, with the exception of Satire and the poetic Epistle, they struck out no new forms of poetic composition, yet those adopted by them assumed something of a new type, owing to the weight of their contents, the massive structure of the

Roman language, the fervour and gravity of the Roman temperament, and the practical bent and logical mould of the Roman understanding.

They were not equally successful in all the forms which they attempted to reproduce. They were especially inferior to their masters in tragedy. They betray the inferiority of their dramatic genius also in other fields of literature, especially in epic and idyllic poetry, and in philosophical dialogues. They express passion and feeling either directly from their own hearts and experience, or in great rhetorical passages, attributed to the imaginary personages of their story—to Ariadne or Dido, to Turnus or Mezentius. But this occasional utterance of passion and sentiment is not united in them with a vivid delineation of the complex characters of men; and it is only in their comic poetry that they are quite successful in reproducing the natural and lively interchange of speech. There is thus, as compared with Homer and Theocritus, a deficiency of personal interest in the epic, descriptive, and idyllic poetry of Virgil. The natural play of characters, acting and reacting upon one another, scarcely, if at all, enlivens the divinely-appointed action of the Aeneid, nor adds the charm of human associations to the poet's deep and quiet pictures of rural beauty, and to his graceful expression of pensive and tender feeling.

The Romans, as a race, were wanting also in speculative capacity; and thus their poetry does not rise, or rises only in Lucretius, to those imaginative heights from which the great lyrical and dramatic poets of Greece contemplated the wonder and solemnity of life. Yet both the epic and the lyrical poetry of Rome have a character and perfection of their own. The Aeneid, with many resemblances in points of detail to the poems of Homer, is yet, in design and execution, a true national monument. The lyrical poetry of Rome, if inferior to the choral poetry of Greece in range of thought and in ethereal grace of expression, and scarcely equalling the few fragments of the early Aeolic poetry in the force of passion, is yet an instrument of varied power, capable of investing the lighter moods or more transient joys of life with an unfading charm, and rising into fuller and more commanding tones to express the national sentiment and moral dignity of Rome. Didactic poetry obtained in Lucretius and Virgil ampler volume and profounder meaning than in their Greek models, Empedocles and Hesiod. It was by the skill of the two great Latin poets that poetic art was made to embrace within its province the treatment of a great philosophical argument, and of a great practical pursuit. The Satires and Epistles of Horace showed, for the first time, how the didactic spirit could deal in poetry with the conduct and familiar experience of life. The elegiac poets of the Augustan age, while borrowing the outward form of their compositions from the early poets of Ionia and the later writers at the court of Alexandria, have taken the substance of their poetry to a great extent from their own lives and interests; and have treated their materials with a fluent brilliancy of style, and often with a graceful tenderness of feeling, unborrowed from any foreign source. It may thus be generally affirmed that the Roman poets, although adding little to the great discoveries or inventions in literature, and although not equally successful in all their adaptations of the inventions of their predecessors, have yet left the stamp of their own genius and character on some of the great forms which poetry has hitherto assumed.

The metres of Roman poetry are also seen to be adaptations to the Latin language of the metres previously employed in the epic, lyrical, and dramatic poetry of Greece. The Italian race had, in earlier times, struck out a native measure, called the Saturnian,—of a rapid and irregular movement,—in which their religious emotions, their festive and satiric raillery, and their commemorative instincts found a rude expression. But after this measure had been rejected by Ennius, as unsuited to the gravity of his greatest work, the Roman poets continued to imitate the metres of their Greek predecessors. But, in their hands, these became characterised by a slower, more stately, and regular movement, not only differing widely from the ring of the native Saturnian rhythm, but also, with every improvement in poetic accomplishment, receding further and further from the freedom and variety of the Greek measures. The comic and tragic measures, in which alone the Roman writers observed a less strict rule than their models, never attained among them to any high metrical excellence. The rhythm of the Greek poets, owing in a great measure to the frequency of vowel sounds in their language, is more flowing, more varied, and more richly musical than that of Roman poetry. Thus, although their verse is constructed on the same metrical laws, there is the most marked contrast between the rapidity and buoyancy of the Iliad or the Odyssey, and the stately and weighty march of the Aeneid. Notwithstanding their outward conformity to the canons of a foreign language, the most powerful and characteristic measures of Roman poetry,—such as the Lucretian and the Virgilian hexameter, and the Horatian alcaic,—are distinguished by a grave, orderly, and commanding tone, symbolical of the genius and the majesty of Rome. In such cases, as the Horatian sapphic and the Ovidian elegiac, where the structure of the verse is too slight to produce this impressive effect, there is still a remarkable divergence from the freedom and manifold harmony of the early Greek poets to a uniform and monotonous cadence.

The language, also, of Roman poetry betrays many traces of imitation. Some of the early Latin tragedies were literal translations from the works of the Athenian dramatists; and fragments of the rude Roman copy may still be compared with the polished expression of the original. Some familiar passages of the Iliad may be traced among the rough-hewn fragments of the Annals of Ennius. Even Lucretius, whose diction, more than that of most poets, produces the impression of being the immediate creation of his own mind, has described outward objects, and clothed his thoughts, in language borrowed from Homer and Empedocles. The short volume of Catullus contains translations from Sappho and Callimachus, and frequent imitations of other Greek poets; and, from the extant fragments of Alcaeus, Anacreon, and others of the Greek lyric poets, it may be seen how frequently Horace availed himself of some turn of their expression to invest his own experience with old poetic associations. Virgil, whose great success is, in no slight measure, due to the skill and taste with which he used the materials of earlier Greek and native writers, has reproduced the heroic tones of Homer in his epic, and the mellow cadences of Theocritus in his pastoral poems; and has blended something of the antique quaintness and oracular sanctity of Hesiod with the golden perfection of his Georgics.

But besides the direct debt which each Roman poet owed to the Greek author or authors whom he imitated, it is difficult to estimate the extent to which the taste of the later Romans was formed by the familiar study of a foreign language so much superior to the rude speech spoken by their fathers. The habitual study of any foreign language has an influence not on style only, but even on the structure of thought and the development of emotion. The Roman poets first learned, from the study of Greek poetry, to feel the graceful combinations and the musical power of expression, and were thus stimulated and trained to elicit similar effects from their native language. It is for this gift, or power over language, that Lucretius prays in his invocation to the creative power of Nature,—

> Quo magis aeternum da dictis, diva, leporem;

and it is this which Catullus claims as the characteristic excellence of his own poems.

The Augustan poets attained a still greater success in the variations of words and rhythm; but this success was gained with some loss of direct force and freshness in the expression of feeling. And it may be said generally that the Latin language, in its adaptation to poetry, lost some of its powers as an immediate vehicle of thought. In Virgil and in Horace, words are combined in a less natural order than in Homer and the Attic dramatists. Their language does not strike the mind with the spontaneous force of Greek poetry, nor does it seem equally capable of being rapidly followed by a popular audience. Catullus alone among the great Roman poets combines perfect grace with the happiest freedom and simplicity. Yet the studied and compact diction of Latin poetry, if wanting in fluency, ease, and directness, lays a strong hold upon the mind, by its power of marking with emphasis what is most essential and prominent in the ideas and objects presented to the imagination. The thought and sentiment of Rome have thus been engraved on her poetical literature, in deep and enduring characters. And, notwithstanding all manifest traces of imitation, the diction of the greatest Roman poets attests the presence of genuine creative power. A strong vital force is recognised in the direct and vigorous diction of Ennius and Lucretius; and, though more latent, it is not less really present under the stateliness and chastened splendour of Virgil, and the subtle moderation of Horace.

Roman poetry owes also a considerable part of its contents to Greek thought, art, and traditions. This is the chief explanation of that conventional character which detracts from the originality of some of the masterpieces of Roman genius. The old religious belief of Rome and Italy became merged in the poetical restoration of the Olympian Gods; the story of the origin of Rome was inseparably connected with the personages of Greek poetry; the familiar manners of a late civilisation appear in unnatural association with the idealised features of the heroic age. Even the expression of personal feeling, experience, and convictions is often coloured by light reflected from earlier representations. Hence a great deal in Latin poetry appears to come less directly from the poet's heart, and to fit less closely to the facts of human life, than the best poetry both of Greece and of modern nations. This imitative and composite workmanship is more apparent in the later than in the earlier poets. The substance and thought of Ennius, Lucretius, and Catullus, even when they reproduce Greek materials, appear to be more vivified by their own feeling than the substance and thought of the Augustan poets. The beautiful and stately forms of Greek legend, which lived a second life in the young imagination of Catullus, were becoming trite and conventional to Virgil:—

> Cetera, quae vacuas tenuissent carmina mentes,
> Omnia jam vulgata.

The ideal aspect of the golden morning of the world has been seized with a truer feeling in the Epithalamium of Peleus and Thetis than in the episode of the 'Pastor Aristaeus' in the Georgics. Not only are the main features in the story of the Aeneid of foreign origin, but the treatment of the story betrays some want of vital sympathy with the heterogeneous elements out of which it is composed. The poem is a religious as well as a great national work; but the religious creed which is expressed in it is a composite result of Greek mythology, of Roman sentiment, and of ideas derived from an eclectic philosophy. The manners represented in the poem are a medley of the Augustan and of the Homeric age, as seen in vague proportions, through the mists of antiquarian learning. It must, indeed, be remembered that Greek traditions had penetrated into the life of the whole civilised world, and that the belief in the connexion of Rome with Troy had rooted itself in the Roman mind for two centuries before the time of Virgil. Still, the tale of the settlement of Aeneas in Latium, as told in the great Roman epic, bears the mark of the artificial construction of a late and prosaic era, not of the spontaneous growth of imaginative legend, in a lively and creative age. So, also, in another sphere of poetry, while there are genuine touches of nature in all the odes of Horace, yet the mythological accessories of some of those which celebrate the praises of a god, or the charms of a mistress, seem to stand in no vital relation with the genuine convictions of the poet.

Roman poetry, from this point of view, appears to be

the old Greek art reappearing under new conditions: or rather the new art of the civilised world, after it had been thoroughly leavened by Greek thought, taste, and education. The poetry of Rome was, however, a living power, after the creative energy of Greece had disappeared, so that, were it nothing more, that literature would still be valuable as the fruit of the later summer of antiquity. As in Homer, the earliest poet of the ancient world, there is a kind of promise of the great life that was to be; so, in the Augustan poets, there is a retrospective contemplation of the life, the religion, and the art of the past,—a gathering up of 'the long results of time.' But the Roman poets had also a strong vein of original character and feeling, and many phases of national and personal experience to reveal. They had to give a permanent expression to the idea of Rome, and to perpetuate the charm of the land and life of Italy. In their highest tones, they give utterance to the patriotic spirit, the dignified and commanding attributes, and the moral strength of the Imperial Republic. But other elements in their art proclaim their large inheritance of the receptive and emotional nature which, in ancient as in modern times, has characterised the Southern nations. As the patrician and plebeian orders were united in the imperial greatness of the commonwealth, as the energy of Rome and of the other Italian communities was welded together to form a mighty national life, so these apparently antagonistic elements combined to create the majesty and beauty of Roman poetry. Either of these elements would by itself have been unproductive and incomplete. The pure Roman temperament was too austere, too unsympathetic, too restrained and formal, to create and foster a luxuriant growth of poetry: the genial nature of the south, when dissociated from the control of manlier instincts and the elevation of higher ideas, tended to degenerate into licentious effeminacy, both in life and literature. The fragments of the earlier tragic and epic poets indicate the predominance of the gravity and the masculine strength inherent in the Roman temper, almost to the exclusion of the other element. Roman comedy, on the other hand, gave full play to Italian vivacity and sensuousness with only slight restraint from the higher instincts inherited from ancient discipline. In Lucretius, Virgil, and Horace, moral energy and dignity of character are most happily combined with susceptibility to the charm and the power of Nature. Catullus and the elegiac poets of the Augustan age abandoned themselves to the passionate enjoyment of their lives, under little restraint either from the pride or the virtue of their forefathers. Their vices, and still more their weaknesses, are of a type apparently most opposed to the tendencies of the higher Roman character. Yet even these may be looked upon as a kind of indirect testimony to the ancient vigour of the race. Catullus, in his very coarseness, betrays the grain of that strong nature, out of which, in a better time, the freedom and energy of the Republic had been developed. Ovid, even in his libertinism, displays his vigorous and ardent vitality. The effeminacy of Tibullus looks like the reaction of a nature, enervated by the circumstances of his age, from the high standard of manliness, which a sterner time had maintained.

Among the most truly Roman characteristics of Latin poetry, national and patriotic sentiment is prominently conspicuous. Among the poets of the Republic, Naevius and Lucilius were animated by strong political as well as national feeling. The chief work of Ennius was devoted to the commemoration of the ancient traditions, the august institutions, the advancing power, and the great character of the Roman State. In the works of the Augustan age, the fine episodes of the Georgics, the whole plan and many of the details of the Aeneid, show the spell exercised over the mind of Virgil by the ancient memories and the great destiny of his country, and bear witness to his deep love of Italy, and his pride in her natural beauty and her strong breed of men. Horace rises above his irony and epicureanism, to celebrate the imperial majesty of Rome, and to bear witness to the purity of the Sabine households, and to the virtues exhibited in the best types of Roman character. The Fasti of Ovid, also, is a national poem, owing its existence to the strong interest which was felt by the Romans in their mythical and early story, so long as any living memory of their political life remained.

The poets of the latest age of the Republic alone express little sympathy with national or public interests. The time in which they flourished was not favourable to the pride of patriotism or to political enthusiasm. The contemplative genius of Lucretius separated him from the pursuits of active life; and his philosophy taught the lesson that to acquiesce in any government was better than to engage in the strife of personal ambition;—

> Ut satius multo jam sit parere quietum
> Quam regere imperio res velle et regna tenere.

Catullus, while eagerly enjoying his life, seems, in regard to all the grave public questions of his time, to 'daff the world aside, and bid it pass': yet there is, as has been well said [1], a rough republican flavour in his careless satire; and he retained to the last, and boldly asserted, what was the earliest, as well as the latest, instinct of ancient liberty—the spirit of resistance to the arbitrary rule of any single man.

Roman poetry is pervaded also by a peculiar vein of imaginative emotion. There is no feeling so characteristic of the works of Roman genius as the sense of majesty. This feeling is called forth by the idea or outward manifestation of strength, stability, vastness, and order; by whatever impresses the imagination as the symbol of power and authority, whether in the aspect of Nature, or in the works, actions, and institutions of man. It is in their most serious and elevated writings, and chiefly in their epic and didactic poetry, that the Romans show their peculiar susceptibility to this grave and dignified emotion. Even the plain and rude diction of Ennius rises into rugged grandeur when he is moved by the vastness or massive strength of outward things, by 'the pomp and circum-

---

[1] Smith's Dict. of Greek and Roman Biography, Art. Catullus.

stance' of war, or by the august forms and symbols of government. The majestic tones of Lucretius seem to give a voice to the deep feeling of the order and immensity of the universe, which possessed him. The sustained dignity of the Aeneid, and the splendour of some of its finest passages—such for instance as that which brings before us the solemn and magnificent spectacle of the fall of Troy —attest how the imagination of Virgil was moved to sympathy with the attributes of ancient and powerful sovereignty[1].

Further, in the fervour and dignity of their moral feeling, the Roman poets are true exponents of the genius of Rome. Their spirit is more authoritative, and less speculative than that of Greek poetry. They speak rather from the will and conscience than from the wisdom that has searched and understood the ways of life. Greek poetry strengthens the will or purifies the heart indirectly, by its truthful representation of the tragic situations in human life; Roman poetry appeals directly to the manlier instincts and more magnanimous impulses of our nature. This glow of moral emotion pervades not the poetry only, but the oratory, history, and philosophy of Rome. It has cast a kind of religious solemnity around the fragments of the early epic, tragic, and satiric poetry: it has given an intenser fervour to the stern consistency and desperate fortitude of Lucretius: it has added the element of strength to the pathos and fine humanity in the Æneid. It is by his moral, as well as his national enthusiasm, that Horace reveals the Roman gravity that tempered his genial nature. The language of Lucan, Persius, and Juvenal still breathed the same spirit in the deadening atmosphere of the Empire. Of all the great poets of

[1] The following lines might be quoted as a specimen of the *majesty* of the Aeneid:—

> Haec finis Priami fatorum; hic exitus illum
> Sorte tulit, Troiam incensam et prolapsa videntem
> Pergama, tot quondam populis terrisque superbum
> Regnatorem Asiae.—Aen. ii. 554–7.

Rome, Catullus alone shows little trace of this grave ardour of feeling, the more usual accompaniment of the firm temper of manhood than of the prodigal genius of youth.

There are, however, as was said above, other feelings expressed in Roman poetry, which are, perhaps, more akin to modern sympathies. In no other branch of ancient literature is so much prominence given to the enjoyment of Nature, the passion of love, and the joys, sorrows, tastes, and pursuits of the individual. The gravity and austerity of the old Roman life, and the predominance of public over private interests in the best days of the Republic, tended to repress, rather than to foster, the birth of these new modes of emotion. They are like the flower of that more luxuriant but less stately Italian life which spread itself abroad under the shadow of Roman institutions, and came to a rapid maturity after her conquests had brought to Rome the accumulated treasures of the world, and left to her more fortunate sons ample leisure to enjoy them.

The love of natural scenery and of country life is certainly more prominently expressed in Roman than in Greek poetry. Homer, indeed, among all the poets of antiquity, presents the most vivid and true description of the outward world; and the imagination of Pindar and the Attic dramatists appears to have been strongly, though indirectly, affected both by the immediate aspect and by the invisible power of Nature. Thucydides and Aristophanes testify to the enjoyment which the Athenians found in the ease and abundance of their country life, and to the affection with which they clung to the old religious customs and associations connected with it. The conscious enjoyment of Nature as a prominent motive of poetry first appears in the Alexandrian era. The great poets of earlier times were too deeply penetrated by the thought of the mystery and the grandeur in human life, to dwell much on the spectacle of the outward world. Though their delicate sense of beauty was unconsciously cherished and refined by the air which they breathed, and the scenes by which they were surrounded, yet they do not, like the Roman poets, yield to the passive pleasures derived from contemplating the aspect of the natural world; nor do they express the happiness of passing out of the tumult of the city into the peaceful security of the country. The difference between the two nations in social temper and customs is connected with this difference in their aesthetic susceptibility. The spirit in which a Greek enjoyed his leisure, was one phase of his sociability, his communicativeness, his constant passion for hearing and telling something new,—a disposition which made the λέσχη a favourite resort so early as the time of Homer, and which is seen still characterising the most typical representatives of the race in the days of St. Paul. The Roman statesman, on the other hand, prized his *otium* as the healthy repose after strenuous exertion. The chief relaxation to his proud and self-dependent temper consisted in being alone, or at ease with his household and his intimate friends. This desire for rest and retirement was one great element in the Roman taste for country life;—a taste which was manifested among the foremost public men, such as the Scipios and Laelius, long before any trace of it is betrayed in Roman poetry. But, as the practice of spending the unhealthy months of autumn away from Rome became general among the wealthier classes, and as new modes of sentiment were fostered by greater leisure and finer cultivation, a genuine love of Nature,—taking the form either of attachment to particular places, or of enjoyment in the life and beautiful forms of the outward world,—was gradually awakened in the more susceptible minds of the Italian race.

The poetry of the Augustan age and of that immediately preceding it is deeply pervaded by this new emotion. Each of the great poets manifests the feeling in his own way. Lucretius, while contemplating the majesty of Nature's laws, and the immensity of her range, is, at the same time, powerfully moved to sympathy with her ever-varying life. He feels the charm of simply living in fine weather, and looking on the common aspects of the world, —such as the sea-shore, fresh pastures and full-flowing rivers, or the new loveliness of the early morning. He represents the punishment of the Danaides as a symbol of the incapacity of the human spirit to enjoy the natural charm of the recurring seasons of the year. Catullus, too, although his active social temper did not respond to the spell which Nature exercised over the contemplative and pensive spirits of Lucretius and Virgil, has many fine images from the outward world in his poems. He delights in comparing the grace and the passion of youth with the bloom of flowers and the stateliness of trees; he associates the beauty of Sirmio with his bright picture of the happiness of home; he feels the return of the genial breezes of spring as enhancing his delight in leaving the dull plains of Phrygia, and in hastening to visit the famous cities of Asia. Virgil's early art was characterised by his friend and brother poet in the lines,—

> Molle atque facetum
> Vergilio annuerunt gaudentes rure camenae[1].

The love of natural, and especially of Italian, beauty blends with all his patriotic memories, and with the charm which he has cast around the common operations of rustic industry. The freedom and peace of his country life, among the Sabine hills, kept the heart of Horace fresh and simple, in spite of all the pleasures and flatteries to which he was exposed; and enabled him, till the end of his course, to mingle the clear fountain of native poetry,—'ingeni benigna vena,'—with the stiller current of his meditative wisdom.

The passion of love was a favourite theme both of the early lyrical poets of Greece, and of the courtly writers of Alexandria; but the works of the former have reached us only in inconsiderable fragments; and the latter, with the exception of Theocritus, are much inferior to the Roman poets who made them their models. It is in Latin litera-

---

[1] Horace, Sat. i. 10. 45.

ture that we are brought most near to the power of this passion in the ancient world. Few among the poets who have recorded their own experience of love, in any age, have expressed a feeling so true or so intense as Catullus. He has all the ardent, self-forgetful devotion, if he wants the chivalry and purity, of modern sentiment. He has painted the love of others, also, with graceful fidelity. He has shown the finest sense in discerning, and the finest power in delineating the charm of youthful passion, when first awakening into life, or first unfolding into true affection. It is by his delineation of the agony of Dido that Virgil has imparted the chief personal interest to the story of the Aeneid. If he has failed to embody any complex type of character, he has described the agitation and pathos of this particular passion at least with a powerful hand. Horace is the poet of the lighter and gayer moods of love. Without ever becoming a slave to it, he experienced enough of its pains and pleasures, to enable him to paint the fascination or the waywardness of a mistress with the equable feeling of an epicurean, but, at the same time, with the refined observation of a poet. The elegiac poets of the Augustan age, making pleasure the chief pursuit of their lives, have made the more ignoble and transient phases of this passion the predominant motive of their poetry. Yet the effeminacy of Tibullus is redeemed by real tenderness of heart; there is ardent emotion expressed by Propertius for his living mistress, and true affection in the lines in which he recalls her memory after death; the profligacy of Ovid is, if not redeemed, at least relieved, by his buoyant wit and his brilliant fancy.

Roman poetry is also interesting as the revelation of personal experience and character. The biographies of ancient authors are, for the most part, meagre and untrustworthy; and thus it is chiefly through the conscious or unconscious self-portraiture in their writings that the actual men of antiquity are brought into close contact with the modern world. Few men of any age or country are so well known to us as Horace; and it is from his own writings, exclusively, that this intimate knowledge has been obtained. The lines in which he describes Lucilius are more applicable to himself than to any extant writer of Greece or Rome,—

> Ille velut fidis arcana sodalibus olim
> Credebat libris: neque si male cesserat, unquam
> Decurrens alio, neque si bene: quo fit, ut omnis
> Votiva pateat veluti descripta tabella
> Vita senis[1].

He has described himself, his tastes and pursuits, his thoughts and convictions, with perfect frankness and candour, and without any of the triviality or affectation of literary egotism. Catullus, although sometimes wanting in proper reticence, and altogether devoid of that meditative art with which Horace transmutes his own experience into the common experience of human nature, is known also as a familiar friend, from the force of feeling with which he realised, and the transparent sincerity with which he recorded, all the pain and the pleasure of his life. The elegiac poets of the Augustan age have written, neither from so strong a heart as that of Catullus, nor with the good taste and self-respect of Horace; but yet one of the chief sources of interest in their poetry, as of that of Martial in a later age, arises from their strong realisation of life, their unreserved communicativeness, and the light they thus throw on one phase of personal and social manners in ancient times.

Nor are these indications of individual character confined to the poets who profess to communicate their own feelings, and to record their own fortunes. All the works of Roman poetry bear emphatically the impress of their authors. While the finest Greek poetry seems like an almost impersonal emanation of genius, Roman poetry is, to a much greater extent, the expression of character. The great Roman writers manifest that kind of self-

---

[1] 'He used from time to time to intrust all his secret thoughts to his books, as to trusty friends; it was to them only he turned in evil fortune or in good; and thus it is, that the whole life of the old poet lies before our eyes, as if it were portrayed on a votive picture.'—Sat. ii. 1. 30.

consciousness which accompanies resolute and successful effort; while the Greeks enjoy that happy self-forgetfulness which attends the unimpeded exercise of a natural gift. The epitaphs composed for themselves by Naevius, Plautus, Ennius, and Pacuvius, and the assertion of their own originality and of their hopes of fame, which occurs in the poetry of Lucretius, Virgil, and Horace, were dictated by a strong sense of their own personality, and of the importance of the task on which they were engaged. Catullus, although he is much preoccupied with, and most frank in communicating his feelings and pursuits, has much less of the consciousness of genius, is much more humble in his aspirations, and more modest in his estimate of himself. In this, as in other respects, he approaches nearer to the type of Greek art than any of his brother-poets of Rome.

It is a common remark that the very greatest poets are those about whose personal characteristics least is known. It is impossible in their case to determine where they have expressed their real sympathies or convictions. They rise above the prejudices of their country and the accidents of their time, and can see the good and evil inseparably mixed in all human action. No criticism can throw any trustworthy light on the personal position, the pursuits and aims, the outward and inward experience of Homer. It cannot even be determined with certainty how much of the poetry which bears his name is the creation of one, seemingly, inexhaustible genius; and how much is the 'divine voice' of earlier singers still 'floating around him.' Such inquiries are ever attracting and ever baffling a high curiosity. They leave the mind perplexed with the doubt whether it is discerning, in the far distance, the outline of solid mountain-land, or only the transient shapes of the clouds. Hesiod, on the other hand, a poet of perhaps equal antiquity, but of an infinitely lower order of genius, has left his own likeness graphically delineated on his remains. There is much to interest a reader in the old didactic poem, 'The Works and Days,' but it is not the interest of studying a work of art or of creative genius. The charm of the book consists partly in its power of calling up the ideas of a remote antiquity and of human life in its most elemental conditions; partly in the distinct impression which it bears of a character of an antique and primitive and yet not unfamiliar type;—a character of deep natural piety and righteousness, but with a quaint intermixture of other qualities, homespun sagacity and worldly wisdom;—genuine thrift, and horror of idleness, of war, of seafaring enterprise;—sardonic dislike of the airs and vices of women, and a grim discontent with his own condition, and with the poor soil which it was his lot to till[1]. It is through his want of those gifts of genius which have made Homer immortal as a poet, and a mere name as a man, that Hesiod has left so distinct a picture of himself to the latest times. In like manner Roman poetry, while never rising to the heights of creative and impersonal genius, from this very defect, is a truer revelation of the poets themselves. The Aeneid supplies ample materials for understanding the affections and convictions of Virgil. Lucretius makes his personal presence felt through the whole march of his argument, and supports every position of his system not with his logic only, but with the whole force of his nature. The fragments of Ennius and of Lucilius afford ample evidence by which we may judge what kind of men they were.

It thus appears that, over and above their higher and finer excellencies, the Roman poets have this additional source of interest, that, more than any other authors in the vigorous times of antiquity, they satisfy the modern curiosity in regard to personal character and experience. These poets have themselves left the most trustworthy record of their happiest hours and most real interests; of their standard of conduct, their personal worth, and their strength of affection; of the studies and the occupations

[1] The parallel which Mr. Ruskin draws (Modern Painters, vol iii. p. 194), between an ancient Greek and 'a good, conscientious, but illiterate Scotch Presbyterian Border farmer of a century or two back,' becomes intelligible if we regard Hesiod as a normal type of the Greek mind.

in which they passed their lives, and of the spirit in which they awaited the certainty of their end.

It remains to say a few words in regard to the historical progress of this branch of literature. The history of Roman poetry may be divided into four great periods:—

I. The age of Naevius, Ennius, Lucilius, etc., extending from about B.C. 240 till about B.C. 100:

II. The age of Lucretius and Catullus, whose active poetical career belongs to the last age of the Republic, the decennium before the outbreak of the Civil War between Caesar and Pompey:

III. The Augustan age:

IV. The whole period of the Empire after the time of Augustus.

The poetry of each of these periods is distinctly marked in form, style, and character. There is evidently a great progress in artistic accomplishment and in poetical feeling, from the rude cyclopean remains of the annals of Ennius to the stately proportions and elaborate workmanship of the Aeneid. Yet this advance was attended with some loss as well as gain. With infinitely less accomplishment and less variety, the older writers show signs of a robuster life and a more vigorous understanding than some at least of those who adorn the Augustan era. They endeavoured to work in the spirit of the great masters, who had made the most heroic passions and most serious interests of men the subject of their art. They were men also of the same fibre as the chief actors on the stage of public affairs, living with them in familiar friendship, while at the same time maintaining a close sympathy with popular feeling and the national life. Their fragments are thus, apart from their intrinsic merits, especially valuable as the contemporary language of that great time, and as giving some expression to the strength, the dignity, and the freedom which were stamped upon the old Republic.

For more than a generation after the death of Accius and Lucilius, no new poet of any eminence appeared at

Rome. The vivid enjoyment of life, and the sense of security which usually accompany and foster the successful cultivation of art, had been rudely interrupted by the convulsions of the State. A new birth of Roman poetry took place during the brief lull between the storms of the first and second civil wars. The new poets arose independently of the old literature. They appealed not to popular favour, but to the tastes of the few and the educated: they gave expression not to any public or national sentiment, but to their individual thought and feeling. Their works reflect the restless agitation of a time of revolution; but they show also all the vigour and sincerity of republican freedom. While greatly superior to the fragments of the older poetry in refinement of style, and in depth and variety of poetical feeling, they want the simple strength of moral conviction, and the interest in great practical affairs, which characterised their predecessors. They are inferior to the poets of the Augustan age in artistic skill; but they show more force of thought, or more intensity of passion, a stronger and livelier inspiration, a bolder and more independent character.

The short interval between the death of Catullus and the appearance of the Bucolics of Virgil marks the beginning of a new era in literature and in history:

> Magnus ab integro saeclorum nascitur ordo.

Catullus, dying only a few years before the extinction of popular freedom, is, in every nerve and fibre, the poet of a republic. Virgil, even before the final success of Augustus, proclaimed the advent of the new Empire; and he became the sincere admirer and interpreter of its order and magnificence. Most of the other poets of that age, though born before the overthrow of the Republic, show the influence of their time, not only by sympathy with or acquiescence in the new order of things, but by a perceptible lowering in the higher energies of life. Still, the poetry of the Augustan age, if inferior in natural force to that of the Republic, is the culmination of all the previous efforts of Roman art; and is, at the same time, the most complete and elaborate representation of Roman and Italian life.

The chief interest of Roman poetry, considered as the work of men of natural genius and cultivated taste, and as the expression of great national ideas or of individual thought and impulse, ceases with the end of the Augustan age. Under the continued pressure of the Empire, true poetical inspiration and pure feeling for art were lost. One certain test of this decay is the absence of musical power and sweetness from the verse of the later poets. Yet some of the poets of the Empire have their own peculiar greatness. Lucan and Juvenal recall in their vigorous rhetoric the masculine tone and fervid feeling of the old Roman character, liberalised by the progress of thought and education. In the Satires of Persius, there is an atmosphere of purer morality than in any earlier Roman writer, with the exception of Cicero. There is much vigour, sense, wit, and keen appreciation of life, intermingled with the coarseness of Martial. Yet it is owing rather to their rhetorical or their intellectual ability and to their historical value, than to their poetical genius, that these writers are still read and admired. The artificial epics of Silius Italicus and Valerius Flaccus may be occasionally read in the interests of learning; but it is hardly probable that they will, or desirable that they should, ever be permanently restored from the neglect and oblivion into which they have long been sinking.

This review of Roman poetry will bring before us the origin and progressive growth of a branch of literature, moulded, indeed, on the forms of a foreign art, but executed with native energy, and expressive of native character. In this poetry not the genius only, but the inner nature and sympathies of some of the more interesting men of antiquity are displayed. It throws light on the impulses of thought and feeling which influenced the action of different epochs in Roman history. The great qualities of Rome are seen to mould and animate her poetry. These qualities are found in harmonious union with the spirit of enjoyment and the sense of exuberant life, fostered by the genial air of Italy; and with a refinement of taste drawn from the purest source of human culture which the world has ever enjoyed. After all deductions have been made for their want of inventiveness, it still remains true, that the Roman poets of the last days of the Republic and of the Augustan age have added to the masterpieces of literature some great works of native feeling as well as of finished execution.

CHAPTER II.

VESTIGES OF EARLY INDIGENOUS POETRY IN ROME AND ANCIENT ITALY.

THE Romans themselves traced the origin of their poetry, as of all their literary culture, to their contact with the mind of Greece.

> Graecia capta ferum victorem cepit, et artes
> Intulit agresti Latio.

The first productive literary impulse was communicated to the Roman mind by the Greek slave, Livius Andronicus, who, in the year B.C. 240—one year after the end of the First Punic War—brought out, before a Roman audience, a drama translated or imitated from the Greek. From this time Roman poetry advanced along the various channels which the creative energy of Greek genius had formed.

But it has been maintained, in recent times, that this was but the second birth of Roman poetry, and that a golden age of native minstrelsy had preceded this historical development of literature. The most distinguished supporters of this theory were Niebuhr and Macaulay. In the preface to his *Lays of Rome*, Macaulay says that 'this early literature abounded with metrical romances, such as are found in every country where there is much curiosity and intelligence, but little reading and writing.' Niebuhr went so far as to assert that the Romans in early times possessed epic poems, 'which in power and brilliance of imagination leave everything produced by the Romans in later times far behind them.' He held that the flourishing period of this native poetry was the fifth century after the foundation of the city. He supposed that the early lays were of plebeian origin, strongly animated by plebeian sentiment, and familiarly known among the mass of the people; that they disappeared after the ascendency of the new literature, chiefly through the influence of Ennius; and that his immediate predecessor, Naevius, was the last of the genuine native minstrels. He professed to find clear traces of these ballads and epic poems in the fine legends of early Roman history. His theory was supported by arguments founded on the testimony of ancient writers, on indications of the early recognition of poetry by the Roman State (as, for instance, the worship of the Camenae), on the poetical character of early Roman story, and on the analogy of other nations.

Although there may be no more ground for believing in a golden age of early Roman poetry than in a golden age of innocence and happiness, yet the question raised by Niebuhr deserves attention, not only on account of the celebrity which it obtained, but also as opening up an inquiry into the nature and value of the rude germs of literature which the Latin soil spontaneously produced. Though there is no substantial evidence of the existence among the Romans of anything corresponding to the modern ballad or the early epic of Greece, yet certain kinds of metrical composition did spring up and flourish among the Italians, previous to and independent of their knowledge of Greek literature. It is worth while to ascertain what these kinds of composition were, as they throw light on some natural tendencies of the race, which ultimately obtained their adequate expression, and helped to impart a native and original character to Latin literature.

It was observed in the former chapter that while the metres of all the great Roman poets were founded on the earlier metres of Greece, there was a native Italian metre, called the Saturnian, which was employed apparently in various kinds of composition, and was quite different in character from the heroic and lyric measures adopted by the cultivated poets of a later age. This metre was used not only in rude extemporaneous effusions, but also in the long poem of Naevius, on the First Punic War. Horace indicates his sense of the roughness and barbarism of the metre, in the lines,

> Sic horridus ille
> Defluxit numerus Saturnius, et grave virus
> Munditiae pepulere [1].

Ennius speaks contemptuously of the verse of Naevius, as that employed by the old prophetic bards, before any of the gifts of poetry had been received or cultivated—

> Quum neque musarum scopulos quisquam superarat
> Nec dicti studiosus erat.

The irregularity of the metre may be inferred from a saying of an ancient grammarian, that, in the long epic of Naevius he could find no single line to serve as a normal specimen of its structure. From the few Saturnian lines remaining, it may be inferred that the verse had an irregular trochaic movement; and it seems first to have come into use as an accompaniment to the beating of the foot in a primitive rustic dance. The name, connected with Saturnus, the old Land-God of Italy, points to the rustic origin of the metre. It was known also by the name of Faunian, derived from another of the Divinities worshipped in the rural districts of Italy. It seems first to have been employed in ritual prayers and thanksgiving for the fruits of the earth, and in the grotesque raillery accompanying the merriment and license of the harvest-home. It is of the Saturnian verse that Virgil speaks in the lines of the second Georgic—

> Nec non Ausonii, Troja gens missa, coloni
> Versibus incomptis ludunt risuque soluto [2].

As the long roll of the hexameter and the stately march of the alcaic were expressive of the gravity and majesty of the Roman State, so the ring and flow of the Saturnian

---

[1] Epist. ii. 1. 157.   [2] Georg. ii. 385.

verse may be regarded as indicative of the freedom and genial enjoyment of life, characterising the old Italian peasantry.

The most important kinds of compositions produced in this metre, under purely native influences, may be classed as,

1. Hymns or ritual verses.
2. Prophetic verses.
3. Festive and satiric verses, uttered in dialogue or in rude mimetic drama.
4. Short gnomic or didactic verses.
5. Commemorative odes sung or recited at banquets and funerals.

1. The earliest extant specimen of the Latin language is a fragment of the hymn of the Fratres Arvales, a priestly brotherhood, who offered, on every 15th of May, public sacrifices for the fertility of the fields. This fragment is variously written and interpreted, but there can be no doubt that it is the expression of a prayer, for protection against pestilence, addressed to the Lares and the god Mars, and that it was uttered with the accompaniment of dancing. The following is the reading of the fragment, as given by Mommsen:—

> Enos, Lases, juvate.
> Ne veluerve, Marmar, sins incurrere in pleores.
> Satur fu, fere Mars.
> Limen sali.
> Sta berber.
> Semunis alternis advocapit conctos.
> Enos, Marmar, juvato.
> Triumpe, triumpe, triumpe, triumpe, triumpe [1].

The address to Mars 'Satur fu,' or, according to another reading, 'Satur furere,' 'be satisfied or done with raging,'

---

[1] It is thus interpreted by the same author:—Nos, lares, juvate. Ne malam luem, Mamers, sinas incurrere in plures. Satur esto, fere Mars. In limen insili. Desiste verberare (limen)! Semones alterni advocate cunctos. Nos, Mamers, juvato. Tripudia.

'Help us, Lares. Suffer not, Mamers, pestilence to fall on the people. Be satisfied, fierce Mars. Leap on the threshold. Cease beating it. Call, in turn, on all the demigods. Help us, Mamers.'—Mommsen, Röm. Geschichte, vol. i. ch. xv.

probably refers to the severity of the winter and early spring[1]. The words have reference to the attributes of the God in the old Italian religion, in which the powers of Nature were deified and worshipped long before Mars was identified with the Greek Ares. The other expressions in the prayer appear to be, either directions given to the dancers, or the sounds uttered as the dance proceeded.

Another short fragment has been preserved from the hymn of the Salii, also an ancient priesthood, supposed to date from the times of the early kings. The hymn is characterised by Horace, among other specimens of ancient literature, as equally unintelligible to himself and to its affected admirers[2].

From the extreme antiquity of these ceremonial chants it may be inferred that metrical expression among the Romans, as among the Greeks and other ancient nations, owed its origin to a primitive religious worship. But while the early Greek hymns or chants in honour of the Gods soon assumed the forms of pleasant tales of human adventure, or tragic tales of human suffering, the Roman hymns retained their formal and ritual character unchanged among all the changes of creed and language. In the lines just quoted there is no trace of creative fancy, nor any germ of devotional feeling, which might have matured into lyrical or contemplative poetry. They sound like the words of a rude incantation. They are the obscure memorial of a primitive, agricultural people, living in a blind sense of dependence on their gods, and restrained by a superstitious formalism from all activity of thought or fancy. Such compositions cannot be attributed to the inspiration or skill of any early poet, but seem to have been copied from the uncouth and spontaneous shouts of a simple, unsophisticated priesthood, engaged in a rude ceremonial dance. If these hymns stand in any relation to Latin literature, they may perhaps be regarded as spring-

---

[1] Such is the interpretation of Corssen, *Origines Poesis Romanae.*
[2] Epist ii. 1. 86.

ing from the same vein of public sentiment, as called forth the hymn composed by Livius Andronicus during the Second Punic War, and as rude precursors of those composed by Catullus and Horace, and chanted by a chorus of youths and maidens in honour of the protecting Deities of Rome.

2. The verses of the Fauns and Vates spoken of by Ennius, with allusion to the poem of Naevius, in the lines,

> Scripsere alii rem,
> Versibu' quos olim Fauni vatesque canebant,

were probably as far removed from poetry as the ritual chants of the Salii and the Fratres Arvales. The Fauni were the woodland gods of Italy, and were, besides their other functions, supposed to be endowed with prophetic power[1]. The word *Vates*, a word of Celtic origin, originally means not a poet, but a soothsayer. The Camenae or Casmenae (another form of which word appears in Carmenta, the prophetic mother of Evander) were worshipped, not as the inspirers of poetry, but as the foretellers of future events[2]. Both Greeks and Romans sought to obtain a knowledge of the future, either through the interpretation of omens, or through the voice of persons supposed to be divinely endowed with foresight. But the Greeks, even in the regard which they paid to auguries and oracles, were influenced, for the most part, by their lively imagination: while the Romans, from the earliest to the latest eras of their history, in all their relations to the supernatural world, adhered to a scrupulous and unimaginative ceremonialism. The notices in Latin literature of the functions of these early Vates—as, for instance, the counsel of the Etrurian seer to drain the Alban Lake during the war with Veii, and the prophecy of Marcius uttered during the Second Punic War,

> Amnem Trojugena Cannam Romane fuge, etc.[3],

---

[1] Cf. Virg. Aen. vii. 81, 82:—
  At rex sollicitus monstris, oracula Fauni,
  Fatidici genitoris adit.
[2] Cf. Schwegler, Röm. Gesch. i. 24, note 1.   [3] Livy xxv. 12.

suggest no more idea of poetical inspiration than the occasional notices, in Latin authors, of the oracles of the Sibylline books. The language of prophecy naturally assumes a metrical or rhythmical form, partly as an aid to the memory, partly, perhaps, as a means of giving to the words uttered the effect of a more solemn intonation. In Greece, the oracles of the Delphian priestess, and the predictions of soothsayers, collected in books or circulating orally among the people, were expressed in hexameter verse and in the traditional diction of epic poetry; but they were never ranked under any form of poetic art. The verses of the Vates, so far as any inference can be formed as to their nature, appear to have been products and proofs of unimaginative superstition, rather than of any imaginative inspiration among the early inhabitants of Latium.

3. Another class of metrical compositions, of native origin, but of a totally opposite character, was known by the name of the 'Fescennine verses.' These arose out of a very different class of feelings and circumstances. Horace attributes their origin to the festive meetings and exuberant mirth of the harvest-home among a primitive, strong, and cheerful race of husbandmen. He points out how this rustic raillery gradually assumed the character of fierce lampoons, and had to be restrained by law:—

> Fescennina per hunc inventa licentia morem
> Versibus alternis opprobria rustica fudit;
> Libertasque recurrentes accepta per annos
> Lusit amabiliter, donec jam saevus apertam
> In rabiem coepit verti jocus et per honestas
> Ire domos impune minax. Doluere cruento
> Dente lacessiti; fuit intactis quoque cura
> Conditione super communi; quin etiam lex
> Poenaque lata, malo quae nollet carmine quemquam
> Describi; vertere modum, formidine fustis
> Ad bene dicendum delectandumque redacti [1].

[1] 'The Fescennine raillery in this way, arose and poured forth its rustic banter in responsive strains; the spirit of freedom, made welcome, as the season came round, first played a kindly part; but soon the jests grew cruel, then changed into sheer fury, and began, with impunity, to threaten and assail honourable households. Men smarted under the sharp edge of its cruel tooth: even those who were unassailed felt concern for the common weal. A law was

The change in character, here described, from coarse and good-humoured bantering to libellous scurrility, may be conjectured to have taken place when the Fescennine freedom passed from villages and country districts to the active social and political life within the city. That this change had taken place in Rome at an early period, is proved by the fact that libellous verses were forbidden by the laws of the Twelve Tables[1]. The original Fescennine verse appears, from the testimony of Horace, to have been in metrical dialogue. This rude amusement, in which a coarse kind of banter was interchanged during their festive gatherings, was in early times characteristic of the rural populations of Greece and Sicily, as well as Italy, and was one of the original elements out of which Greek comedy and Greek pastoral poetry were developed. These verses had a kindred origin with that of the Phallic Odes among the Greeks. They both appear to have sprung out of the rudest rites and the grossest symbolism of rustic paganism. The Fescennine raillery long retained traces of this original character. Catullus mentions the 'procax Fescennina locutio' among the accompaniments of marriage festivals; and the songs of the soldiers, in the extravagant license of the triumphal procession, betrayed unmistakably this primitive coarseness.

These rude and inartistic verses, which took their name either from the town of Fescennia in Etruria or from the word fascinum[2], were the first expression of that aggressive and censorious spirit which ultimately animated Roman satire. But the original satura, which also was familiar to

passed, and a penalty enforced, forbidding any one to be branded in libellous verses. Thus they changed their style, and were brought back to a kindly and pleasant tone, under fear of a beating.'—Epist. ii. 1. 144-55.

[1] Sei quis ocentasit, casmenue condisit, quod infamiam faxsit flacitiomque alterei, fuste feritor.

[2] Teuffel quotes from Festus: Fescennini versus qui canebantur in nuptiis, ex urbe Fescennina dicuntur allati, sive ideo dicti quia fascinum putabantur arcere. It seems more natural to connect the name of these verses, which were especially characteristic of the Latian peasantry, with fascinum (the phallic symbol) than with any particular town of Etruria, though the name of that town may probably have the same origin.

the Romans before they became acquainted with Greek literature, was somewhat different both from the Fescennine verses, and from the lampoons which arose out of them. The more probable etymology[1] of the word *satura* connects it in origin with the *satura lanx*, a plate filled with various kinds of fruit offered to the gods. If this etymology be the true one, the word meant originally a medley of various contents, like the Italian *farsa*[2], and it evidently had not lost this meaning when first employed in regular literature by Ennius and Lucilius. The original satura was a kind of dramatic entertainment, accompanied with music and dancing, differing from the Fescennine verses in being regularly composed and not extemporaneous, and from the drama, in being without a connected plot. The origin of this composition is traced by Livy[3] to the representation of Etrurian dancers, who were brought to Rome during a pestilence. The Roman youth, according to his account, being moved to imitation of these representations, in which there was neither acting nor speaking, added to them the accompaniment of verses of a humorous character; and continued to represent these jocular medleys, combined with music (*saturas impletas modis*), even after the introduction of the regular drama.

These scenic saturae, which, from Livy's notice, appear to have been accompanied with good-humoured hilarity rather than with scurrilous raillery, prepared the way for the reception of the regular drama among the Romans, and will, to some extent, account for its early popularity among them. The later Roman satire long retained traces of a connexion with this primitive and indigenous satura, evinced both by the miscellaneous character of its topics, and by its frequent employment of dramatic dialogue.

4. The didactic tendency which is so conspicuous in the cultivated literature of Rome manifested itself also in the indigenous compositions of Italy. The popular maxims

---

[1] Mommsen's explanation, 'the masque of the full men' ('saturi'), does not seem to meet with general acceptance.
[2] Cf. Teuffel, vi. 2.   [3] vii. 2.

and precepts preserved by the old agricultural writers and afterwards embodied by Virgil in his Georgics, were handed down from generation to generation in the Saturnian rhythm. But, apparently, the first metrical composition committed to writing was a poem of an ethical or didactic character, written two generations before the first dramatic representation of Livius Andronicus, by Appius Claudius Caecus, who is also the earliest known to us in the long line of Roman orators[1].

5. But it was not from any of these sources that Niebuhr supposed the poetical character of early Roman history to be derived. Nor is there any analogy between the religious hymns, or the Fescennine verses of Italy, and the modern ballad. But there is evidence of the existence, at one time, of other metrical compositions of which scarcely anything is definitely ascertained, except that they were sung at banquets, to the accompaniment of the flute, in celebration of the praises of great men. There is no direct evidence of the time when these compositions, some of which were believed by Niebuhr to have attained the dimensions of Epic poems, existed, or when they fell into disuse. Cato, as quoted by Cicero in the Tusculan Disputations, and in the Brutus[2], is our earliest authority on the subject. His testimony is to the effect that many generations before his time, the guests at banquets were in the habit of singing, in succession, the praises of great men, to the music of the flute. Cicero, in the Brutus, expresses a wish that these songs still existed in his own day; 'utinam exstarent illa carmina, quae multis saeculis ante suam aetatem in epulis esse cantitata a singulis convivis de clarorum virorum laudibus in Originibus scriptum reliquit Cato.' Varro again is quoted, to the effect, that boys used to be present at banquets, for the purpose of singing 'ancient poems,' celebrating the praises of their ancestors. Valerius Maximus mentions 'that the older men used at banquets to celebrate in song the illustrious deeds of their ancestors,

---

[1] Cf. Teuffel, Wagner's Translation, p. 102
[2] Tusc. Disp. iv. 2 ; Brutus, 19.

in order to stimulate the youth to imitate them.' Passages are quoted also from Horace, from Dionysius, and from Tacitus, implying a belief in the ancient existence of these compositions.

Besides the odes sung or recited at banquets, there were certain funeral poems, called *Naeniae*, originally chanted by the female relatives of the deceased, but afterwards by hired women. As the practice of public speaking advanced, these gradually passed into a mere form, and were superseded by funeral orations.

The facts ascertained about these commemorative poems amount to no more than this,—that they were sung at banquets and the funerals of great men,—that they were of such length as to admit of several being sung in succession,—and that they fell into disuse some generations before the age of Cato. The inferences that may fairly be drawn from these statements are opposed to some of the conclusions of Niebuhr. The evidence is all in favour of their having been short lyrical pieces, and not long narrative poems. As they were sung at great banquets and funerals, it seems probable that, like the custom of exhibiting the ancestral images on the same occasions, they owed their origin to the patrician pride of family, and were not likely to have been animated by strong plebeian sentiment. If they had been preserved at all, they were thus more likely to have been preserved by members of the great houses living within the city walls, than by the peasantry living among the outlying hills and country districts. If ever there were any golden age of early Roman poetry, it had passed away long before the time of Ennius and Cato.

The fact, however, remains, that the Romans did possess, in early times, some kind of native minstrelsy, in which they honoured the memory and the exploits of their great men. And this impulse of hero-worship became in later times an important factor in their epic poetry. But is there any reason to suppose that these compositions were of the nature and importance assigned to them by Niebuhr, and had any value in respect of invention and execution? It is difficult to believe that such a native force of feeling and imagination, pouring itself forth in stirring ballads and continuous epic poems, could have been frozen so near its source; or that a rich, popular poetry, not scattered through thinly-peopled districts, but the possession of a great commonwealth — one most tenacious of every national memorial — could have entirely disappeared, under any foreign influence, in the course of one or two generations. But even on the supposition that a great national poetry might have passed from the memory of men—as, possibly, the poems existing before the time of Homer may have been lost or merged in the greater glories of the Iliad and the Odyssey—this early poetry could not have perished without leaving permanent influence on the Roman language. The growth of poetical language necessarily accompanies the growth of poetical feeling and inspiration. The sensuous, passionate, and musical force by which a language is first moulded into poetry is transmitted from one generation of poets to another. The language of Homer, by its natural and musical flow, by its accumulated wealth of meaning, by the use of traditional epithets and modes of expression, that penetrate far back into the belief, the feelings, and the life of an earlier time, implies the existence of a long line of poets who preceded him. On the other hand, the diction of the fragments of Ennius, in its strength and in its rudeness, is evidently, in great measure, the creation of his own time and his own mind. He has no true discernment of the characteristic difference between the language of prose and of poetry. The materials of his art had not been smoothed and polished by any long, continuous stream of national melody, but were rough-hewn and adapted by his own energy to the rugged structure of his poem.

While, therefore, it appears that the actual notices of the early commemorative poems do not imply that they were the products of imagination or poetical feeling, or that they excited much popular enthusiasm, and were an important element in the early State, their entire disappearance among a people so tenacious of all their gains, and, still more, the unformed and prosaic condition of the language and rhythm used by Naevius, Ennius, and the other early poets, lead to the presumption, that they were not much valued by the Romans at any time, and that they were not the creations of poetic genius and art. This presumption is further strengthened by such indications as there are of the recognition, or rather the non-recognition, of poets or of the poetic character at Rome in early times.

The worship of the Camenae was indeed an old and genuine part of the Roman or Italian religion; but, as was said before, their original function was to predict future events, and to communicate the knowledge of divination; not like that of the Greek Muses, to imagine bright stories of divine and human adventure,—

λησμοσύνην τε κακῶν ἄμπαυμά τε μερμηράων.

Even the names by which two of the Camenae were known—Postvorta and Antevorta—suggest the prosaic and practical functions which they were supposed to fulfil. The Romans had no native word equivalent to the Greek word ἀοιδός, denoting the primary and most essential of all poetical gifts, the power to awaken the music of language. The word *vates*, as was seen, denoted a prophet. The title of *scriba* was applied to Livius Andronicus; and Naevius, who has by some been regarded as the last of the old race of Roman bards, applies to himself the Greek name of *poeta*,—

Flerent divae Camenae Naevium poetam.

The commemorative odes appear to have been recited or sung at banquets, not by poets or rhapsodists, but by boys or guests. There is one notice, indeed, of a class of men who practised the profession of minstrelsy. This passage, which is quoted by Aulus Gellius from the writings of Cato, implies the very lowest estimation of the position and character of the poet, and points more naturally to the composers of the libellous verses forbidden by the laws of the Twelve Tables, than to the authors of heroic and national lays:—'Poetry was not held in honour; if anyone devoted himself to it, or went about to banquets, he was called a vagabond[1].'

It appears that, on this ground also, there is no reason for believing in the existence of any golden age of Roman poetry before the time of Ennius, or in the theory that the legendary tales of Roman history were created and shaped by native minstrels. To what cause, then, can we attribute their origin? These tales have a strong human interest, and represent marked and original types of antique heroism. They have the elements of true tragic pathos and moral grandeur. They could neither have arisen nor been preserved except among a people endowed with strong capacities of feeling and action. But the strength of the Roman mind consisted more in retentive capacity than in creative energy. Their art and their religion, their family and national customs, aimed at preserving the actual memory of men and of their actions: not like the arts, ceremonies, and customs of the Greeks, which aimed at lifting the mind out of reality into an ideal world. As one of the chief difficulties of the Homeric controversy arises from our ignorance of the power of the memory during an age when poetry and song were in the fullest life, but the use of letters was either unknown, or extremely limited; so there is a parallel difficulty in all attempts to explain the origin of early Roman history, from our ignorance of the power of oral tradition in a time of long established order, but yet unacquainted with any of the forms of literature. The indifference of barbarous tribes to their past history can prove little or nothing as to the tenacity of the national memory among a people far advanced towards civilisation like the Romans after the establishment of their Republican form of government. Nor can the analogy of early Greek traditions be fairly applied to those of Rome, owing to the great difference in the circumstances and the genius of the two nations.

[1] Noct. Att. xi. 2. A similar character at one time attached to minstrels in Scotland.

Many real impressions of the past might fix themselves indelibly in the grave and solid temperament of the Romans, which would have been lost amid the inexhaustible wealth of fancy that had been lavished upon the Greeks. The strict family life and discipline of the Romans, the continuity of their religious colleges, the unity of a single state as the common centre of all their interests, the slow and steady growth of their institutions, their strong regard for precedent, were all conditions more favourable to the preservation of tradition than the lively social life, the numerous centres of political organization, and the rapid growth and vicissitudes of the Greek Republics.

It cannot, indeed, be disputed that although the legendary tales of Roman history may have drawn more of their colour from life than from imagination, yet there is no criterion by which the amount of fact contained in them can be separated from the other elements of which they were composed. Oral tradition among the Romans, as among other nations, was founded on impressions originally received without any careful sifting of evidence; and these first impressions would naturally be modified in accordance with the feelings and opinions of each generation, through which they were transmitted. Aetiological myths, or the attempt to explain some institution or memorial by some concrete fact, and the systematic reconstruction of forgotten events, have also entered largely into the composition of Roman history. But these admissions do not lead to the conclusion that the art or fancy of any class of early poets was added to the unconscious operation of popular feeling in moulding the impressive tales of early heroism, partly out of the memory of real events and personages, partly out of the ideal of character, latent in the national mind. It has been remarked by Sir G. C. Lewis that many even of the Greek myths, abounding 'in striking, pathetic, and interesting events,' existed as prose legends, and were handed down in the common speech of the people. In like manner, such tales as those of Lucretia and Virginia, of Horatius and the Fabii, of Cincinnatus, Coriolanus, and

Camillus, which stand out prominently in the twilight of Roman history, may have been preserved in the *fama vulgaris*, or among the family traditions of the great houses, till they were gathered into the poem of Ennius and the prose narratives of the early annalists[1]. In so far as they are shaped or coloured by imagination, they do not bear traces of the conscious art of a poet, but rather of an unconscious conformity to the national ideal of character. The most impressive of these legendary stories illustrate the primitive virtues of the Roman character, such as chastity, frugality, fortitude, and self-devotion; or the national characteristics of patrician pride and a stern exercise of parental authority. There is certainly no internal evidence that any of them originated in a pure poetic impulse, or gave birth to any work of poetic art deserving a permanent existence in literature.

The analogy of other nations might suggest the inference that a race which in its maturity produced a genuine poetic literature must, in the early stages of its history, have given some proof of poetic inspiration. It is natural to associate the idea of poetry with youth both in nations and individuals. Yet the evidence of their language, of their religion, and of their customs, leads to the conclusion that the Romans, while prematurely great in action and government, were, in the earlier stages of their national life, little moved by any kind of poetical imagination. The state of religious feeling or belief which gives birth to or co-exists with primitive poetry has left no trace of itself upon the early Roman annals. It is generally found that a fanciful mythology, of a bright, gloomy, or grotesque character, in accordance with the outward circumstances and latent spirit or humour of the particular race among whom it originates, precedes and for a time accompanies

[1] Some of these tales may have been originally aetiological, but the human interest even in these was probably drawn originally from actual incidents and personages of the Early Republic. Some of the aetiological myths, such as that of Attus Navius the augur, have no human interest, though they have an historical interest in connexion with early Roman religion or institutions.

the poetry of romantic action. The creative faculty produces strange forms and conditions of supernatural life out of its own mysterious sympathy with Nature, before it learns to invent tales of heroic action and of tragic calamity out of its sympathy with human energy and passion, and its interest in marking the course of destiny, and the vicissitudes of life. The development of the Roman religion betrays the absence, or at least the weaker influence of that imaginative power which shaped the great mythologies of different races out of the primeval worship of nature. The later element introduced into Roman religion was due not to imagination but to reflection. The worship of Fides, Concordia, Pudicitia, and the like, marks a great progress from the early adoration of the sun, the earth, the vault of heaven, and the productive power of nature; but it is a progress in understanding and moral consciousness, not in poetical feeling nor imaginative power. It shows that Roman civilisation advanced without this vivifying influence, that the mind of the race early reached the maturity of manhood, without passing through the dreams of childhood or the buoyant fancies of youth.

The circumstances of the Romans, in early times, were also different from those by which the growth of a romantic poetry has usually been accompanied. Though, like all races born to a great destiny, they had much latent imaginative ardour of feeling, this was employed by them, unconsciously, in elevating and purifying the ideal of the State and the family, as actually realised in experience. Their orderly organisation,—the early establishment of their civic forms,—the strict discipline of family life among them,—the formal and ceremonial character of their national religion, —and their strong interest in practical affairs,—were not calculated either to kindle the glow of individual genius, or to dispose the mass of the people to listen to the charm of musical verse. The wars of the young Republic, carried on by a well-trained militia, for the acquisition of new territory, formed the character to solid strength and steady discipline, but could not act upon the fancy in the same way as the distant enterprise, the long struggles for national independence, or the daring forays, which have thrown the light of romance around the warlike youth of other races. The tillage of the soil, in which the brief intervals between their wars were passed, was a tame and monotonous pursuit compared with the maritime adventure which awoke the energies of Greece, or with the wild and lonely, half-pastoral, half-marauding life, out of which a true ballad poetry arose in modern times. Some traces of a wilder life, or some faint memories of their Sabine forefathers, may be dimly discerned in the earliest traditions of the Roman people; but their youth was essentially practical,— great and strong in the virtues of temperance, gravity, fortitude, reverence for law and the majesty of the State, combined with a strong love of liberty and sturdy resistance to wrong. These qualities are the foundations of a powerful and orderly State, not the root nor the sap by which a great national poetry is nourished [1].

If the pure Roman intellect and discipline had spontaneously produced any kind of literature, it would have been more likely to have taken the form of history or oratory than of national song or ballad. It was from men of the Italian provinces, and not from her own sons, that Rome received her poetry. The men of the most genuinely Roman type and character long resisted all literary progress. The patrons and friends of the early poets were the more liberal members of the aristocracy, in whom the austerity of the national character and narrowness of the national mind had yielded to new ideas and a wider experience. The art of Greece was communicated to 'rude Latium,' through the medium of those kindred races who had come into earlier contact with the Greek language and civilisation. With less native strength, but with greater flexibility, these races were more readily moulded by foreign influences; and, leading a life of greater ease and freedom, they were more susceptible to all the impulses of Nature. While they were thus more readily prepared to

[1] Cf. Schwegler, Röm. Gesch. i. 1. 24.

catch the spirit of Greek culture, they had learned, through long years of war and subsequent dependence, to understand and respect the imperial State in which their own nationality had been merged. It is important to remember that the time in which Roman literature arose was not only that of the first active intercourse between Greeks and Romans, but also that in which a great war, against the most powerful State outside of Italy, had awakened the sense of an Italian nationality, of which Rome was the centre. The great Republic derived her education and literature from the accumulated stores of Greek thought and feeling ; but these were made available to her through the willing service of poets who, though born in other parts of Italy, looked to Rome as the head and representative of their common country.

CHAPTER III.

THE BEGINNING OF ROMAN LITERATURE—LIVIUS ANDRO-
NICUS—CN. NAEVIUS, B.C. 240–202.

THE historical event which first brought the Romans into familiar contact with the Greeks, was the war with Pyrrhus and with Tarentum, the most powerful and flourishing among the famous Greek colonies in lower Italy. In earlier times, indeed, through their occasional communication with the Greeks of Cumae, and the other colonies in Italy, they had obtained a vague knowledge of some of the legends of Greek poetry. The worship of Aesculapius was introduced at Rome from Epidaurus in B.C. 293, and the oracle of Delphi had been consulted by the Romans in still earlier times. As the Sibylline verses appear to have been composed in Greek, their interpreters must have been either Greeks or men acquainted with that language[1]. The identification of the Greek with the Roman mythology had probably commenced before Greek literature was known to the Romans, although the works of Naevius and Ennius must have had an influence in completing this process. Greek civilisation had come, however, at an earlier period into close relation with the south of Italy; and the natives of that district, such as Ennius and Pacuvius, who first settled at Rome, were spoken of by the Romans as 'Semi Graeci.' But, until after the fall of Tarentum, there appears to have been no familiar intercourse between the two great representatives of ancient civilisation. Till the war with Pyrrhus, the knowledge that the two nations had of

[1] Cf. Lewis, Credibility of Early Roman History, vol. i. chap. ii. 14.

one another was slight and vague. But, immediately after that time, the affairs of Rome began to attract the attention of Greek historians[1], and the Romans, though very slowly, began to obtain some acquaintance with the language and literature of Greece.

Tarentum was taken in B.C. 272, but more than thirty years elapsed before Livius Andronicus represented his first drama before a Roman audience. Twenty years of this intervening period, from B.C. 261 to B.C. 241, were occupied with the First Punic War; and it was not till the successful close of that war, and the commencement of the following years of peace, that this new kind of recreation and instruction was made familiar to the Romans.

> Serus enim Graecis admovit acumina chartis;
> Et post Punica bella quietus, quaerere coepit
> Quid Sophocles et Thespis et Aeschylus utile ferrent[2].

Two circumstances, however, must in the meantime have prepared the minds of the Romans for the reception of the new literature. Sicily had been the chief battle-field of the contending powers. In their intercourse with the Sicilian Greeks, the Romans had great facilities for becoming acquainted with the Greek language, and frequent opportunities of being present at dramatic representations. Many Greeks also had been brought to Rome as slaves after the capture of Tarentum, and were employed in educating the young among the higher classes. Thus many Roman citizens were prepared, by their circumstances and education, to take interest in the legends and in the dramatic form of literature introduced from Greece; while the previous existence of the saturae, and other scenic exhibitions at Rome, tended to make the new drama acceptable to the great mass of the population.

The earliest period of Roman poetry extends from the close of the First Punic War till the beginning of the first

---

[1] Cf. Lewis, Credibility of Early Roman History, vol. i. chap. ii. 14, 15.
[2] Horace, Epist. ii. 1. 161-3.

century B.C. During this period of about a century and a half, in which Roman oratory, history, and comedy, were also actively cultivated, we hear only of five or six names as eminent in different kinds of serious poetry. The whole labour of introducing and of keeping alive, among an unlettered people, some taste for the graver forms of literature thus devolved upon a few men of ardent temperament, vigorous understanding, and great productive energy; but with little sense of art, and endowed with faculties seemingly more adapted to the practical business of life than to the idealising efforts of genius. They had to struggle against the difficulties incidental to the first beginnings of art and to the rudeness of the Latin language. They were exposed, also, to other disadvantages, arising from the natural indifference of the mass of the people to all works of imagination, and from the preference of the educated class for the more finished works already existing in Greek literature.

Yet this long period, in which poetry, with so much difficulty and such scanty resources, struggled into existence at Rome, is connected with the age of Cicero by an unbroken line of literary continuity. Naevius, the younger contemporary of Livius, and the first native poet, was actively engaged in the composition of his poems till the time of his death; about which period his greater successor first appeared at Rome. For about thirty years, Ennius shone alone in epic and tragic poetry. The poetic successor of Ennius was his nephew, Pacuvius. He, in the later years of his life, lived in friendly intercourse with his younger rival Accius, who, again, in his old age, had frequently conversed with Cicero[1]. The torch, which was first lighted by Livius Andronicus from the decaying fires of Greece, was thus handed down by these few men, through this long period, until it was extinguished during the stormy times which fell in the youth of the great orator and prose writer of the Republic.

The forms of serious poetry, prevailing during this

[1] Cic. Brutus, ch. 28.

period, were the tragic drama, the annalistic epic, and satire. Tragedy was earliest introduced, was received with most favour, and was cultivated by all the poets of the period, with the exception of Lucilius and the comic writers. The epic poetry of the age was the work of Naevius and Ennius. It has greater claims to originality and national spirit, both in form and substance, and it exercised a more powerful influence on the later poetry of Rome, than either the tragedy or comedy of the time. The invention of satire, the most purely original of the three, is generally attributed to Lucilius; but the satiric spirit was shown earlier in some of the dramas of Naevius; and the first modification of the primitive satura to a literary shape was the work of Ennius, who was followed in the same style by his nephew Pacuvius.

No complete work of any of these poets has been preserved to modern times. Our knowledge of the epic, tragic, and satiric poetry of this long period is derived partly from ancient testimony, but chiefly from the examination of numerous fragments. Most of these have been preserved, not by critics on account of their beauty and worth, but by grammarians on account of the obsolete words and forms of speech contained in them,—a fact, which probably leads us to attribute to the earlier literature a more abnormal and ruder style than that which really belonged to it. A few of the longest and most interesting fragments have come down in the works of the admirers of those ancient poets, especially of Cicero and Aulus Gellius. The notion that can be formed of the early Roman literature must thus, of necessity, be incomplete. Yet these fragments are sufficient to produce a consistent impression of certain prevailing characteristics of thought and sentiment. Many of them are valuable from their own intrinsic worth; others again from the grave associations connected with their antiquity, and from the authentic evidence they afford of the moral and intellectual qualities, the prevailing ideas and sympathies of the strongest race of the ancient world, about, or shortly after, the time when they attained the acme of their moral and political greatness.

The two earliest authors who fill a period of forty years in the literary history of Rome, extending from the end of the First to the end of the Second Punic War, are Livius Andronicus and Cn. Naevius. Of the first very little is known. The fragments of his works are scanty and unimportant, and have been preserved by grammarians merely as illustrative of old forms of the language. The admirers of Naevius and Ennius, in ancient times, awarded only scanty honours to the older dramatist. Cicero, for instance, says of his plays 'that they are not worth reading a second time[1].' There is no ground for believing that Livius was a man of original genius. The importance which attaches to him consists in his being the accidental medium through which literary art was first introduced to the Romans. He was a Greek, and, as is generally supposed, a native of Tarentum. If he was among the captives taken after the fall of that city, he must have resided thirty years at Rome before he ventured to reproduce a Greek drama in the Latin language. He educated the sons of his master, M. Livius Salinator, from whom he afterwards received his freedom. The last thirty years of his life were devoted to literature, and chiefly to the reproduction of the Greek drama in a Latin dress. His tragedies appear all to have been founded on Greek subjects; most of them, probably, were translations. Among the titles, we hear of the *Aegisthus, Ajax, Equus Trojanus, Tereus, Hermione,* etc.—all of them subjects which continued to be popular with the later tragedians of Rome. No fragment is preserved sufficient to give any idea of his treatment of the subjects, or of his general mode of thought and feeling. Little can be gathered from the scanty remains of his works, except some idea of the harshness and inelegance of his diction.

In addition to his dramas, he translated the Odyssey into Saturnian verse. This work long retained its place as

[1] Brutus, 18.

a school-book, and is spoken of by Horace as forming part of his own early lessons under the rod of Orbilius [1]. One or two lines of the translation still remain, and exemplify its bald and prosaic diction, and the extreme irregularity of the Saturnian metre. The lines of the Odyssey [2],

οὐ γὰρ ἔγωγέ τί φημι κακώτερον ἄλλο θαλάσσης
ἄνδρα γε συγχεῦαι, εἰ καὶ μάλα καρτερὸς εἴη;

are thus rendered:—

>   Namque nilum pejus
> Macerat hemonem, quamde mare saevom, viris quoi
> Sunt magnae, topper confringent importunae undae.

He was appointed also, on one occasion, near the end of the Second Punic War, to compose a hymn to be sung by 'virgines ter novenae,' which is described by Livy, the historian, as rugged and unpolished [3].

Livius was the schoolmaster of the Roman people rather than the father of their literature. To accomplish what he did required no original genius, but only the industry, knowledge, and tastes of an educated man. If his long residence among his grave and stern masters, and the hardships and constraint of slavery, had subdued in him the levity and gaiety of a Tarentine Greek, they did not extinguish his love of his native literature and the intellectual cultivation peculiar to his race. In spite of the disadvantage of writing in a foreign language, and of addressing an unlettered people, he was able to give the direction which Roman poetry long followed, and to awaken a new interest in the legends and heroes of his race. It was necessary that the Romans should be educated before they could either produce or appreciate an original poet. Livius performed a useful, if not a brilliant service, by directing those who followed him to the study and imitation of the great masters who combined, with an unattainable grace and art, a masculine strength and heroism of sentiment congenial to the better side of Roman character.

Cn. Naevius is really the first in the line of Roman

[1] Epist. ii. 1. 71.   [2] viii. 138.   [3] xxvii. 17.

poets, and the first writer in the Latin language whose fragments give indication of original power. He is believed to have been a Campanian by birth, on the authority of Aulus Gellius, who characterised his famous epitaph as 'plenum superbiae Campanae.' Though the arrogance of Campania may have been proverbial, yet the expression could scarcely with propriety have been applied, except to a native of that district. If not a Roman by birth, he at least belonged to a district which had become thoroughly Latinised long before his time, and he showed himself to be, like his successor Ennius, thoroughly Roman in his sympathies. He served as a soldier in the First Punic War, and recorded his services in his epic poem on that subject. The earliest drama of Naevius was brought out in B.C. 235, five years after the first representation of Livius Andronicus. The number of dramas which he is known to have composed affords proof of great industry and activity, from that time till the time of his banishment from Rome. He was more successful in comedy than in tragedy, and he used the stage, as it had been used by the writers of the old Attic comedy, as an arena of popular invective and political warfare. A keen partisan of the commonalty, he attacked with vehemence some of the chiefs of the great senatorian party. A line, which had passed into a proverb in the time of Cicero, is attributed to him,—

Fato Metelli Romae fiunt consules;

to which the Metelli are said to have replied in the pithy Saturnian,

Dabunt malum Metelli Naevio poetae.

It is, however, doubted whether the first of these lines was really written by Naevius, as the Metelli did not enjoy their rapid succession of consulships till nearly a century after his death; but even at the time of the Second Punic War they were powerful enough to procure the imprisonment of the poet, in consequence of some offence which he had given them. Plautus[1] alludes to this event, in one of

[1] Miles Gloriosus, ii. 2. 27.

the few passages in which Latin comedy deviates from the conventional life of Athenian manners to notice the actual circumstances of the time. While in prison, he composed two plays (the *Hariolus* and *Leon*), which contained some retractation of his former attacks, and he was liberated through the interference of the Tribunes of the Commons. Being afterwards banished, he took up his residence at Utica, where he is said by Cicero, on the authority of ancient records, to have died, in B.C. 204[1], though the same author adds that Varro, 'diligentissimus investigator antiquitatis,' believed that he was still alive for some time after that date[2]. It is inferred, from a passage in Cicero[3], that his poem on the First Punic War was composed in his old age. Probably it was written in his exile, when removed from the sphere of his active literary efforts. As he served in that war, some time between B.C. 261 and B.C. 241, he must have been well advanced in years at the time of his death.

The best known of all the fragments of Naevius, and the most favourable specimen of his style, is his epitaph:—

> Mortales immortales flere si foret fas,
> Flerent divae Camenae Naevium poetam,
> Itaque postquam est Orcino traditus thesauro,
> Obliti sunt Romae loquier Latina lingua.

It has been supposed that this epitaph was written as a dying protest against the Hellenising influence of Ennius; but as Ennius came to Rome for the first time about B.C. 204, it is not likely, even if the life of Naevius was prolonged somewhat beyond that date, that the fame and influence of his younger rival could have spread so rapidly as to disturb the peace of the old poet in his exile. It might as fairly be regarded as proceeding from a jealousy of the merits of Plautus, as from hostility to the innovating tendency of Ennius. The words of the epitaph are simply expres-

---

[1] Brutus, 15.
[2] Mommsen remarks that he could not have retired to Utica till after it fell into the possession of the Romans.
[3] De Senectute, 14.

sive of the strong self-assertion and independence which Naevius maintained till the end of his active and somewhat turbulent career.

He wrote a few tragedies, of which scarcely anything is known except the titles,—such as the *Andromache*, *Equus Trojanus*, *Hector Proficiscens*, *Lycurgus*,—the last founded on the same subject as the Bacchae of Euripides. The titles of nearly all these plays, as well as of the plays of Livius, imply the prevailing interest taken in the Homeric poems, and in all the events connected with the Trojan War. The following passage from the Lycurgus has some value as containing the germs of poetical diction :—

> Vos, qui regalis corporis custodias
> Agitatis, ite actutum in frundiferos locos,
> Ingenio arbusta ubi nata sunt, non obsita [1].

He composed a number of comedies, and also some original plays, founded on events in Roman history,— one of them called *Romulus*, or *Alimonia Romuli et Remi*. The longest of the fragments attributed to him is a passage from a comedy, which has been, with less probability, attributed to Ennius. It is a description of a coquette, and shows considerable power of close satiric observation :—

> Quasi pila
> In choro ludens dadatim dat se, et communem facit:
> Alii adnutat, alii adnictat, alium amat, alium tenet;
> Alibi manus est occupata, alii percellit pedem;
> Alii spectandum dat annulum ; a labris alium invocat;
> Cum alio cantat, attamen dat alii digito literas [2].

The chief characteristic illustrated by the scanty fragments of his dramas is the political spirit with which they were

---

[1] 'Ye who keep watch over the person of the king, hasten straightway to the leafy places, where the copsewood is of nature's growth, not planted by man.'

[2] 'Like one playing at ball in a ring, she tosses about from one to another, and is at home with all. To one she nods, to another winks ; she makes love to one, clings to another. Her hand is busy here, her foot there. To one she gives a ring to look at, to another blows a kiss; with one she sings, with another corresponds by signs.'

The reading of the passage here adopted is that given by Munk.

animated. Thus Cicero[1] refers to a passage in one of his plays (*ut est in Naevii ludo*) where, to the question, 'Who had, within so short a time, destroyed your great commonwealth?' the pregnant answer is given,

> Proveniebant oratores novi, stulti adolescentuli[1].

The nobles, whose enmity he provoked, were probably attacked by him in his comedies. One passage is quoted by Aulus Gellius, in which a failing of the great Scipio is exposed[1]. Other fragments are found indicative of his freedom of speech and bold independence of character:—

> Quae ego in theatro hic meis probavi plausibus,
> Ea nunc audere quemquam regem rumpere?
> Quanto libertatem hanc hic superat servitus[3]?

and this also[4]:—

> Semper pluris feci potioremque ego
> Libertatem habui multo quam pecuniam.

He is placed in the canon of Volcatius Sedigitus immediately after Plautus in the rank of comic poets. He has more of the stamp of Lucilius than of his immediate successor Ennius. By his censorious and aggressive vehemence, by boldness and freedom of speech, and by his strong political feeling, Naevius in his dramas represents the spirit of Roman satire rather than of Roman tragedy. He holds the same place in Roman literature as the Tribune of the Commons in Roman politics. He expressed the vigorous independence of spirit that supported the Commons in their long struggle with the patricians, while Ennius may be regarded as expressing

---

[1] De Senectute, 6.

[2] Etiam qui res magnas manu saepe gessit gloriose,
  Cujus facta viva nunc vigent, qui apud gentes solus praestat,
  Eum suus pater cum pallio ab amica abduxit uno.

[3] 'What I in the theatre here have made good by the applause given to me, to think that any of these great people should now dare to interfere with! How much better thing is the slavery *here*' (*i.e.* represented in this play), 'than the liberty we actually enjoy?'

[4] I have always held liberty to be of more value and a better thing than money.' The reading is that given by Munk.

the majesty and authority with which the Roman Senate ruled the world.

But the work on which his fame as a national and original poet chiefly rested was his epic or historical poem on the First Punic War. The poem was originally one continuous work, written in the Saturnian metre; though, at a later time, it was divided into seven books. The earlier part of the work dealt with the mythical origin of Rome and of Carthage, the flight of Aeneas from Troy, his sojourn at the court of Dido, and his settlement in Latium. The mythical background of the poem afforded scope for imaginative treatment and invention. Its main substance, however, appears to have been composed in the spirit and tone of a contemporary chronicle. The few fragments that remain from the longer and later portion of the work, evidently express a bare and literal adherence to fact, without any poetical colouring or romantic representation.

Ennius and Virgil are both known to have borrowed much from this poem of Naevius. There are many passages in the Aeneid in which Virgil followed, with slight deviations, the track of the older poet. Naevius (as quoted by Servius) introduced the wives of Aeneas and of Anchises, leaving Troy in the night-time,—

> Amborum
> Uxores noctu Troiade exibant capitibus
> Opertis, flentes abeuntes lacrimis cum multis.

He represents Aeneas as having only one ship, built by Mercury,—a limitation which did not suit Virgil's account of the scale on which the war was carried on, after the landing in Italy. The account of the storm in the first Aeneid, of Aeneas consoling his followers, of Venus complaining to Jupiter, and of his comforting her with the promise of the future greatness of Rome (one of the cardinal passages in Virgil's epic), were all taken from the old Saturnian poem of Naevius. He speaks also of Anna and Dido, as daughters of Agenor, though there is no direct evidence that he anticipated Virgil in telling the tale of Dido's unhappy love. He mentioned also the Italian

Sibyl and the worship of the Penates—materials which Virgil fused into his great national and religious poem. Ennius followed Naevius in representing Romulus as the grandson of Aeneas. The exigencies of his chronology compelled Virgil to fill a blank space of three hundred years with the shadowy forms of a line of Alban kings.

Whatever may have been the origin of the belief in the connexion of Rome with Troy, it certainly prevailed before the poem of Naevius was composed, as at the beginning of the First Punic War the inhabitants of Egesta opened their gates to Rome, in acknowledgment of their common descent from Troy. But the story of the old connexion of Aeneas and Dido, symbolising the former league and the later enmity between Romans and Carthaginians, most probably first assumed shape in the time of the Punic Wars. The belief, as shadowed forth in Naevius, that the triumph of Rome had been decreed from of old by Jupiter, and promised to the mythical ancestress of Aeneas, proves that the Romans were possessed already with the idea of their national destiny. How much of the tale of Aeneas and Dido is due to the imagination of Naevius it is impossible to say; but his treatment of the mythical part of his story,—his introduction of the storm, the complaint of Venus, etc.,—merits the praise of happy and suggestive invention, and of a real adaptation to his main subject. There was more meaning in the mythical foreshadowing of the deadly strife between Romans and Carthaginians, at a time when the two nations were fighting for their very existence, and for the ultimate prize of the empire of the world, than in the age of Virgil, when the power of Carthage was only a memory of the past, and the immediate danger from which Rome had escaped had arisen not so much from any foreign enemy, as from the fierce passions of her own sons.

The mythical part of the poem was a prelude to the main subject, the events of the First Punic War. Naevius and Ennius, like others among the Roman poets of a later date, allowed the provinces of poetry and of history to run into one another. They composed poetical chronicles without any attempt to adhere to the principles and practice of the Greek epic. The work of Naevius differed from that of Ennius in this respect, that it treated of one particular portion of Roman history, and did not profess to unfold the whole annals of the State. The slight and scanty fragments that remain from the latter part of the poem, are expressed with all the bareness, and, apparently, with the fidelity of a chronicle. They have the merit of being direct and vigorous, but are entirely without poetic grace and ornament. Rapid and graphic condensation is their chief merit. There is a dash of impetuosity in some of them, suggestive of the bold, impatient, and energetic temperament of the poet; as for instance in the lines

> Transit Melitam Romanus exercitus, insulam integram
> Urit, populatur, vastat, rem hostium concinnat[1].

But the fragments of the poem are really too unimportant to afford ground for a true estimate of its general merit. They supply some evidence in regard to the irregularity of the metre in which it was written. The uncertainty which prevails as to its structure may be inferred from the fact that different conjectural readings of every fragment are proposed by different commentators. A saying of an old grammarian, Atilius Fortunatianus, is quoted to the effect that he could not adduce from the whole poem of Naevius any single line, as a normal specimen of the pure Saturnian verse. Cicero bears strong testimony to the merits of the poem in point of style. He says in one place, 'the Punic War delights us like a work of Myron[2].' In the dialogue 'De Oratore,' he represents Crassus as comparing the idiomatic purity which distinguished the conversation of his mother-in-law, Laelia, and other ladies of rank, with the style of Plautus and Naevius. 'Equidem quum audio socrum meam Laeliam (facilius enim mulieres

---

[1] Mommsen remarks that, in the fragments of this poem, the action is generally represented in the *present tense*.

[2] Brutus, 19.

incorruptam antiquitatem conservant, quod, multorum sermonis expertes, ea tenent semper, quae prima didicerunt); sed eam sic audio, ut Plautum mihi aut Naevium videar audire. Sono ipso vocis ita recto et simplici est, ut nihil ostentationis aut imitationis afferre videatur; ex quo sic locutum ejus patrem judico, sic majores[1].' Expressions from his plays were, from their weight and compact brevity, quoted familiarly in the days of Cicero; and one of them 'laudari a laudato viro,' like so many other pithy Latin sayings, is still in use to express a distinction that could not be characterised in happier or shorter terms. It is to be remarked also that the merit, which he assumes to himself in his epitaph, is the purity with which he wrote the Latin language.

Our knowledge of Naevius is thus, of necessity, very limited and fragmentary. From the testimony of later authors it may, however, be gathered that he was a remarkable and original man. He represented the boldness, freedom, and energy, which formed one side of the Roman character. Like some of our own early dramatists, he had served as a soldier before becoming an author. He was ardent in his national feeling; and, both in his life and in his writings, he manifested a strong spirit of political partisanship. As an author, he showed great productive energy, which continued unabated through a long and vigorous lifetime. His high self-confident spirit and impetuous temper have left their impress on the few fragments of his dramas and of his epic poem. Probably his most important service to Roman literature consisted in the vigour and purity with which he used the Latin language. But the conception of his epic poem seems to imply some

---

[1] 'I, for my part, as I listen to my mother-in-law, Laelia (for women more easily preserve the pure idiom of antiquity, because, from their limited intercourse with the world, they retain always their earlier impressions), in listening, I say to her, I fancy that I am listening to Plautus or Naevius. The very tones of her voice are so natural and simple, that she seems absolutely free from affectation or imitation; from this I gather that her father spoke, and her ancestors all spoke, in the very same way.'—Cicero, De Oratore iii. 12.

share of the higher gift of poetical invention. He stands at the head of the line of Roman poets, distinguished by that force of speech and vehemence of temper, which appeared again in Lucilius, Catullus, and Juvenal; distinguished also by that national spirit which moved Ennius and, after him, Virgil, to employ their poetical faculty in raising a monument to commemorate the power and glory of Rome.

CHAPTER IV.

ENNIUS.

THE impulse given to Latin literature by Naevius was mainly in two directions, that of comedy and of a rude epic poetry, drawing its subjects from Roman traditions and contemporary history. In comedy the work begun by him was carried on with great vigour and success by his younger contemporary Plautus: and, in a strictly chronological history of Roman literature, his plays would have to be examined next in order. But it will be more convenient to defer the consideration of Roman comedy, as a whole, till a later chapter, and for the present to direct attention to the results produced by the immediate successor of Naevius in epic poetry, Q. Ennius.

The fragments of Ennius will repay a more minute examination than those of any author belonging to the first period of Roman literature. They are of more intrinsic value, and they throw more light on the spirit of the age in which they were written. It was to him, not to Naevius or to Plautus, that the Romans looked as the father of their literature. He did more than any other man to make the Roman language a vehicle of elevated feeling, by forcing it to conform to the metrical conditions of Greek poetry; and he was the first fully to elicit the deeper veins of sentiment latent in the national imagination. The versatility of his powers, his large acquaintance with Greek literature, his sympathy with the practical interests of his time, the serious purpose and the intellectual vigour with which he carried out his work, enabled him to be in letters, what Scipio was in action, the most vital representative of his epoch. It has happened too that the fragments from his writings and the testimonies concerning him are more expressive and characteristic than in the case of any other among the early writers. There are none of his contemporaries, playing their part in war or politics, and not many among the writers of later times, of whom we can form so distinct an image.

I. LIFE, TIMES, AND PERSONAL TRAITS.

I. He was born at Rudiae, a town of Calabria, in B.C. 239, the year after the first representation of a drama on the Roman stage. He first entered Rome in B.C. 204, in the train of Cato, who, when acting as quaestor in Sardinia, found the poet in that island serving, with the rank of centurion, in the Roman army. In the poem of Silius Italicus, he is fancifully represented as distinguishing himself in personal combat like one of the heroes of the Iliad. After this time he resided at Rome, 'living,' according to the statement of Jerome, 'very plainly, on the Aventine' (the Plebeian quarter of the city), 'attended only by a single maid-servant[1],' and supporting himself by teaching Greek and by his writings. He accompanied M. Fulvius Nobilior in his Aetolian campaign. Through the influence of his son, he obtained the honour of Roman citizenship, probably at the time when the colony of Pisaurum was planted in B.C. 184. This distinction Ennius has himself recorded in a line of the Annals:—

Nos sumu' Romani, qui fuvimus ante Rudini.

He lived on terms of intimacy with influential members of the noblest families in Rome, and became the familiar friend of the great Scipio. When he died at the age of seventy, his bust was believed to be placed in the tomb of the Scipios, between those of the conqueror of Hannibal and of the conqueror of Antiochus. He died in the year B.C. 169. The most famous of his works were his Tragedies and the Annals, a long historical poem written in eighteen

[1] Parco admodum sumptu contentus et unius ancillae ministerio.

books. But, in addition to these, he composed several miscellaneous works, of which only very scanty fragments have been preserved.

Among the circumstances which prepared him to be the creator of a national literature, his birthplace and origin, the kind of education available to him in his early years, and the experience which awaited him when first entering on life, had a strong determining influence. His birthplace, Rudiae, is called by Strabo 'a Greek city;' but it was not a Greek colony, like Tarentum and the other cities of Magna Graecia, but an old Italian town, (the epithet *vetustae* is applied to it by Silius) which had been partially Hellenised, but still retained its native traditions and the use of the Oscan language. Ennius is thus spoken of as 'Semi-Graecus.' He laid claim to be descended from the old Messapian kings, a claim which Virgil is supposed to acknowledge in the introduction of Messapus leading his followers in the gathering of the Italian races,

Ibant aequati numero regemque canebant.

This claim to royal descent indicates that the poet was a member of the better class of families in his native district; and the consciousness of old lineage, which prompted the claim, probably strengthened the high self-confidence by which he was animated, and helped to determine the strong aristocratic bias of his sympathies. He bore witness to his nationality in the saying quoted by Gellius[1] that 'in the possession of the Greek, Oscan, and Latin speech, he possessed three hearts.' Of these three languages the Oscan, as the one of least value to acquire for the purposes of literature or of social intercourse, was most likely to have been his inherited tongue. Rudiae, from its Italian nationality, from its neighbourhood to the cities of Magna Graecia, and from its relation of dependence on Rome, must have been in the time of the boyhood of Ennius a meeting-place, not only of three different languages,—that of common

[1] xvii. 17.

life, that of culture and education, that of military service—but of the three different spirits or tendencies which were operative in the creation of the new literature. To his home among the hills overlooking the Grecian seas—referred to in a line of the Annals,—

> Ad patrios montes et ad incunabula nostra—

in the expression of Ovid,—

> Calabris in montibus ortus—

and in the phrase of Silius,—

> Hispida tellus
> Miserunt Calabri; Rudiae genuere vetustae

the poet owed the 'Italian heart' the virtue of a race still uncorrupted and unsophisticated, the buoyant energy and freshness of feeling which enabled him to apprehend all the novelty and the greatness of the momentous age through which he lived. The South of Italy afforded, at this time, means of education, which were denied to Rome or Latium; and the peace enjoyed by his native district for the first twenty years of the life of Ennius granted leisure to avail himself of these means, which he could not have enjoyed had he been born a few years later. In the short account of his life in Jerome's continuation of the Eusebian Chronicle, it is stated that he was born at Tarentum. Though this is clearly an error, it seems probable that the poet may have spent the years of his education there. Though Tarentum had lost its political importance since its capture by the Romans, it still continued to be a centre of Greek culture and of social pleasure. Dramatic representations had been especially popular among a people who had drifted far away 'ex Spartana dura illa et horrida disciplina[1]' of their ancestors. From the intimate knowledge of the Attic tragedians displayed by Ennius in his later career it is likely that he had witnessed representations of their works on a Greek stage, before he began, in middle life, to direct his own genius to dramatic composition. The knowledge and admiration of Homer which stimulated him to the composition of his greatest work, might have

[1] Livy xxxviii. 17.

been acquired in any centre of Greek culture. But the intellectual interests indicated in some of his miscellaneous writings have a kind of local character, distinguishing them alike from the older philosophies of Athens and from the more recent science of Alexandria. His acceptance of the doctrine of the transmigration of souls and the physical fancies expressed in some of the fragments of the Epicharmus probably came to him from the teaching of the Neo-Pythagoreans, who were widely spread among the Greeks of Southern Italy. The rationalistic speculations of Euhemerus, which appear in strange union with the 'somnia Pythagorea' of the Annals, were of Sicilian origin. The gastronomic treatise, which Ennius afterwards translated into Latin, was the work of Archestratus of Gela. The class of persons for whom such a work would originally be written was likely to be found among the luxurious livers of Sicily and Magna Graecia. Thus while the serious poetry of Ennius was inspired by the older and nobler works of Greek genius, the influence of a more vulgar and prosaic class of teachers, transmitted by him to Roman thought and literature, was probably derived from the place of his early education.

His Italian spirit, and the Greek culture acquired by him in early youth, were two of the conditions out of which the new literature was destined to arise. The third condition was his steadfast and ardent Roman patriotism. Born more than a generation after his native district had ceased to be at war with Rome, he grew up to manhood during the years of peace between the first and second Carthaginian wars, when the supremacy of Rome was loyally accepted. Between early manhood and middle life he was a witness of and an actor in the protracted and long doubtful struggle between the two great Imperial States, on the issue of which hung the future destinies of the world:—

> Omnia cum belli trepido concussa tumultu
> Horrida contremuere sub altis aetheris oris;
> In dubioque fuere utrorum ad regna cadendum
> Omnibus humanis esset terraque marique[1].

[1] 'When the Carthaginians were coming from all sides to the conflict, and

Though during that struggle the loyalty of some of the Italian communities was shaken, yet the aristocratic party in every city, and the Greek States generally, were true to the Roman alliance[1]. Thus his political sympathies, as well as his Greek education, would incline Ennius to identify himself with the cause of Rome, and his ardent imagination apprehended the grandeur and majesty with which she played her part in the contest. It was in the Second Punic War that the ideal of what was greatest in the character and institutions of Rome was most fully realised. Her good fortune supplied from among the contingent furnished to the war by her Messapian allies a man of a nature so sympathetic with her own and an imagination so vivid as to gain for the ideal thus created a permanent realization.

Of the share which Ennius had in the war we know only that he served in Sardinia with the rank of centurion. That he had become a man of some note in that capacity is suggested by the fact that he attracted the attention of the Roman quaestor Cato, and accompanied him to Rome. A certain dramatic interest attaches to this first meeting of the typical representative of Roman manners and traditions and great enemy of foreign innovations, with the man by whom, more than by any one else, the mind of Rome was enlarged and liberalised, and many of her most cherished convictions were most seriously undermined. This actual service in a great war left its impress on the work done by Ennius. Fragments both of his tragedies and his Annals prove how thoroughly he understood and appreciated the best qualities of the soldierly character. This fellowship in hardship and danger fitted him to become the national poet of a race of soldiers. He has drawn from his own observation an image of the fortitude and discipline of the Roman armies, and of the patriotic devotion and resolution of the men by whom these armies were led.

all things, beneath high heaven, confounded by the hurry and tumult of war, shook with alarm: and men were in doubt to which of the two the empire of the whole world, by land and sea, should fall.'—Lucret. iii. 833–7.

[1] Mommsen, book iii. ch. 5.

There is a strong realism in the expression of martial sentiment in Ennius, marking him out as a man familiar with the life of the camp and the battle-field, and quite distinct from the idealising enthusiasm of Livy and Virgil [1].

Ennius entered on his career as a writer at a time when the long strain of a great struggle was giving place to the confidence and security of a great triumph. He lived for thirty-five years longer, witnessing the rapid advance of Roman conquest in Greece and Asia, and over the barbarous tribes of the West. He died one year before the crowning victory of Pydna. During all his later life his sanguine spirit and patriotic enthusiasm were buoyed up by the success of the Roman and Italian arms abroad; while his political sympathies were in thorough accord with the dominant influences in the government of the State. At no other period of Roman history was the ascendency of the Senate and of the great houses more undisputed, or, on the whole, more wisely and ably exercised. In the lists of those who successively fill the great curule magistracies, we find almost exclusively the names of members of the old patrician or of the more recent plebeian nobility. At no other period does the tribunician opposition to the senatorian direction of affairs and to the authority of the magistrate appear weaker or more intermittent. It was not till a generation after the death of Ennius that the moral corruption and political and social disorganisation —the ultimate results of the great military successes gained under the absolute ascendency of the Senate,—became fully manifest. It is difficult to say how far the aristocratic and antipopular bias of all Roman literature may have been determined by the political conditions of the time in which that literature received the most powerful impulse, and by the personal relations and peculiar stamp of character of the man by whom that impulse was given.

Along with the military and political activity of the

---

[1] The author of Caesar's Spanish War quotes Ennius in his account of the critical moment in the Battle of Munda:—'Hic, ut ait Ennius, "pes pede premitur, armis teruntur arma."' Bell. Hisp. xxxi.

time, during which Ennius lived in Rome, the stirring of a new intellectual life was apparent. Even during the war dramatic representations continued to take place, and the most active part of the career of Naevius, and a considerable part of that of Plautus, belong to the years during which Hannibal was still in Italy. After the cessation of the war, we note in the pages of Livy that much greater prominence is given to the celebration of public games, of which at this time dramatic representations formed the chief part. The regular holidays for which the Aediles provided these entertainments became more numerous; and the art of the dramatist was employed to enhance the pomp of the spectacle on the occasion of a great triumph, or of the funeral of an illustrious man. The death of Livius Andronicus and the banishment of Naevius, which must have happened about the time that Ennius arrived at Rome, had deprived the Roman stage of the only writers of any name, who had attempted to introduce upon it the works of the Greek tragedians. Ennius had, indeed, rather to create than to revive the taste for tragedy. The prologue to the Amphitryo[1] shows how much more congenial the reproduction of the ordinary life of the Greeks was to the uneducated audiences of Rome than the higher effort to familiarise them with the personages and adventures of the heroic age. The great era of Roman comedy was coincident with the literary career of Ennius. It was then that the best extant plays of Plautus were produced, and that Caecilius Statius, whom ancient critics ranked as his superior, flourished. The quality attributed to the latter in the line of Horace,

> Vincere Caecilius gravitate, Terentius arte,

indicates a closer affinity with the spirit of Ennius, than the moral and political indifference of the older dramatist. The aim of Ennius was to raise literature from being a mere popular recreation, and to bring it into accord with

---

[1] Amphit. 52–3—
> Quid contraxistis frontem, quia tragoediam
> Dixi futuram hanc?

the higher mood of the nation; to use it as a medium both of elevation and enlightenment. In carrying out this aim he appealed to the temper and to the newly awakened interests of members of the aristocratic class, who were coming into close contact with educated Greeks, and were beginning to appreciate the treasures of art and literature now opened up to them. The career of Q. Fabius Pictor, the first historian of Rome, and the first who made a name for himself in painting, who lived at this time, attests this twofold attraction. The friendly relations which Roman generals, such as T. Quintius Flamininus, established with the famous Greek cities, in which they appeared as liberators rather than conquerors, were the result of intellectual enthusiasm as much as of a definite policy. With the wars of Pyrrhus and the capture of Tarentum, the first stage of the process described in the lines of Horace began[1]: the end of the Second Punic War was the second stage in the process. It is to this period, rather than to the progress of the war, that the words of the Grammarian, Porcius Licinus, most truly apply,

> Poenico bello secundo Musa pinnato gradu
> Intulit se bellicosam in Romuli gentem feram.

The more frequent and closer contact with the mind of Greece not only refined the taste and enlarged the intelligence of those capable of feeling its influence, but produced at the same time a change in men's deepest convictions. Though the definite tenets of Stoicism and Epicureanism did not acquire ascendency till a later time, the dissolving force of Greek speculative thought and Greek views of life forced its way into Rome through various channels,—especially through the adaptations of the tragedies of Euripides and of the comedy of Menander. All these tendencies of the time acted on Ennius, stimulating his mental activity in various directions. His natural temperament and his acquired culture brought him into harmony with the spirit of his age without raising him too much above it. A poet of more delicacy of taste and

[1] Graecia capta ferum victorem cepit, &c.

perfection of execution would have been unintelligible to his contemporaries. A more systematic thinker would have been out of harmony with the conditions of life by which he was surrounded. Breadth, vigour, a spirit clinging to what was most vital in the old state of things, and yet readily adapting itself to what was new, were the qualities needed to establish a literature true to the genius of Rome in the second century B.C., and containing the promise of the more perfect accomplishment of a later age. And these qualities belonged to Ennius by natural gifts and the experience and culture of his earlier years.

There is no reason to believe that he had obtained any eminence in literature before he settled in middle age at Rome. His genius was of that robust order which grows richer and livelier with advancing years. The Annals was the work of his old age,—the ripe fruit of a strong and energetic manhood, prolonged to the last in hopeful activity. Cicero speaks of 'the cheerfulness with which he bore the two evils of old age and poverty[1].' Wherever the poet speaks of himself, his words reveal a sanguine and contented spirit; as, in that fine simile, where he compares himself, at the close of his active and successful career, to a brave horse which has often won the prize at the Olympian games, and in old age obtains his well-deserved repose:—

> Sicut fortis equus, spatio qui saepe supremo
> Vicit Olimpia, nunc senio confectu' quiescit.

In none of his fragments is there any trace of that melancholy after-thought which pervades the poetry of his greatest successors, Lucretius and Virgil. From the humorous exaggeration of Horace,

> Ennius ipse pater nunquam, nisi potus, ad arma
> Prosiluit dicenda;

and from the poet's own confession,

> Nunquam poetor, nisi si podager,

it may be inferred that he belonged to the class of poets

[1] De Senectute, 5.

of a lusty and social nature, of which Dryden is a type in modern times, who enjoyed the pleasures of wine and good fellowship. The well-known anecdote, told by Cicero, of the interchange of visits between Scipio Nasica and Ennius[1], though not a brilliant specimen of Roman wit, is interesting from the light which it throws on the easy terms of intimacy in which the poet lived with the members of the most eminent Roman families. Such testimonies and traits of personal character make us think of Ennius as a man of genial and social temper, as well as of 'an intense and glowing mind.'

It was probably through his position as a teacher of Greek that Ennius first became known to the leading men of Rome. If this position was at first one of dependence, similar to that in which in earlier times the client stood to his patron, it soon changed into one of mutual esteem and admiration. We can best understand the relation in which he stood to men eminent in the state and in the camp, from a passage from the seventh book of the Annals quoted by Aulus Gellius. In that passage the poet is stated, on the authority of L. Aelius Stilo[2] (an early grammarian, a friend of Lucilius, and one of Cicero's teachers), to have drawn his own portrait, under an imaginary description of a confidential friend of the Roman general, Servilius Geminus. The portrait has the air of being drawn from the life, with a rapid and forcible hand, and with a minuteness of detail significant of close personal observation:—

>   Haece locutu' vocat quocum bene saepe libenter
>   Mensam sermonesque suos rerumque suarum
>   Congeriem partit, magnam cum lassu' diei
>   Partem fuisset de summis rebu' regendis
>   Consilio, indu foro lato sanctoque senatu:
>   Cui res audacter magnas parvasque jocumque
>   Eloqueretur, cuncta simul malaque et bona dictu
>   Evomeret, si qui vellet, tutoque locaret.

---

[1] De Oratore, ii. 68.
[2] 'L. Aelium Stilonem dicere solitum ferunt Q. Ennium de semet ipso haec scripsisse, picturamque istam morum et ingenii ipsius Q. Ennii factam esse.'—Gell. xii. 4.

>   Quocum multa volup ac gaudia clamque palamque:
>   Ingenium cui nulla malum sententia suadet
>   Ut faceret facinus levis aut malu', doctu', fidelis,
>   Suavis homo, facundu', suo contentu', beatus,
>   Scitu,' secunda loquens in tempore, commodu', verbum
>   Paucum, multa tenens antiqua sepulta, vetustas
>   Quem fecit mores veteresque novosque tenentem,
>   Multorum veterum leges divumque hominumque;
>   Prudenter qui dicta loquive tacereve possit.
>   Hunc inter pugnas Servilius sic compellat[1].

There are many touches in this picture, which suggest the kind of intimacy in which Ennius may have lived with Fulvius Nobilior when accompanying him in his Aetolian campaign, or his bearing when taking part in the light or serious talk of the Scipios. The learning and power of speech, the knowledge of antiquity and of the manners of the day, attributed to this friend of Servilius, were gifts which we may attribute to the poet both on ancient testimony and on the evidence afforded by the fragments of his writings. The good sense, tact, and knowledge of the world, the cheerfulness in life and conversation, the honour and integrity of character represented in the same passage, are among the personal qualities which, in all ages, form a bond of union between men eminent in great practical affairs and men eminent in literature. Such were the qualities which, according to his own account, recommended Horace to the intimate friendship of Maecenas. Many expressive fragments from the lost poetry of Ennius give assurance that he was a man in whom learning and the

---

[1] 'He finished: and summons to him one with whom often, and right gladly, he shared his table, his talk, and the whole weight of his business, when weary with debate, throughout the day, on high affairs of state, within the wide Forum and the august Senate,— one to whom he could frankly speak out serious matters, trifles, and jest; to whom he could pour forth and safely confide, if he wanted to confide in any one, all that he cared to utter, good or bad; with whom, in private and in public, he had much entertainment and enjoyment,— a man of that nature which no thought ever prompts to baseness through levity or malice: a learned, honest, pleasant man, eloquent, contented, and cheerful, of much tact, speaking well in season; courteous and of few words; with much old buried lore; whom length of years had made versed in old and recent ways; in the laws of many ancients, divine and human; one who knew when to speak and when to be silent. Him, during the battle, Servilius thus addresses.'

ardent temperament of genius were happily united with the worth and sense described in this nameless portrait.

By his personal merit he broke through the strongest barriers ever raised by national and family pride, and made the name of poet, instead of a reproach, a name of honour with the ruling class at Rome. The favourable impression which he produced on the 'primitive virtue' of Cato, by whom he was first brought to Rome, was more probably due to his force of character and social qualities than to his genius and literary accomplishment,—qualities seemingly little valued by his earliest patron, who, in one of his speeches, reproached Fulvius Nobilior with allowing himself to be accompanied by a poet in his campaign. But the strongest proof of the worth and the wisdom of Ennius is his intimate friendship with the greatest Roman of the age, and the conqueror of the greatest soldier of antiquity. It is honourable to the friendship of generous natures, that the poet neither sought nor gained wealth from this intimacy, but continued to live plainly and contentedly on the Aventine. Yet after death it was believed that the two friends were not divided; and the bust of the provincial poet found a place among the remains of that time-honoured family, the record of whose grandeur has been preserved, even to the present day, in the august simplicity of their monumental inscriptions.

The elder Africanus may have been attracted to Ennius not only by his passion for Greek culture, but by a certain community of nature. The mystical enthusiasm, the high self-confidence, the direct simplicity combined with majesty of character, impressed on the language of the poet were equally impressed on the action and bearing of the soldier. The feeling which Ennius in his turn entertained for Scipio was one of enthusiastic admiration. While paying due honour to the merits and services of other famous men, even of such as Cato and Fabius, who were most opposed to his idol, of Scipio he said that Homer alone could worthily have uttered his praises [1].

---

[1] Σκιπίωνα γὰρ ᾄδων καὶ ἐπὶ μέγα τὸν ἄνδρα ἐξᾶραι βουλόμενος φησὶ μόνον ἂν

In addition to the part which he assigned to him in the Ninth Book of the Annals, he devoted a separate poem to commemorate his achievements. He has left also two short inscriptions, written in elegiac verse, in which he proclaims in words of burning enthusiasm the momentous services and transcendent superiority of the 'great world's victor's victor'—

> Hic est ille situs cui nemo civi' neque hostis
> Quivit pro factis reddere opis pretium[1];

and this also,

> A sole exoriente supra Maeoti' paludes
> Nemo est qui factis me aequiperare queat.
> Si fas endo plagas coelestium ascendere cuiquam est,
> Mi soli caeli maxima porta patet[2].

With many marked differences, which distinguish a man of active, social, and national sympathies from a student of Nature and a thinker on human life, there is a certain affinity of character and genius between Ennius and Lucretius. Enthusiastic admiration of personal greatness is one prominent feature in which they resemble one another. But while Lucretius is the ardent admirer of contemplative and imaginative greatness, it is greatness in action and character which moves the admiration of Ennius. They resemble each other also in their strong consciousness of genius and their high estimate of its function and value. Cicero mentions that Ennius applied the epithet *sanctus* to poets. Lucretius applies the same epithet to the old philosophic poets, as in the lines of strong affection and reverence which he dedicates to Empedocles,

> Nil tamen hoc habuisse viro praeclarius in se,
> Nec *sanctum* magis, et mirum carumque videtur[3].

Ὅμηρον ἐπαξίους ἐπαίνους εἰπεῖν Σκιπίωνος.—Aelian, as quoted by Suidas, vol. i. p. 1258. Ed. Gaisford. Cf. Vahlen.

[1] 'Here is he laid, to whom no one, either countryman or enemy, has been able to pay a due meed for his services.'

[2] 'From the utmost east, beyond the Maeotian marsh, there is no one who in actions can vie with me. If it is lawful for any one to ascend to the realms of the gods, to me alone the vast gate of heaven is opened!'

[3] 'Yet nothing more glorious than this man doth it (the island of Sicily) seem to have contained, nor aught more holy, nor more wonderful and beloved.'

The inscription which Ennius composed for his own bust directly expresses his sense of the greatness of his work, and his confident assurance of fame, and of the lasting sympathy of his countrymen—

> Aspicite, O cives, senis Enni imagini' formam,
>   Hic vestrum panxit maxima facta patrum.
> Nemo me lacrimis decoret nec funera fletu
>   Faxit. Cur? Volito vivu' per ora virum[1].

Two lines from one of his satires—

> Enni poeta salve qui mortalibus
> Versus propinas flammeos medullitus[2],

indicate in still stronger terms his burning consciousness of power.

Some of the greatest of modern poets, such as Dante, Milton, and Wordsworth, have manifested a feeling similar to that expressed by Ennius and Lucretius. Although appearing in strange contrast with the self-suppression of the highest creative art (as seen in Homer, in Sophocles, and in Shakspeare), this proud self-confidence, 'disdainful of help or hindrance,' is the usual accompaniment of an intense nature and of a genius exercised with some serious moral, religious, or political purpose. The least pleasing side of the feeling, even in men of generous nature, is the scorn,—not of envy, but of imperfect sympathy,—which they are apt to entertain towards rival genius or antagonistic convictions. Something of this spirit appears in the disparaging allusion of Ennius to his predecessor Naevius:—

> Scripsere alii rem
> Versibu', quos olim Fauni vatesque canebant,
> Quum neque Musarum scopulos quisquam superarat
> Nec dicti studiosus erat[3].

---

[1] 'Behold, my countrymen, the bust of the old man, Ennius. He penned the record of your fathers' mighty deeds. Let no one pay to me the meed of tears, nor weep at my funeral. And why? because I still live, as I speed to and fro, through the mouths of men.'

[2] 'Hail, poet Ennius, who pledgest to mortals thy fiery verse from thy inmost marrow.'

[3] 'Others have treated the subject in the verses, which in days of old the Fauns and bards used to sing, before any one had climbed the cliffs of the Muses, or gave any care to style.'

The contempt here expressed for the metre employed by the older poet seems to be the counterpart of his own exultation in being the first to introduce what he called 'the long verses' into Latin literature.

Another point in which there is some affinity between Ennius and Lucretius is their religious temper and convictions. There is indeed no trace in Ennius of the rigid intellectual consistency of Lucretius, nor in Lucretius any gleam of the mysticism which Ennius inherited from the speculations of Pythagoras. But in both deep feelings of awe and reverence are combined with a scornful disbelief of the superstition of their time. They both apply the principles of Euhemerism to resolve the bright creations of the old mythology into their original elements. Ennius, like Lucretius, seems to deny the providence of the gods. He makes one of the personages of his dramas give expression to the thought which perplexed the minds of Thucydides and Tacitus—the thought, namely, of the apparent disconnexion between prosperity and goodness, as affording proof of the divine indifference to human well-being—

> Ego deum genus esse semper dixi et dicam caelitum,
> Sed eos non curare opinor, quid agat humanum genus;
> Nam si curent, bene bonis sit, male malis, quod nunc abest[1]:

and he exposed, with caustic sense, the false pretences of augurs, prophets, and astrologers. His translation of the Sacred Chronicle of Euhemerus exercised a permanent influence on the religious convictions of his countrymen. But while led to these conclusions by the spirit of his age, and by the study of the later speculations of Greece, he believed in the soul's independence of the body, and of its continued existence, under other conditions, after death. He declared that the spirit of Homer, after many changes, —at one time having animated a peacock[2], again, having

---

[1] 'I have always said and will say that the gods of heaven exist, but I think that they heed not the conduct of mankind; for, if they did, it would be well with the good and ill with the bad; and it is not so now.'

[2] Cor jubet hoc Enni, postquam destertuit esse
Maeonides, Quintus pavone ex Pythagoreo.
          Persius, vi. 10 (Ed. Jahn).

been incarnate in the sage of Crotona,—had finally passed into his own body: and he told how the shade—which he regards as distinct from the soul or spirit—of his great prototype had appeared to him from the invisible world,—

> Quo neque permaneant animae neque corpora nostra
> Sed quaedam simulacra modis pallentia miris,

and explained to him the whole plan of nature. These dreams of the imagination may not have been without effect in enabling Ennius to escape from the gloom which 'eclipsed the brightness of the world' to Lucretius. The light in which the world appeared to the older poet was that of common sense strangely blended with imaginative mysticism. He thus seems to stand midway between the spiritual aspirations of Empedocles and the negation of Lucretius. Born in the vigorous prime of Italian civilisation he came into the inheritance of the bold fancies of the earlier Greeks and of the dull rationalism of their later speculation. His ideas on what transcends experience appear thus to have been without the unity arising from an unreflecting acceptance of tradition, or from the basis of philosophical consistency.

II. HIS WORKS.—(1) MISCELLANEOUS WORKS.

II. (1) In laying the foundations of Roman literature, Ennius displayed not only the fervent sympathies and active faculty of genius, but also great energy and industry, and a many-sided learning. The composition of his tragedies and of the Annals, while making most demand on his original gifts, implied also a diligent study of Homer and of the Greek tragedians, and a large acquaintance with the traditions and antiquities of Rome. But besides the works on which his highest poetical faculty was employed, other writings, of a philosophical, didactic, and miscellaneous character, gave evidence of the versatility of his powers and interests. It does not appear that he was the author of any prose writing. His version of the Sacred Chronicle of Euhemerus was more probably a poetical adaptation than a literal prose translation of that work. The work of Euhemerus was conceived in that spirit of vulgar rationalism, which is condemned by Plato in the Phaedrus. He explained away the fables of mythology, by representing them as a supernatural account of historical events. Several extracts of the work quoted by Lactantius, as from the translation of Ennius, look as if they had been reduced from a form originally metrical into the prose of a later era[1]. There is thus no evidence, direct or indirect, to prove that Ennius had any share in forming the style of Latin prose. But if verse was the sole instrument which he used, this was certainly not due to the poetical character of all the topics which he treated, but, more likely, to the fact that his acquired aptitude, and the state of the Latin language in his time, made metrical writing more natural and easy than prose composition.

One of his works in verse was a treatise on good living, called Hedyphagetica, founded on the gastronomic researches of Archestratus of Gela,—a sage who is said to have devoted his life to the study of everything that contributed to the pleasures of the table, and to have recorded his varied experience and research with the grave dignity of epic verse. A few lines from this translation or adaptation of Ennius, giving an account of the coasts on which the best fish are to be found, have been preserved by Apuleius. The lines are curious as exemplifying that tone of half-serious enthusiasm, which all who treat, either in prose or verse, of the pleasures of eating seem naturally to adopt[2]. The language in which the *scarus*, a fish unhappily lost to the modern epicure, is described as 'the brain almost of almighty Jove,' fits all the requirements of gastronomic rapture:—

> Quid turdum, merulam, melanurum umbramque marinam
> Praeterii, atque scarum, cerebrum Jovi' paene supremi?
> Nestoris ad patriam hic capitur magnusque bonusque[3].

---

[1] Vahlen. [2] E.g. Horace, Sat. ii. 4.

He wrote also a philosophical poem in trochaic septenarian verse, called Epicharmus, founded on writings attributed to the old Sicilian poet, which appear to have resolved the gods of the Greek mythology into natural substances[1]. A few slight fragments have been preserved from this poem. They speak of the four elements or principles of the universe as 'water, earth, air, the sun'; of 'the blending of heat with cold, dryness with moisture'; of 'the earth bearing and supporting all nations and receiving them again back into herself.' The following is the longest fragment from the poem:—

> Istic est is Jupiter quem dico, quem Graeci vocant
> Aërem: qui ventus est et nubes; imber postea
> Atque ex imbre frigus: ventus post fit, aër denuo,
> Haece propter Jupiter sunt ista quae dico tibi,
> Quoniam mortalis atque urbes beluasque omnis juvat[2].

These fragments and a passage from the opening lines of the Annals, where the shade of Homer was introduced as discoursing to Ennius (like the shade of Anchises to Aeneas), on 'the nature of things,' are specimens of that vague curiosity about the facts and laws of Nature, which, in ancient times, supplied the absence of scientific knowledge. Such physical speculations possessed a great attraction for the Roman poets. The spirit of the Epicharmus, as well as of the Sacred Chronicle of Euhemerus, reappears in the poem of Lucretius. Ennius was the first among his countrymen who expressed that curiosity as to the ultimate facts of Nature and that sense of the mysterious life of the universe, which acted as the most

---

[1] 'The poetical philosophy, which the later Pythagoreans had extracted from the writings of the old Sicilian comedian, Epicharmus of Megara, or rather had, at least for the most part, circulated under cover of his name, regarded the Greek gods as natural substances, Zeus as the atmosphere, the soul as a particle of Sun-dust, and so forth.'—Mommsen's Hist. of Rome, Book iii. ch. 15. (Dickson's Translation.)

[2] 'This is that Jupiter which I speak of, which the Greeks call the air; it is first wind and clouds; afterwards rain, and after rain, cold; next it becomes wind, then air again. All those things which I mention to you are Jupiter, because it is he who supports mortals and cities and all animals.'

powerful intellectual impulse on the mind of Lucretius, and which fascinated the imagination of Virgil.

Another of his miscellaneous works, probably of a moral and didactic character, was known by the name of Protreptica. It is possible that all of these works[1], as well as the Scipio, formed part of the Saturae, or Miscellanies, under which title Ennius composed four, or, according to another authority, six books. The Romans looked upon Lucilius as the inventor of satire in the later sense of that word[2];—he having been the first to impress upon the satura the character of censorious criticism, which it has borne since his time. But there was another kind of satura, of which Ennius and Pacuvius in early times, and Varro at a somewhat later time, were regarded as the principal authors. This was really a miscellany treating of various subjects, in various metres, and, as employed by Varro, was written partly in prose, partly in verse. This kind of composition, as well as the Lucilian satire, arose out of the old indigenous satura or dramatic medley, familiar to the Romans before the introduction of Greek literature. When the scenic element in the original satura was superseded by the new comedy introduced from Greece, the old name was first applied to a miscellaneous kind of composition, in which ordinary topics were treated in a serious but apparently desultory way; and even as employed by Lucilius and Horace the satura retained much of its original character. The satires of Ennius were written in various metres, iambic, trochaic, and hexameter, and treated of various topics of personal and public interest. The few passages which ancient authorities quote as fragments from them are not of much value in themselves, but when taken in connexion with the testimonies as to their character, they are of some interest as showing that this kind of composition was a form intermediate between the old dramatic satura and the satire of Lucilius and Horace. It is recorded that in one of these pieces, Ennius introduced a

---

[1] Mommsen.   [2] 'Inventore minor.'—Horace.

dialogue between Life and Death;—thus transmitting in the use of dialogue (which appears very frequently in Horace and Persius) some vestige of the original scenic medley. Ennius also appears, like Lucilius and Horace, to have communicated in his satires his own personal feelings and experience, as in the fragment already quoted:—

> Nunquam poetor, nisi si podager.

Further satire, in the hands of its chief masters, aimed at practical moral teaching, not only by precept, ridicule, and invective, and by portraiture of individuals and classes, but also by the use of anecdotes and fables. This last mode of combining amusement with instruction is common in Horace. It appears, however, to have been first used by Ennius. Aulus Gellius mentions that Aesop's fable of the field-lark and the husbandman 'is very skilfully and gracefully told by Ennius in his satires'; and he quotes the advice, appended to the fable, 'Never to expect your friends to do for you what you can do for yourself:'

> Hoc erit tibi argumentum semper in promptu situm:
> Nequid expectes amicos, quod tute agere possies[1].

These miscellaneous works of Ennius were the fruits of his learning and literary industry, rather than of his genius. Such works might have been written in prose, if the art of prose composition had been as familiar as that of verse. It is in the fragments of his dramas, and still more of the Annals, that his poetic power is most apparent, and that the influence which he exercised over the Roman mind and literature is discerned.

---

[1] Another passage, ascribed to Ennius, descriptive of the greed of a parasite, occupies the ground common to Roman comedy and to Roman satire:—

> Quippe sine cura laetus lautus cum advenis
> Insertis malis, expedito bracchio
> Alacer, celsus, lupino expectans impetu,
> Mox cum alterius obligurias bona,
> Quid censes domino esse animi? pro divum fidem!
> Ille tristis cibum dum servat, tu ridens voras.

(2) DRAMAS.

(2) Before the time of Ennius, the Roman drama, both tragic and comic, had established itself at Rome, in close imitation of the tragedy and the new comedy of Athens. The latter had been most successfully cultivated by Naevius and his younger contemporary, Plautus. The advancement of tragedy to an equal share of popular favour was due to the severer genius of Ennius. He appears however to have tried, though without much success, to adapt himself to the popular taste in favour of comedy. The names of two of his comedies, viz. *Cupuncula* and *Pancratiastae*, have come down to us; but their fragments are too insignificant to justify the formation of any opinion on their merits. His admirers in ancient times nowhere advance in his favour any claim to comic genius. Volcatius Sedigitus, an early critic, who wrote a work *De Poetis*, and who has already been referred to as assigning the third rank in the list of comic poets to Naevius, mentions Ennius as tenth and last, solely 'antiquitatis causa.' Any inference that might be drawn from the character exhibited in the other fragments of Ennius, would accord both with the negative and positive evidence of antiquity, as to his deficiency in comic power. He has nothing in common with that versatile and dramatic genius, in which occasionally the highest imagination has been united with the most abundant humour. The real bent of his mind, as revealed in his higher poetry, is grave and intense, like that of Lucretius or Milton. Many of the conceits, strained effects, and play on words, found in his fragments, imply want of humour as well as an imperfect poetic taste. Thus, in the following fragment from one of his satires, the meaning of the passage is more obscured than pointed by the forced iteration and play upon the word *frustra*:—

>   Nam qui lepide postulat alterum frustrari,
>   Quom frustrast, frustra illum dicit frustra esse.
>   Nam qui se frustrari quem frustra sentit,
>   Qui frustratur frustrast, si ille non est frustra [1].

[1] The meaning of the passage amounts to no more than this, that the man who tries to 'sell' another, and fails, is himself 'sold.'

The love of alliteration and assonance, which is conspicuous also in Plautus and in the fragments of Pacuvius and Accius, and which seems to have been the natural accompaniment of the new formative energy imparted to the Latin language by the earliest poets and orators, appears in its most exaggerated form in such lines as the

O Tite tute Tati tibi tanta tiranne tulisti,

quoted from the Annals. Many of his fragments show indeed that he possessed the caustic spirit of a satirist; but it was in the light of common sense, not of humour, that he viewed the follies of the world.

The general character of Roman tragedy, so far as it can be ascertained from ancient testimony and the extant fragments of the early tragedians, will be examined in the following chapter. It is not possible to determine what dramatic power Ennius may have displayed in the evolution of his plots or the delineation of his characters. His peculiar genius is more distinctly stamped on his epic than on his dramatic fragments. Still many of the latter, in their boldness of conception and expression, and in their strong and fervid morality, are expressive of the original force of the poet, and of the Roman temper of his mind. Some of them will be brought forward in the sequel, along with passages from the Annals, as important contributions to our estimate of the poet's genius and intellect.

It was certainly due to Ennius that Roman tragedy was first raised to that pitch of popular favour which it enjoyed till the age of Cicero. While actively employed in many other fields of literature, he carried on the composition of his tragedies till the latest period of his life. Cicero records that the *Thyestes* was represented at the celebration of the Ludi Apollinares, shortly before the poet's death[1]. The titles of about twenty-five of his tragedies are known, and a few fragments remain from all of them. About one half of these bear the titles of the heroes and heroines connected with the Trojan cycle of

---

[1] Brutus, 20.

events, such as the *Achilles, Achilles Aristarchi, Ajax, Alexander, Andromache Aechmalotis, Hectoris Lutra, Hecuba, Iphigenia, Phoenix, Telamo*. One at least of his tragedies, the *Medea*, was literally translated from the Greek of Euripides, whom he seems to have made his model, in preference to the older Attic dramatists. Cicero[1] speaks of it, along with the Antiope of Pacuvius, as being translated word for word from the Greek; and a comparison of the fragments of the Latin with the passages in the Medea of Euripides shows how closely Ennius followed his original. In one place he has mistranslated his author,—the passage (Eur. Med. 215),

οἶδα γὰρ πολλοὺς βροτῶν
σεμνοὺς γεγῶτας, τοὺς μὲν ὀμμάτων ἄπο
τοὺς δ' ἐν θυραίοις,

being thus rendered in Latin,—

Multi suam rem bene gessere et publicam patria procul.

The opening lines of the Medea of Ennius may be quoted as probably a fair specimen of the degree of faithfulness with which the early Roman tragedians translated from their originals. There is some nervous force, but little either of poetical grace or musical flow in the language:—

Utinam ne in nemore Pelio securibus
Caesa cecidisset abiegna ad terram trabes,
Neve inde navis inchoandae exordium
Coepisset, quae nunc nominatur nomine
Argo, quia Argivi in ea dilecti viri
Vecti petebant pellem inauratam arietis
Colchis, imperio regis Peliae, per dolum;
Nam nunquam era errans mea domo ecferret pedem
Medea, animo aegra, amore saevo saucia[2].

---

[1] De Fin. i. 2.
[2] Cf. Eur. Med. 1-8:—

Εἴθ' ὤφελ' Ἀργοῦς μὴ διαπτάσθαι σκάφος
Κόλχων ἐς αἶαν κυανέας Συμπληγάδας,
μηδ' ἐν νάπαισι Πηλίου πεσεῖν ποτε
τμηθεῖσα πεύκη, μηδ' ἐρετμῶσαι χέρας
ἀνδρῶν ἀριστέων, οἳ τὸ πάγχρυσον δέρος
Πελίᾳ μετῆλθον· οὐ γὰρ ἂν δέσποιν' ἐμὴ
Μήδεια πύργους γῆς ἔπλευσ' Ἰωλκίας
ἔρωτι θυμὸν ἐκπλαγεῖσ' Ἰάσονος.

In his Hecuba, also, and probably in his Iphigenia, Ennius made free use of the dramas founded on the same subjects by Euripides. But in many of his dramatic fragments the sentiment expressed is clearly that of a Roman, not of a Greek mind[1]. The subjects of many of his dramas, such as the Achilles, the Ajax, the Hectoris Lutra, the Telamon, the Iphigenia, afforded scope for the exhibition of the soldierly character. Cicero[2] adduces the wounded Eurypylus as an example of the kind of fortitude and superiority to pain produced by the discipline of the Roman armies. The same author quotes with great admiration scenes from the Alexander and from the Andromache Aechmalotis, in which pathos is the predominant sentiment. He adds to his quotations the comments 'O poema tenerum, et moratum, et molle;' and again, 'O poetam egregium, quamquam ab his cantoribus Euphorionis contemnitur! Sentit omnia repentina et necopinata esse graviora . . . praeclarum carmen est enim et rebus et verbis et modis lugubre[3].' In the former of these scenes Cassandra, under the influence of Apollo, reluctant and *ashamed* (perhaps in this feeling the hand of a Roman rather than of a Greek poet may be recognised), yet mastered by prophetic fury, bursts forth in these wild, agitated tones :—

> Adest, adest fax obvoluta sanguine atque incendio :
> Multos annos latuit: cives ferte opem et restinguite.
> Iamque mari magno classis cita
> Texitur: exitium examen rapit.
> Advenit, et fera velivolantibus
> Navibus complevit manus litora[4].

[1] Several of these fragments will be examined later.

[2] Tusc. Disp. ii. 16.

[3] 'How tender, how true to character, how affecting!' De Div. i 31. 'What a great poet, though he is despised by those admirers of Euphorion. He understands that sudden and unlooked-for calamities are more grievous. A noble poem,—pathetic in matter, in language, in melody.' Tusc. Disp. iii. 19.

[4] 'Here it is; here, the torch, wrapped in fire and blood. Many years it hath lain hid; help, citizens, and extinguish it. For now, on the great sea, a swift fleet is gathering. It hurries along a host of calamities. They come: a fierce host lines the shores with sail-winged ships.' Exitium = exitiorum, cf. Cic. Orator. 46. Itaque idem poeta, qui inusitatius contraxerat 'Patris mei meum factum' pudet pro 'meorum factorum' et 'Texitur: exitium examen rapit' pro 'exitiorum.'

We see in this passage how the passionate character of the situation is enhanced by the mysterious power attributed to Cassandra. A similar excitement of feeling, produced by supernatural terror, appears in a fragment of the Alcmaeon, quoted also by Cicero, and of another the motive is the awe associated with the dim and pale realms of the dead[1]. In these and similar passages we note the power of expressing the varying moods of passion by varied effects of metre. Horace characterises his ordinary verse in the line,

<blockquote>In scaenam missos cum magno pondere versus;</blockquote>

and this slow and weighty movement seems to have been the general character of his metre in the calmer parts of his dramas. But in a large number of the fragments of the dialogue, where there is any excitement of feeling or intensity of thought, we find him using the more rapid trochaic septenarian, with quick transitions to the anapaestic dimeter or tetrameter, as the passion passes beyond the control of the speaker.

In two of his dramas, the Sabinae and Ambracia, he made use of materials supplied by the early legendary history of Rome, and by a great contemporary event. The first of these, like the Romulus of Naevius, belonged to the class of 'fabulae Praetextatae,' and was founded on the intervention of the Sabine women in the war between Romulus and Tatius. The second, representing the capture of the town of Ambracia, in the Aetolian war, may, like the Clastidium of the older poet (written in celebration of the victory of Marcellus over the Gauls), have had more of the character of a military pageant and, in all probability, was composed for representation at the games celebrated on the triumphal return of M. Fulvius Nobilior from that war.

(3) THE ANNALS.

(3) But the poem which was the chief result of his life, and made an epoch in Latin literature, was the Annals.

---

[1] Acad. ii. 28.

On the composition of this work he rested his hopes of popular and permanent fame—

> Hic vestrum panxit maxima facta patrum :

and again, apparently at the opening of the poem, he wrote,—

> Latos per populos terrasque poemata nostra
> Clara cluebunt.

At its conclusion, he claimed for his old age the repose due to a brave and triumphant career. He composed the eighteenth book, the last, in his sixty-seventh year, three years before his death[1]. The great length to which the poem extended, and the vast amount of materials which it embraced, imply a long and steady concentration of his powers on the task. It was one requiring much learning as well as original conception. The fragments of the poem afford proofs of a familiarity with Homer, and of acquaintance with the Cyclic poets[2]. It is impossible to say how much of the early Roman history, as it has come down to modern times, is due to the diligence of Ennius in collecting, and to his genius in giving life to the traditions and ancient records of Rome. He was certainly the earliest writer who gathered them up, and united them in a continuous narrative. The work accomplished by him required not only the antiquarian lore of a man

> Multa tenens, antiqua, sepulta,

and the power of imagination to give a new shape to the past, but an intimate knowledge of the great events and the great men of his own time, and a sympathetic insight into the spirit by which they were animated.

The poem was written in eighteen books. Of these books about six hundred lines have been preserved in fragments, varying from about twenty lines to half a line in length. From the minuteness with which comparatively unimportant matters are described, it is inferred that the separate books extended to a much greater length than

---

[1] Gellius, xvii. 21.

[2] He speaks of Eurydice as the wife of Aeneas. This statement he is supposed to have derived from the *Cypria*.

those either of the Iliad or of the Aeneid. Of the first book there remain about 120 lines, including the dream of Ilia in seventeen lines, and the auspices of Romulus in twenty lines. In it were narrated the mythical events from the time

> Quum veter occubuit Priamus sub marte Pelasgo,

to the death and deification of Romulus;

> Romulus in caelo cum dis genitalibus aevum
> Degit.

There is no allusion in these fragments to the Carthaginian adventures of Aeneas, which Naevius had introduced into his poem on the First Punic War. Aeneas seems at once to have been brought to Hesperia, a land,

> Quam prisci casci populi tenuere Latini.

Ilia is represented as the daughter of Aeneas. The birth and infancy of Romulus and Remus appear to have been described at great length. In commenting on Virgil's lines at Aeneid viii. 630—

> Fecerat et viridi fetam Mavortis in antro
> Procubuisse lupam: geminos huic ubera circum
> Ludere pendentes pueros, et lambere matrem
> Impavidos; illam terreti cervice reflexam
> Mulcere alternos, et corpora fingere lingua,—

Servius says 'Sane totus hic locus Ennianus est.' The second and third books contained the history of the remaining Roman kings. Virgil imitated the description given in these books of the destruction of Alba (the story of which is told by Livy also with much poetic power, perhaps reproduced from the pages of Ennius), in his account of the capture of Troy, at Aeneid ii. 486—

> At domus interior gemitu miseroque tumultu, etc.

One short fragment of the third book contains a picturesque notice of the founding of Ostia—

> Ostia munita est; idem loca navibu' pulchris
> Munda facit; nautisque mari quaesentibu' vitam.

This line also

> Postquam lumina sis oculis bonus Ancu' reliquit

is familiar from its reappearance in one of the most impressive passages of Lucretius.

The fourth and fifth books contained the history of the State from the establishment of the Republic till just before the beginning of the war with Pyrrhus. One short fragment is taken from the night attack of the Gauls upon the Capitol. The sixth book was devoted to the war with Pyrrhus; the seventh, eighth, and ninth, to the First and Second Punic Wars. In the fragments of the sixth are found a few lines of the speeches of Pyrrhus, and of Appius Claudius Caecus. In the account of the First Punic War, the disparaging allusion to Naevius occurs—

> Scripsêre alii rem, etc.

It is mentioned by Cicero that Ennius borrowed much from the work of Naevius; and also that he passed over (*reliquisse*) the First Punic War, as it had been treated by his predecessor. Several fragments however must certainly refer to this war; but it is probable that that part of the subject was treated more cursorily than either the war with Pyrrhus, or the later wars. The passage in which the poet is supposed to have painted his own character, under the form of a friend of Servilius Geminus, occurred in the seventh book. Two well-known passages have been preserved from the ninth book—viz., that characterising the 'sweet-speaking' orator, M. Cornelius Cethegus—

> Fos delibatus populi suadaeque medulla,

and the lines in honour of Q. Fabius Maximus,

> Unus homo nobis cunctando restituit rem, etc.

The tenth and eleventh books, beginning with a new invocation to the muse—

> Insece Musa manu Romanorum induperator
> Quod quisque in bello gessit cum rege Philippo,

treated of the Macedonian war, and of the deeds of T. Quintius Flamininus. In the later books, Ennius told the history of the war with Antiochus, of the Aetolian War carried on by his friend, M. Fulvius Nobilior, of the exploits of L. Caecilius Denter and his brother (of whom scarcely anything is known except that the sixteenth book of the Annals was written in consequence of the poet's especial admiration for them), and lastly, of the Istrian War, which took place within a few years of the author's death.

Neither in general design nor in detail could the Annals be regarded as a pure epic poem. Like the Aeneid, which connects the mythical story of Aeneas with the glories of the Julian line and the great destiny of Rome, the poem of Ennius treated of fabulous tradition, of historical fact, and of great contemporary events; but it did not, like the Aeneid, unite these varied materials in the representation of the fortunes of one individual hero. The action of the poem, instead of being limited to a few days or months, extended over many generations. Nor could the poem terminate with any critical catastrophe, as its object was to unfold the continuous, still advancing progress of the State. From the name it might be inferred that the Annals must have been more like a metrical chronicle than like an epic poem; yet, as being inspired and pervaded by a grand and vital idea, the work was elevated above the level of matter of fact into the region of poetry. The idea of a high destiny, unfolding itself under the old kingly dynasty and the long line of consuls,—through the successive wars with the Italian races, with Pyrrhus and the Carthaginians, —rapidly advancing, though not fully accomplished in the age when the poem was written,—gave unity of plan and consistency of form to its rude and colossal structure. The word Annales, as applied to Roman story, suggests something more than the mere record of events in regular annual sequence. It involves also the idea of unbroken continuity. In the Roman Republic, the unity and vital action of the State were maintained and manifested by the delegation of the functions of government on magistrates appointed from year to year, just as the life of a monarchical state is maintained and manifested in its line of kings. In the spirit animating the work,—in the conception of a past history, stretching back in unbroken grandeur until it is lost in fable, but yet vitally linked to the interests of the present time,—the Annals of Ennius may be compared with the dramas in which Shakspeare has represented the national life of England—in all its greatness and vicissitudes—with the glory and splendour, as well as the dark and tragic colours with which that story is inwoven.

The poem, although laying no claim to the perfection of epic form, had thus something of the genuine epic inspiration. While treating both of a mythical past and of real historical events, it was pervaded by a living and popular idea,—faith in the destiny of Rome. It was through the power and presence of that same idea in his own age, that Virgil was able to impart a vital and enduring meaning to a fabulous tradition, and to create, out of the imaginary fortunes of a Trojan hero, a poem most truly representative of his age and country. It is the absence of any such living idea which renders the artificial epics of refined and civilised eras,—such poems, for instance, as the *Thebais* of Statius, or the *Argonautics* of Valerius Flaccus,—in general so flat and unprofitable. Regarded, on the other hand, as a historical poem, the Annals was written under more favourable conditions than the *Pharsalia* of Lucan, or the *Punic Wars* of Silius Italicus—in being the work of an age to which the past had come down as popular tradition, not as recorded history. The imagination of the poet employs itself more happily and legitimately in filling up or modifying a story that has been shaped by the fancies and feelings of successive generations, than in venturing to recast the facts that stand out prominently in the actual march of human affairs. By treating of contemporary events, the poem must have receded still further from the pure type of epic poetry; yet the later fragments of the work, while written with something of the minute and literal fidelity of a chronicle, may yet lay claim to poetic inspiration. They prove that the author was no unconcerned spectator and reporter of the events going on around him, but that his imagination was fired and his sympathies keenly interested by whatever, in speech or action, was worthy to live in the memory of the world.

There must have been many drawbacks to the popularity of the poem in a more critical time, when strong enthusiasm and forcible conception fail to interest, unless they are combined with the harmonious execution of a work of art. Even from the extant fragments the rude proportions and the unwieldy mass of the original work may be inferred. It is still possible to note the bare, annalistic style of many passages which sink below the level of dignified prose, the barbarisms of taste shown by a fondness for alliterative lines and plays upon words, the more common faults of careless haste and redundance of expression, and of a rugged and irregular cadence. There must have been some peculiar excellencies or adaptation to the Roman taste, through which, in spite of these defects, the popularity of the poem was sustained far into the times of the Empire. This late popularity may have been due in part to antiquarian zeal or affectation, but some degree of it, as well as the favour of the age in which the poem was written, must have been founded on more substantial grounds. Apart from other literary interest, this poem first drew forth and established, for the contemplation of after times, the ideal latent in the national mind. The patriotic tones of Virgil have the same kind of ring as these in the older poet—

> Audire est operae pretium procedere recte
> Qui rem Romanam Latiumque augescere vultis;

and this other line which Cicero compared to the utterance of an oracle—

> Moribus antiquis stat res Romana virisque.

While in his other works Ennius was the teacher of an alien culture to his countrymen, in his Annals he represented them. He set before them an image of what was most real in themselves;—an image combining the strength and commanding features of his own time, with the proud memories and traditional traits of the past. As it is by sympathy with what is most vital and of deepest meaning in actual experience that a great poet forms his ideal of what transcends experience, so it is by a vivid apprehension of the present, that he is able to re-animate the past. Dante and Milton gained their vision of other worlds through their intense feeling of the spiritual meaning of this life; and, in another sphere of art, Scott was enabled to immortalise the romance and humour of past ages, partly through the chivalrous and adventurous spirit which he inherited from them, partly through the strong interest and enjoyment with which he entered into the actual life and pursuits of his contemporaries. It is in ages of transition, such as were the ages of Sophocles, of Shakspeare, and of Scott, in which the traditions of the past seem to blend with and colour the activity and enjoyment of a new time in which great issues are involved, that representative works of genius are produced. Living in such an era, deeply moved by all the memories, the hopes, and the impulses which acted upon his contemporaries, living his own life happily and vigorously in the chief centre of the world's activity, Ennius was enabled to gather the life of centuries into one representation, and to tell the story of Rome, if without the accomplished art, yet with something of the native force and spirit of early Greece; to fix in language the patriotic traditions which had hitherto been kept alive by the statues, monuments, and commemorative ceremonies of earlier times; to uphold the standard of national character with a fervent enthusiasm; and to address the understanding of his contemporaries with a practical wisdom like their own, and a large knowledge both of 'books and men:'—

> Vetustas
> Quem fecit mores veteresque novosque tenentem.

The manifest defects, as well as the peculiar power of the poem, show how widely it departed from the standard of the Greek epic which it professed to imitate. Its vast dimensions and solid structure are proofs of that capacity of long labour and concentrated interest on one great object, which was the secret of Roman success in other spheres of action. So large a mass of materials held in union only by a pervading national enthusiasm would have been utterly repugnant to Greek taste, intolerant above all things of monotony, and most exacting in its demands of artistic unity and completeness. The fragments of the poem give no idea of careful finish; they produce the impression of massiveness and energy, strength and uniformity of structure, unaccompanied by beauty, grace, or symmetry. The creation of an untutored age may be recognised in the rudeness of design,—of a Roman mind in the national spirit, the colossal proportions, and the strong workmanship of the poem.

The originality of the Roman epic will be still more apparent if we compare the fragments of the Annals, in some points of detail, with the complete works of the poet, whom Ennius regarded as his prototype. There was, in the first place, a marked difference between Homer and the Roman poet in their modes of representing human life and character. The personages of the Iliad and of the Odyssey are living and forcible types of individual character. In Achilles, in Hector, and in Odysseus,—in Helen, Andromache, and Nausicaa, we recognise embodiments the most real, yet the most transcendent, of the grandeur, the heroism, the courage, and strong affection of manhood, and of the grace, the gentleness, and the sweet vivacity of woman. The work of Ennius, on the other hand, instead of presenting varied types of human nature, appears to have unfolded a long gallery of national portraits. The fragments of the poem still afford glimpses of the 'good Ancus'; 'of the man of the great heart, the wise Aelius Sextus'; 'of the sweet speaking orator,' Cethegus, 'the marrow of persuasion.' The stamp of magnanimous fortitude is impressed on the fragmentary words of Appius Claudius Caecus; and sagacity and resolution are depicted in the lines which have handed down the fame of Fabius Maximus. This idea of the poem, as unfolding the heroes of Roman story in regular series, may be gathered also from the language of Cicero: 'Cato, the ancestor of our present Cato, is extolled by him to the skies; the honour of the

Roman people is thereby enhanced: finally all those Maximi, Fulvii, Marcelli, are celebrated with a glory in which we all participate[1].' This portraiture of the kings and heroes of the early time, of the orators, soldiers, and statesmen of the Republic, could not have exhibited the variety, the energy, the passion, and all the complex human attributes of Homer's personages. The men who stand prominently out in the annals of Rome were of a more uniform type. They were men of one common aim, —the advancement of Rome; animated with one sentiment, —devotion to the State. All that was purely personal in them seems merged in the traditional pictures which express only the fortitude, dignity, and sagacity of the Republic.

Ennius also followed Homer in introducing the element of supernatural agency into his poem. The action of the Annals, as well as of the Iliad, was made partially dependent on a divine interference with human affairs, though exercised less directly, and, as it were, from a greater distance. Yet how great is the difference between the life-like representation of the eager, capricious, and passionate deities of Homer's Olympus and that outline which may still be traced in Ennius, and which is seen filled up in Virgil and Horace, of the gods assembled, like a grave council of state, to deliberate on the destiny of Rome. In one fragment, containing the familiar line,—

> Unus erit quem tu tolles in caerula caeli
> Templa,—

they are introduced as debating, 'tectis bipatentibus,' on the admission of Romulus into heaven. Again, in the account of the Second Punic War, Jupiter is introduced as promising to the Romans the destruction of Carthage; and Juno abandons her resentment against the descendants of the Trojans,—

> Romanis coepit Juno placata favere.

It may be remarked, as a strong proof of the hold which their mythology had on the minds of the ancients, that

[1] Cicero, Arch. 9.

men so sincere as Ennius and Lucretius, while openly expressing opposition to that system of religious belief, cannot separate themselves from its influence and associations in their poetry. But it is not to be supposed that Ennius, in the passages just referred to, was merely using an artificial machinery to which he attached no meaning. In this representation of the councils of the gods, he embodies that faith in the Roman destiny, which was at the root of the most serious convictions of the Romans, in the most sceptical as well as the most believing ages of their history. This, too, is the real belief, which gives meaning to the supernatural agency in the Aeneid. Aeneas is little more than a passive instrument in the hands of Fate; Jupiter merely foreknows and pronounces its decrees; the parts assigned to Juno and Venus, in thwarting and advancing these decrees, seem to be an artistic addition to this original conception, suggested perhaps as much by the experience of female influence and intrigue in the poet's own age as by the memories of the Iliad.

Homer makes his personages known to us in speech as well as in action. Among epic poets he alone possessed the finest dramatic genius. But over and above the natural dialogue or soliloquy, in which every feeling of his various personages is revealed, he has invested his heroes with the charm of fluent and powerful oratory, in the council of chiefs and before the assembled people. The words of his speakers pour on, as he says of the words of Odysseus,—

νιφάδεσσιν ἐοίκοτα χειμερίῃσι,

in the rapid vehemence of passion or the subtle fluency of persuasion. The fragments of Ennius, on the other hand, scarcely afford sufficient ground for attributing to him a genuine dramatic faculty. But, as the citizen of a republic in which action was first matured in council, and living in the age when public speech first became a recognised power in the State, it was incumbent on him to embody in 'his abstract and chronicle of the time' the speech of the orator no less than the achievement of the soldier. In his estimate of character this power of speech is honoured as the fitting accompaniment of the wisdom of the statesman. In the following lines, for instance, he laments the substitution of military for civil preponderance in public affairs.

> Pellitur e medio sapientia, vi geritur res:
> Spernitur orator bonus, horridu' miles amatur:
> Haut doctis dictis certantes, sed maledictis
> Miscent inter sese inimicitiam agitantes;
> Non ex jure manu consertum, sed magi' ferro
> Rem repetunt, regnumque petunt, vadunt solida vi.[1]

Many lines of the Annals are evidently fragments of speeches. The most remarkable of these passages is one from a speech of Pyrrhus, and is characterised by Cicero as expressing 'sentiments truly regal and worthy of the race of the Aeacidae[2].' This fragment, although evincing nothing of the fluency, the passion, or the argumentative subtlety of debate, yet suggests the power of a great orator by its grave authoritative appeal to the moral dignity of man:—

> Nec mi aurum posco, nec mi pretium dederitis:
> Non cauponantes bellum, sed belligerantes,
> Ferro non auro vitam cernamus utrique.
> Vosne velit an me regnare era quidve ferat Fors,
> Virtute experiamur. Et hoc simul accipe dictum:
> Quorum virtutei belli fortuna pepercit,
> Eorundem libertati me parcere certum est.
> Dono ducite, doque volentibu' cum magnis dis.[3]

Of the same severe and lofty tone is that appeal of Appius Claudius, blind and in extreme old age, to the Senate,

---

[1] 'Wisdom is banished from amongst us, violence rules the day: the good orator is despised, the rough soldier loved; striving, not with words of learning, but with words of hate, they get embroiled in feuds, and stir up enmity one with another. The battle is fought, not according to law, but wi·h the sword they demand their rights, assail the sovereign power, advance by sheer force.'

[2] Cic. De Off. i. 12.

[3] 'Neither do I ask gold for myself, nor offer ye to me a ransom. Let us wage the war, not like hucksters, but like soldiers—with the sword, not with gold, putting our lives to the issue. Whether our mistress Fortune, wills that you or I should reign, or what her purpose be, let us prove by valour. And hearken too to this saying,—The brave men, whom the fortune of battle spares, their liberty I have resolved to spare. Take my offer, as I grant it, under favour of the great gods.'

when wavering in its resolution, and inclined to make peace with Pyrrhus—

> Quo vobis mentes rectae quae stare solebant
> Antehac, dementes sese flexere viai.[1]

As Milton, in his representation of the great debate in Pandemonium, idealised and glorified the stately and serious speech of his own time, so Ennius, in his graphic delineation of the age in which he lived, gave expression to that high magnanimous mood in accordance with which the acts of Roman statesmen were assailed or vindicated, and the policy of the State was shaped before Senate and people—

> indu foro lato sanctoque senatu—

The great poets of human action and passion are for the most part to be ranked among the great poets of the outward world. If they do not seem to have penetrated with so much personal sympathy into the inner secret of the life of Nature, as the great contemplative poets of ancient and modern times, yet they show, in different ways, that their sense and imagination were powerfully affected both by her outward beauty and by her manifold energy. Homer, not so much by direct description of the scenes in which the action of his poems is laid, as by many indirect touches, by vivid imagery and picturesque epithets, reveals the openness of his mind to every impression from the outward world, and the fresh delight with which his imagination reproduced the impressions immediately received from the 'world of eye and ear.' If he has left any personal characteristic stamped upon his poetry, it is the trace of adventure and keen enjoyment in the open air, among the most stirring sights and sounds and forces of Nature. The imagery of Virgil is of a more peaceful cast. It seems rather to be 'the harvest of a quiet eye,' gathered in the conscious contemplation of rural beauty, and stored up for after use along with the

---

[1] 'Whither have your minds, which heretofore were wont to stand firm, madly swerved from the straight course?'

products of his study and meditation. The fragments of Ennius, on the other hand, afford few indications either of active toil and unconscious enjoyment among the solitudes of Nature, or of the luxurious and pensive susceptibility to beauty by which the poetry of Virgil is pervaded. He was the poet, not of the woods and rivers, but, essentially, of the city and the camp. No sentiment could appear less appropriate to him than that of Virgil's modest prayer,—

> Flumina amem silvasque inglorius.

Yet both in his illustrative imagery and in his narrative, he occasionally reproduces with lively force, if not with much poetical ornament, some aspects of the outward world, as well as many real scenes from the world of action.

His imagery is sometimes borrowed from that of Homer; as, for instance, the following simile, which is also imitated by Virgil :—

> Et tum sic ut equus, qui de praesepibu' fartus,
> Vincla suis magnis animis abrupit, et inde
> Fert sese campi per caerula laetaque prata
> Celso pectore, saepe jubam quassat simul altam,
> Spiritus ex anima calida spumas agit albas.[1]

Other illustrations are taken from circumstances likely to have been familiar to the men of his own time, but without any apparent intention of adding poetical beauty to the object he is representing. Thus the silent expectation

---

[1] A comparison with the original passage (Iliad, vi. 506), will show that Ennius, while reproducing much, though not all, of the force and life of Homer's image, has added also some touches of his own :—

> ὡς δ' ὅτε τις στατὸς ἵππος, ἀκοστήσας ἐπὶ φάτνῃ
> δεσμὸν ἀπορρήξας θείῃ πεδίοιο κροαίνων,
> εἰωθὼς λούεσθαι εὐρρεῖος ποταμοῖο,
> κυδιόων· ὑψοῦ δὲ κάρη ἔχει, ἀμφὶ δὲ χαῖται
> ὤμοις ἀΐσσονται· ὁ δ' ἀγλαΐηφι πεποιθώς,
> ῥίμφα ἑ γοῦνα φέρει μετά τ' ἤθεα καὶ νομὸν ἵππων.

Cf. irgil, Aen. xi. 492 :—

> Qualis ubi abruptis fugit praesepia vinclis
> Tandem liber equus, campoque potitus aperto
> Aut ille in pastus armentaque tendit equarum,
> Aut adsuetus aquae perfundi flumine noto
> Emicat, arrectisque fremit cervicibus alte
> Luxurians, luduntque jubae per colla, per armos.

with which the assembled people watch the rival auspices of Romulus and Remus is brought before the mind by an illustration suggested by, and suggestive of, the passionate eagerness with which the public games were witnessed by the Romans of his own age :—

> Expectant vel uti consul cum mittere signum
> Volt, omnes avidi spectant ad carceris oras,
> Quam mox emittat pictis e faucibu' currus.[1]

There may be noticed also, in fragments of the narrative, occasional expressions and descriptive touches implying some sense of what is sublime or picturesque in the familiar aspects of the outward world. The sky, with its starry host, is poetically presented in that expression, which has been adopted by Virgil, 'stellis ingentibus aptum ;' and in the following line,

> Vertitur interea caelum cum ingentibu' signis.

In the description of the auspices of Romulus, the scene is enlivened by this vivid flash, 'simul aureus exoritur Sol,' following instantaneously upon the appearance of the first bird of omen. A lively sense of natural scenery is implied in these lines from the dream of Ilia—

> Nam me visus homo pulcher per amoena salicta
> Et ripas raptare locosque novos ;

in this description of a river, afterwards imitated both by Lucretius and Virgil—

> Quod per amoenam urbem leni fluit agmine flumen ;

and in these lines which recall a familiar passage in the Aeneid :—

> Jupiter hic risit tempestatesque serenae
> Riserunt omnes risu Jovis omnipotentis.[2]

The rhythm and the diction of these fragments suggest another point of contrast between the father of Greek and

---

[1] 'They watch, as when the consul is going to give the signal, all look eagerly to the barrier, to see how soon he may start the chariots from the painted entrance.'

[2]   Olli subridens hominum sator atque deorum
   Voltu, quo caelum tempestatesque serenat.—Aen. i. 254.

the father of Roman literature. For the old Saturnian verse of the Fauns and Bards, which had been employed by Livius Andronicus and Naevius, Ennius substituted the heroic hexameter, which he moulded to the use of Roman poetry, with little art and grace, but with much energy and weight. As he imitated the metre of Homer, he has in several places (as in a simile already quoted, and again in describing the conduct of a brave tribune in the Istrian war), attempted to reproduce his language. Nothing, however, can show more clearly the vast original difference between the genius of Greece and of Rome than the contrast presented between the rhythm and style of their earliest epic poets. In their regard for law and civil order, in military and political organisation, in practical power of understanding, and in the command which that power gave them over the world, the Romans of the second century B.C. had made a great and permanent advance beyond the Greeks of the time of Homer. But the Greeks, when they first become known to us, appear in possession of a gift to which all later generations have been unable to attain. The genius of poetry has never, since the time of Homer, appeared in union with a faculty of expression so true and spontaneous, so faultless in purity, so inexhaustible in resources. It is difficult to imagine a greater contrast than that between the varied and harmonious power of the earliest Greek epic, and the rugged rhythm and diction of the Annals. Yet the very rudeness of that work is significant of the energy of a man who had to accomplish a gigantic task by his own unaided efforts. His ear had not been passively trained by the musical echoes transmitted by earlier minstrels; nor did he inherit the fluency and richness of expression which a long line of poets hands on to their successors. While professing to imitate the structure of the Homeric verse, he was unable to seize its finer cadences. Nor had he learned the stricter conditions under which that metre could be adapted to the powerful and weighty movement of the Latin language. If he did much to establish Latin prosody on principles deviating considerably from those observed by the contemporary comic poets, yet many points which were regulated unalterably for Virgil were left quite unsettled by Ennius. There are found occasionally in these fragments lines without any *caesura* before the fifth foot, as the following, in one of the longest and least imperfect of his remains—

> Corde capessere : semita nulla pedem stabilibat.

and this in a passage in which the sound seems intended to imitate the sense—

> Poste recumbite vestraque pectora pellite tonsis.

And though such marked violations of harmony are rare, yet there is a large proportion of lines in which the laws for the caesura observed by later poets are violated. Again, while the final 's' is in most cases not sounded before a word beginning with a consonant (a usage which finally disappears only in the Augustan poets) the final m, on the other hand, is sometimes left without elision before a vowel, as in the following line—

> Miscent inter sese inimicitiam agitantes.

The quantity of syllables and the inflexions of words were so far unsettled, that such lines as the following are read,

> Partem fuisset de summis rebu' regendis ;

and this,

> Noenum rumores ponebat ante salutem ;

and

> Volturus in spinis miserum mandebat homonem.

Among the ruder characteristics of his diction, his use of prosaic and technical terms is especially to be noticed. The following lines, for instance, read more like the bare statement of a chronicle, or of a legal document, than an extract from a poetical narrative :—

> Cives Romani tunc facti sunt Campani ;

and this

> Appius indixit Karthaginiensibu' bellum ;

and these lines enumerating the various priesthoods established by Numa,—

> Volturnalem Palatualem Furrinalem
> Floralemque Falacrem et Pomonalem fecit
> Hic idem.

Yet, in spite of these imperfections, both his rhythm and language produce the impression of power and originality. With all the roughness and irregularity of his measure, and notwithstanding the inharmonious structure of continuous passages, his lines often have a weighty and impressive effect, like that produced by some of the great passages in Lucretius and Virgil. It is said of the rhetorician Aelian that he excessively admired in Ennius both 'the greatness of his mind and the grandeur of his metre[1].' Something of this sonorous grandeur may be recognised in a fragment descriptive of the havoc made by woodcutters in a great forest,—a passage in which the language of Ennius again appears as a connecting link between that of Homer and of Virgil :—

> Incedunt arbusta per alta, securibu' caedunt,
> Percellunt magnas quercus, exciditur ilex,
> Fraxinu' frangitur, atque abies consternitur alta.
> Pinus proceras pervortunt: omne sonabat
> Arbustum fremitu siluai frondosai.[2]

In the longest consecutive passages,—the dream of Ilia, the auspices of Romulus, and that from book seventh, already quoted as illustrative of the poet's character,—there is, notwithstanding the roughness of the lines, something also of Homeric rapidity;—a quality which the Latin hexameter never afterwards attained in elevated poetry.

The diction also of the Annals is generally fresh and forcible, sometimes vividly imaginative. But perhaps the most admirable quality of its style is a grave simplicity and sincerity of tone. Especially is this the case in pas-

---

[1] Ἔννιος Ῥωμαῖος ποιητής· ὃν Αἰλιανὸς ἐπαινεῖν ἄξιόν φησι . . . . δῆλον δὲ ὡς ἐτεθήπει τοῦ ποιητοῦ τὴν μεγαλόνοιαν καὶ τῶν μέτρων τὸ μεγαλεῖον καὶ ἀξιάγαστον. —Suidas, vol. i. p. 1258, ed. Gaisford.

[2] Cf. Iliad, xxiii. 114-120; and also Virgil, Aen. vi. 179 :—
> Itur in antiquam silvam, stabula alta ferarum,
> Procumbunt piceae, sonat icta securibus ilex,
> Fraxineaeque trabes cuneis et fissile robur
> Scinditur, advolvunt ingentis montibus ornos.

sages expressing appreciation of strength and grandeur of character, as in those fragments from the speeches of Pyrrhus and of Appius Claudius Caecus, already quoted, and in the famous lines commemorative of the resolute character and momentous services of Fabius Maximus.

> Unus homo nobis cunctando restituit rem:
> Noenum rumores ponebat ante salutem:
> Ergo plusque magisque viri nunc gloria claret.[1]

These lines leave on the mind the same impression of antique majesty, as is produced by the unadorned record of character and work accomplished inscribed on the tombs of the Scipios.

This truly Roman quality of style, depending on a strong imaginative sense of reality, is one of the great elements of power in the language of Lucretius.

III. CHIEF CHARACTERISTICS OF HIS GENIUS AND INTELLECT.

III.—From a review of the extant fragments both of the Tragedies and the Annals of Ennius, it appears that his prominent place in Roman literature, and influence over his countrymen, were due much more to a great productiveness and activity, and to an original force of mind and character, than to any artistic skill displayed in the conception or execution of his works. A consideration of the spirit and purpose of his greatest works has led to the conclusion that they were, in a considerable measure, inspired by the genius of Rome, and were thus rather the starting-point of a new literature than the mechanical reproduction of the literature of the Greeks. It remains to consider what inference may be formed from these fragments as to the character of his genius, of his imaginative sentiment and moral sympathies, and of his intellectual power.

---

[1] 'One man, by biding his time, restored the commonwealth. He cared not for what men said of him, as compared with our safety: therefore now his fame waxeth brighter day by day.'

The force of many single expressions in these fragments, and the power with which various incidents, situations, and characters, are brought before the mind indicate an active imagination. A sense of energy and life-like movement is the prevailing impression produced by a study of the language and the longer passages in these remains. Many single lines and expressions that have been gathered accidentally, as mere isolated phrases, disjoined from the context in which they originally occurred, bear traces of the ardour with which they were cast into shape. In longer passages, the whole heart, sense, and understanding of the writer seem to be thrown into his narrative. He has not the eye of a poetic artist who observes, as it were, from a distance, and fixes as in a picture, some phase of passionate feeling or some beautiful aspect of repose. He suggests rather the idea of a man of practical energy, who has been present and taken part in the action described, who enters with living interest into every detail, and watches it at the same time with a sagacious discernment and a strong enthusiasm. His power as a narrative poet is the power of forcibly reproducing the outward movement and the inward meaning of an action, and of identifying himself with the hearts and minds of the actors on the scene. Several passages, wanting altogether in poetical beauty, yet arrest the attention by this energy and realism of conception; as, for example, this short and rugged fragment, descriptive of a commander in the crisis of a battle (probably that of Cynoscephalae),—

> Aspectabat virtutem legioni' suai,
> Expectans, si mussaret, quae denique pausa
> Pugnandi fieret, aut duri fini' laboris.[1]

Even in the abrupt dislocation from their context these lines leave on the mind an impression of the calm vigilance of a general, and of his confidence, not unmixed with anxiety, in 'the long-enduring hearts' of his men. The same truth and energy of conception, with more poetical

[1] 'He watched the courage of his force, to see if any murmur should arise for some pause to the long battle, some rest from their weary toil.'

accompaniment, may be recognised in the longer passages, from Book vii. and Book i., already quoted or referred to.

But the imaginative power which gives poetical meaning to familiar objects and ideas is revealed by the force of many single expressions and by the delineation of more passionate situations. Such expressions as the following, most of which reappear with an antique lustre in the gold of Virgil's diction, are indicative of this higher power.

> Musae quae pedibus magnum pulsatis Olympum.
> Transnavit cita per teneras caliginis auras.
> Postquam discordia taetra
> Belli ferratos postes portasque refregit.
> Quem super ingens
> Porta tonat caeli.
> Spiritus austri imbricitor. Naves velivolae, etc. etc.

These and similar phrases, some of which have already been quoted, imply poetical creativeness. They tend to justify the estimate of the genius of Ennius, indicated in the language of high admiration applied to him by Lucretius,—

> Ennius ut noster cecinit, qui primus amoeno
> Detulit ex Helicone perenni fronde coronam,
> Per gentes Italas hominum quae clara clueret;[1]

and in the signs of the careful study of the Annals which may be traced in the elaborate workmanship of the Aeneid.

The longest specimen of narrative vivified by poetical feeling, from the hand of Ennius, is the passage in which the vestal Ilia relates to her sister the dream that portended her great and strange destiny:—

> Excita cum tremulis anus attulit artubu' lumen,
> Talia commemorat lacrimans, exterrita somno.
> Eurudica prognata, pater quam noster amavit,
> Vires vitaque corpu' meum nunc deserit omne.
> Nam me visus homo pulcher per amoena salicta
> Et ripas raptare locosque novos; ita sola
> Postilla, germana soror, errare videbar

---

[1] 'As sang our Ennius, the first who brought down from pleasant Helicon a chaplet of unfading leaf, the fame of which should be bruited loud through the nations of Italian men.'

> Tardaque vestigare et quaerere te neque posse
> Corde capessere: semita nulla pedem stabilibat.
> Exin compellare pater me voce videtur
> His verbis: 'O gnata, tibi sunt ante ferendae
> Aerumnae, post ex fluvio fortuna resistet.'
> Haec ecfatu' pater, germana, repente recessit
> Nec sese dedit in conspectum, corde cupitus,
> Quanquam multa manus ad caeli caerula templa
> Tendebam lacrimans et blanda voce vocabam:
> Vix aegro cum corde meo me somnu' reliquit.[1]

Though these lines are rough and inharmonious as compared with the rhythm of Catullus or Virgil, yet they flow more smoothly and rapidly than any of the other fragments preserved from Ennius. The impression of gentleness and tender affection produced by the speech of Ilia, implies some dramatic skill in the conception of character. And there is real imaginative power shown in the sense of hurry and surprise, of vague awe and helplessness conveyed in the lines—

> Nam me visus homo pulcher per amoena salicta, etc.

From this passage Virgil has borrowed one of the finest touches in his delineation of the passion of Dido, the sense of horror and desolation haunting the Carthaginian queen in her dreams—

> Agit ipse furentem
> In somnis ferus Aeneas: semperque relinqui
> Sola sibi, semper longam incomitata videtur
> Ire viam, et Tyrios deserta quaerere terra.

---

[1] 'When the old dame had risen, and with trembling limbs had brought the light, thus she (Ilia), roused in terror from her sleep, with tears tells her tale: "Daughter of Eurydice, whom our father loved, my strength and life now fail me through all my frame. For methought that a goodly man was bearing me off through the pleasant willow-groves, by the river-banks, and places strange to me. Thereafter, O my sister, I seemed to be wandering all alone, and with slow steps to track my way, to be seeking thee, and to be unable to find thee near; no footpath steadied my step. Afterwards methought I heard my father address me in these words—'Daughter, trouble must first be borne by thee; afterwards thy fortune shall rise up again from the river.' With these words, O sister, he suddenly departed, nor gave himself to my sight, though my heart yearned to him, though I kept eagerly stretching my hands to the blue vault of heaven, weeping, and calling on him with loving tones. With pain and weary heart at last sleep left me."'

Another of the most impressive passages in the early books of the Aeneid—the dream in which Hector appears to Aeneas[1]—was evidently suggested by the description which Ennius gave of the appearance of the shade of Homer to himself. Some of his dramatic fragments, also, as for instance the scene between Hecuba and Cassandra already referred to, show a real power of conceiving and representing passionate situations.

Among the modes of imaginative sentiment by which the poetry of Ennius is pervaded, those kindled by patriotic enthusiasm are most conspicuous. In the manifestation of his enthusiasm, he shows an affinity to Virgil in ancient, and to Scott in modern times. He resembles them in their mingled feelings of veneration and affection which they entertain towards the national heroes of old times, and the great natural features of their country, associated with historic memories and legendary renown. Such feelings are shown by Ennius in the lines of tender regret and true hero-worship, which express the sorrow of Senate and people at the death of Romulus—

> Pectora . . . tenet desiderium, simul inter
> Sese sic memorant, O Romule, Romule die
> Qualem te patriae custodem di genuerunt!
> O pater, O genitor, O sanguen dis oriundum!
> Tu produxisti nos intra luminis oras.[2]

They appear also in the language applied by him to the sacred river of Rome, which had preserved the founder of the city from his untimely fate, and which was thus inseparably identified with the national destiny—

> Teque pater Tiberine tuo cum flumine sancto.

and also in this fragment—

> Postquam consistit fluvius qui est omnibu' princeps
> Qui sub caeruleo.

---

[1] Aen. ii. 270.

[2] 'Regret and sorrow fill their hearts, while thus they say to one another, O Romulus, God-like Romulus, how great a guardian of our country did the gods create in thee! O father, author of our being, O blood sprung from the gods! it is thou that hast brought us forth within the realms of light.'

The enumeration of the great warlike races in the line

> Marsa manus, Peligna cohors, Vestina virum vis,

may recall the pride and enthusiasm which are kindled in the heart of Virgil by the names of the various tribes of Italy, and of places renowned for their fame in story, or their picturesque environment [1]. This fond use of proper names recalling old associations or the charm of natural scenery is also among the most familiar characteristics of the poetry of Scott.

It was seen in the introductory chapter that the Roman mind was peculiarly susceptible of that kind of feeling, which perhaps may best be described as the *sense of majesty*. This vein of poetical emotion is also conspicuous in the fragments of Ennius. His language shows a deep sense of greatness and order, both in the material world and in human affairs. Thus his style appears animated not only by vital force, but by an impressive solemnity, befitting the grave and dignified emotion which responds to such ideas. This susceptibility of his genius appears in such expressions as these—

> Magnum pulsatis Olympum.   Indu mari magno.
> Litora lata sonant.
> Latos per populos terrasque.
> Magnae gentes opulentae.
> Quis potis ingentis oras evolvere belli?
> Vertitur interea caelum cum ingentibu' signis;

and again in the following—

> Indu foro lato sanctoque senatu.
> Augusto augurio postquam incluta condita Roma est.
> Omnibu' cura viris uter esset induperator,

and in the epithet which Cicero quotes as applied to cities—

> Urbes magnas atque *imperiosas*.

[1] E. g. passages such as the following:—
> Quique altum Praeneste viri, quique arva Gabinae
> Junonis gelidumque Anienem et roscida rivis
> Hernica saxa colunt, quos dives Anagnia pascit,
> Quos, Amasene pater.—Aen. viii. 682-5.

His imagination appears also to have been impressed by that sense of outward pomp and magnificence which exercised a strong spell on the Roman mind in all ages, and obtained its most complete and permanent realisation in the architecture of the Empire. A short passage from one of his tragedies, the Andromache, may be quoted as illustrative of this influence, even in the writings of Ennius, though naturally it is much more apparent in the style of those poets who witnessed the grandeur of Rome in her later era :—

> O pater, O patria, O Priami domus,
> Saeptum altisono cardine templum!
> Vidi ego te, astante ope barbarica,
> Tectis caelatis, lacuatis,
> Auro ebore instructum regifice![1]

While his peculiar poetical feeling is present chiefly in the fragments of the Annals, the moral elements of his poetry may be gathered both from his epic and dramatic remains. Strength and dignity of character are the qualities with which his own nature was most in sympathy. Yet in delineating the agitation of Ilia, the shame of Cassandra, and the sorrow of Andromache, he reveals also much tenderness of feeling,—the not unusual accompaniment of the manly genius of Rome. A similar tenderness is found in union with the grave tones of Pacuvius and Accius, and in still greater measure with the fortitude of Lucretius and the majesty of Virgil. The masculine qualities which most stir his enthusiasm are the Roman virtues of resolution (constantia), sincerity, magnanimity, capacity for affairs. Thus a latent glow of feeling may be discerned in the lines which record the brave resolution of the Roman people during the first hardships of the war with Pyrrhus—

> Ast animo superant atque aspera prima
> Volnera belli dispernunt;[2]

---

[1] 'O father! O fatherland! O house of Priam, palace, closing on high-sounding hinge, I have seen thee, guarded by a barbaric host, with carved and deep-fretted roof, with ivory and gold royally adorned.'

[2] 'But they rise superior in spirit, and spurn the first sharp wounds of war.'

and in this strong and scornful triumph over natural sorrow, from the Telamon:—

> Ego cum genui tum morituros scivi, et ei rei sustuli:
> Praeterea ad Trojam cum misi ob defendendam Graeciam,
> Scibam me in mortiferum bellum, non in epulas mittere.[1]

The generosity and courage of a magnanimous nature are stamped upon the kingly speech which he puts into the mouth of Pyrrhus. A frank sincerity of character reveals itself in such passages as the following:—

> Eo ego ingenio natus sum,
> Aeque inimicitiam atque amicitiam in frontem promptam gero.[2]

There is no subtlety nor rhetorical point in the expression of his serious convictions. The very style of the tragedies, which, as Cicero says[3], 'does not depart from the natural order of the words,' is a symbol of frankness and straightforwardness.

He shows also, in his delineations of character, high appreciation of practical wisdom, and of its most powerful instrument in a free State, the persuasive power of oratory. This appreciation is expressed in the lines so much admired by Cicero and Aulus Gellius[4], though ridiculed by the purism of Seneca:

> Is dictus 'st ollis popularibus olim
> Qui tum vivebant homines, atque aevum agitabant,
> Flos delibatus populi suadaeque medulla.[5]

He seems to admire the sterling qualities of character and intellect rather than the brilliant manifestations of impulse and genius. He celebrates the heroism of brave

---

[1] 'When I begat them, I knew that they must die, and to that end I bred them. Besides, when I sent them to Troy to fight for Greece, I was well aware that I was sending them, not to a feast, but to a deadly war.'

[2] 'Such is my nature. Enmity and friendship equally I bear stamped on my forehead.'

[3] 'Ennio delector, ait quispiam, quod non discedit a communi ordine verborum.'—Orator, 11.

[4] Cicero, Brutus, 15; Aulus Gellius, xii. 2.

[5] 'He was called by those, his fellow-countrymen, who flourished then and enjoyed their day, the chosen flower of the people, and the marrow of persuasion.'

endurance rather than of chivalrous daring[1]; the fortitude that, in the long run, wins success, and saves the State[2], rather than the impetuous valour which achieves a barren glory; the sincerity and simplicity which are stronger than art, yet that know when to speak and when to be silent[3]; the sagacity which enables men to understand their circumstances, and to turn them to the best account[4].

Many of his fragments, again, show traces of that just and vigorous understanding of human life, and that shrewdness of observation, which constitute a great satirist. The didactic tone of satire appears, for instance, in the following lines—

> Otioso in otio animus nescit quid velit;
> Hic itidem est: enim neque domi nunc nos neque militiae sumus,
> Imus huc, illuc hinc, cum illuc ventum est, ire illinc lubet;
> Incerte errat animus: praeter propter vitam vivitur[5],—

a fragment which might be compared with certain passages in the Epistles of Horace, which give expression to the *ennui* experienced as a result of the inaction and luxurious living of the Augustan age. But a closer parallel will be found in a passage where Lucretius has assumed something of the caustic tone of Roman satire—

> Exit saepe foras magnis ex aedibus ille
> Esse domi quem pertaesum 'st, subitoque revertit,
> Quippe domi nihilo melius qui sentiat esse,' etc.[6]

While Ennius, like Lucretius, gives little indication of humour, yet the folly and superstition of his times provoke

---

[1] Compare his account of the Tribune in the Istrian war:
  'Undique conveniunt velut imber, tela tribuno,' etc.
[2] Cf. 'Unus homo nobis cunctando restituit rem,' etc.
[3] Cf. 'Ita sapere opino esse optimum, ut pro viribus
    Tacere ac fabulare tute noveris;'
also
  'Ea libertas est quae pectus purum et firmum gestitat.'
[4] 'Egregie cordatus homo catus Aeliu' Sextus.'
[5] 'In idleness the mind knows not what it wants. This is now our case. We are neither now at home nor abroad. We go hither, back again to the place from which we came,—when we have reached it we desire' to leave it again. Our mind is all astray—existence goes on outside of real life.'
[6] iii. 1059-67.

him into tones of contemptuous irony, especially where he has to expose the arts of false prophets and fortune-tellers. The men of the manliest temper and the strongest understanding in ancient times were most intolerant of this mischievous form of imposture and credulity. Thus Thucydides, in general so reserved in his expression of personal feeling, treats, with a manifest irony, all supernatural pretences to foresee or control the future. The tone in which Ennius writes of such professions reminds us of Milton's grim contempt for

> Eremites and friars
> White, black, and grey, with all their trumpery.

Thus, in a fragment of Book xi. of the Annals, the fears excited by the prophets and diviners at the commencement of the war with Antiochus are encountered with the pertinent question—

> Satin' vates verant aetate in agenda?

Thus too the pretensions and the ignorance of astrologers are exposed in a line of one of the dramas—

> Quod est ante pedes nemo spectat: caeli scrutantur plagas.

And the following passage may be quoted as applicable to charlatans of every kind, in every age and country—

> Sed superstitiosi vates, impudentesque arioli,
> Aut inertes aut insani, aut quibus egestas imperat,
> Qui sibi semitam non sapiunt, alteri monstrant viam,
> Quibus divitias pollicentur, ab eis drachmam ipsi petunt.[1]

There are passages of the same spirit to be found among the fragments of Pacuvius and Accius.

There is not much indication of speculative thought in any of these fragments. The blunt sentiment which Ennius puts into the mouth of Neoptolemus probably

---

[1] 'But your superstitious prophets and impudent fortune-tellers, idle fellows, or madmen, or the victims of want, who cannot discern the path for themselves, yet point the way out to others, and ask a drachma from the very persons to whom they promise a fortune.'

expressed his own mental attitude towards the schools of philosophy—

> Philosophari est mihi necesse, at paucis : nam omnino haut placet.

His observations on life are neither of an imaginative, of a deeply reflective, nor of a purely satiric character. Unlike the thoughts of the Greek dramatists, they make no attempt to solve the painful riddle of the world; they want the universality and systematic basis of philosophical truths; they are expressed neither with the pointed wit nor with the ironical humour of satire. They are the maxims of a strong common sense and the dictates of a grave rectitude of will. They are practical, not speculative. They have their origin in a sense of duty rather than of consequences. They are in conformity with the ideal realised in the best types of Roman character; and they bear witness to the sterling worth combined with the ardent enthusiasm, and the practical sense united to the strong imagination of the poet.

Such appear to be the chief attributes of genius and imaginative sentiment, and the chief moral and intellectual features indicated in the fragments of Ennius. It is not indeed possible, from the tenor of single passages, to judge of the composition of a whole drama or of a continuous book of the Annals. No single scene or speech can afford sufficient grounds for inferring the amount of creative power with which his characters were conceived and sustained in all their complex relations. Yet enough has appeared in these fragments, which, from the accidental mode of their preservation, must be regarded as the ordinary samples and not chosen specimens of his style, to confirm the ancient belief in his pre-eminence and to determine the prevailing characteristics of his genius. There is ample evidence of the great popularity which he enjoyed among his countrymen, and of the high estimate which many of the best Roman writers formed of his power. It is recorded that great crowds ('magna frequentia') attended the public reading of the Annals.

Virgil was said to have introduced many lines into the Aeneid, with the view of pleasing a public devoted to Ennius ('populus Ennianus'). The title of Ennianista was assumed by a public reader of the Annals in the time of Hadrian [1]. Cicero often speaks of the poet as 'noster Ennius,' and quotes him with all the signs of hearty admiration and affection. The numerous references in his works to the Annals and the Tragedies imply also a thorough familiarity with these poems on the part of the readers for whom his philosophical and rhetorical treatises were written. The criticism of Quintilian, 'Ennium sicut sacros vetustate lucos adoremus, in quibus grandia et antiqua robora jam non tantam habent speciem quantam religionem[2],' expresses a sentiment of traditional reverence as well as of personal appreciation. Aulus Gellius, a writer of the time of Hadrian, often quotes and comments upon him with hearty and genial sympathy. The greatest among the Roman poets also, directly and indirectly, acknowledge their admiration. The strong testimony of Lucretius, the most imaginative poet and the most powerful thinker whom Rome produced, is alone sufficient to establish the fame of Ennius as a man of remarkable force and genius. The spirit of the Annals still lives in the antique charm and national spirit which make the epic poem of Virgil the truest representation of Roman feeling which has come down to modern times. By Ovid he is characterised as—

Ennius, ingenio maximus, arte rudis.

Horace, although more reluctant and grudging in his admiration, yet allows the 'Calabrian Muse' to be the

[1] 'And there it is announced to Julianus that a certain public reader, an accomplished man, with a very well-trained and musical voice, read the Annals of Ennius publicly in the theatre. Let us go, says he, to hear this "Ennianista," whoever he is,—for by that name he chose to be called.'—Aulus Gellius, xviii. 5.

The following line of Martial (v. 10. 7) implies also his popularity under the Empire—

'Ennius est lectus, salvo tibi, Roma, Marone.'

[2] 'Let us venerate Ennius like the groves, sacred from their antiquity, in which the great and ancient oak-trees are invested not so much with beauty as with sacred associations.'—Inst. Or. x. i. 88.

best preserver of the fame of the great Scipio. Even the disparaging lines—

> Ennius et sapiens et fortis et alter Homerus,
> Ut critici dicunt, leviter curare videtur
> Quo promissa cadant et somnia Pythagorea,[1]

are a strong testimony in favour of the esteem in which the vigour and sagacity of Ennius were held by those who had all his works in their hands. As one of the founders of Roman literature, it was impossible that he could have rivalled the careful and finished style of the Augustan poets; but, by his rude and energetic labours, he laid the strong groundwork on which later poets built their fame.

He has been exposed to more serious detraction in modern times, as the corrupter of the pure stream of early Roman poetry. It is alleged against him by Niebuhr, that through jealousy he suppressed the ballad and epic poetry of the early bards. The answer to this charge has already been given. There is no evidence to prove that any such poems were in existence in the time of Ennius. By other modern scholars he is disadvantageously compared with Naevius, who is held up to admiration as the last of the genuine Roman minstrels. Naevius appears indeed to have been a remarkable and original man, yet his very scanty fragments do not afford sufficient evidence to justify the reversal of the verdict of antiquity on the relative greatness and importance of the two poets. The old Roman party, in opposition to whom Ennius and his friends are supposed to have introduced the new taste and suppressed the old, never showed any zeal in favour of poetry of any kind. Cato, their only literary representative, wrote prose treatises on antiquities and agriculture, and in one of his speeches reproached Fulvius Nobilior for the consideration which he showed to Ennius. The evidence of these epic and dramatic frag-

---

[1] 'Ennius, the wise and strong, and the second Homer, as his critics will have it, seems to care little for the issue of all his promises and Pythagorean dreams.'—Epist. II. i. 50-2.

ments which have just been considered, is all in favour of the high verdict of antiquity on the importance and pre-eminence of the author of the Annals. Whatever in the later poets is most truly Roman in sentiment and morality appears to be conceived in the spirit of Ennius.

He stands out prominently in that early time as a man of true genius, and of a strong and original character. His lot was not cast, like that of the Augustan poets, in the midst of a refined and courtly society, with all the aids and appliances of literary leisure, and in secure exemption from any harsh collision with the world. Neither was he a poetical artist, like Catullus, yielding himself up to the enjoyment of beauty, and reproducing in his verse the charm which he had found in life, in Nature, and in earlier art. His poetry was the serious product of a manly and energetic life, and of a vital interest in the great affairs of his time. Till middle life he is dimly discerned as an obscure Messapian soldier, claiming descent from an old race of kings, and a stranger to the great city which in after times regarded him as the father of her literature. In mature manhood, and in a kindly old age, he is seen exercising a constant literary industry in manifold ways, living plainly and in cheerful independence, applauded by his fellow-citizens, and honoured by the friendship of the greatest among his contemporaries.

The variety and extent of his works bear witness to remarkable learning, as well as a strong productive energy. With a wide knowledge of Greek literature, he combined the heart and will of a Roman; and to the study of the best books he added a close contact with men. Expressions in his remains indicate the opposite religious feelings and convictions of a mystic and a sceptic. In his temper and character a high self-consciousness appears united with a true simplicity and hearty appreciation of others, and a great gravity of tone and purpose with a cheerful and sanguine spirit. His moral sympathies are most deeply moved by such qualities as fortitude, magnanimity, and practical wisdom; and the transparent sincerity of his words gives assurance that he himself was formed out of the same true metal which he recognised in 'the old manners and men' of his adopted country.

In his poetry he represented the traditions and the steady continuous growth of the Roman State, and expressed the confidence which the people reposed in their destiny, their institutions, and their leading men. His dramas, although founded on Greek models, and dealing with Greek legends and personages, yet had a real national air in the type of character they presented, in the sentiments they expressed, and in the lessons of life they inculcated. His epic poem was in form, spirit, and substance, inspired by the genius of his country, and was finished with the strong and massive execution of Roman workmanship[1]. While discarding the native Saturnian measure, as unequal to the elevated tone of a long narrative poem, he moulded the Latin language to the conditions of a new metre, which, in later times, was successfully wrought into the most expressive organ of the majesty of Rome. In his reproduction of the Homeric mythology, he has embodied the idea of the national destiny. The characteristic sentiment of his poetry indicates his affinity not to Homer and Sophocles, but to Lucretius and Virgil. There are gleams also of true creative power in these fragments. If wanting in the fine accomplishment and the contemplative faculty of a poetic artist, he seems to have possessed a strength and energy of conception unsurpassed by any of his successors. He was endowed also with that living power which gives new meaning to familiar things; which, without distorting or exaggerating the truth, discerns and reveals the glory and grandeur in the actual march of events.

[1] The name *Romais* given to the Annals in a later age indicates the appreciation of this national inspiration.

CHAPTER V.

EARLY ROMAN TRAGEDY—M. PACUVIUS, B.C. 219–129;
L. ACCIUS, B.C. 170–ABOUT B.C. 90.

THE powerful impulse given to Roman tragedy by Ennius was sustained till about the beginning of the first century B.C. first by his nephew M. Pacuvius and after him by L. Accius. The popularity of the drama during this period may be estimated from the fact that, of the early writers of poetry, Lucilius alone contributed nothing to the Roman stage. The plays of the three tragedians who have just been mentioned were not only performed during the lifetime of their authors, but, as appears from many notices of them in Cicero, they held their place on the stage with much popular applause, and were read and admired as literary works till the last days of the Republic. This popularity implies either some adaptation of Roman tragedy to the time in which it was produced, or some special capacity for awakening new interests and ideas in a people hitherto unacquainted with literature. Yet, on the other hand, the want of permanence, and the want of any power of development in the Roman drama, would indicate that it was less adapted to the genius of the nation than either the epic or the satiric poetry of this era. If the dramatic art of Pacuvius and Accius had been as true an expression of the national mind as either the epic poem of Ennius or the satire of Lucilius, it might have been expected that it would have flourished in greater perfection in the eras of finer literary accomplishment. The efforts of Naevius and Ennius were crowned with the fulfilment of Virgil, and the spirit and manner of Lucilius still live in the satires of Horace and Juvenal; but Roman tragedy dwindled away till it became a mere literary exercise of educated men, and remains only in the artificial and rhetorical compositions attributed to the philosopher Seneca.

From the fact that early Roman tragedy left no literary heir, it is more difficult to discern its original features and character than those of the epic or satiric poetry of the period. A further difficulty arises out of the very nature of dramatic fragments. Isolated passages in a drama afford scanty grounds for judging of the conduct of the action, or the force and consistency with which the leading characters are maintained. There is, moreover, very slight direct evidence bearing on the dramatic genius of the early tragic poets. Roman critics seem to have paid little attention to, or had little perception of this kind of excellence. They quote with admiration the fervid sentiment and morality—'the rugged maxims hewn from life'—expressed on the Roman stage; but they have not preserved the memory of any great typical character, or of any dramatic plot creatively conceived or powerfully sustained.

The Roman drama was confessedly a reproduction or adaptation of the drama of Athens. The titles of the great majority of Roman tragedies indicate that they were translated or copied from Greek originals, or were at least founded on the legends of Greek poetry and mythology. The *Medea* of Ennius and the *Antiope* of Pacuvius are known, on the authority of Cicero, to have been directly translated from Euripides. Other dramas were more or less close adaptations from his works, or from those of the other Attic tragedians. All of the Roman tragic poets indeed produced one or more plays founded on Roman history or legend: but, with the exception of the Brutus of Accius, none of these seem to have been permanently popular. This failure to establish a national drama seems to imply a want of dramatic invention in the conduct of a plot and the exhibition of character on the part of the poets. As their own history was of supreme interest to the Romans at all times, it is difficult on any other supposition to explain the failure of the 'fabula praetextata' in gaining the public ear. There is, however, distinct evidence that in their adaptations from the Greek the Roman poets in some cases departed considerably from their originals. Something of a Roman stamp was perhaps unconsciously impressed on the Greek personages who were represented. Many of the extant fragments seem to breathe the spirit of Rome more than of Athens. They are expressed not with the subtlety and reflective genius of Greece, but in the plain and straightforward tones of the Roman Republic. The long-continued popularity of Roman tragedy implies also that it was something more than an inartistic copy of the masterpieces of Athenian genius. Mere imitations of Aeschylus, Sophocles, and Euripides might possibly have obtained some favour with a few men of literary education, but could never have been listened to with applause, for more than a century and a half, by miscellaneous audiences.

The following questions suggest themselves as of most interest in connexion with the general character of early Roman tragedy:—How far may it have reproduced not the materials and form only, but the spirit and ideas of the Greek drama? What was its bearing on the actual circumstances of Roman life, and what were the grounds of the favour with which it was received? What cause can be assigned for the cessation of this favour with the fall of the Republic?

The materials or substance of Roman tragedy were almost entirely Greek. The stories and characters represented were, except in the few exceptional cases referred to above, directly derived from the Greek tragedians or from Homer and the cyclic poets. In point of form also and some of the metres employed, Roman tragedy endeavoured to imitate the models on which it was founded, with probably as little perception of the requirements of dramatic art as of refinement in expression and harmony in rhythm. But while generally conforming to their models, the early Roman poets departed in some important respects from their practice. Thus they banished the Chorus from the orchestra, assigning to it merely a subsidiary part in the dialogue. Although some simple lyrical metre, accompanied with music, continued to be employed in the more rapid and impassioned parts of the dialogue, there was no scope, on the Roman stage, for the great lyrical poetry of the Greek drama, and for the nobler functions of the chorus. On the other hand, there seems to have been more opportunity both for action and for oratorical declamation. The acting of a Roman play must have been more like that on a modern stage than the stately movement and the statuesque repose of the Greek theatre. Again, in imitating the iambic and trochaic metres of the Greek drama, the Roman poets were quite indifferent to the laws by which their finer harmony is produced. Any of the feet admissible in an iambic line might occupy any place in the line, with the exception of the last. There is thus little metrical harmony in the fragments of Roman tragedy; but, on the other hand, it may be remarked that the order of the words in these fragments appears more natural and direct than in the more elaborate metres of the later Roman poets.

But it was as impossible for the Roman drama to reproduce the inner spirit of the noblest type of Greek tragedy as to rival its artistic excellence. Greek tragedy, in its mature glory, was not only a purely Greek creation, but was the artistic expression of a remarkable phase through which the human mind has once passed;—a phase in which the vivid fancies and emotions of a primitive age met and combined with the thought, the art, the social and political life of the greatest era of ancient civilisation. The Athenian dramatists, like the great dramatists of other times, imparted a new and living interest to ancient legends; but this was but one part, perhaps not the most important part, of their functions. They represented before the people the destiny and sufferings of national heroes and demigods, sanctified by long association in the feelings of many generations, still honoured by a vital worship, and appealed to as a present help in danger. Thus a highly idealised and profoundly religious character was imparted to the tragic representation of human passion and destiny on the Athenian stage. This view of life, represented and contemplated with solemnity of feeling in the age of Pericles, would have been altogether unmeaning to a Roman of the age of Ennius. Such a one would understand the natural heroism of a strong will, but not the new force and elevation imparted to the will by reliance on the hidden powers and laws overruling human affairs He might be moved to sympathy with the sufferers or actors on the scene; but he would be altogether insensible to the higher consolation which overcomes the natural sorrow for the mere earthly catastrophe in a great dramatic action. The inward strength and dignity of a Roman senator might enable him to appreciate the magnanimity and kingly nature of Oedipus; but the deeper interest of the great dramas founded on the fortunes of the Theban king, especially the interest arising from his trust in final righteousness, his sense of communion with higher powers, from the thought of his elevation out of the lowest earthly state into perpetual sanctity and honour, was widely remote from the tangible objects of a Roman's desire, and the direct motives of his conduct. Or perhaps a Roman would have a fellow-feeling with the proud and soldierly bearing of Ajax; but he would be blind to the inward lesson of self-knowledge and self-mastery, which Sophocles represents as forced upon the spirit of the Greek hero through the stern visitation of Athene. Equally remote from the ordinary experience and emotions of a Roman would be the feeling of awe, gloom, and mystery, diffused through the great thoughts and imaginations of Aeschylus. Both in Aeschylus and in Sophocles the light and the gloom cast over the human story are not of this world. But in the fragments of the Roman tragedians, though there is often found the expression of magnanimous and independent sentiment, and of a very dignified and manly morality, there is little trace of any sense of the relation of the individual to a Divine power; and there are some indications not only of a scorn for common superstition, but also of disbelief in the foundations of personal religion. The thought of the insecurity of life, of the vicissitudes of human affairs, and of the impotence of man to control his fate, which forced the Greek poets and historians of the fifth century B.C. into deeper speculations on the question of Divine Providence, was utterly alien to the natural temperament of Rome, and to the confidence inspired by uniform success during the long period succeeding the Second Punic War.

The contemplative and religious thought of Greek tragedy was thus as remote from the practical spirit of the Romans as the political license and the personal humours of the old Athenian comedy were from the earnestness of public life and the dignity of government in the great aristocratic Republic. And thus it happened that, as the comic poets of Rome reproduced the new comedy of Athens, which portrayed the passions of private not of political life, and the manners rather of a cosmopolitan than of a purely Greek civilisation, so the tragic poets found the art of Euripides and of his less illustrious successors more easy to imitate than that of Aeschylus and Sophocles. The interest of tragedy, as treated by Euripides, turns upon the catastrophes produced by human passion: the religious meaning has, in a great measure, passed out of it; the characters have dwindled from their heroic stature to the proportions of ordinary life; his thought is the result of the analysis of motives, and the study of familiar experience. He has more affinity with the ordinary thoughts and moods of men than either of the older poets. The older and the later Greek writers have a nearer relation to the spirit of other eras of the world's history than those who represent Athenian civilisation in its maturity. It requires a longer familiarity with the mind and heart of antiquity to realise and enjoy the full meaning of Sophocles, Thucydides, or Aristophanes, than of Homer, Euripides, or Theocritus. Homer is indeed one of the truest, if not the truest, representative of the genius of Greece,—the representative also of the ancient world in the same sense as Shakspeare is of the modern world,—but he is, at the same time, directly intelligible and interesting to all countries and times from his being the most natural and powerful exponent of the elementary feelings and forces of human nature. The later poets, on the other hand, such as Euripides and the writers of the new comedy, were not indeed more truly human, but were less distinctively Greek than their immediate predecessors. They had advanced beyond them in the analytic knowledge of human nature; but, with the decay of religious belief and political feeling, they had lost much of the genius and sentiment by which the old Athenian life was characterised. Both their gain and their loss bring them more into harmony with later modes of thought and feeling. Thus it happened that, while the influence of Aeschylus and Sophocles, of Thucydides and Aristophanes, is scarcely perceptible in Roman literature, Homer and the early lyrical poets who flourished before Greek civilisation exhibited its most special type, and Euripides who, though a contemporary of Sophocles and Aristophanes, yet belonged in spirit and tone to a younger generation, the writers of the new comedy, and the Alexandrine poets who flourished when the purely Greek ideas and character were being merged in a cosmopolitan civilisation, exercised a direct influence on Roman taste and opinion in every age of their literature. The early tragic poets of Rome could not rival or imitate the dramatic art, the pathetic power, the clear and fluent style, the active and subtle analysis of Euripides; but they could approach nearer to him than to any of his predecessors, by treating the myths and personages of the heroic time apart from the sacred associations and ideal majesty of earlier art, and as a vehicle for inculcating the lessons and the experience of familiar life.

The primary attraction, by means of which the tragic drama established itself at Rome, must have been the power of scenic representations to convey a story, and to produce novel impressions on a people to whom reading was quite unfamiliar. In Homer, the cyclic poets, and the Attic dramatists, there existed for the Romans of the second century B.C. a new world of incident and human interest quite different from the grave story of their own annals. This new world, which was becoming gradually familiar to their eyes through the works of plastic and pictorial art, was made more living and intelligible to them in the representations of their tragic poets. It cannot be supposed that these poets attempted to reproduce the antique Hellenic character of the legends on which they founded their dramas. In this early stage of literary culture, the harmonious cadences of rhythm, the fine and delicate shades of expression, the main requirements of dramatic art,—such as the skilful construction of a plot, the consistent keeping of a character, the evolution of a tragic catastrophe through the meeting of passion and outward accident,—would have been lost upon the unexacting audiences who thronged the temporary theatres on occasional holidays. The fragments of the lost dramas indicate that the matter was presented in a straightforward style, little differing in sound and meaning from the tone of serious conversation. Although little can be known or conjectured as to the general conduct of the action in a Roman drama, yet there are indications that in some cases a series of adventures, instead of one complete action, were represented[1]. But while failing, or not attempting to reproduce the Greek spirit and art of their originals, the Roman poets seem to have animated the outlines of their foreign story and of their legendary characters with something of the spirit of their own time and country. They imparted to their dramas a didactic purpose and rhetorical

[1] E. g. the *Dulorestes* of Pacuvius.

character which directly appealed to Roman tastes. The fragments quoted from their works, the testimonies of later Roman writers, and the natural inference to be drawn from the moral and intellectual characteristics of the people, all point to the conclusion that the long-sustained popularity of tragedy rested mainly on the satisfaction which it afforded to the ethical sympathies, and to the oratorical tastes of the audience.

The evidence for this popularity is chiefly to be found in Cicero; and it is mainly, though not solely, to the popularity which the tragic drama enjoyed in his own age that he testifies. The loss of the earlier writings renders it impossible to adduce contemporary evidence of the immediate success of this form of literature. But the activity with which tragedy was cultivated for about a century, and the favour with which Ennius, Pacuvius, and Accius, were regarded by the leading men in the State, suggest the inference that the popularity of the drama in the age of Cicero, after the writers themselves had passed away, and when more exciting spectacles occupied public attention, was only a continuation of the general favour which these poets enjoyed in their lifetime. Cicero in many places mentions the great applause with which the expression of feeling in different dramas was received, and speaks of the great crowds ('maximus consessus' or 'magna frequentia'), including women and children, present at the representation. Varro states that, in his time, 'the heads of families had gradually gathered within the walls of the city, having quitted their ploughs and pruning-hooks, and that they liked to use their hands in the theatres and circus better than on their crops and vineyards[1].' The large fortunes amassed and the high consideration enjoyed by the actors Aesopus and Roscius afford further evidence of the favour with which the representation of tragedy and comedy was received in the age of Cicero.

According to his testimony, these lively demonstrations of popular approbation were chiefly called out by the moral

[1] De Re Rustica, Lib. ii. Praef. Quoted also by Columella, Praef. 15.

significance or the political meaning attached to the words, and by the oratorical fervour and passion with which the actor enforced them. Thus Laelius is represented, in the treatise *De Amicitia*, as testifying to the applause with which the mutual devotion of Pylades and Orestes, as represented in a play of Pacuvius, was received by the audience[1]: 'What shouts of applause were heard lately through the whole body of the house, on the representation of a new play of my familiar friend, M. Pacuvius, when, the king being ignorant which of the two was Orestes, Pylades maintained that it was he, while Orestes persisted, as was indeed the case, that he was the man! They stood up and applauded at this imaginary situation.' Again, in his speech in defence of Sestius[2], the same author says, 'amid a great variety of opinions uttered, there never was any passage in which anything said by the poet might seem to bear on our time, which either escaped the notice of the people, or to which the actor did not give point.' In a letter to Atticus (ii. 19) he states that the actor Diphilus had applied to Pompey the phrase 'Miseria nostra tu es magnus,' and that he was compelled to repeat it a thousand times amid the shouts of the whole theatre. He mentions further, in the speech in defence of Sestius[3] that the actor Aesopus had applied to Cicero himself a passage from a play of Accius (the Eurysaces), in which the Greeks are reproached for allowing one who had done them great public service to be driven into exile; and that the same actor, in the Brutus, had referred to him by name in the words, 'Tullius qui libertatem civibus stabiliverat;' he adds that these words 'were *encored* over and over again,' 'millies revocatum est.' These and similar passages testify primarily to the intense political excitement of the time at which they were written, but also to the meaning which was looked for by the audience in the words addressed to them on the stage, and which was enforced by the emphasis given to them by the actor.

---

[1] De Amicitia, 7.   [2] Cic. Pro P. Sestio, 65.
[3] Chap. 57.

Besides these and other passages in Cicero, the fragments themselves of Roman tragedy testify to its moral and didactic tone, and its occasional appeal to national and political feeling.

In so far as it served any political end we may infer from the personal relations of the poets, from the approving testimony of Cicero, and from the personages and the nature of the situations represented, that, unlike the older comedy of Naevius and Plautus, it was in sympathy with the spirit of the dominant aristocracy. The 'boni' or 'optimates' regarded themselves as the true guardians of law and liberty, and it would be to their partisans that the resistance to, and denunciations of tyrannical rule, expressed in such plays as the Atreus, the Tereus, and the Brutus of Accius, must have been most acceptable. Members of the aristocracy, eminent in public life and accomplished as orators, became themselves authors of tragedies. Of these two are mentioned by Cicero, C. Julius Caesar, a contemporary and friend of the orator Crassus, and C. Titius, a Roman Eques, also distinguished as an orator[1]. These instances, and the comments Cicero makes upon them, indicate the close affinity of Roman tragedy to the training and accomplishments which fitted men for public life at Rome.

Passages already referred to, and others which will be brought forward later, imply also that the audience were easily moved by the dramatic art and the elocution of the actor. We hear of the pains which the best actors took to perfect themselves in their art, and of the success which they attained in it. Cicero specifies among the accomplishments of an orator, the 'voice of a tragedian, the gestures and bearing of a consummate actor.' The stage may be said to have been to the Romans partly a school of prac-

---

[1] Cicero, Brutus, 48-45; De Orat. iii. 8. 30. 'Quid noster hic Caesar nonne novam quandam rationem attulit orationis et dicendi genus induxit prope singulare? Quis unquam res praeter hunc tragicas paene comica, tristes remisse, severas hilare, forenses scaenica prope venustate tractavit atque ita, ut neque iocus magnitudine rerum excluderetur nec gravitas facetiis minueretur.'

tical life, partly a school of oratory. Spirited declamation, the expression, by voice and gesture, of vehement passion, of moral and political feeling, and of practical wisdom, would gratify the same tastes that were fostered by the discussions and harangues of the Forum [1].

The testimony of later writers points to the conclusion that the early Roman tragedy, like Roman oratory, was characterised both by great moral weight and dignity, and also by a fervid and impassioned character. The latter quality is suggested by the line of Horace,

> Nam spirat tragicum satis et feliciter audet;

and also by the epithets 'altus' and 'animosus' applied by him and Ovid to the poet Accius. Quintilian describes the ancient tragedies as superior to those of his own time in the management of their plots ('oeconomia'), and adds that 'manliness and solemnity of style' ('virilitas et sanctitas')[2], were to be studied in them. He states also that Accius and Pacuvius were distinguished by 'the earnestness of their thought, the weight of their language, the commanding bearing of their personages [3].' The fragments of all the tragic poets bear further evidence to the union of these qualities in their thought and style.

These considerations may afford some explanation of the fact, that the early Roman tragedy, although having less claim to originality, and less capacity of development than any other branch of Roman literature, yet exercised a more immediate and more general influence than either the epic, lyrical, or satiric poetry of the Republic. For more than a century new tragedies were written and represented at the various public games, and afforded the sole kind of serious intellectual stimulus and education to the mass of the people. During

---

[1] Cf. Cic. de Orat. iii. 7. 'Atque id primum in poetis cerni licet quibus est proxima cognatio cum oratoribus quam sint inter sese Ennius, Pacuvius, Acciusque dissimiles.'

[2] 'Sanctitas certe, et, ut sic dicam, virilitas, ab iis petenda est, quando nos in omnia deliciarum vitia dicendi quoque ratione defluximus.'—Quintil. Inst. Or. i. 8. 9.

[3] Inst. Or. x. i. 97.

the lifetime of the old dramatists, there was no regular theatre, but merely structures of wood raised for each occasion. A magnificent stone theatre was at last built by Pompey from the spoils of the Mithridatic War; but this, instead of giving a new impulse to dramatic art, was fatal to its existence. The attraction of a gorgeous spectacle superseded that afforded by the works of the older dramatists; and dancers like Bathyllus soon obtained the place in popular favour which had been enjoyed by the 'grave Aesopus and the accomplished Roscius.' The composition of tragedy passed from the hands of popular poets, and became a kind of literary and rhetorical exercise of accomplished men. We hear that Quintus Cicero composed four tragedies in sixteen days, and in the Augustan age Virgil and Horace eulogise the dramatic talent of their friend and patron Asinius Pollio. The 'Ars Poetica' implies that the composition of tragedy was the most fashionable form of literary pursuit among the young aspirants to poetic honour at that time, and the Thyestes of Varius and the Medea of Ovid enjoyed a great literary reputation. These were, however, futile attempts to impart artificial life to a withered branch; they obtained no general favour, and left no name or fame behind them. Of all forms of poetry the drama is most dependent on popular sympathy and intelligence. With the loss of contact with public feeling the Roman drama lost its vital power. One cause of the change in public taste was the passion for more frivolous and coarser excitement, such as was afforded by the mimes and by gladiatorial combats and shows of wild beasts to a soldiery brutalised by constant wars, and to the civic masses degraded by idleness and by intermixture from all quarters of the world. Other causes may have acted on the poets themselves, such as the exhaustion of the mine of ancient stories fit for dramatic purposes, and the truer sense, acquired through culture, of the bent of Roman genius. But another cause was the loss of mutual sympathy between the poet and the people, arising from the decay and final extinction of political life. In ancient, as occasionally also in modern times, the contests and interests of politics were the means of affording the highest intellectual stimulus of which they were capable to the large classes on whom literary influences act only indirectly. So long as the old republican sense of citizenship remained, there was a bond of common feelings, ideas, and sympathies between the body of the people and some of the foremost and most highly educated men in Rome. There was an immediate sympathy between the political orator and his audiences within the Senate or in the public assemblies; there was a sympathy, more remote, but still active, between the poet of the Republic, who had the strong feelings of a Roman citizen, and the great body of his countrymen. With the overthrow of free government, this bond of union between the educated and the uneducated classes was destroyed. The former became more refined and fastidious, but lost something in breadth and genuine strength by the want of any popular contact. The latter became more debased, coarser, and more servile. Poetic works were more and more addressed to a small circle of men of rank and education, sharing the same opinions, tastes, and pleasures. They thus became more finished as works of art, but had less direct bearing on the passions and great public interests of their time.

The origin and the earliest stage of the Roman drama have been examined in a previous chapter. For about a century after the close of the Second Punic War new tragedies continued to be represented at Rome with little interruption, first by Ennius, afterwards by his nephew Pacuvius and by Accius. The older poets, Livius and Naevius, had produced both tragedy and comedy: Ennius neglected or failed to attain success in comedy; and his two successors appear to have devoted themselves more exclusively than any of their predecessors to the composition of tragedy. While the fame of Ennius chiefly rested on his epic poem[1], Pacuvius and Accius are classed

---

[1] Cf. Cic. Opt. Gen. Orat. 'Itaque licet dicere et Ennium summum epicum poetam si cui ita videtur, et Pacuvium tragicum, et Caecilium fortasse comicum.'

together as representatives of the tragic poetry of the Republic. Though in point of age there was a difference of fifty years between them, yet Cicero mentions, on the authority of Accius himself, that they had brought out plays under the same Aediles, when the one was eighty years of age and the other thirty.

M. Pacuvius, nephew, by the mother's side, of Ennius, was born at Brundusium, in the south of Italy, about 219 B.C., and died at Tarentum about 129 B.C., at the age of ninety. He obtained some distinction as a painter[1], and he is supposed to have written his tragedies late in life. Jerome records of him, 'picturam exercuit et fabulas vendidit.' Cicero represents Laelius as speaking of him as a friend, 'amici et hospitis mei.' A pleasing anecdote is told by Aulus Gellius[2] of his intercourse with his younger rival, L. Accius. 'When Pacuvius, at a great age, and suffering from disease of long standing, had retired from Rome to Tarentum, Accius, at that time a considerably younger man, on his journey to Asia, arrived at that town, and stayed with Pacuvius. And being kindly entertained, and constrained to stay for several days, he read to him, at his request, his tragedy of Atreus. Then, as the story goes, Pacuvius said, that what he had written appeared to him sonorous and elevated but somewhat harsh and crude. 'It is just as you say,' replied Accius; 'and in truth I am not sorry for it, for I hope that I shall write better in future. For, as they say, the same law holds good in genius as in fruit. Fruits which are originally harsh and sour afterwards become mellow and pleasant; but those which have a soft and withered look, and are very juicy at first, become soon rotten without ever becoming ripe. It appears, accordingly, that there should be left something in genius also for the mellowing influence of years and time.' This anecdote, while giving a pleasing impression of the friendly relation subsisting between the older and younger poets, seems to add some corroboration to the opinion that the

---

[1] Pliny. Hist. Nat. xxxv. 7.   [2] xiii. 2.

Romans valued more the oratorical style than the dramatic art of their tragedies. It affords support also to the testimony of Horace and Quintilian in regard to the distinction which the admirers of the old poetry drew between the excellence of Pacuvius and Accius:

> Ambigitur quoties uter utro sit prior, aufert
> Pacuvius docti famam senis, Accius alti.

Aulus Gellius quotes the epitaph of Pacuvius, written by himself to be inscribed on his tombstone, with a tribute of admiration to 'its modesty, simplicity, and fine serious spirit'—'Epigramma Pacuvii verecundissimum et purissimum dignumque ejus elegantissima gravitate.'

> Adolescens, tametsi properas, te hoc saxum rogat,
> Ut se aspicias, deinde quod scriptum est, legas,
> Hic sunt poetae Pacuvi Marci sita
> Ossa. Hoc volebam nescius ne esses. Vale[1]

With its quiet and modest simplicity of tone this inscription is still significant of that dignified self-consciousness which characterised all the early Roman poets, though the feeling may have been displayed with more prominence by Naevius and Plautus, by Ennius, Accius, and Lucilius, than by Pacuvius.

Among the testimonies to his literary qualities the best known is that of Horace, quoted above. Cicero, in speaking of the age of Laelius as that of the purest Latinity, does not allow this merit to Pacuvius and to the comic poet Caecilius. He says of them, 'male locutos esse[2].' Pacuvius seems to have attempted to introduce new forms of words, such as 'temeritudo,' 'geminitudo,' 'vanitudo,' 'concorditas,' 'unose'; and also to have carried to a greater length than any of the older poets the tendency to form such poetical compounds as 'tardigradus,' 'flexanimus,' 'flexidicus,' 'cornifrontis'—a tendency which the Latin language continued more and more to repudiate in the hands of its most perfect masters. One

---

[1] 'Young man, though thou art in haste, this stone entreats thee to regard it, and then read what is written:—Here are laid the bones of the poet Marcus Pacuvius. This I desired to be not unknown to thee. Farewell.'
[2] Brutus, 74.

line is quoted in which the tendency probably reached the extremest limits it ever did in any Latin author,—

> Nerei repandirostrum incurvicervicum pecus.

We find also such inflexions as 'tetinerim,' for 'tenuerim,' 'pegi' for pepigi,' 'cluentur' for 'cluent.' These peculiarities are ridiculed in the fragments of Lucilius, and also in a passage of Persius. Another author[1] contrasts the *sententiae* of Ennius with the *periodi* of Pacuvius,—a distinction probably connected with the progress of oratory in the interval between the poets. Persius applies the term 'verrucosa' (an epithet not inapplicable to his own style) to the Antiope of Pacuvius, which, on the other hand, was much admired by Cicero[2]. Lucilius refers to this harshness of style in the line,

> Verum tristis contorto aliquo ex Pacuviano exordio.

Pacuvius is known to have been the author of about twelve tragedies, founded on Greek subjects; and of one, *Paulus*, founded on Roman history. Among these, the *Antiope* was perhaps the most famous and most admired. It was, like the Medea of Ennius, a translation from Euripides. The principal characters in it were the brothers Zethus and Amphion, the one devoted to hunting, the other to music. Their dispute as to the respective advantages of music and philosophy is referred to by Cicero and Horace, and by other authors. The Zethus of Pacuvius is described by Cicero[3] as one who made war on all philosophy; and the author of the treatise addressed to Herennius describes their controversy as beginning about music, and ending about philosophy and the use of virtue. Two dramas, the *Dulorestes* and the *Chryses*, the latter being a continuation of the first, represented the adventures of Orestes in his wanderings with his friend

---

[1] The writer of the treatise on Rhetoric addressed to C. Herennius.

[2] 'Quis enim tam inimicus paene nomini Romano est, qui Ennii Medeam aut Antiopam Pacuvii spernat aut rejiciat, quod se eisdem Euripidis fabulis delectari dicit.'—Cic. De Fin. i. 2.

[3] De Oratore, ii. 37.

Pylades, after the murder of his mother. The former play, in which Orestes was represented as on the point of being sacrificed by his sister Iphigenia, contained the passage already referred to, in which Pylades and Orestes contend as to which should suffer for the other. The Chryses was founded on their subsequent adventures, and the title of the play was apparently taken from the old Homeric priest of Apollo, Chryses, who bore a prominent part in it. Another of the plays of Pacuvius, the *Niptra*, was founded on, though not translated from, one of Sophocles[1]; and the title seems to have been suggested by the story of the recognition of Ulysses by his nurse, Eurycleia, told at Odyssey xix. 386, etc. The subjects of his other dramas may be inferred from the following titles:—*Armorum Judicium, Atalanta, Hermione, Ilione, Io, Medus* (son of Medea), *Pentheus, Periboea, Teucer*.

The fragments of Pacuvius amount to about four hundred lines. Many of these are single lines, preserved by grammarians in illustration of old forms and usages of words, and thus are of little value in the way of illustrating his poetical or dramatic power. Several of them, however, are interesting, from the light which they throw on his mode of thought, his moral spirit, and his artistic faculty.

A remarkable passage is quoted from the Chryses, showing the growth of that interest in physical philosophy, which was first expressed in the Epicharmus of Ennius, and which continued to have a powerful attraction for many of the Roman poets:—

> Hoc vide, circum supraque quod complexu continet
> Terram
> Solisque exortu capessit candorem, occasu nigret,
> Id quod nostri caelum memorant, Graii perhibent aethera:
> Quidquid est hoc, omnia animat, format, alit, auget, creat,
> Sepelit recipitque in sese omnia, omniumque idem est pater,
> Indidemque eadem quae oriuntur, de integro aeque eodem incidunt.[2]

---
[1] Cic. Tusc. Disp. ii. 21.
[2] 'Behold this, which around and above encompasseth the earth, and puts on brightness at the rising of the sun, becomes dark at his setting; that which our people call Heaven, and the Greeks Aether. Whatever this is, it is to all

The following fragment illustrates the dawning interest in ethical speculation, which became much more active in the age of Cicero, under the influence of Greek studies :—

> Fortunam insanam esse et caecam et brutam perhibent philosophi
> Saxoque instare in globoso praedicant volubili:
> Insanam autem esse aiunt, quia atrox, incerta, instabilisque sit:
> Caecam ob eam rem esse iterant, quia nil cernat quo sese adplicet:
> Brutam quia dignum atque indignum nequeat internoscere.
> Sunt autem alii philosophi, qui contra fortunam negant
> Esse ullam, sed temeritate res regi omnis autumant.
> Id magis veri simile esse usus reapse experiundo edocet:
> Velut Orestes modo fuit rex, factu'st mendicus modo.[1]

These lines again from the Chryses show that Pacuvius, like Ennius, exposed and ridiculed the superstition of his time—

> Nam isti qui linguam avium intelligunt
> Plusque ex alieno jecore sapiunt quam ex suo,
> Magis audiendum quam auscultandum censeo;[2]

and this is to the same effect—

> Nam si qui, quae eventura sunt, provideant, aequiparent Jovi.

This tendency to physical and ethical speculation may be the reason for which Horace applies to Pacuvius the epithet 'doctus.'

The fragments of Pacuvius show not only the cast of

things the source of life, form, nourishment, growth, existence; it is the grave and receptacle of all things, and the parent, too, of all things: all things which arise from it equally lapse into it again.' Compare with this passage Lucretius, ii. 991—
'Denique caelesti sumus omnes semine oriundi' etc.
Both may be traced to a fragment of the Chrysippus of Euripides, quoted by Ribbeck, Röm. Trag. p. 257; and also by Munro, Lucret. p. 455, third edition.

[1] 'Philosophers say that Fortune is mad, blind, and senseless, and represent her as set on a round rolling stone. They say that she is mad, because she is harsh, fickle, untrustworthy; blind, for this reason, that she can see nothing to which to attach herself; senseless, because she cannot distinguish between the worthy and unworthy. Other philosophers again deny the existence of Fortune, but hold that all things are ruled by chance. That this is more probable, common experience proves, as Orestes was but the other day a king, and is now a beggar'

[2] 'For those men who understand the language of birds, and have more wisdom from examining the liver of other beings than from their own (i. e. understanding), I think should be heard rather than listened to.'

understanding, but also the grave and dignified tone of morality, which was found to be one of the most Roman characteristics of Ennius. They indicate also a similar humanity of feeling. The moral nobleness of the situation, in which Pylades and Orestes contend which should sacrifice himself for the other, has already been noticed: 'stantes plaudebant in re ficta.' Again, in the Tusculan Disputations (ii. 21), Cicero commends Pacuvius for deviating from Sophocles, who had represented Ulysses, in the Niptra, as utterly overcome by the power of his wound; while, in Pacuvius, those who are supporting him, 'personae gravitatem intuentes,' address this reproof to him, 'leviter gementi':—

> Tu quoque Ulysses, quanquam graviter
> Cernimus ictum, nimis paene animo es
> Molli, qui consuetu's in armis
> Aevom agere![1]

The strong tones of Roman fortitude are heard in this grave rebuke; and the lines in which Ulysses, at the point of death, reproves the lamentations of those around him, have the unstudied directness that may be supposed to have characterised the serious speech of the time:—

> Conqueri fortunam adversam, non lamentari decet:
> Id viri est officium, fletus muliebri ingenio additus.[2]

The following maxim is quoted by Aulus Gellius with the remark 'that a Macedonian philosopher, a friend of his, an excellent man, thought it deserving of being written in front of every temple':—

> Ego odi homines ignava opera et philosopha sententia.

There are other fragments the significance of which is political rather than ethical, as for instance the following:—

> Omnes qui tam quam nos severo serviunt
> Imperio callent dominum imperia metuere.

---

[1] 'Thou, too, Ulysses, although we see thee sore wounded, art yet almost too much cast down; thou, who hast been used to pass thy life in arms!'

[2] 'To complain of adverse fortune is well, but not to lament over it. The one is the act of a man; it is a woman's part to weep.'

A passage from his writings was sung at games in honour of Caesar, in order to rouse a feeling of indignation against the conspirators. The prominent words of the passage were,—

> Men' servasse ut essent qui me perderent.[1]

Other passages again appear to be fragments of spirited dialogue, and well adapted to show the art and the elocution of the actor. Cicero[2] quotes from the Teucer of Pacuvius the reproach of Telamon, couched in much the same terms as those which Teucer himself anticipates in the Ajax of Sophocles :—

> Segregare abs te ausu's aut s'ne illo Salamina ingredi,
> Neque paternum aspectum es veritus, quom aetate exacta indigem
> Liberum lacerasti orbasti extinxti, neque fratris necis
> Neque ejus gnati parvi, qui tibi in tutelam est traditus—?[3]

In commenting on these lines, Cicero speaks of the passion displayed by the actor ('so that even out of his mask the eyes of the actor appeared to me to burn'), and of the sudden change to pathos in his voice as he proceeded. He adds the further comment, 'Do we suppose that Pacuvius, in writing this passage, was in a calm and passionless mood?'—one of many proofs that the 'gravity' of the old tragedians was that of strong and ardent, not of phlegmatic natures, and that their strength was tempered by a pathos and humanity of feeling which were gradually gaining ascendency over the old Roman austerity. The language in such passages has not only the straightforward directness which is the general characteristic of the early literature, but a force and impetuosity added to its gravity, recalling the style of some fragments of the older orators [4].

The fragments of Accius afford the first hint of that

---

[1] Sueton. Caes. 84.   [2] De Orat. ii. 46.

[3] 'Didst thou venture to let him part from thee, or to enter Salamis without him; and didst thou not fear to see thy father's face, when in his old age, bereft of his children, thou hast torn him with anguish, robbed, crushed him; nor didst thou feel for thy brother's death, and his child, who was trusted to thy protection—?'

[4] Compare especially the fragments of the speeches of C. Gracchus.

enjoyment of natural beauty which enters largely into the poetry of a later age; but one or two fragments of Pacuvius, like several passages in Ennius, show the power of observing and describing the sublime and terrible aspects of Nature. The description of the storm which overtook the Greek army after sailing from Troy is perhaps the best specimen in this style :—

> Profectione laeti piscium lasciviam
> Intuentur. nec tuendi capere satietas potest.
> Interea prope jam occidente sole inhorrescit mare,
> Tenebrae conduplicantur, noctisque et nimbum occaecat nigror,
> Flamma inter nubes coruscat, caelum tonitru contremit,
> Grando mista imbri largifico subita praecipitans cadit,
> Undique omnes venti erumpunt, saevi existunt turbines,
> Fervit aestu pelagus [1].

There are also, in the same style, these rough and graphic lines, exemplifying the impetuous force which the older Roman poets impart to their descriptions by the figure of speech called 'asyndeton,'—

> Armamentum stridor, flictus navium,
> Strepitus fremitus clamor tonitruum et rudentum sibilus.[2]

Virgil must have had this passage in his mind when he wrote the line—

> Insequitur clamorque virum, stridorque rudentum.

The effect of alliteration and assonance may be illustrated by a passage from the 'Niptra,' in which Eurycleia addresses the disguised Ulysses :—

> Cedo tamen pedem tuum lymphis flavis flavum ut pulverem
> Manibus isdem quibus Ulixi saepe permulsi abluam,
> Lassitudinemque minuam manuum mollitudine.[3]

---

[1] 'Glad at their starting, they watch the play of the fish, and are never weary of watching them. Meanwhile. nearly at sunset, the sea grows rough, darkness gathers, the blackness of night and of the storm-clouds hides the world, the lightning flashes between the clouds, the heaven is shaken with the thunder, hail mixed with torrents of rain dashes down in sudden showers; from all quarters all the winds burst forth, the wild whirlwinds arise, the sea boils with the surging waters.'—Quoted partly from Cic. De Div. i. 14; partly from De Orat. iii. 39.

[2] 'The groaning of the ships' tackling, the dashing together of the ships, the uproar, the crash, the rattle of the thunder, and the whistling of the ropes.'

[3] 'Give me your foot, that with the brown waters I may wash away the brown dust with those hands with which I have often rubbed gently the feet of Ulysses, and with my hands' softness soothe your weariness.'

Pacuvius composed one drama on a Roman subject, the title of which was 'Paulus.' Although the name does not indicate whether the principal character of the drama was the Aemilius Paulus who fell at Cannae, whom Horace commemorates as one of the national heroes in the words—

Animaeque magnae
Prodigum Paulum, superante Poeno,

or his more fortunate son who conquered the Macedonians at Pydna, yet it would seem much more probable that the poet should celebrate a great triumph of his own time, achieved by one in whom, from his connexion with Scipio, the nephew of Ennius would feel a special interest, than that he should recall a great calamity of a past generation, neither near enough to excite immediate attention, nor sufficiently remote to justify an imaginative treatment. The Fabulae Praetextatae, of which this was one, were, as Niebuhr[1] has pointed out, historical plays rather than tragedies. Such a drama would not naturally or necessarily require a tragic catastrophe, but would represent the traditions of the earlier annals, or the great events of current history, in accordance with the dictates of national feeling. No important fragment of this drama has been preserved, but the fact of its having been written by Pacuvius is interesting, as affording a parallel to the celebration of the victory of Marcellus in the Clastidium of Naevius, and of the success of M. Fulvius Nobilior in the Ambracia of Ennius.

Neither the fragments nor the ancient notices of Pacuvius produce on a modern reader so distinct an impression of his peculiar genius and character as may be formed of Naevius, Ennius, and Lucilius. His remains are chiefly important as throwing light on the general features of the Roman tragic drama; and few critics would attempt to determine from internal evidence alone

---

[1] 'It represented the deeds of Roman kings and generals: hence it is evident that at least it wanted the unity of time of the Greek tragedy; that it was a history like Shakspeare's.'—Niebuhr's Roman History, vol. i. note 1150.

whether any particular passage came from the lost works of Pacuvius or of Accius. The main points that are known in his life are his provincial origin, and his relationship to Ennius; the fact of his supporting himself, first by painting, afterwards by the payment he received from the Aediles for his plays; his friendship with Laelius, the centre of the literary circle in Rome during the latter part of the second century B.C.; his intimacy with his younger rival Accius; the facts also that, like Sophocles, he preserved his poetical power unabated till a great age, and that, like Shakspeare, he retired to spend his last years in his native district. The language of his epitaph is suggestive of a kindly and modest temper, and of the calm and serious spirit of age; while that of many of his dramatic fragments bears evidence to his moral strength and worth, and to the manly fervour as well as the gentle humanity of his temperament.

L. Accius (or Attius) was born in the year 170 B.C., of parentage similar to that of Horace—'parentibus libertinis.' He was a native of the Roman colony of Pisaurum in Umbria, founded in 184 B.C.; and an estate in that district was known in after times by the name 'fundus Accianus.' Like Pacuvius, he lived to a great age, though the exact date of his death is uncertain. Cicero, who was born B.C. 106, speaks of the oratorical and literary accomplishment of D. Junius Brutus—Consul, along with P. Scipio Nasica, B.C. 138, and one of the most famous soldiers and chiefs of the senatorian party in that age— on the authority of what he had himself often heard from the poet: 'ut ex familiari ejus L. Accio poeta sum audire solitus[1].' The meeting of the old tragic poet and of the great orator is remarkable, as a link connecting the two epochs in literature, which stand so widely apart in the spirit and style by which they are respectively characterised. Cicero again, in the speech

[1] Brutus, 28.

in defence of Archias, mentions the intimacy subsisting between D. Brutus and the poet[1]. The expressions 'familiari ejus' and 'amicissimi sui,' like that of 'hospitis et amici mei,' applied by Laelius, in Cicero's dialogue, to Pacuvius, indicate that the relation between the poets (men of humble or provincial origin) and eminent statesmen and soldiers, was in that age one of familiar intimacy rather than of patronage and dependence.

Although Cicero's notice of his own acquaintance with Accius, which is not likely to have existed before the former assumed the toga virilis, is a proof of the great age which the poet attained, it is not certain how long he continued the practice of his art. Seneca, in quoting from the Atreus of this poet the well-known tyrant's maxim, 'oderint dum metuant'—a maxim, according to Suetonius, constantly in the mouth of Caligula,—adds the remark that 'any one could see that it was written in the days of Sulla.' But Aulus Gellius, on the other hand, states that the Atreus was the play which had been read by the poet in his youth to Pacuvius at Tarentum. The termination of the literary career of Accius must have been soon after the beginning of the first century B.C., so that nearly half a century elapses between the last of the works of the older poets and the appearance of the great poem of Lucretius. The journey of Accius to Asia shows the beginning of that taste for foreign travel which became prevalent among the most educated men in a generation later, and grew more and more easy with the advance of Roman conquest, and more attractive from the increased cultivation of Greek literature. Accius is the first of the Roman poets who seems to have possessed a country residence; and some taste for country life and the beauties of Nature first betrays itself in one or two of his fragments. He possessed apparently all the self-esteem and high spirit of the earlier poets. Pliny

---

[1] 'Decimus quidem Brutus, summus ille vir et imperator, Accii, amicissimi sui, carminibus templorum ac monumentorum aditus exornavit suorum.'—Chap. 11.

mentions that though a very little man, he placed a colossal statue of himself in a temple of the Muses[1].

Another story is told by Valerius Maximus, that on the entrance of C. Julius Caesar (the author of a few tragedies, and a member of one of the great patrician houses), into the place of meeting of the 'Poets' Guild' on the Aventine, he refused to rise up as a mark of deference, thus asserting his own superiority in literature in opposition to the unquestionable claims of rank on the part of his younger rival.

He was much the most productive among the early tragic poets. The titles of his dramas are variously reckoned from about 37 to about 50 in number. Like Ennius, he seems to have made great use of the Trojan cycle of events; and to have appealed largely to the martial sympathies of the Romans in his representation of character and action. Two of his dramas, the Brutus, treating of the downfall of the Tarquinian dynasty, and the Aeneadae, or Decius, founded on the story of the second Decius, who devoted himself at the battle of Sentinum, belonged to the class of Fabulae Praetextatae. He followed the example of Ennius in composing a national epic, called Annales, in three books. He was the author also of what seem to have been works of grammar and literary criticism and history, written in trochaic and other metres, and known by the name Didascalica and Pragmatica, and Parerga. The subjects of these last works, as well as those of some of the satires of Lucilius, and of the poems of Porcius Licinus and Volcatius Sedigitus, written in trochaic and septenarian verse, show the attention which was given about this time by Roman authors to the principles of composition. The literary and grammatical studies of the time of Accius must have prepared the way for the rapid development of style which characterised the first half of the first century B.C. In some of the fragments of Accius distinctions in the meaning of words—e.g. of 'pertinacia' and 'pervicacia'—are prominently brought out. We note also in his remains,

---

[1] Hist. Nat. xxxiv. 10: 'Notatum ab auctoribus, et L. Accium poetam in Camenarum aede maxima forma statuam sibi posuisse, cum brevis admodum fuisset.'

as in those of Pacuvius, a great access of formative energy in the language, especially in abstract words in -*tas* and -*tudo*, many of which afterwards dropped out of use. The antagonism manifested by Lucilius to Accius seems in a great measure to have arisen from his claims to a kind of literary dictatorship in questions of criticism and style.

The literary qualities most conspicuous in the fragments of Accius, and attributed to him by ancient writers, are of the same kind as those which the dramatic fragments of Ennius and Pacuvius exhibit. Cicero testifies to his oratorical force, to his serious spirit, and to the didactic purpose of his writings. His most important remains illustrate these attributes of his style, along with the shrewd sense and vigorous understanding of the older writers, and afford some traces of a new vein of poetical emotion, which is scarcely observable in earlier fragments. Horace applies the epithet 'altus,' Ovid that of 'animosus' to Accius. Cicero characterises him as 'gravis et ingeniosus poeta,' and attests the didactic purpose of a particular passage in the words, 'the earnest and inspired poet wrote thus with the view of stimulating, not those princes who no longer existed, but us and our children to energy and honourable ambition[1].' The style of a passage from the Atreus is described by the same author in the dialogue '*De Oratore*,' as 'nervous, impetuous, pressing on with a certain impassioned gravity of feeling[2].' Oratorical fervour and dignity seem thus to have been the most distinctive characteristic of his style. Virgil, whose genius made as free use of the diction and sentiment of native as of Greek poets, has cast the ruder language of the old poet into a new mould in some of the greatest speeches of the Aeneid, and seems to have drawn from the same source something of the high spirit and lofty pathos with which he has animated the personages of his story. The famous address, for instance—

>   Disce puer virtutem ex me verumque laborem,
>   Fortunam ex aliis,

---

[1] Pro Plancio 24.　　　　　　　　[2] De Orat. iii. 58.

though originally found in the Ajax of Sophocles, was yet familiar to Virgil in the line of Accius—

> Virtuti sis par, dispar fortunis patris.

The address of Latinus to Turnus—

> O praestans animi juvenis, quantum ipse feroci
> Virtute exsuperas, tanto me impensius aequum est
> Consulere atque omnis metuentem expendere casus,

is quoted by Macrobius as an echo of these lines of the old tragic poet—

> Quanto magis te istius modi esse intelligo,
> Tanto, Antigona, magis me par est tibi consulere ac parcere.

The same author quotes two other passages, in which the sentiment and something of the language of Accius are reproduced in the speeches of the Aeneid. The lofty and fervid oratory which is one of the most Roman characteristics of that great national poem, and is quite unlike the debates, the outbursts of passion, and the natural interchange of speech in Homer, recalls the manner of the early tragic poets rather than the style of the oratorical fragments in the Annals of Ennius. The following lines may give some idea of the passionate energy which may be recognised in many other fragments of Accius—

> Tereus indomito more atque animo barbaro
> Conspexit in eam amore vecors flammeo,
> Depositus: facinus pessimum ex dementia
> Confingit.[1]

He gives expression also to great strength of will and to that most powerful kind of pathos which arises out of the commingling of compassion for suffering with the admiration for heroism, as in these fragments of the Astyanax and the Telephus,—

> Abducite intro; nam mihi miseritudine
> Commovit animum excelsa aspecti dignitas;[2]

---

[1] 'Tereus, in his wild mood and savage spirit, gazed upon her, maddened with burning passion, quite desperate; in his madness, he resolves a cursed deed.'

[2] 'Withdraw him within: for the lofty dignity of his aspect has moved my mind to compassion.'

and—

> Nam huius demum miseret, cuius nobilitas miserias
> Nobilitat.¹

He shows a further power of directly seizing the real meaning of human life, and setting aside false appearances and beliefs. The following may be quoted as exhibiting something of his moral strength, humanity, and direct force of understanding :—

> Scin' ut quem cuique tribuit fortuna ordinem,
> Nunquam ulla humilitas ingenium infirmat bonum.²
>
> Erat istuc virile, ferre advorsam fortunam facul.³
>
> Nam si a me regnum fortuna atque opes
> Eripere quivit, at virtutem non quit.⁴
>
> Nullum est ingenium tantum, neque cor tam ferum,
> Quod non labascat lingua, mitiscat malo.⁵

The following, again, like similar passages already quoted from Ennius and Pacuvius, is expressive of contempt for that form of superstition which had most practical hold over the minds of the Roman people :—

> Nil credo auguribus, qui auris verbis divitant
> Alienas, suas ut auro locupletent domos.⁶

Again, the view of common sense in regard to dreams is expressed by the interpreter to whom Tarquinius applies when alarmed by a strange vision—

> Rex, quae in vita usurpant homines, cogitant, curant, vident,
> Quaeque agunt vigilantes agitantque, ea si cui in somno accidunt
> Minus mirum est.⁷

---

¹ 'That man indeed we pity whose nobleness gives distinction to his misery.'

² 'Dost thou not know, that whatever rank fortune has assigned to a man, no meanness of station ever weakens a fine nature?'

³ 'This was the part of a man, to bear adversity easily.'

⁴ 'Though fortune could strip me of kingdom and wealth, it cannot strip me of my virtue.'

⁵ 'No nature is so strong, no breast so savage, which is not shaken by words, does not melt at misfortune.'

⁶ 'I trust not those augurs, who enrich the ears of others with their words, that they may enrich their own houses with gold.' There is of course a pun on the *auris* and *auro*.

⁷ 'O king, what men usually do in life, what they think about, care about, see,—their pursuits and occupations, when awake,—if these occur to any one in sleep, it is not wonderful.'

Besides the characteristics already exemplified, one or two passages may be appealed to, as implying the more special gifts of a poet—force of imagination, and some sense of natural beauty. There is considerable descriptive power in the following lines, for instance, in which a shepherd, who had never before seen a ship, announces the first appearance of the Argo—

> Tanta moles labitur
> Fremebunda ex alto, ingenti sonitu et spiritu:
> Prae se undas volvit, vortices vi suscitat:
> Ruit prolapsa, pelagus respergit, reflat.[1]

There is an imaginative apprehension of the active forces of nature in this fragment—

> Sub axe posita ad stellas septem, unde horrifer
> Aquilonis stridor gelidas molitur nives.[2]

There is a fresh breath of the early morning in the lines from the Oenomaus—

> Forte ante Auroram, radiorum ardentum indicem,
> Cum e somno in segetem agrestis cornutos cient,
> Ut rorulentas terras ferro rufidas
> Proscindant, glebasque arvo ex molli exsuscitent.[3]

This is perhaps the first instance in Latin poetry of a descriptive passage which gives any hint of the pleasure derived from contemplating the common aspects of Nature. Several other short fragments betray the existence of this new vein of poetic sensibility, as, for instance, the following :—

> Saxum id facit angustitatem, et sub eo saxo exuberans
> Scatebra fluviae radit ripam.[4]

---

[1] 'So huge a mass is approaching—sounding from the deep with a mighty rushing noise; it rolls the waves before it, forces through the eddies, plunges forward, throws up and dashes back the sea.'—Quoted in Cic. De Nat. Deor. ii. 35.

[2] 'Lying beneath the pole by the seven stars, whence the blustering roar of the north-wind drives before it the chill snows.'

[3] 'By chance before the dawn, harbinger of burning rays, when the husbandmen bring forth the oxen from their rest into the fields, that they may break the red, dew-sprinkled soil with the plough, and turn up the clods from the soft soil.'

[4] 'That rock makes the passage narrow, and from beneath that rock a spring gushing out sweeps past the river's bank.'

The early expression of this kind of emotion seems to have been accompanied with some degree of affectation, or unnatural straining after effect, as in this fragment:—

> Hac ubi curvo litore latratu
> Unda sub undis labunda sonit.

The following lines, quoted by Cicero (Tusc. Disp. i. 28) without naming the author, are probably from Accius—

> Caelum nitescere, arbores frondescere,
> Vites laetificae pampinis pubescere,
> Rami bacarum ubertate incurviscere,
> Segetes largiri fruges, florere omnia,
> Fontes scatere, herbis prata convestirier.

We note also many instances of plays on words, alliteration, and asyndeton, reminding us of similar modes of conveying emphasis in Plautus, as in the following:—

> Pari dyspari, si impar esses tibi, ego nunc non essem miser.
> Pro se quisque cum corona clarum cohonestat caput.
> Egredere, exi, ecfer te, elimina urbe.

It remains to sum up the most important results as to the early tragic drama of Rome, which have been obtained from a consideration of ancient testimony and of the fossil remains of this lost literature, as we find them collected and arranged from the works of ancient critics and grammarians. The Roman tragedies seem to have borne much the same relation to the works of the Attic tragedians as Roman comedy to the new comedy of Athens. The expression of Quintilian, 'in comoedia maxime claudicamus[1],' following immediately on the praise which he bestows on Pacuvius and Accius, implies that in his opinion the earlier writers had been more successful in tragedy than in comedy. But a comparison between the fragments of the tragedians and the extant works of Plautus and Terence, proves that, in style at least, Roman comedy was much the most successful; and this superiority is no doubt one main cause of its partial preservation. The style of Roman tragedy appears to have been direct and

[1] Inst. Or. x. i. 99.

vigorous, serious, often animated with oratorical passion, but singularly devoid of harmony, subtlety, poetical refinement and inspiration. There is no testimony in favour of any great dramatic conceptions or impersonations. The poets appear to have aimed at expressing some particular passion oratorically, as Virgil has done so powerfully in his representation of Mezentius and Turnus, but not to have created any of those great types of human character such as the world owes to Homer, Sophocles, and Shakspeare. The popularity and the power of Roman tragedy, during the century preceding the downfall of the Republic, are to be attributed chiefly to its didactic and oratorical force, to the Roman bearing of the persons represented, to the ethical and occasionally the political cast of the sentiments expressed by them, and to the plain and vigorous style in which they are enunciated. The works of the tragic poets aided the development of the Roman language. They communicated new ideas and experience, and fostered among the mass of the Roman people the only taste for serious literature of which they were capable. They may have exercised a beneficial influence also on the thoughts and lives of men. They kept the national ideal of duty, the 'manners of the olden time,' the 'fas et antiqua castitudo' (to use an expression of Accius), before the minds of the people: they inculcated by precept and by representations great lessons of fortitude and energy: they taught the maxims of common sense, and touched the minds of their audiences with a humanity of feeling naturally alien to them. No teaching on the stage could permanently preserve the old Roman virtue, simplicity, and loyalty to the Republic, against the corrupting and disorganising effects of constant wars and conquests, and of the gross forms of luxury, that suited the temperament of Rome: but, among the various influences acting on the mind of the people, none probably was of more unmixed good than that of the tragic drama of Ennius, Pacuvius, and Accius.

CHAPTER VI.

ROMAN COMEDY.   PLAUTUS.   ABOUT 254 TO 184 B.C.

THE era in which Roman epic and tragic poetry arose was also the flourishing era of Roman comedy. A later generation looked back on the age of Ennius and Plautus as an age of great poets, who had passed away:—

> Ea tempestate flos poetarum fuit
> Qui nunc abierunt hinc in communem locum.[1]

And among these poets the writers of comedy were both most numerous and apparently the most popular in their own time[2]. Besides the names of Naevius, Plautus, Caecilius, and Terence, we know the names of other comic poets of less fame[3], and from allusions in the extant plays of Plautus[4] and in the prologues of Terence we infer that there were other competitors for public favour whose names were unknown to a later generation. In the Ciceronian age the works of these forgotten playwrights were for the most part attributed to Plautus, probably with the view of gaining some temporary popularity for them. In the time of Gellius no fewer than 130 plays passed under his name; among these, twenty-one were regarded as undoubtedly his, nineteen more as probably genuine, and the rest as spurious. They were however all of the

---

[1] Prologue to Casina, 18, 19.
[2] Prologue to Amphitryo, 52.
[3] Licinius and Atilius are placed before Terence in the Canon of Volcatius Sedigitus.
[4] E. g. Pseudolus, 1081:
> 'Nugas theatri: verba quae in comoediis
> Solent lenoni dici, quae pueri sciunt.'
Cf. also Captivi, 778.

class of *palliatae*; and as the *fabulae togatae* seem, after the time of Terence, to have been composed in much greater number than those founded on Greek originals, most of them must have belonged to the first half of the second century B.C. Plays of a later date would have clearly shown by their diction that they were not the work of Plautus.

Although this form of literature has little in common with the higher Roman mood, and exercised comparatively slight influence on the style and sentiment of later Roman poetry[1], yet no review of the creative literature of the Republican period would be complete without some attempt to estimate the value of the comedy of Plautus and Terence. The difficulty of doing so adequately arises from an opposite cause to that which makes our judgment on the art and genius of the Roman tragic poets so incomplete. In the latter case we know what was the character of their Greek models; but we can only conjecture from a number of unconnected fragments, how far the copy deviated in tone and spirit from the original. On the other hand, while we have between twenty and thirty specimens of Latin comedy, we have no finished work of Greek art in the same style, with which to compare them. It makes a great difference in our opinion, not only of the genius of the Roman poets, but of the productive force of the Roman mind, whether we regard Plautus and Terence as facile translators, or as writers of creative originality who filled up the outlines which they took from the new comedy of Athens with matter drawn from their own observation and invention. It makes a great difference in the literary interest of these works, whether we regard them as blurred copies of pictures from later Greek life, or, like so much else in Roman literature, as compositions which, while Greek in form, are yet in no slight degree Roman or Italian in substance, character, life,

---

[1] The influence of Plautus may be traced in the style of Catullus, and perhaps in the sentiment of the passage in Lucretius, iv. 1121, etc.; and that of Terence also in Catullus, and in the Satires, Epistles, and some of the Odes of Horace.

and sentiment. How far can we answer these questions, either by general considerations, or by a special attention to the actual products of Latin comedy which we possess?

We have seen that there was a certain aptitude in the graver Roman spirit for tragedy:—

> Nam spirat tragicum satis et feliciter audet.

The rhetorical character of Roman education and the rhetorical tendencies of the Roman mind secured favour for this kind of composition till the age of Quintilian. His dictum 'in comoedia maxime claudicamus,' on the other hand, implies that the educated taste of Romans under the Empire did not find much that was congenial in the works of Plautus, Caecilius, or Terence. The tone of Horace is more contemptuous towards Plautus than towards Ennius and the tragic poets. While tragedy continued to be cultivated by eminent writers in the Augustan age and early Empire, few original comedies seem to have been written after the beginning of the first century B.C. The higher efforts of the comic muse were almost, if not entirely, superseded by the Mimus. These considerations show that comedy was not congenial to the educated or the uneducated taste of Romans in the last years of the Republic, and in the early Empire. But, on the other hand, the popularity enjoyed by the old comedy between the time of Naevius and of Terence, and even down to the earlier half of the Ciceronian age, when some of the great parts in Plautus continued to be performed by the 'accomplished Roscius,' and the admiration expressed for its authors by grammarians and critics, from Aelius Stilo down to Varro and Cicero, shows its adaptation to an earlier and not less vigorous, if less refined stage of intellectual development; while the actual survival of many Roman comedies can only be accounted for by a more real adaptation to human nature, both in style and substance, than was attained by Roman tragedy in its straining after a higher ideal of sentiment and expression.

The task undertaken by Naevius and Plautus was indeed a much easier one than that accomplished by the early writers of tragedy. They were not called upon to create a new taste, or to gratify a taste recently acquired in Sicily and the towns of Magna Graecia. They had only to give ampler and more defined form, fuller and more coherent substance, to a kind of entertainment which was indigenous in Italy. The improvised 'Saturae'—'dramatic medleys or farces with musical accompaniment'—had been represented on Roman holidays for more than a century before the first performance of a regular play by Livius Andronicus. And these 'Saturae' had been themselves developed partly out of the older Fescennine dialogues—the rustic raillery of the vintage and the harvest-home,—partly out of mimetic dances imported from Etruria. Another kind of dramatic entertainment, the 'Oscum ludicrum,' which was developed into the literary form of the 'fabulae Atellanae,' with its standing characters of Maccus, Pappus, Bucco, and Dossennus, had been transferred to the city from the provinces of southern Italy, and ultimately became so popular as to be performed, not by professional actors, but by the free-born youth of Rome. The extant comedies of Plautus show considerable traces of both of these kinds of entertainment, both in the large place assigned to the 'Cantica,' which were accompanied by music and gesticulation[1], and in the farcical exaggeration of some of his characters, which provoked the criticism of Horace,—

   Quantus sit Dossennus edacibus in parasitis.

The mass of Roman citizens, both rural and urban, was thus prepared by their festive traditions and habits to welcome the introduction of comedy, just as they were prepared by their political traditions and aptitudes to welcome the appearance of a popular orator.

Naevius and Plautus might thus be poets of the people more truly than any later Roman poet could be. The career of Naevius, and the public and personal elements which he

---

[1] E. g. the dance of Pseudolus. Pseud 1246, etc.

introduced into his plays, afford evidence of his desire to use his position as a popular poet for political ends. His imprisonment and subsequent banishment equally attest the determination of the governing class to allow no criticism on public men or affairs, nor anything derogatory to the majesty of the State and the dignified forms of Roman life, to be heard on the stage. Plautus, though prevented either by his own temperament or the vigilance of state-censorship from directly acting on the political sympathies of the commons, maintained the thoroughly popular character of Roman comedy, and poured a strongly national spirit into the forms which he adopted from Greece. Between the death of Plautus and that of Terence there was no cessation in the productiveness of Roman comedy; but the little that is known of Caecilius, and the evidence afforded by the plays of Terence, show that Roman comedy had now begun to appeal to a different class of sympathies. The ascendency of Ennius in Roman literature immensely widened the gulf which always separates an educated from an uneducated class. One of the great sources of interest in Plautus is that he flourished before this separation became marked, while the upper classes were yet comparatively rude and simple in their requirements, and the mass of the people were yet hearty and vigorous in their enjoyments. The popularity of his plays revived again after the death of Terence, and maintained itself till nearly the end of the Republic, a proof that his genius was not only in harmony with his own age, but satisfied a permanent vein of sentiment in his countrymen, so long as they retained anything of their native vigour and republican spirit. The fact that Roman comedy was not congenial to the educated taste of the early Empire is no proof of its want of originality. It was in harmony with an earlier stage in the development of the Roman people. Had that been all, it might have been completely lost, or preserved only in fragments like those of the Satire of Lucilius. But as being the heir of an older popular kind of composition it enjoyed the advantage, possessed by none of the more artificial forms of poetry introduced at this period, of a fresh, copious, popular, and idiomatic diction. The comic poets of Rome alone inherited, like the epic poets of Greece, a vehicle of expression formed by the improvised utterance of several generations. The greater fluency of style and the greater ease of rhythmical movement, thus enjoyed by the early comedy, is the most obvious explanation of its permanent hold on the world. But the mere merits of language would scarcely have secured permanence to these compositions apart from the cosmopolitan human interest derived from the Greek originals on which they were founded, and from the strong vitality which the earlier Roman poet drew from the great time into which he was born, and the refined art for which the younger poet was partly indebted to the circle of high-born, aspiring, and accomplished youths into which he was admitted.

Our chief authorities for the life of Plautus are a short statement of Jerome, one or two slight notices in Cicero, and a somewhat longer passage in Aulus Gellius (iii. 3. 14). As he died at an advanced age, in the year 184 B.C.[1] (during the censorship of Cato), he must have been born about the middle of the third century B.C. He was thus a younger contemporary of Naevius, and somewhat older than Ennius. His birthplace was Sarsina in Umbria. That this district must have been thoroughly Latinised in the time of Plautus, is attested by the idiomatic force and purity of his style, a gift which no foreigner seems ever to have acquired[2]. He probably came early to Rome, and was at first engaged 'in operis artificum scenicorum,'— in some kind of employment connected with the stage. He saved money in this service, and lost it all in foreign trade,—what he himself calls 'marituma negotia[3].' Returning to Rome in absolute poverty, he was reduced to work

---
[1] Cic. Brut. 15. 60; De Senec. 14. 50.
[2] Cf. Cicero's testimony to the purity of the style of Naevius and Plautus with his criticism on the style of Caecilius and Pacuvius.
[3] 'Puplicisne adfinis fuit an maritumis negotiis?'—Trinum. 331.

as a hired servant in a mill; and while thus employed he first began to write comedies. The names of two of these early works, *Saturio* and *Addictus*, have been preserved by Gellius. From this time till his death he seems to have been a most rapid and productive writer. We have no means of determining at what date he began to write. A passage quoted from Cicero has been thought to imply that he was writing for the stage during the life-time of P. and Cn. Scipio, i.e. before 212 B.C. But the earliest allusion to contemporary events that we find in any of his extant plays, is that in the Miles Gloriosus, to the imprisonment of Naevius, about 207 B.C. We have no certainty that any of the extant plays were written before this date, although the mention of Hiero in the Menaechmi, and the use of some more than usually archaic inflexions in that play, have been supposed to indicate an earlier date for it. Of the other plays, the Cistellaria and Stichus were written within a year or two of the end of the Second Punic War[1]. The larger number of the extant comedies belong to the last ten years of the poet's life. His plays do not seem to have been published as literary works during his life-time, but to have been left in possession of the acting companies, by whom passages may have been interpolated and others omitted, before they were finally reduced into a literary shape. Most of the prologues to his plays belong to a later time, probably that of the generation after his death[2]. Of the twenty-one plays which Varro accepted, on the ground of their intrinsic merits, as certainly genuine, we possess twenty, and fragments of the remaining one, the *Vidularia*. The names of some other

---

[1] Cf. the line at the end of the Prologue to the Cistellaria (Act i. Sc. 3)—
'Vt vobis victi Poeni poenas sufferant.'
The 'Didascalia' to the Stichus is one of the few preserved. From it we learn that the play was acted P. Sulpicio, C. Aurelio, Cos., i. e. 200 B.C.

[2] This is shown in some cases by reference to seats in the theatre, which were not introduced till 155 B.C. In the Prologue to the Casina it is said that only the older men present could remember the first production of that play in the lifetime of the poet. The Prologues to the Aulularia, Trinummus, and Rudens, are probably genuine, and also the speech of *Auxilium* in the Cistellaria.

genuine plays, such as the *Saturio, Addictus,* and *Commorientes,* are also known to us.

How far are we able to fill up this meagre outline by personal indications of the poet left on his works? In the case of any dramatist this is always difficult; and Plautus is not in form only, but in spirit, essentially dramatic. Nothing marks the difference between the popular and the aristocratic tendencies of Roman thought and literature more than the entire absence of any didactic tendency in his plays. He does not think of making his hearers better by his representations, nor does he believe that it is possible to do so[1]. He identifies himself as heartily for the time being with his rogues of both sexes as with his rarer specimens of honest men and virtuous women. He seldom indulges in reflexions on life. When he does so it is by the mouth of a slave, who winds up the unfamiliar process in some such way as Pseudolus, 'sed iam satis est philosophatum[2],' or in the lyrical self-reproaches of some prodigal, whose good resolutions vanish on the re-appearance of his mistress. Among the innumerable terms of reproach which one slave addresses to another, none is expressive of more withering contempt than the term 'philosophe[3].' But even if we could trace any predominant sympathies in Plautus, or any special vein of reflexion which might seem to throw light on his own experience, some doubt would always remain as to whether he was not in these passages reproducing his original. The loss of many of his prologues deprives us of the kind of knowledge of his circumstances and position which Terence affords us in his prologues. Even the 'asides' to the spectators, which often occur in Plautus, may in many cases be due to the comedians of a later time.

[1] Cf. Rudens, 1249—
    Spectavi ego pridem comicos ad istum modum
    Sapienter dicta dicere atque is plaudier,
    Quom illos sapientis mores monstrabant poplo.
    Set quom inde suam quisque ibant divorsi domum
    Nullus erat illo pacto ut illi iusserant.
[2] Pseud. 687.   [3] E.g. Rudens, 986.

Yet perhaps it is not impossible to enlarge our notion of his personal circumstances and characteristics by tracing some hints of them in his extant works.

We find one reference to his birthplace, in the form of a bad pun altogether devoid of any trace of sentiment or affection[1]. He mentions other districts or towns in Italy in the tone of half-humorous, half-contemptuous indifference, which a Londoner of last, or a Parisian of the present century, might adopt to the provinces[2]. More than one allusion indicates that the citizens of Praeneste were especially regarded as butts by the wits of Rome[3]. The contempt of the town for the country also appears unmistakeably in the dialogue between Grumio and Tranio in the 'Mostellaria[4],' and in the boorish manners of the country lover in the 'Truculentus.' In the eyes of a town-bred wit the chief use of the country is to supply elm-rods for the punishment of pert or refractory slaves. A large number of his illustrations are taken from the handicrafts of the city, but very few are indicative of familiarity with rustic occupations. There is no breath of the poetry of rural nature in Plautus. If he betrays any poetical sensibility to natural influences at all, it is to be found in passages in which the aspects of the sea, in calm or storm, are recalled. Mommsen speaks of 'a most remarkable analogy in many external points between Plautus and Shakespeare[5].' Yet there is contrast rather than analogy in the impression left upon their respective works by the associations of their early homes.

On the other hand we find, in many of his plays, traces

---

[1] 'Quid? Sarsinatis ecquast, si Umbram non habes.' Mostel. 757.
[2] 'Post Ephesi sum natus, noenum in Apulis, noenum Aminulae.'
Mil. Glor. 653.
'Quid tu per barbaricas urbes iuras? *Erg.* Quia enim item asperae
Sunt ut tuum victum autumabas esse.' Captiv. 884–5.
[3] Capt. 879; Trinum. 609; Truc. iii. 2. 23; Bacch. 24.
[4] 'Quid tibi, malum, hic ante aedis clamitatiost?
An ruri censes te esse? apscede ab aedibus.' Most. 6. 7.
[5] Vol. ii. p. 440; Eng. Trans.

of intimate familiarity with the adventures of a mercantile life. It is most probable that some of the passages in which these appear would have been found in his originals had they been preserved to us. Yet the emotions of thankfulness for a safe return to harbour, or of curiosity and pleasure in landing at a strange town [1], are expressed so frequently and with such liveliness as to seem like the reminiscence of personal experience. We get, somehow, the impression of one who had travelled widely, had 'seen the cities of many men and learned their minds,' had marked with humorous observation many varieties of character, had taken note, but without any special aesthetic sensibility, of the works of art which were scattered throughout the Hellenic cities, had shared in the pleasures which these cities held out freely to their visitors, and had encountered the dangers of the sea not without some sense of their sublimity and picturesqueness [2]. The God most frequently appealed to in prayer or thanksgiving is Neptune [3]. The colloquial use of Greek phrases in many of his plays seems to imply a familiar habit of employing them, in active intercourse with Greeks on his maritime adventures. The day-dream of Gripus, after finding his treasure, might almost be taken as a humorous comment on the various motives of curiosity and mercantile enterprise by which he himself was prompted to become engaged in maritime speculation :—

> Navibus magnis mercaturam faciam : aput reges rex perhibebor.
> Post animi causa mihi navem faciam atque imitabor Stratonicum,
> Oppida circumvectitabor, ubi nobilitas mea erit clara,
> Oppidum magnum conmoenibo : ei ego urbi Gripo indam nomen.[4]

---

[1] Cf. Trinum. 820, etc.; Menaechmi, 228, etc.; Stichus, 402, etc.
[2] 'Ita iam quasi canes, haud secus circumstabant navem turbine venti,
    Imbres, fluctus, atque procellae infensae (fremere) frangere malum,
    Ruere antennas, scindere vela, ni pax propitia foret praesto.'
                                                   Trinum. 835-7.
[3] E. g. Rudens, 906; Trinum. 820.
[4] 'I shall trade in big ships : at the courts of princes I shall be styled a prince. Afterwards for my amusement I shall build a ship and imitate Stratonicus; I shall visit towns in my voyages : when I shall have become famous, I'll build a big town, and call it Gripus.'—Rudens, 931-5.

He shows much greater familiarity with the life of the lower and middle classes than with that of those above them in station. He is not always happy in his embodiment of the character of a gentleman. Nothing, for instance, can be meaner than the conduct of the second Menaechmus, who is intended to interest us, in his relations to Erotion. And this failure is equally conspicuous in another of his favourite characters, Periplecomenus, the 'lepidus senex' of the Gloriosus. His indecorous geniality is scarcely compatible with the respectability, not to say the dignity, of age. We recognise in his characters and illustrations a vigorous and many-sided contact with life, but no influence derived from association with members of the governing class. In this respect he stood in marked contrast to Ennius and Terence, and probably to Caecilius. The two latter, being freedmen, were naturally brought into closer association with, and dependence on, their social superiors. Plautus writes in the spirit of an 'ingenuus,' in good-humoured sympathy with the mass of the citizens, and with no feeling of bitterness towards the aristocracy, or indeed to any human being whatsoever. He is at home with all kinds of men, except the highest in rank. He takes a good-natured ironical delight in his slaves, courtesans, parasites, and sycophants. He is not shocked by anything they can do or say. He feels the enjoyment of a man of strong animal spirits in laughing at and with them. Even the 'leno,' the least estimable character in the repertory of ancient comedy, he treats rather as a butt than as an object of detestation. He does not by a single phrase show any sign of having been soured or depressed by the misfortunes and vicissitudes of his life. We feel, in his dialogues, the presence of irrepressible animal spirits, and a sense of boundless resource and lively intelligence in his characters, especially in his slaves. From no scrape does it seem hopeless for them to find some means of extrication. Like them, he himself has the buoyancy of one, 'fortunae immersabilis undis.'

From the zest with which he writes of them, we might

infer that he had a keen personal enjoyment in eating and drinking, and in the coarser forms of conviviality. His favourite dishes,—

> Pernam callum glandium sumen etc.[1]

find no place in the more fastidious gastronomy of our own times, but they were capable of giving great satisfaction to the larger and robuster appetites of the ancient Italians,— of a people who had been, till the sudden influx of luxury in his own time, described as 'barbarous porridge-eaters[2].' Horace has criticised the extravagant gusto with which he makes his parasites dilate on their peculiar pleasures[3]; and the important part which the preparation for the 'prandium' or the 'cena' plays in several of his dramas is perhaps significant of the attention which he himself bestowed on them in the days of his prosperity. The early revels of Philolaches and Callidamates in the Mostellaria, the manner in which Pseudolus celebrates his triumph over Ballio[4], and Sagarinus and Stichus the return of their masters from abroad[5], the tastes which the poet attributes to the old women in his pieces, as to Staphyla in the Aulularia,— show that the Romans had not learned, in his time, the more cultivated enjoyment of wine, which they brought to perfection in the days of Horace. The experience to which Plautus bears witness, like that attributed to his contemporaries in the lines

> Ennius ipse pater numquam nisi potus ad arma
> Prosiluit dicenda,

and

> Narratur et prisci Catonis
> Saepe mero caluisse virtus,

is indicative rather of the convivial 'abandon' of men of vigorous constitutions, than of the more deliberate and fastidious epicureanism of the poets of a later age.

---

[1] Pseud. 166.
[2] 'Non enim haec pultifagus opufex opera fecit barbarus.'
    Mostel. 815.
[3] 'Quantus sit Dossennus edacibus in parasitis.'
[4] Pseud. 1229, etc.   [5] Stichus, 682, etc.

Another criticism of Horace upon Plautus—

> Gestit enim nummum in loculos demittere—

may very probably be true, and is by no means to his discredit. The same charge has been brought against some of the most facile and productive creators in modern times, such as Scott, Dickens, and Balzac, and, to a certain extent, even Shakespeare. To the poets of Nature, or of the higher thought and emotions of men, the pure enjoyment of their art may afford sufficient happiness. In so far as they are true to their higher genius, they are, or ought to be, more independent than any other class of men of the pleasures which money can give. But artists whose power consists in vividly realising and representing the various activities, passions, and enjoyments of life, may feel, in their own experience, some of the craving and of the satisfaction which they are called on to describe. Nor is it unnatural that they should take any legitimate means of securing for themselves some share in the objects of desire, which are the moving forces of their imaginary world. In the large place which the details of good living fill in his plays, Plautus exaggerates a tendency which is discernible in the more decorous fictions of Scott and Dickens. In the important part which he assigns to money in many of his dramas, in his business-like mention of specific sums, in the frequency of his illustrations from the practice of keeping accounts, he shows a resemblance to Balzac. The experience of his life must have impressed upon him the value of money. The fact that he saved enough in his early employment in connexion with the stage to embark on mercantile speculations is a proof of early thrift and prudence and of a wish to raise himself in the world. In all this he was merely exhibiting one of the most common characteristics of the middle class among his countrymen.

Horace adds the further criticism, that so long as he could make money he was indifferent to the artistic merits of his pieces,—

> Securus cadat an recto stet fabula talo ;—

and this criticism is to a great extent true. His object was to give the largest amount of immediate amusement[1]. He was not a careful artist like Terence, studying either finish of style, perfect consistency in the development of his characters, or the working out of his plots to a harmonious conclusion. It was owing to the irrepressible vitality and strong human nature which he could not help imparting to his careless execution, that his plays have survived many more elaborate compositions. Yet he shows a rude kind of consciousness of his art in such passages as that in which he makes Pseudolus compare himself to the poet who creates out of nothing—

> Set quasi poeta, tabulas quom cepit sibi,
> Quaerit quod nusquamst gentium, reperit tamen;[2]

and he speaks of the pleasure which he took in his play 'Epidicus[3].' Cicero also testifies to the joy which he derived from two of the works of his old age, the Pseudolus and the Truculentus[4]. But his delight was that of a vigorous creator, not of a painstaking artist.

Many allusions in his plays attest his acquaintance with works of art, with the stories of Greek mythology or the subjects of Greek tragedies, and with the names, at least, of Greek philosophers. His extraordinary productiveness in adapting works from the new comedy shows that he had a complete command of the Greek language. He not only uses Greek phrases, but has endeavoured to enrich the native vocabulary with a considerable number of Greek words in a Latin form[5]. Yet the knowledge he betrays is that which a man of versatile intelligence, lively curiosity, and retentive memory, would pick up in his varied intercourse with his contemporaries, without any special study of books, except such as were

---

[1] Cf. Pseud. 720 :—
> 'Horum causa haec agitur spectatorum fabula,
> Hi sciunt qui hic adfuerunt; vobis post narravero.'

[2] Pseud. 401-2. [3] Bacchid. 214. [4] De Senec. 14.

[5] E. g. graphicus, doulice, euscheme, morus, logos, techinae, prothyme, basilicus, etc., etc.

needed for his immediate purpose. The more recondite learning of Ennius was probably as strange to him as that of Ben Jonson was to Shakspeare.

The great movement of his age acted on the mind of Plautus in a manner different from that in which it affected Ennius. To the younger poet the triumphant close of the Second Punic War brought the sense of a mighty future awaiting the Roman Republic. He appealed to the higher national aspirations stirring the hearts of the governing class. Plautus felt the strong rebound of spirits from a long-continued state of tension, from a time of anxiety and self-sacrifice, in a less noble manner. He appealed to the craving which the mass of the citizens felt for a more unrestrained enjoyment of the pleasures of life. In the spirit which moved him we seem to recognise the same kind of impulse which prompted the repeal of the Oppian law, and which led to the great increase of public amusements of every kind. The newly-acquired peace and ease awoke in him a sense of the immense capacities of the individual for enjoyment. In a passage of one of his later plays he seems to claim this indulgence as the natural concomitant of victory:—

> Postremo in magno populo, in multis hominibus,
> Re placida atque otiosa, victis hostibus,
> Amare oportet omnes, qui quod dent habent.[1]

With this new sense of freedom and of fullness of life, the old restraints of religion and of the morality bound up with it were relaxed. The commons began to exercise less and less influence in the state. Their political indifference finds an echo in the slighting allusions which Plautus makes to the duties of public life[2]. The increased contact

---

[1] Truculentus, 55-57. Weise condemns the passage as spurious. But whether written by Plautus or not it is in the spirit of the Plautine comedy. In a passage of the Poenulus (act iii. 1. 21) another reference is made to the sense of security enjoyed since their victory:—

> 'Praesertim in re populi placida, atque interfectis hostibus,
> Non decet tumultuari.'

[2] Cp. the remark of the parasite in the Persa, 75, 76—

> 'Set sumne ego stultus qui rem curo publicam
> Ubi sint magistratus, quos curare oporteat?'

with the mind and life of the Greeks powerfully stimulated intellectual curosity, but at the same time was a great solvent of faith, manners, and morals. The frequent use of the words *congraecari, pergraecari*, etc., in Plautus, shows that while the highest Roman minds were learning new lessons of wisdom and humanity from the great Greek writers of the past, the ordinary Roman was learning lessons of idleness and dissoluteness from the living Greeks of the time. The armies which returned from the Macedonian wars, and still more from that with Antiochus, brought with them new fashions and new appliances of luxury. Plautus shows a large indulgence, not unmixed with a vein of saturnine humour, for these new ways on which both young and old were eagerly entering. We see in him the unchecked exuberance of animal life, but no sign of the recklessness or the satiety of exhausted passions. Though there is more decorum, more refined sentiment, in the life of pleasure as presented by Terence, there is more often in Plautus an expression of a struggle between the new temptations and the old Roman ideas of thrift, active duty, and self-restraint. The conscience, though easily lulled to sleep, is still capable of feeling the sting of the thought contained in the Lucretian line—

> Desidiose agere aetatem lustrisque perire.

If we turn now to the extant plays we find that all belong to the class of *palliatae*. We find that they are adaptations or combinations from the works of Menander, Diphilus, Philemon, and other writers of the new comedy. The action is generally supposed to take place in Athens, sometimes in other Greek towns, in Epidamnus, Ephesus, Cyrene, etc. The plays of Plautus, unlike those of Terence and most of those of Caecilius, have generally Latin titles, but nearly all his personages have Greek names. One or two of his parasites (Peniculus, Saturio, Curculio) are

and that of the parasite in the Captivi, 'that only those who were unable to procure invitations to luncheon should be expected to attend public meetings and elections'; and such jokes as 'Plebiscitum non est scitius.'

exceptions to this rule: but the absence of all *gentile* designations among his richer personages would alone prove that he had no intention of presenting to his audience the outward conditions of Roman or Italian life. The social circumstances implied in all his plays are those of well-to-do citizens engaged in foreign commerce, or retired from business after having made their fortunes. The only differences in station among his personages are those of rich and poor, free and slave. There is no recognition of those great distinctions of birth, privilege, and political status, which were so pervading a characteristic of Roman life. Old men are indeed spoken of as 'senati columen'; and it is made a ground of reproach to a young man that he is not already a candidate for public office, or making a name for himself by defending cases in the law-courts. But such passages are probably to be classed among the frequent Roman allusions to be found in Plautus, which had no equivalent in his original. The new comedy of Menander was based on the philosophy of Epicurus, which taught the lesson of abstention from all public duties[1]. The life of the young men is almost entirely a life of pleasure, varied perhaps by some participation in their father's foreign business, or occasional service in the army. But the dislike of a military life among the 'easy livers' of Athens in the beginning of the third century B.C. is shown as much by the indifference of these young men to their honour as soldiers[2], as by the ridicule which is heaped upon the 'Captain Bobadils' who served as mercenaries in the military monarchies of the successors of Alexander. Even a slave regards enlisting as a soldier as the last refuge of a ruined man. The other characters are of Greek origin, though some of them became naturalised in Rome. The ordinary Roman client on the one hand—such as the Volteius Mena of Horace,—and the scurra of Roman satire on the other (Volanerius or Maenius), had a certain likeness to the Greek parasite;

---

[1] The Comedy of Terence, which represents that of Menander, is completely non-political.
[2] Cf Epidicus, 30, etc., and Captivi, 262.

though the position of the first was more respectable[1], and the last was a more formidable element in society than a Gelasimus or an Artotrogus. The 'fallax servus' of comedy, though a wonderful conception of a humorous imagination, is a character hardly compatible with any social conditions; but it is undoubtedly an exaggeration of Greek mendacity and intelligence, the very antithesis of Italian rusticity. The commanding part they play in the affairs of their masters seems like a grotesque anticipation of the part played under the empire by Greek freedmen,—

>Viscera magnarum domuum dominique futuri.

The 'meretrix blanda' of Menander was probably more refined, but not essentially different from the 'libertina' of Rome. Among the rare glimpses into social life which Livy affords behind the stately but somewhat monotonous pageant of consuls and imperators, armies in the field, senators in council, and political assemblies of the people, none is more interesting than that given in the enquiries into the horrors of the Bacchanalia at Rome[2]. The relations between P. Aebutius and the freedwoman Hispala Fecenia bring to mind those existing between the Philematiums, the Phileniums, or Planesiums of comedy and their lovers. The 'leno insidiosus' and the 'improba lena' are probably much the same in all times and countries; but there is a vigorous brutality and inhuman hardness about Ballio and Cleaereta which seem more true to Roman than to Greek life. The kind of life which comedy represents must have had great attractions for a race of vigorous organisation like the Romans, after continued

---

[1] The advocati in the Poenulus, who are evidently clients, show a certain spirit of independence. Cf. Act iii. 6. 13:—
>'Et tu vale.
>Iniuriam illic insignite postulat:
>Nostro sibi servire nos censet cibo.
>Verum ita sunt omnes isti nostri divites:
>Si quid bene facias, levior pluma est gratia;
>Si quid peccatum est, plumbeas iras gerunt.'

[2] Livy, xxxix. 9, etc.

success and prosperity had broken down the old restraints on conduct and desire, and the accumulated wealth of the world had become the prize of their energy. Yet their inherited instincts for industry and frugality must have made it difficult for them to realise gracefully the hollow life of light-hearted enjoyment which came easily to a Greek in the third century B.C. They learned to exaggerate the profligacy without acquiring the more refined and humane qualities of their teachers.

It might perhaps have been expected that a writer of such prodigal invention and so popular and national a fibre as Plautus would have chosen rather to set before his countrymen a humorous image of themselves, than to transport them in imagination to Athens and to exhibit to them these well-used conventional types of Greek life and manners. But, in the first place, the mere fact that it was more easy for him to adapt than to create would have been a sufficient motive to so careless and unconscious an artist. Again, the state-censorship exercised by the magistrates who exhibited the games would naturally deter a poet, who did not wish to encounter the fate of Naevius, from any direct dealing with the delicate subject of Roman social and family life. The later writers of the *fabulae togatae* seem for the most part to have reproduced the life and personages of the provincial towns in Italy. The position not only of the magistrate but even of the citizen at Rome was invested with a kind of dignity and even sanctity, which it would have been dangerous to violate in a public spectacle. Further, the very novelty and unfamiliarity of the ways of Greek life would be more stimulating to the rude imagination of that age than a reproduction of the everyday life of Rome. It requires a more cultivated fancy to recognise incidents, situations and characters suited for art in actual experience, than to appreciate the conventional types of older dramatists. It is a noticeable fact that Shakespeare places the scene of only one of his comedies in England, and that he too introduces the English names and characteristics of

Bottom, Snug, Peter Quince, etc., as Plautus does those of Saturio or Curculio into an imaginary representation of Athenian life. But whatever were his motives for doing so, Plautus professes to introduce his hearers to a representation of Greek manners and morals. His frequent use of the word *barbarus* in reference to Italian or Roman ways, his use of Latinised Greek words and actual Greek phrases, the Greek names of his personages, the dress in which they appeared, the invariable reference to Greek money, perhaps the actual scene presented to the eye, the frequent mention of ships unexpectedly arriving in harbour, the names of the foreign towns visited, etc., would all tend to remind the audience that they were listening to an action and witnessing a spectacle of Greek life.

But while the outward conditions of his dramas are professedly taken from Greek originals, much of the manner and spirit of his personages is certainly Roman. The language in which they express themselves in the first place is thoroughly their own. This is shown by the large number of his puns and plays on words. These by their spontaneity, sometimes by their grotesqueness, sometimes by a Latin play on a Greek word—such as Archidemides[1] or Epidamnus,—show their native origin. No writer, again, abounds so much in alliterations, assonances, asyndeta[2], which are characteristic of all early Roman

---

[1] 'Quom mi ipsum nomen eius Archidemides
Clamaret dempturum esse si quid crederem.' Bacchid. 285.
'Propterea huic urbi nomen Epidamno inditumst
Quia nemo ferme sine damno huc devortitur.' Menaech. 264.
Cf also the play on Chrysalus and Crucisalus; and the following may serve as a specimen of his perpetual puns:—
'Non enim es in senticeto, eo non sentis.' Captivi, 857.

[2] Alliterations and assonances:—'Vi veneris vinctus.' 'Cottabi crebri crepent.' 'Laetus, lubens, laudes ago.' 'Collus collari caret'
'Atque mores hominum moros et morosos efficit,' etc., etc.
Asyndeta:—
'Laudem, lucrum, ludum, iocum, festivitatem, ferias.'
'Vorsa, sparsa, tersa, strata, lauta, structaque omnia ut sint.' etc., etc.
These are not occasional, but constantly recurring characteristics of his style. The thought and matter they express must, in a great measure, be due to his own invention.

poetry down even to Lucretius, and which have no parallel in the more refined and natural diction of the Greek dramatists. Further, we constantly meet with Roman formulae[1], Roman proverbs[2], expressions of courtesy[3], and the like. The very fluency, copiousness, and verve of his language are impossible to a translator, at least in the early stages of a literature. Nothing can be more spontaneous and natural than the dialogue in Plautus. There is, on the other hand, considerable appearance of effort in the reflective passages of the 'cantica'; and this is exactly what we should expect in a Roman writer of originality. Reflexion on life was altogether strange to a Roman in the age of Plautus; to a Greek it was easy and hackneyed. In the prolixity and slow beating out of the thought in some of the 'cantica' we note the beginning of a process unfamiliar to the Roman mind, for which the forms of the Latin language were not yet adapted. The facility of expressing reflexion appears much more developed in Terence. If Plautus were reproducing a Greek original in such passages as Mostell. 85–145, Trinummus 186–273, the thought and the illustration would have lost much in freshness and naiveté, but they would have been expressed with much more point and conciseness.

But it is not only in his language and manner that Plautus shows his independence of his originals. The poems taken from Greek life are in a large measure filled up with matter taken from the life around him. The Greek personages of his play, without apparently any sense of artistic incongruity, speak as Romans would do of the places familiar to Romans — towns in Italy[4], streets, markets, gates, in Rome[5]; of Roman magistrates and other officials,

---

[1] Roman formulae:—'Quae res bene vortat.' 'Conceptis verbis.' 'Quod bonum felix, faustum, fortunatumque sit.' 'Ut gesserit rempublicam ductu, imperio, auspicio suo,' etc., etc.

[2] Proverbs:—'Sarta tecta.' 'Sine sacris haereditas.' 'Inter saxum et sacra.' 'Vae victis.' 'Ad incitas redactust,' etc.. etc.

[3] Expressions of courtesy:—'Tam gratiast.' 'Benigne.' 'Num quid vis?' etc.

[4] E. g. Pistoria, Placentia, Praeneste, Sutrium, Sarsina, etc.

[5] E g. Vicus Tuscus, Velabrum, Macellum, Porta Trigemina, Porta Metia; and compare the long passage in the Curculio (462), which directly refers to Rome.

Quaestors, Aediles, Praetors, Tresviri, Publicani; they allude to the public business of the senate, comitia, and law-courts,— to colonies[1], praefecturae, and the provincia of a magistrate,—to public games in honour of the dead,—to the distinctive dress worn by matrons,—to the forms of bargaining and purchasing, of summoning an antagonist into court, of pleading a case at law,—to the times of vacation from business[2],—to the emancipation of slaves,—peculiar to the Romans. The special characteristics of Roman religion appear in the number of abstract deities referred to, such as Salus, Opportunitas, Libentia, etc. A new divinity is invented in the interests of lovers, under the name of Suavisuaviatio[3]. Other better-known objects of Roman worship, such as Jupiter Capitolinus, Laverna, the Lar Familiaris, are also introduced. We find also references to recent events in Roman history—such as the subjugation of the Boii[4], the treatment inflicted on the Campanians after the second Punic War, the importation of Syrian slaves after the war with Antiochus[5], the introduction of foreign luxuries at the same time[6], the extreme frequency with which triumphs were granted in the first twenty years of the second century B.C.[7] Allusion is made to particular Roman laws, such as the lex alearia[8], probably passed about this time to resist the progress of Greek demoralisation. The state of feeling aroused, on both sides, by the repeal of the Oppian law, and the state of society which led to the original enactment of that law, are reflected in many

---

[1]   'Quid ego cesso Pseudolum
   Facere ut det nomen ad Molas coloniam.' Pseud. 1082.
[2] 'Mancupio dare,' 'stipulatio,' 'antestatio,' 'sponsio,' 'ubi res prolatae sunt.'
[3] Bacchid. 120. [4] Captivi, 888.
[5] Trinummus, 545–6.
[6]   'Non omnes possunt olere unguenta exotica.' Mostell. 42.
[7] Cf. Bacch. 1072:
   'Set, spectatores, vos nunc ne miremini
   Quod non triumpho: peruolgatumst, nil moror.
   Verum tamen accipientur mulso milites.'
[8] Mil. Glor. 164, 6. Cf. Hor. 'Seu malis vetita legibus alea.'

passages of the plays of Plautus. A remark of one of the better class of matrons—

> Non matronarum officium est, sed meretricium,
> Viris alienis, mi vir, subblandirier[1]—

may serve as a comment on the arguments with which Cato opposed the repeal of the law: 'Qui hic mos est in publicum procurrendi, et obsidendi vias, et viros alienos appellandi? ... An blandiores in publico quam in privato, et alienis quam vestris estis[2]?' The imperiousness of a 'dotata uxor,' and the spirit of rebellion thereby aroused in the mind of her husband, are themes treated with grim humour in many of the dramas. The stale jokes against the happiness of married life were as applicable to Greek as to Roman life; and Greek husbands may have stood in as much dread of their wives' extravagance in dress, and in as great awe of their surveillance, as were experienced by the elderly husbands of Latin comedy. But the fact that similar criticisms appear in the satirical and oratorical fragments of the second century B.C. indicate that such jokes, whether or not originally due to the Greek writer, came equally home to a Roman audience.

Again, the great fertility of Plautus and his many-sided contact with life are apparent in the number and variety of his metaphors and illustrations from, and other references to, many varieties of human occupation. These have, for the most part, both a national and a popular origin. The number of those taken from military operations, and from legal and business transactions, is a clear indication that they were of fresh Roman coinage. There is no character which a slave, who has to conduct some intrigue to a successful issue, is so fond of assuming as that of the general of an army. In one passage one of his confederates addresses him as 'Imperator.' He takes the auspices, he brings his engines to bear on the citadel of the enemy, he brings up his supports, he lays his ambush and avoids that

---

[1] Casina, iii. 3. 22.   [2] Livy, xxxiv. 2.

laid for him, he leads his army round by some unknown pass, cuts off the enemy's communications, keeps open his own, invests and takes the hostile position, and divides the booty among his allies. The following passage for instance is freshly coloured with all the recent experience of the Hannibalian war :—

> Viden hostis tibi adesse, tuoque tergo obsidium? Consule,
> Arripe opem auxiliumque ad hanc rem, propere hoc non placide decet.
> Anteveni aliqua aut aliquo saltu circumduce exercitum,
> Coge in obsidium perduellis, nostris praesidium para.
> Interclude conmeatum inimicis, tibi moeni viam,
> Qua cibatus conmeatusque ad te et legionis tuas
> Tuto possit pervenire. Hanc rem age: res subitariast.[1]

The illustrations from the practice of keeping accounts, from banking and business operations, and the references to law forms, such as the mode of pleading a case by sponsio[2], would come home to the experience and habits which were fostered more in Rome than in any other ancient community[3]. Though the Romans never were a mercantile community, like the Carthaginians or the Greek States in their later days, yet from the earliest times they understood the uses of the accumulation and skilful application of capital. Another large class of metaphors, generally expressive of some form of roguery, and taken from the trade of various artisans—such as the smith, carpenter, butcher, weaver, etc.[4]—speaks to the popular as well as

---

[1] 'Do you see that the enemy is close upon you, and that your back will soon be invested. Quick! seize some help and succour: it must be done speedily, not peacefully. Get before them somehow; lead round your forces by some pass or other. Invest the enemy; bring relief to our own troops; cut off the enemy's supplies; make a road for yourself, by which provisions or supplies may reach yourself or your legions safely: give your whole heart to the business—it is a sudden emergency.'—Mil. Glor. 219-225.

The end of many of the prologues also shows that they were addressed to a people constantly engaged in war.

[2] Menaech. 590.

[3] Cf. such expressions and lines as :—'Salva sumes indidem' (Mil. Glor. 234); 'locare argentum;' 'fenerato.'

'Mihi quod credideris, sumes ubi posiueris.' Trinum. 145.

'Nequaquam argenti ratio comparet tamen.' Ib. 418.

'Bene igitur ratio accepti atque expensi inter nos convenit.' Mostel. 292.

[4] For a list of these, cp. the edition of the Mostellaria by the late Professor Ramsay.

the national characteristics of his dramas. If these metaphorical phrases had been mere translations, they would, as thus applied, have had no meaning to a Roman audience. They must have been more or less of slang phrases, formed by and for the people, and suggested by an intimate familiarity with many varieties of trickery and swindling on the one hand, and with the skill and trade of various classes of artisans on the other.

The exuberant use of terms of endearment and of abuse in Plautus may be also mentioned as an original and Roman characteristic of his genius. His lovers' phrases[2], though used by him with a saturnine humour, remind us of the passionate use of similar phrases in Catullus. The slave or cook of Greek comedy may probably have indulged freely in the vituperation of his fellows; but there is an idiomatic heartiness in the interchange of curses and verbal sword-thrusts among the slaves, panders, and cooks of Plautus, which seems congenial to the race who enjoyed the spectacles of the amphitheatre. The inexhaustible fund of merriment supplied by references to or practical exemplifications of the various modes of punishing and torturing slaves, tells of a people not especially cruel, but practically callous either to the infliction or the suffering of pain. The Greek nature was, when roused to passion, capable of fiercer and more cowardly cruelty than the Roman, but was too sensitively organised to enjoy the spectacle or the imagination of inflictions which form the subject of the stalest jokes in Plautus. The spirit of the new comedy as it existed in Greece, was not, on the whole, calculated to elevate, but it certainly was capable of humanising the Roman character.

We are less able to speak of his originality in the selection of incidents and dramatic situations, in the general management of his plots, and his conception of characters. Though more varied than Terence in the subjects which he chooses for dramatic treatment, yet there is great sameness, both of incident, development, and character,

---

[1] E. g. 'Mellitus, ocelle, mea anima, medullitus amare.'

in many of them. His favourite subject is a scheme by which a slave, in the interests of his young master, and his mistress, cheats a father, a mercenary captain, or a 'leno,' who are treated, though in different degrees, as enemies of the human race and legitimate objects of spoliation. Some of the best of his plays—the Pseudolus, Bacchides, the Mostellaria, and the Miles Gloriosus—turn entirely upon incidents of this kind,—'frustrationes in comoediis' as they are called. There is nothing on which the chief agent in such plots prides himself so much as on his success 'in shearing,' 'planing away,' or 'wiping the nose' of, his antagonist in the game: there is no indignity about which the sense of honour is so sensitive as that of having had 'words palmed off upon one,' and having thus been made an object of ridicule. The invariable enlisting of sympathy in favour of the cheat and against the dupe is a trait more illustrative of the countrymen of Ulysses than of Fabricius: but the 'Tusci turba impia vici' at Rome had, no doubt, their own native aptitude for cheating and lying.

The 'Pseudolus' is perhaps the best and the most typical specimen of a play the interest of which turns on this kind of intrigue. In it the plot is skilfully worked out, the characters are conceived with the greatest liveliness, and admirably sustained and contrasted, and the incidents and motives on which the personages act are never strained beyond the limits of probability. A more fastidious age might have objected to the celebration by Pseudolus of his triumph, as a grotesque excrescence: but it serves to bring out the sensual geniality underlying the audacity and roguery of his character, in contrast to the sensual brutality underlying the audacity and villainy of Ballio. When we consider the vigorous life and even the art with which the whole piece is worked out, we understand why Plautus, with good reason, took, in his old age, especial pleasure in this play. There is not much to offend a robust morality in the piece; for though the result accomplished cannot be called the triumph of virtue over vice, it is at least the triumph of a more amiable over a more detestable form of depravity.

In the 'Bacchides' the slave Chrysalus plays a part similar to that of Pseudolus, with perhaps more subtlety but less vigour and liveliness. The mode in which both the 'pater attentus' and the 'senex lepidus' of the piece (Nicobulus and Philoxenus) succumb to the blandishments of the two sisters, and in the end become the rivals of their sons, is still less edifying than the winding up of the Pseudolus: but the dénouement is brought about not unskilfully or extravagantly. It is difficult to say whether Plautus, like the author of Gil Blas, felt a moral indifference to the characters he brought on the stage, so long as he could make them amusing; or whether, like Balzac, but with more humour and less cynicism, he had a peculiar delight in following human corruption into its last retreats. The moral with which the piece winds up—

> Hi senes nisi fuissent nihili jam inde ab adulescentia,
> Non hodie hoc tantum flagitium facerent canis capitibus,

implies that he recognised the difference between right and wrong, or at least between good and bad taste in such matters, but that he did not, perhaps, attach much importance to it. The 'Asinaria,' which also turns on a scheme by which a slave defrauds his mistress in behalf of his young master, winds up with a scene in which a father is enjoying himself as the rival of his complaisant son, till he is summoned away by the apparition of his wife, and the wrathful and scornful reiteration of 'Surge, amator, i domum.' The moral expressed there by the 'Caterva' implies less sympathy with outraged virtue than with the disappointed delinquent—

> Hic senex siquid clam uxorem suo animo fecit volup
> Neque novom neque mirum fecit nec secus quam alii solent.

There are two or three other plays in which a father appears as the rival of his son. None of the characters in Plautus, not even Ballio, or Labrax, or Cleaereta,—the worst of his 'lenones' and 'lenae,'—excite more unmitigated disgust than Stalino in the 'Casina.'

The 'Miles Gloriosus' and the 'Mostellaria' are much less objectionable in point of morality, or at least good taste, than either the 'Bacchides' or the 'Asinaria.' They are among the most popular of the plays of Plautus. There is a great variety of humorous situations in the 'Miles': and, although the principal character transcends all natural limits in his self-glorification, his stupid insensibility, and his pusillanimity, the intrigue is carried out with the greatest vivacity by Palaestrio and his army of accomplices; and the humour with which the fidelity and veracity of the slave Sceledrus are played upon almost merges into pathos in the despairing tenacity with which he cannot bring himself to disbelieve the evidence of his eyes—

> Noli minitari: scio crucem futuram mihi sepulchrum:
> Ibi mei sunt maiores siti, pater, avos, proavos, abavos.
> Non possunt tuis minaciis hisce oculi mi ecfodiri.[1]

Tranio in the 'Mostellaria' is, in readiness of resource and resolute mendacity, a not unworthy member of the fraternity to which Pseudolus, Chrysalus, and Palaestrio belong. He is, besides something of a fop and a fine gentleman, and all his relations with his young and old master, with Simo and the Banker, are conducted with perfect urbanity. Yet the 'Mostellaria' is certainly one of those plays to which the criticism of Horace—

> Securus cadat an recto stet fabula talo,—

is peculiarly applicable. No less suitable 'Deus ex machina' than the crapulous Callidamates can well be imagined for the purpose of reconciling a justly incensed father and master of a household to the profligate extravagance of his son, and the audacious mystification of his slave.

Several other plays turn upon similar 'frustrationes.' Two of the best of these are the 'Curculio' and the 'Epidicus.' Though there are lively and humorous scenes in nearly all his plays, and the language is generally

---

[1] 'Don't threaten me; I know that the cross will be my tomb: there lie my ancestors, father, grandfather, great-grandfather, great-great-grandfather: but your threats can't dig these eyes out of my head.'—Mil. Glor. 372-5.

sparkling and vigorous, yet the sameness of situation and character, and the unrelieved tone of light-hearted merriment and mendacity with which this class of play is pervaded soon pall upon the taste. A few, the 'Cistellaria' and the 'Poenulus,' for instance, turn upon the incident of a free-born child being stolen in infancy, and recognised by her parents before she has fatally committed herself to the occupation for which she has been destined. But these are not among the best executed of the Plautine plays. In the 'Stichus' we enjoy the unwonted satisfaction of making acquaintance with two wives who really care for their husbands: and the parasite Gelasimus in that play is as amusing as the characters of the same kind in the Captivi, Curculio, Menaechmi, Persa, etc. But the absence of incident, coherent plot, and adequate dénouement, must prevent this play from being ranked among the more important compositions of Plautus. A few however still remain to be noticed as among the most serious or the most imaginative efforts of his genius. The 'Aulularia,' 'Trinummus,' 'Menaechmi,' 'Rudens,' 'Captivi,' and 'Amphitryo,' are much more varied in their interest than most of those already mentioned, and each of them has its own characteristic excellence.

The interest of the 'Aulularia' turns entirely on the character of Euclio. Whether or not this embodiment of the miser owes much to the original creation of Plautus, it is certainly realised by him with the greatest truth and vivacity. The whole conception is thoroughly human and original; and though nothing can be more complete than the hypochondriacal possession which his one idea has over his imagination, the character is not presented in an odious or despicable light. In this respect it differs from the frequent presentment of the miserly character in Roman satire, and in most modern works of fiction. Perhaps, except Silas Marner and Père Goriot, there is no other case of a miser being conceived with any human-hearted sympathy. His exaggerated sense of the value of the smallest sum of money is like a hallucination, arising out of the unexpected discovery of a great treasure after a life of poverty has made pinching and sparing a second nature to him. But this hallucination has left him shrewdness, honesty, pluck, a certain dignity, shown in his relation to Megadorus, and abundance of a grim humour; and it seems to have cleared away, in the dénouement of the piece, under the influence of fatherly affection [1]. There are none of the baser or more brutal characters of the Plautine comedies introduced into this play. Eunomia is a rare specimen of a virtuous woman; Megadorus of a worthy and kindly old man, with a didactic tendency which makes him a little wearisome; the 'young lover' shows an honourable loyalty in the reparation of his fault. Though none of these subsidiary characters are conceived with anything like the force and vivacity of Euclio, yet after reading the humours of ancient life, as exhibited in the 'Asinaria,' 'Casina,' and 'Truculentus,' we feel a sense of relief in finding ourselves in such respectable company. The genius with which the chief character of the play is conceived and executed is sufficiently attested by the fact that it served as a model to the greatest of purely comic dramatists of modern times.

The 'Trinummus,' if less amusing than most of the other plays of Plautus, is one of the most unexceptionable in moral tendency; and one at least of the personages in it, Philto, in his union of shrewd sense and old-fashioned severity with a sarcastic humour and real humanity of nature is quite a new type, distinguishable from the hard fathers, the disreputably genial old men, and the mere worthy citizens, who are among the stock characters of the Plautine comedy. There is no play in which the struggle between the stricter morals of an older time and the new temptations is more clearly exhibited: and though vice is finally condoned, or at least visited only with the mild penalty of an unsolicited marriage, the sympathies of the

[1] The conclusion of the Aulularia is lost, but the play seems to have ended with the old man's consigning his treasure into the hands of his son-in-law and daughter.

audience are entirely enlisted on the side of virtue. Lesbonicus is a prodigal of the type of Charles Surface, whose folly and extravagance are redeemed by good feeling and a latent sense of honour: and if it is not easy to acquit Lysiteles of a too conscious virtue, one must remember how difficult it always is for a comic dramatist to make the character of a thoroughly respectable young man lively and entertaining. But the whole piece, from the prologue, which indicates the way which all prodigals go, to the end,—the good sense, worth of character, and friendly confidence exhibited in the relations of Megaronides and Callicles,—the honourable love of Lysiteles for the dowerless sister of his friend,—the pious humanity and humility of such sentiments as these in the mouth of Philto—

> Di divites sunt, deos decent opulentiae
> Et factiones: verum nos homunculi
> Scintillula animae, quam quom extemplo emisimus,
> Aequo mendicus atque ille opulentissimus
> Censetur censu ad Acheruntem mortuos,[1]—

the denunciation by Megaronides of the 'School for Scandal,' which seems to have flourished in Athens as similar institutions do in our modern cities,—enable us to believe that the citizen life of the Greek communities, after the loss of their independence, may not have been so utterly hollow and disreputable as some of the representations of ancient comedy would lead us to suppose.

There is much greater originality of plot, incident, and character, though, at the same time, a much less unexceptionable moral tendency in the 'Menaechmi,' the model after which Shakspeare's Comedy of Errors was composed. The plot turns upon the likeness of twins, who have been separated from each other from childhood: and granting this original supposition,—one perfectly conformable to experience,— the many lively and humorous situations arising out of their undistinguishable resemblance to one

---

[1] 'The Gods only are rich: great wealth and high connexions are for the Gods; but we, poor creatures, are but a tiny spark of life, and so soon as that is gone, the beggar and the richest man, when dead, are rated alike by the shores of Acheron.'—Trin. 490-4.

another, are natural and lifelike. We feel, in the incidents which Plautus brings before us, none of that sense of unreality which the complication of the two Dromios adds to the 'Comedy of Errors.' The play is enlivened also by the element of personal adventure, arising out of the experiences of the second Menaechmus in his search for his brother over all the coasts of the Mediterranean. The two brothers (whether or not this was intended by the poet) are like in character, as well as in outward appearance; and they are both, in their hardness and knowledge of the world, in the unscrupulousness with which they gratify their love of pleasure, and the superiority which they maintain over their dependents, entirely distinct from the weak and vacillating 'amantes ephebi' of most of the other plays. The character of the 'parasite' is not very different from that in some of the other plays, except that in his vindictiveness for the loss of his 'déjeuner,' and his love of mischief-making, he comes nearer to the type of the 'scurra' than of the faithful client of the house, who is best represented by the Ergasilus of the 'Captivi.' But in the fashionable physician who is called in by the wife and father-in-law of the first Menaechmus, to examine into and prescribe for his condition, we are introduced to a new type of character which certainly seems to be drawn from the life. After reading the scene in which this personage is introduced, one might be inclined to fancy that, notwithstanding the advance of medical science, certain characteristics of manner and procedure had become long ago stereotyped in the profession.

These three plays show Plautus at his best in regard to the delineation of character, to moral tendency, to the conduct of a story by means of humorous incidents and situations. The three which still remain to be considered assert his claim to some share of poetic feeling and genius, and to at least some sympathy with the more elevated motives and sentiments which dignify human life. The 'Rudens' is inferior to several of the other plays in purely dramatic interest; but it has all the charm and freshness of a sea-idyl. The outward picture imprinted on the imagination is that of a bright morning after a storm, of which the effects are still apparent in the unroofing of the villa of Daemones, in the wild commotion of the sea[1], in the desolation of the two shipwrecked women wandering about among the lonely rocks where they have been cast ashore, in the touching complaint of the poor fishermen deprived by the storm of their chance of earning their daily bread. The action, which consists in the rescue of innocence from villainy, and in the recognition of a lost daughter by her father, entirely enlists both the moral and the humane sympathies. There is imaginative as well as humorous originality in the soliloquies of Gripus, and in his altercation with Trachalio; and a sense of sardonic satisfaction is experienced in contemplating the plight of Labrax (a weaker and meaner ruffian than Ballio) and his confederate chattering with cold and bewailing the loss of their ill-gotten gains. But the peculiar charm of the play, as compared with any of those which has been already noticed, is the sentiment of natural piety—not unlike that expressed in the 'rustica Phidyle,' of Horace[2]—by which the drama is pervaded. This key-note is struck in the prologue uttered by Arcturus, whose function it is to shine in the sky during the night, and during the day to wander over the earth, and report to Jove on the good and evil deeds of men.

> 'Quist imperator divom atque hominum Iuppiter,
> Is nos per gentis hic alium alia disparat,
> Hominum qui facta, mores, pietatem et fidem
> Noscamus, ut quemque adjuvet opulentia.[3]

The affinity of piety to mercy is exhibited in the part played by the priestess of Venus—

> Manus mihi date, exurgite a pedibus ambae,
> Misericordior nulla mest feminarum;[4]

---

[1] 'Non vidisse undas me maiores censeo.' Rudens, 167.
'Atque ut nunc valide fluctuat mare, nulla nobis spes est.' Ib. 303.
[2] Cf. 'Atque hoc scelesti [illi] in animum inducunt suum
Iovem se placare posse donis, hostiis:
Et operam et sumptum perdunt. id eo fit quia
Nihil ei accemptumst a periuris supplici,' etc.—22-5.
[3] 9-12.   [4] 280, 1.

and the natural trust of innocence and good faith in divine protection is exemplified by the confidence with which the shipwrecked women take refuge at the altar of Venus.

> Tibi auscultamus et, Venus alma, ambae te opsecramus
> Aram amplexantes hanc tuam lacrumantes, genibus nixae,
> In custodelam nos tuam ut recipias et tutere, etc.[1]

Even the moral sentiment expressed is of a finer quality than the maxims of rough good sense and probity which we find, for instance, in the Trinummus. When Gripus tells his master that he is poor owing to his scrupulous piety—

> Isto tu's pauper, quom nimis sancte piu's—

the answer is in a higher strain than that familiar to ancient comedy.

> O Gripe Gripe, in aetate hominum plurimae
> Fiunt transennae, [illi] ubi decipiuntur dolis.
> Atque edepol in eas plerumque esca inponitur,
> Quam siquis avidus poscit escam avariter,
> Decipitur in transenna avaritia sua.
> Ille qui consulte, docte atque astute cavet,
> Diutine uti ei bene licet partum bene.
> Mi istaec videtur praeda praedatum irier,
> Majore ut cum dote abeat hinc quam advenerit.
> Egone ut quod ad me adlatum esse alienum sciam
> Celem? minume istuc faciet noster Daemones.
> Semper cavere hoc sapientes aequissumum'st,
> Ne conscii sint ipsi maleficii suis.
> Ego nisi quom lusim nil morer ullum lucrum.[2]

The 'Captivi' was pronounced by the greatest critic of last century to be the best constructed drama in existence. Though probably few will now be found to assign to it so high a place, yet, if not the best, it certainly is

---

[1] 694, etc.

[2] 'O Gripus, Gripus! in the life of man are laid many snares, by which they are trapped; and for the most part a bait is laid on them, and whoso in his greed greedily craves for it, by reason of his greed he is caught in the trap. But whoso warily, wisely, craftily takes heed, to him it is given long to enjoy what has been well earned. That prize of yours, I fancy, will be so made prize of, as to bring a larger dower in going from us than when it came to us. To fancy that I should be capable of keeping secret possession of what I know to be another's property? Far will that be from our friend Daemones! It is the absolute duty of a wise man to be on his guard against ever being privy to any wrong done by his own people. I never would care for any gain, except when I am in the game.'—Rudens, 1235-48.

among the very best plays of Plautus, in respect both of plot and the dramatic irony of its situations. But it possesses a still higher claim to our admiration in the presentment of at least one character of true nobleness. And the originality of the conception is all the greater from the fact that this heroism is embodied in the person of one who has been brought up from childhood as a slave. There are not many of the plays of Plautus calculated to raise our ideas of human nature; but the loyal affection of Tyndarus for his young master, his self-sacrifice, the buoyancy, courage, and ready resource with which he first meets his dangers, and the manly fortitude with which he accepts his doom—

> Dum ne ob malefacta, peream: parvi id aestimo.
> Si ego hic peribo, ast ille, ut dixit, non redit,
> At erit mi hoc factum mortuo memorabile,
> Me meum erum captum ex servitute atque hostibus
> Reducem fecisse liberum in patriam ad patrem,
> Meumque potius me caput periculo
> Hic praeoptavisse quam is periret ponere[1]—

enable us to feel that some of the glory of the older and nobler Greek tragedy still lingered in the Athens of Menander, and has been reproduced by Plautus with imaginative sympathy. Yet perhaps even to this play the criticism of Horace,

> Quam non adstricto percurrat pulpita socco,

in part applies. The old slave-tricks of mendacity and unseasonable joking, which are a legitimate source of amusement in the Pseudolus and similar plays, jar on our feelings as inconsistent with the simple dignity of the character of Tyndarus and the heroic part which he has to play.

There are none of the plays of Plautus which it is so difficult to criticise from a modern point of view as the 'Amphitruo.' On the one hand the humour of the scenes

---

[1] 'Provided it be not for wrong done, let me perish, I care not. If I shall perish here, while he returns not, as he promised, yet even after death this will be a memorable act, that I restored my master from captivity and his enemies to his father and his home, and chose rather to emperil my own life here than that he should perish.'—Captivi, 682-8.

between Mercury and Sosia is not surpassed in any of the other comedies. There is no passage in any other play in which such power of imagination is exhibited, as that in which Bromia tells the tale of the birth of Alcmena's twins—

> Ita erae meae hodie contigit: nam ubi partuis deos sibi invocat,
> Strepitus, crepitus, sonitus, tonitrus: subito ut propere, ut valide tonuit.
> Ubi quisque institerat, concidit crepitu: ibi nescio quis maxuma
> Voce exclamat: 'Alcumena, adest auxilium, ne time:
> Et tibi et tuis propitius caeli cultor advenit.
> Exurgite' inquit 'qui terrore meo occidistis prae metu.'
> Ut iacui, exurgo: ardere censui aedis: ita tum confulgebant.[1]

Nor is there, perhaps, anywhere in ancient literature a nobler realisation of the virtue of womanhood than in the indignant vindication of herself by Alcmena,—

> Non ego illam mihi dotem esse duco, quae dos dicitur,
> Set pudicitiam et pudorem et sedatum cupidinem,
> Deum metum et parentum amorem et cognatum concordiam,
> Tibi morigera atque ut munifica sim bonis, prosim probis.[2]

On the other hand, it is difficult to understand how the part played by Jupiter, and the comments of Mercury upon that part, should not have shocked the religious and moral sense even of the Athenians of the age of Epicurus and of the Romans in the age when they were first made familiar with the Sacred Chronicle of Euhemerus. Perhaps the Romans made a distinction between the Jupiter of Greek mythology and their own Jupiter Optimus Maximus, and may have thought that what was derogatory to the first did not apply to the second. Or, perhaps, some

---

[1] 'So it befell my mistress this day: for when she calls the powers of travail to her aid, lo! there ensues a rumbling, rattling noise, loud uproar and a peal of thunder—all of a sudden how fast, how mightily it thundered! At the crash each one fell on the spot where he stood. Then some one, I know not who, exclaims in a loud voice, "Alcmena, be not afraid; help is at hand: the dweller in the skies draweth nigh with kindly intent to thee and thine. Arise ye who from the dread inspired by me have fallen down in alarm." As I lay, I rose up: methought the house was all on fire, so brightly did it shine.'—Amphitruo, 1060-67.

[2] 'I call not that which is named my dower, my true dower, but chastity and modesty, and passion subdued, fear of the Gods, affection to my parents, amity with my kinsmen, a will to yield to thee, to be bountiful to the good, of service to the worthy.'—Amphitruo, 839-42.

clue to the origin of the Greek play may be found in a phrase of the Rudens,

> Non ventus fuit, verum Alcumena Euripidi.[1]

Was the Greek writer partly parodying, in accordance with the tradition of the old comedy, partly reproducing a tragedy of Euripides? and was the representation first accepted as a recognised burlesque of a familiar piece? In any case its production both at Athens and Rome must be regarded partly as a symptom, partly as a cause, of the rapid dissolution of religious beliefs among both Greeks and Romans.

As in the case of other productive writers there is no absolute agreement as to which are the best of the Plautine plays. Without assigning precedence to any one over the other, a preference may be indicated for these five, as combining the most varied elements of interest with the best execution—*Aulularia, Captivi, Menaechmi, Pseudolus, Rudens*; and for these, as second to the former in interest owing to some inferiority in comic power, artistic execution, or natural *vraisemblance*, or owing to some element in them which offends the taste or moral sentiment—*Trinummus, Mostellaria, Miles Gloriosus, Bacchides, Amphitruo*. These ten plays alone, without taking the others into account, show both in their incidents, scenes, and characters, how much wider Plautus' range of observation was than that of Terence. Even within the narrow limits of the characters most familiar to ancient comedy—the 'amans ephebus,' the 'meretrix blanda,' the 'fallax servus,' the 'bragging captain,' the 'parasite,' the 'leno,' the 'old men'—good, kindly, severe, genial, sensual and disreputable,—we find great individual differences. More than Terence, Plautus maintains a dramatic and ironical superiority over his characters. This is especially shown in his treatment of his young lovers and the objects of their despairing affection. The former exhibit various shades of weakness, from the mere ineffectual struggle between the grain of conscience left

[1] 86.

them and the attractions of pleasure, to the sentimental impulse to end their woes by suicide. The latter show varying degrees of attraction, from a grace and vivacity that reminds German critics of the Mariana and the Philina in 'Wilhelm Meister,' to the hardness and astuteness of the heroines of the 'Truculentus' and the 'Miles Gloriosus.' Plautus cannot be said to care much about any of them except as objects of amusement and of the study of human nature. Nor, on the other hand, has he any hatred of his worst characters. He has the true dramatist's sympathy with the vigorous conception of Ballio—the same kind of sympathy which made that part a favourite one of the actor Roscius. His characters are interesting and amusing in themselves; they are never used as the mere mouthpieces of the writer's reflexion, wit, or sentiment. It is, of course, impossible to determine definitely how far he was an original creator, how far a merely vigorous imitator. But he is so perfectly at home with his characters, he makes them speak and act so naturally, he is so careless about those minutiae of artistic treatment of which a mere translator would be scrupulously regardful, that it seems most probable that the life with which he animates his conventional type is derived from his own exuberant vitality and his many-sided contact with humanity.

In what relation do the plays of Plautus stand to the more serious interests of life? Is he to be ranked among philosophic humourists who had felt deeply the speculative perplexities of this world, whose imagination vividly realised the incongruity between the outward mask that men wear and the reality behind it, and the wide divergence of the actual aims of society from the purified ideal towards which it tends? Is there in him any vein of ironical comment or satirical rebuke? any latent sympathy with any of the objects which move the serious passions of moral and social reformers? Or is he merely a great humourist, revelling in the mirth, the absurdities, the ridiculous phases of character, which show themselves on the surface of life? It must be admitted that it is difficult to find in him any traces of the speculative questioning, of the repressed or baffled enthusiasm, of the rebellion against the common round of the world which tempers or inspires some of the greatest humourists of ancient and modern times. His indifference to the problems of speculative philosophy is expressed in such phrases as the

> Salva res est: philosophatur quoque jam, non mendax modo'st

of Tyndarus in the Captivi[1], and in the

> Sed jam satis est philosophatum

of Pseudolus[2]. Yet to Tyndarus he attributes a sense of religious trust befitting both his character and situation—

> Est profecto deus, qui quae nos gerimus auditque et videt, etc.,[3]

while Pseudolus easily finds an opposite doctrine to suit his ready, self-reliant, and unscrupulous nature—

> Centum doctum hominum consilia sola haec devincit dea,
> Fortuna, etc.[4]

Probably the truth is that living in an age of active enjoyment and energy, he troubled himself very little about the 'problem of existence'; but that he had thought enough and doubted enough to enable him to animate his more elevated characters with sentiments of natural piety, and to conceive of the ordinary round of pleasure and intrigue as quite able to dispense with them. There is rather an indifference to religious influences or beliefs, than such expressions of scepticism or antagonism to existing superstitions as we find in the tragic poets. The political indifference of his plays has been already noticed. Yet the sentiments attributed to some of his best characters, such as Philto in the Trinummus, Megadorus in the Aulularia[5], imply that he recognised in the growing ascend-

---

[1] Captivi, 280.   [2] Pseud. 666.   [3] Captivi, 310.   [4] Pseud. 677.
[5] Cf. Aul. iii. 5. 4-8:—
> 'Nam, meo quidem animo, si idem faciant ceteri,
> Opulentiores pauperiorum filias
> Ut indotatas ducant uxores domum,
> Et multo fiat civitas concordior,
> Et invidia nos minore utamur, quam utimur.'

ency of wealth an element of estrangement between the different classes of the community. His frequent reference to the extravagance and imperiousness of the 'dotatae uxores' seems to imply further his conviction that the curse of money was a dissolving force, not only of the social and political but also of the family life of Rome.

The first aspect of many of his plays certainly produces the impression of their demoralising tendency. But it is perhaps necessary to be on our guard against judging this tendency too severely from a merely modern point of view. These plays were addressed to the people in their holiday mood, and a certain amount of license was claimed for such a mood (as we may see by the Fescennine songs in marriage ceremonies and in triumphal processions), which perhaps was not intended to have more relation to the ordinary life of work and serious business than the lies and tricks of slaves in comedy to their ordinary relations with their masters.

Public festivity in ancient times, which was originally an outlet of religious emotion, became ultimately a rebound from the severer duties and routine of daily life. There are frequent reminders in Plautus that this life of pleasure and intrigue was not altogether worthy or satisfactory. There are no false hues of sentiment thrown around it, as there are in Terence, and still more in the poets of a later age. Nor must we expect in an ancient poet any sense of moral degradation attaching to a life of pleasure. So far as that life is condemned it is on the ground of sloth, weakness, and incompatibility with more serious aims. The maxims which Palinurus addresses to Phaedromus in the Curculio would probably not have shocked an ancient moralist:

> Nemo hinc prohibet nec vetat
> Quin quod palamst venale, si argentumst, emas.
> Nemo ire quemquam puplica prohibet via,
> Dum ne per fundum saeptum faciat semitam:
> Dum ted apstineas nupta vidua virgine
> Iuventute et pueris liberis, ama quod lubet.[1]

[1] Curculio, 33-8.

Something of the same kind is implied in the warning addressed by his father to the young Horace. Any breach of the sanctities of family life is invariably reprobated. On the rare occasions where such breaches occur,—as in the Aulularia — they are repaired by marriage. Any one aspiring to play the part of a Lothario—as in the Miles Gloriosus—is made an object both of punishment and ridicule. In this respect the comedy of Plautus contrasts favourably with our own comic drama of the Restoration. There are no scenes in these plays intended or calculated to stimulate the passions; and although there are coarse expressions and allusions in almost all of them, yet the coarseness of Plautus is not to be compared with that of Lucilius, Catullus, Martial, or Juvenal. It is rather in the absence of any virtuous ideal, than in positive incitements to vice, that the Plautine comedy might be called immoral. Although family honour is treated as secure from violation, there is no pure feeling about family life. Sons are afraid of their fathers, run into debt without their knowledge, deceive them in every possible way, occasionally express a wish that their death might enable them to treat their mistresses more generously. Husbands fear their wives and speak on all occasions bitterly against them. Plautus was evidently more familiar with the ways of the 'libertinae' than of Roman matrons of the better sort; and thus while we see little of the latter, what we hear of them is not to their advantage. The only obligation which young men seem to acknowledge is that of honour and friendly service to one another. So too slaves, while they hold it as their first duty to lie and swindle in behalf of their young masters, feel the duty of absolute devotion and sacrifice of themselves to their interests. Plautus shows scarcely any of the Roman feeling of dignity or seriousness, or any regard for patriotism or public duty. There is everywhere abundance of good humour and good sense, but, except in the Captivi and Rudens, we find scarcely any pathos or elevated feeling. The ideal of character which satisfies most of his personages might almost be expressed in the words of Stalagmus in the Captivi—

> Fui ego bellus, lepidus,—bonus vir nunquam neque frugi bonae
> Neque ero unquam.[1]

But the life of careless freedom and strong animal spirits which Plautus shaped with prodigal power into humorous scenes and representations for the holiday amusements of the mass of his fellow-citizens, does not admit of being tried by any moral or social standard of usefulness. It would be equally unprofitable to search for any consistent vein of irony in him, or any deep intuition into the paradoxes of life. He is to be judged and valued on the grounds put forward in the epitaph, which was in ancient times attributed to himself,—

> Postquam est mortem aptus Plautus, comoedia luget,
> Scaena est deserta, dein risus, ludu' iocusque
> Et numeri innumeri simul omnes conlacrumarunt.

And this leads us to the last question concerning him— What is his value as a poetic artist? The very fact that his imagination plays so habitually on the surface of life, that he has, as compared with the greatest humourists of modern times, so little poetry, elevation, or depth, prevents his being ranked in the very highest class of humorous creators. In the absence of serious meaning or feeling from his writings he reminds us of Le Sage or Smollett rather than of Cervantes or Molière. Nor does he compensate for these defects by careful artistic treatment. The criticisms of Horace on this subject are perfectly true. If the line—

> Plautus ad exemplar Siculi properare Epicharmi

refers to the rapidity with which he hurries on to the dénouement of his plot, it must be admitted that in some cases this quality degenerates into haste and impatience[2]. But, on the other hand, the careless ease and

---

[1] 'I was a fine gentleman, a nice fellow—a good or respectable man I never was nor will be.'—Capt. 956-7.

[2] Cp. the winding up of the Mostellaria, Casina, Cistellaria.

O

prodigal productiveness of his genius entitle him to take certainly a high rank in the second class of humourists. If he shows little of the idealising or contemplative faculty of poetic genius, he has at least the facile power and spontaneous exuberance which distinguish the great creators of human character.

The power of high and true dramatic invention which he occasionally puts forth, and the stray gleams of beauty which light up the coarser and commoner texture of his fancies, suggest the inference that it was owing more to the demands of his audiences than to the original limitation of his own powers, that he did not raise both himself and his countrymen to the enjoyment of nobler productions. A people accustomed to the buffoonery of the indigenous mimic dances required strong and broad effects. Their popular poet, in conforming to the conditions of Greek art, could not altogether forget the Dossennus native to Italy.

But the largest endowment of Plautus, the truest note of his creativeness, is his power of expression by means of action, rhythm, and language. The phrase 'properare' may more probably be explained by the extreme vivacity and rapidity of gesture, dialogue, declamation, and recitative, by which his scenes were characterised, than be taken as an equivalent to 'ad eventum festinare.' The Italian liveliness and mobility of temperament made them admirable mimics: and the favour which the plays of Plautus continued to enjoy with the companies of players, may be in part accounted for by the scope they afforded to the talent of the actor. How far he was expected to bring out the meaning of the poet may be gathered from the lively description given by Periplecomenus of the outward manifestations which accompanied the inward machinations of Palaestrio,—

> Illuc sis vide
> Quem ad modum astitit severo fronte curans, cogitans.
> Pectus digitis pultat: cor credo evocaturust foras.
> Ecce avortit: nisim laevo in femine habet laevam manum.
> Dextera digitis rationem conputat: fervit femur
> Dexterum, ita vehementer icit: quod agat, aegre suppetit.

Concrepuit digitis: laborat, crebro conmutat status.
Eccere autem capite nutat: non placet quod repperit.
Quidquid est, incoctum non expromet, bene coctum dabit.
Ecce autem aedificat: columnam mento suffigit suo.
Apage, non placet profecto mihi illaec aedificatio:
Nam os columnatum poetae esse indaudivi barbaro,
Quoi bini custodes semper totis horis occubant.
Euge, euscheme hercle astitit et dulice et comoedice.[1]

Many other scenes must have lent themselves to this representation of feeling by lively gesture, accompanied sometimes by some kind of mimic dance: of this kind, for instance, is the vigorous recitative of Ballio on his first appearance on the stage, the scene in which Ergasilus tells Hegio of the return of his son, the appearance of Pseudolus when well drunken after celebrating his triumph over Ballio,—

Quid hoc? sicine hoc fit? pedes, statin an non?
An id voltis ut me hinc jacentem aliqui tollat? etc.[2]

His temptation was to exaggerate in this, as in other elements of the dramatist's art; and this is what is probably meant by the word *percurrat* in the criticism of Horace, which has been already quoted. But this tendency to exaggerate is merely the defect of his superabundant share of the vigorous Italian qualities.

It is characteristic of the liveliness of Plautus' temperament, that the lyrical and recitative parts of his plays occupy a place altogether out of proportion to that occu-

---

[1] 'Look there, if you please, how he has taken up his post, with serious brow pondering, meditating; now he taps his breast with his fingers. I fancy he is going to summon his heart outside: look, he turns away; now his left hand is leaning on his left thigh; with his right hand he is making a calculation on his fingers; his right thigh burns, such a violent blow he has struck it; his scheme does not come easily to him:—he cracks his fingers: he is at a loss; he often changes his position: look, there he nods his head: he does not like this new idea. Whatever it is, he will not bring it out till it is ready: he'll serve it up well done. Look again, he is busy building: he props up his chin with a pillar. Away with it! I don't like that kind of building: for I have heard that a foreign poet has his face thus pillared, beside whom two sentinels are every hour on watch. Bravo! by Hercules, now he is in a fine attitude, like a slave, or a man in a play.'—Mil. Glor. 201-14.

[2] Pseud. 1246.

pied by the unimpassioned monologue or dialogue expressed in senarian iambics. The 'Cantica,' or purely lyrical monologues, are much more frequent and much longer in his comedies than in those of Terence. They were sung to a musical accompaniment, and were composed chiefly in bacchiac, anapaestic, or cretic metres, rapidly interchanging with trochaic lines. The bacchiac metre is employed in passages expressive of some sedate or laboured thought, as, for instance, the opening part of the 'Canticum' of Lysiteles in the Trinummus,—

> Multas res simitu in meo corde vorso,
> Multum in cogitando dolorem indipiscor.
> Egomet me coquo et macero et defatigo.

The anapaestic metre was less suited to Latin, and is rarely met with either in the comic poets, or in the fragments of the tragedians. On the other hand, cretic and trochaic metres, from their affinity to the old Saturnian, came most easily to the early dramatists, and are largely employed by Plautus to express lively emotion. As an instance of the first we may take the following song of a lover, addressed to the bolts which barred his mistress's door,—

> Pessuli, heus pessuli, vos saluto lubens,
> Vos amo vos volo vos peto atque obsecro,
> Gerite amanti mihi morem amoenissumi:
> Fite caussa mea ludii barbari,
> Sussulite, obsecro, et mittite istanc foras,
> Quae mihi misero amanti exbibit sanguinem.
> Hoc vide ut dormiunt pessuli pessumi
> Nec mea gratia conmovent se ocius.[1]

These early efforts of the Italian lyrical muse do not approach the smoothness and ease of the Glyconics and Phalaecians of Catullus, nor the dignity of the Alcaics and Asclepiadeans of Horace: but they do, in a rude kind of

---

[1] 'Hear me, ye bolts, ye bolts, gladly I greet you, I love you, I am fond of you; I beg you, I beseech you, most amiably now comply with the desire of me a lover. For my sake become like foreign dancers; spring up, I beseech you, and send her forth, who now is drinking up the life-blood of me her lover. Mark how these vilest bolts are still asleep, and do not stir one whit on my account.'—Curculio, 147-154.

way, show facility and native power in finding a rhythmical vehicle for the emotion or sentiment of the moment. In the longer passages in which they occur, these metres are generally combined with some form of trochaic verse, which again is often exchanged for septenarian or octonarian iambics. Of the rapid transitions with which Plautus passes from one metre to another in the expression of strong excitement of feeling, we have a striking example in the long recitative of Ballio [1], in which trochaics, septenarian, octonarian, and dimeter, are continually varied by the introduction now of one, now of several, octonarian or septenarian iambics. He thus claims much greater freedom than Terence in the combination of his metres. He exercises also greater licence, in substituting two short for one long syllable (in his cretics and trochaics), and in deviating from the laws of position and hiatus accepted by later poets. It is impossible for a modern reader to reproduce the rhythmical flow of passages which must have depended a good deal for their effect on the musical accompaniment, and on the pronunciation of the actor. Yet even though it requires some effort to recognise the legitimate beat of the rhythm 'digito et aure,' it is equally impossible not to recognise the vigour and vehemence of movement of such passages as these—

> Haec, quom ego a foro revortar, facite ut offendam parata,
> Vorsa sparsa tersa strata lauta structaque omnia ut sint.
> Nam mi hodiest natalis dies: eum decet omnis vos concelebrare.
> Magnifice volo me viros summos accipere, ut rem mi esse reantur.[2]

Terence has a more artistic mastery than Plautus of the ordinary metre of comic dialogue: but the latter has the more original poetic gift of adapting and varying his 'numeri innumeri' to the animated moods and lively fancies of his characters.

---

[1] Pseud. 132-238.
[2] 'See that when I return from the Forum, I find everything ready, the floor swept, sprinkled, polished, the couches covered; the plate all clean and arranged: for this is my birthday: this you must all join in keeping: I want to entertain some great people sumptuously, that they may think I am well to do.'—Pseud. 159-62.

But the gift for which Plautus is preeminent above all the earlier, and in whch he is not surpassed by any of the later poets, is the exuberant vigour and spontaneous flow of his diction. No Roman poet shows more rapidity of conception, or greater variety of illustration: and words and phrases are never wanting to body forth and convey with immediate force and freshness the intuitive discernment of his common sense, the quick play of his wit, the riotous exaggerations of his fancy, his vivid observation of facts and of the outward peculiarities of men, his inexhaustible resources of genial vituperation and execration, or bantering endearment. The mannerisms of his style, already mentioned as indicative of the originality with which he deviates from his Greek models, are not laboured efforts, but the spontaneous products of a rich and comparatively neglected soil. His burlesque invention of proper names, even in its wildest exaggeration, as in the high-sounding title assumed by Sagaristio in the Persa—

> Vaniloquidorus, Virginisvendonides,
> Nugipalamloquides, Argentumexterebronides,
> Tedigniloquides, Nummosexpalponides,
> Quodsemelarripides, Nunquampostreddonides—

is a Rabelaisian ebullition, stimulated by the novel contact with the Greek language, of the formative energy which he displays more legitimately in the creation of new Latin words and phrases. In the freedom with which he uses, without vulgarising, popular modes of speech, in the idiomatic verve of his Latin, employed in an age when inflexions still retained their original virtue, and had not been limited by the labours of grammarians to a fixed standard, he has no equal among Latin writers. It is one of the great charms of the Letters to Atticus, and of the shorter poems of Catullus, that they give us back the flavour of this homely native idiom. Where there is difficulty in interpreting Plautus, this arises either from the uncertainty of the reading, or from the wealth of his vocabulary. He saw clearly and realised strongly what he meant to say, and his words and phrases appeared in rapid, close, and orderly

movement to his summons.   He describes his personages,
—Pseudolus for instance,
>Rufus quidam, ventriosus, crassis suris, subniger.
>Magno capite, acutis oculis, ore rubicundo, ad modum
>Magnis pedibus;[1]

Ballio,
>Cum hirquina barba;

Plesidippus, in the Rudens,
>Adulescentem strenua facie, rubicundum, fortem;

Harpax, in the same play,
>Recalvom ac silonem senem, statutum, ventriosum
>Tortis superciliis, contracta fronte, etc.—

in such a way as to show how real they were to his imagination in their outward semblance as well as in the inward springs of their actions. Or he brings before us some peculiarity in the dress or manner of his personages by some graphic touch, as that of the disguised sycophant of the Trinummus,—
>Pol hic quidem fungino generest : capite se totum tegit.
>Illurica facies videtur hominis : eo ornatu advenit;

and later—
>Mira sunt
>Ni illic homost aut dormitator aut sector zonarius.
>Loca contemplat, circumspectat sese, atque aedis noscitat.[2]

He tells an imaginary story or adventure, such as that which Chrysalus invents of the pursuit of his vessel by a piratical craft—
>Ubi portu eximus, homines remigio sequi,
>Neque aves neque venti citius, etc.[3],

or the account which Curculio gives of his encounter with the soldier[4], tersely, rapidly, and vividly, as if he were recalling some scene within his own recent experience. He imitates the style of tragedy—as in the imaginary speech of the Ghost in the Mostellaria—in such a manner as to

---

[1] 'A red-haired fellow, pot-bellied, with thick legs, darkish, with a big head, keen eyes, a red face, and enormous feet.'

[2] 'By Pollux he is of the mushroom sort : he hides himself with his head : he looks like an Illyrian : he is got up like one ;'—
'I should be surprised if he be not either some dreaming fellow (? al. house-breaker) or a cut purse : he takes a good look of the ground, gazes about him, takes note of the house.'—Trinum. 850-862.

[3] Bacchid. 289.   [4] Curculio, 337, etc.

show that he might have rivalled Ennius in the art of tragic rhythm and expression, if his genius had allowed him to pass beyond the province which was peculiarly his own. His plays abound in pithy sayings which have anticipated popular proverbs, or the happy hits of popular poets in modern times, such as the 'nudo detrahere vestimenta,' in the Asinaria, and the 'virtute formae id evenit te ut deceat quidquid habeas[1],' in the Mostellaria. He writes letters with the forms of courtesy, and with the ease and simplicity characteristic of the best epistles of a later age. His resources of language are never wanting for any call which he may make upon them. In a few descriptive passages he shows a command of the language of forcible poetic imagination. But he does not often betray a sense of beauty in action, character, or Nature: and thus if his style altogether wants the peculiar charm of the later Latin poets, and the tenderness and urbanity of Terence, the explanation of this defect is perhaps to be sought rather in the limited play which he allowed to his finer sensibilities, than in any inability to avail himself of the full capabilities of his native language.

Whether the deficiency in the sense of beauty should deny to him the name of a great poet, is to be answered only when agreement has been attained as to the definition of a poet. He was certainly a true and prodigally creative genius. He is also thoroughly representative of his race—not of the gravity and dignity superinduced on the natural Italian temperament by the strict discipline of Roman life, and by the sense of superiority which arises among the governing men of an imperial state—but of the strong and healthy vitality which enabled the Italian to play his part in history, and of the quick observation and ready resource, the lively emotional and social temperament, the keen enjoyment of life, which are the accompaniment of that original endowment.

[1] Cp. the proverbial 'taking the breeches off a Highlander,' and the lines in one of Burns' earliest songs—

'And then there's something in her gait
Gars ony dress look weel.'

CHAPTER VII.

TERENCE AND THE COMIC POETS SUBSEQUENT TO PLAUTUS.

THE names of five or six comic dramatists are known, who fill the space of eighteen years between the death of Plautus and the representation of the earliest play of Terence, the 'Andria.' From one of these, Aquilius, some verses are quoted, which Varro did not hesitate to attribute to Plautus, and which Gellius characterises as 'Plautinissimi.' They are the words of a parasite, complaining of the invention of sun-dials as inconveniently retarding the dinner hour. Among these writers the most famous was Caecilius Statius, an Insubrian Gaul, first a slave, and afterwards a freedman of a member of the Caecilian house. He is mentioned by Jerome as having been a 'contubernalis' of Ennius,—a term which has been explained as meaning that they were together members of the poets' collegium or club, which met in the temple of Minerva on the Aventine. His poetic career very nearly coincides with that of the epic and tragic poet, and he is said to have died one year after him, in 168 B.C. Some Roman critics ranked him above even Plautus as a poet. The line of Horace—

Vincere Caecilius gravitate, Terentius arte—

probably indicates the ground of their preference. He is said also to have been careful in the construction of his plots[1]. Cicero, who often quotes from him, speaks of him

---

[1] 'In argumento Caecilius poscit palmam,' quoted from Varro.

as having written a bad style[1]. He is also mentioned among those poets who 'powerfully moved the feelings.'

He composed about forty plays. Most of them had Greek titles, and a considerable number of these are identical with the titles of comedies by Menander. Two of the longest of his fragments express with more bitterness and less humour the feelings which husbands in Plautus entertain towards their wives. In one of these passages he has adapted his Greek original to the coarser Roman taste with even less fastidiousness than Plautus generally shows[2]. Another passage, from the Synephebi, is more in the spirit of Terence than of Plautus. It is one in which a young lover complains that the 'good nature' (commoditas) of his father made it impossible to cheat him with an easy conscience. Occasionally we find specimens of those short maxims which probably led the Augustan critics to attribute to him the character of *gravitas*, such as the

Serit arbores quae alteri saeclo prosint,

quoted by Cicero in the Tusculan Questions, and this line—

Saepe est etiam sub palliolo sordido sapientia.

He seems to have had nothing of the creative originality of Plautus, nor ever to have enjoyed the same general popularity. He prepared the way for Terence by a more careful conformity to his Greek models than his predecessor had shown, and, apparently, by introducing a more serious and sentimental vein into his representations of life.

With Terence Roman literature takes a new departure. When he appeared, a younger generation had grown up, who not only inherited the enthusiasm for Greek art and letters of the older generation,—of men of the stamp of the elder Scipio, Æmilius Paulus, T. Quintius Flamininus,—but who had been carefully educated from their boyhood in Greek accomplishments. The leading representative of this younger generation, Scipio Aemilianus, was about the same age as Terence, and admitted him to his intimacy; thus showing in his early youth the same enlightened and

---

[1] Ep. ad Attic. vii. 3; Brutus, 74.
[2] Cf. Mommsen, vol. ii. p. 435, English translation.

tolerant spirit and the same cultivated aspiration which made him choose Panaetius and Polybius as the associates of his manhood, and induced him to live in relations of frank unreserve with Lucilius during the latter years of his life. Among the members of the Scipionic circle, Laelius and Furius Philo were also closely associated with Terence; and he is said to have enjoyed the favour of older men of distinction and culture, Sulpicius Gallus, Q. Fabius Labeo, and M. Popillius, men of consular rank and of literary and poetic accomplishment [1] In the interval between Plautus and Terence, the great gap which was never again to be bridged over had been made between the mass of the people and a small educated class. While the former became less capable of intellectual pleasure, and were beginning to prefer the exhibitions of boxers, rope-dancers, and gladiators[2], to the comedies which had delighted their fathers, the latter became more exacting in their demands for correctness and elegance than the men of a former generation. They had acquired through education the fastidiousness of scholars and men of culture, a quality not easily gained and retained without some sacrifice of native force and popular sympathies. Recognising the immense superiority of the Greek originals in literature to the rude Roman copies, they believed that the best way to create a national Latin literature was to deviate as little as possible, in spirit, form, and substance, from the works of Greek genius. But though cosmopolitan, or rather purely Greek, in their literary tastes, they were thoroughly patriotic in devotion to their country's interests. They cherished their native language as the great instrument of social and political life; and they recognised the influence which a cultivated literature might have in rendering that instrument finer and more flexible than natural use had made it. By concentrating attention on form and style, without aiming at originality of invention, Latin literature might become a truer medium of Greek culture, and might,

---

[1] 'Consulari utroque ac poeta.' Life of Terence, by Suetonius.
[2] Cf. Prologue to the Hecyra.

at the same time, impart a finer edge and temper to the rude ore of Latin speech.

The task which awaited Terence was the complete Hellenising of Roman comedy, and the creation of a style which might combine something of Attic flexibility and delicacy with the idiomatic purity of the Latin spoken in the best Roman houses. By birth a Phoenician, by intellectual education a Greek, by the associations of his daily life a foreigner living in Rome, he was more in sympathy with the cosmopolitan mode of thought and feeling which Greek culture was diffusing over the civilised world, than with the traditions of Roman morality or the homely and genial humours of Italian life. As a dependent and associate of men belonging to the most select society of Rome, he had neither the contact with the many sides of life, nor the familiarity with the animated modes of popular speech, which helped to fashion the style of Plautus: but by assimilating the literary grace of the Athenian comedy and the familiar manner of a friendly, courteous, and active-minded society, he gave to Latin, what the Greek language in ancient and the French in modern times have had preeminently, a style which gives dignity and urbanity to conversation, and freedom and simplicity to literary expression. If the oratorical tastes and training of the Romans make the absence of these last qualities perceptible in much both of their prose and verse, we feel the charm of their presence in the Letters of Cicero, the lighter poems of Catullus, the Epistles of Horace, the Epigrams of Martial: and it was owing to the social and intellectual position of Terence that this secret of combining consummate literary grace with conversational ease and spontaneity was discovered.

The biography of Terence written by Suetonius has been preserved in a complete state; so that in regard to the facts of his life, as of that of Horace and Virgil, we have ampler evidence than is afforded in the case of other writers, of whom the only external record is contained in the short summaries of Jerome. We are enabled to go back to the original and nearly contemporary authorities which Suetonius used in his work 'De viris illustribus.' But the result of this fuller information is to increase the distrust which some of the summaries in Jerome naturally arouse. The authorities are found to be inconsistent with one another in several important points. We find also proof that the grammarians and *littérateurs* of the second century B.C. had a pleasure in chronicling the same kind of scandalous gossip which Suetonius has perpetuated in his lives of the Caesars, and his biographies of Virgil and Horace.

He was born at Carthage in the year 185 B.C.[1], and became the slave of Terentius Lucanus, by whom he was liberally educated and soon emancipated. According to the statement of Porcius Licinus he was ruined in fortune by the intimacy of his noble friends, who did nothing to save him from poverty, and retired in disgust to Greece, where he died, at Stymphalus in Arcadia. The same authority adds that he had not even a lodging in Rome, to which a slave might have brought the news of his death. This account is contradicted by other authorities, who give a more probable reason for his journey into Greece—viz. his desire to become more familiar with the life and manners which he represents. In him we note that impulse to travel, stimulated by artistic enthusiasm, which acted on the great Roman poets of a later time. Other conflicting accounts are given of his death: one, that he was never heard of after sailing from Italy; another, that he was lost at sea, on his return from Greece, along with a number of plays which he had translated from Menander; another, that he died in Arcadia or at Leucadia from grief at the loss of his baggage (including a number of new plays), which he had sent forward by sea by a different route. The account given of the extreme poverty into which the neglect of his friends allowed him to sink is contradicted by the statement that he left behind him a property, consisting of gardens to the extent of twenty acres, close to the Appian Way. It seems also inconsistent with

[1] Another reading makes the date ten years earlier.

the fact that his daughter was so well provided for that she ultimately married a Roman knight. The 'animus' of Porcius Licinus against the members of the Scipionic circle is probably the explanation of the conflicting accounts of the poet's circumstances.

The 'Andria,' his earliest play, was exhibited in 166 B.C., when the poet was eighteen or nineteen years of age. A story is told, that before the play was accepted by the aediles, he was desired to read it to Caecilius; that he came to him at supper, and being meanly dressed ('quod erat contemptiore vestitu'), he sat down on a bench at the foot of his couch; but after reading a few lines he was invited to take his place at the table, and afterwards read the whole play, to the great admiration of the older poet. The story probably owes its origin to the tendency which delights to find a point of contact between the beginning of one literary career and the close of another. It is inconsistent with the date assigned for the death of Caecilius: nor does it seem likely that one, admitted to the intimacy of young men of the highest rank, should have appeared on such an occasion 'contemptiore vestitu.' Perhaps however it may be regarded as quite as worthy of credit as the story of the meeting of Accius with Pacuvius at Brundisium.

The next play in order of composition was the 'Hecyra,' first produced in 165, but withdrawn owing to the bad reception which it met. The 'Hautontimorumenos' appeared in 163, and the 'Eunuchus' and 'Phormio' in 161 B.C.; the second and third representations of the 'Hecyra' and the production of the 'Adelphi' took place in 160. The last was represented at the funeral games of L. Aemilius Paulus. It was in this year that Terence sailed for Greece; and he died in the following year when only twenty-five years of age. Two of his plays, 'Phormio' and 'Hecyra,' were translated from Apollodorus, the rest from Menander.

His art is so purely imitative, that for any knowledge of his circumstances and character we have to trust entirely to his 'prologues,' in which he speaks in his own person.

We note in them his apologetic tone, in marked contrast to the confident hold which Plautus has over his audiences. This tone is to be explained partly, perhaps, by the consciousness of his servile origin and his position as an alien; partly by a sense that his art was not congenial to his audiences. He shows great sensitiveness to criticism, and shields himself from the want of popular applause by the sense of the favour and protection of the great[1]. His attitude to his 'noble friends' is not unlike that of Horace to the higher class of his day; but he seems to want the Italian self-confidence and independence of the son of the Venusian freedman. In the prologue to the 'Adelphi' he refers with pride to the charge made against him that he was assisted by his friends in the composition of his plays—

>   Nam quod isti dicunt malivoli, hominis nobilis
>   Eum adiutare adsidueque una scribere:
>   Quod illi maledictum vemens esse existumant,
>   Eam laudem hic ducit maxumam, quom illis placet,
>   Qui vobis univorsis et populo placent,
>   Quorum opera in bello, in otio, in negotio
>   Suo quisque tempore usus't sine superbia.[2]

Traditions both of Scipio and Laelius show that the report was believed in later times; and as his plays lay no claim to original invention, it is quite possible that he may have been directly assisted by them or by other men of rank in the task of translating and adapting. In any case the style in which they are written seems to reflect the simplicity and urbanity, the friendliness and the freedom from intolerance, though not the more serious interests or the

---

[1] Eunuchus, 1-3:
>   'Si quisquamst, qui placere se studeat bonis
>   Quam plurimis et minime multos laedere,
>   In his poeta hic nomen profitetur suom.'
Hecyra, 46:
>   'Nolite sinere per vos artem musicam
>   Recidere ad paucos.'

[2] 'For as to the charge of these ill-natured people, that men of rank aid him, and constantly write along with him, what they regard as a great reproach he considers the greatest compliment, while he enjoys the favour of those who enjoy the favour of all of you and of the people, whose services in war, in your leisure, in your business, each one of you has availed himself of at his own time without pride.'

graver aspirations of young men who, in their maturer years, had to play the greatest parts in the Roman State. In other passages of his prologues he vindicates himself from the reproach of 'contaminatio,' i.e. the combination of scenes from different plays, and also from that of plagiarising from Naevius and Plautus[1]. He contrasts the sobriety of his own art with the sensationalism of his detractor[2]; and in another place[3], he charges his opponent with having, by his bad style and literal adherence to his original, turned good Greek plays into bad Latin ones—

> Qui bene vortendo et easdem scribendo male
> Ex Graecis bonis Latinas fecit non bonas.

In the prologue to the Andria he professes to imitate the carelessness of Naevius, Plautus, Ennius, rather than the 'obscura diligentia' of his detractors.

All these passages show that he was at war with the survivors of the older generation of playwrights; that he was not a popular poet, in the sense in which Plautus was popular; that he made no claim to original invention, or even original treatment of his materials; that he was however not a mere translator but rather an adapter from the Greek; and that his aim was to give a true picture of Greek life and manners in the purest Latin style. He speaks with the enthusiasm not of a creative genius, but of an imitative artist, inspired by a strong admiration of his models. And this view of his aim is confirmed by the result which he attained. He has none of the purely Roman characteristics of Plautus, in sentiment, allusion, or style[4]; none of his extravagance, and none of his vigour. The law which Terence always imposes on himself is the 'ne quid nimis.' He aims at correctness and consistency, and

---

[1] Eunuchus, Prologue.   [2] Prologue to Phormio, l. 5 etc.
[3] Eunuchus, 7.
[4] We have one or two Latin puns. Such as the play of words in *amentium* and *amantium*, *verba* and *verbera*; one or two cases of alliteration and asyndeton, e.g.—
        'Hic est vietus, vetus, veternosus senex,'—
  and
       'Profundat, perdat, pereat, etc. ;'
but such mannerisms, which abound in Plautus, are extremely rare in the younger poet.

rejects nearly every expression or allusion which might remind his hearers that they were in Rome and not in Athens. His plots are tamer and less varied in their interest than those of Plautus, but they are worked out more carefully and artistically. He takes great pains in the opening scenes to make the situation in which the play begins clear, and he allows the action to proceed to the dénouement through the medium of the natural play of character and motive. As a painter of life it is not by striking effects, but by his truth in detail, and his power of delineating the finer distinctions in varying specimens of the same type, that he gains a hold over the reader. There are no strongly-drawn or vividly conceived personages in his plays, but they all act and speak in the most natural manner: and the powers of intrigue and mystification attributed to his slaves are limited by the ordinary resources of human ingenuity. Characters, circumstances, motives, etc., are all in keeping with a cosmopolitan type of citizen life, courteous and humane, taking the world easily, and outwardly decorous in its pleasures, but without any serious interests, any sense of duty, or any high aspirations.

Terence is, accordingly, in substance and form, a 'dimidiatus Menander,'—a Roman only in his language. The aim of his art was to be as purely Athenian as it was possible for one writing in Latin to be. The life of Athens, in the third century B.C., after the loss of her religious belief, her great political activity, her speculative and artistic energy,—or, rather, one of the phases of that life, as it was shaped by Menander for dramatic purposes—supplies the material of all his plays. It is the embodiment of the lighter side of the philosophy of Epicurus, without the elevation of the speculative and scientific curiosity which gave serious interest even to that form of the philosophic life. There is a charm of friendliness, urbanity, social enjoyment, superficial kindness of heart, in the picture presented: and it was a necessary stage in the culture of the best Romans that they should learn to appreciate this charm, and assimilate its influence in their intercourse with one another.

P

The Greek comedy of Menander was a lesson to the Romans in manners, in tolerance, in kindly indulgence to equals and inferiors, and in the cultivation of pleasant relations with one another. The often quoted line,—

> Homo sum; humani nihil a me alienum puto,

might be taken as its motto. The idea of 'human nature,' in its weakness and in its sympathy with weakness, may be said to be the new element contributed to Roman life by the comedy of Terence. The qualities of 'humanitas, clementia, facilitas,'—general amiability and good nature,—are the virtues which it exemplifies. The indulgence of the old to the follies or pleasures of the young is often contrasted with the stricter view of the obligations of life, entertained by an earlier generation, and always in favour of the former. The plea of the passionate modern poet—

> 'To step aside is human'—

is often urged, but without any feeling that this divergence needs an apology. The hollowness of the social conditions on which this superficial agreeability and humanity rested is revealed by passages in these plays which prove that the habitual comfort of a moderately wealthy class was maintained by the practice of infanticide: and a virtuous wife is represented as begging the forgiveness of her husband for having given her child away instead of ordering it to be put to death[1]. In its outward amenity, as well as its inward hollowness, the social and family life depicted in the comedies of Terence was the very antithesis of the old Roman austere and formal discipline. How far this comedy contributed to the subsequent depravation of Roman character, it is difficult to say. The tone in which pleasure or vice is treated seems too feeble and sentimental to have powerfully stimulated the Roman temperament. The writings of Cicero and Horace show that the receptive Italian intellect was able to extract the elements of courtesy, tolerance, and social amiability out of such a delineation without any loss of native manliness and strength of affection. And

[1] In the Heauton Timorumenos.

thus perhaps, apart from their literary charm, the permanent gain to the world from the comedies of Terence and the philosophy which they embody, has been greater than the immediate loss to the weaker members of the Roman youth who may have been misled by the view of life presented in them.

The motive of all the pieces is love. There is generally a double love-story; one, an attachment, which, if not virtuous in the beginning, has become so afterwards, and which ends in marriage and the discovery that the lady is the daughter of a citizen, who has been exposed or carried away in her infancy; the other, an ordinary intrigue, like those which form the subject of most of the comedies of Plautus. In his treatment of love, Terence may be said to be the precursor of Catullus, Propertius, and Tibullus. He has the serious sense of its pains and pleasures which they display, though he wants the passionate intensity of the two first of these. The greatest attraction of his love passages arises from his tenderness of feeling. In this he is like Tibullus. Although the origin of the sentiment, in most of his plays, is nothing deeper than desire, inspired by outward charms and enhanced by compassion, yet we recognise in him, or in the model which he followed, much more than in Plautus, a belief in and appreciation of constancy and fidelity. In his treatment of his 'amantes ephebi' he shows sympathy with, rather than the humourous superiority to their weaknesses which we find in Plautus. But though there is more grossness in the older poet, yet there is occasionally more real indelicacy in Terence; as in the subject of the 'Eunuchus' and in the acceptance by Phaedria, at the end of that play, of the suggestion of Gnatho, which, in its union of mercenary with sentimental motives, is almost more repugnant to natural feeling than the conclusion of the 'Asinaria' and 'Bacchides.'

The characters in Terence, although more consistent and more true to ordinary life, are more faintly drawn than those of Plautus. None of them stand out in our memory with the distinctness and individuality of

Euclio, Pseudolus, Ballio, or Tyndarus. The want of definite personality which they had to the poet himself is implied in the frequent recurrence of the same names in his different pieces. They are products of analysis and reflexion, not of bold invention and creative sympathy. They are embodiments of the good sense which keeps a conventional society together, or of the tamer impulses by which the surface of that society is temporarily ruffled. The predominant tone in their intercourse with one another is one of urbanity. We find none of the rollicking vituperation and execration in which Plautus revels. The encounter of wits between slaves and fathers is conducted with the weapons of polished irony and mutual deference to one another. Davus, Parmeno, Syrus, Geta, speak with the terse and epigrammatic polish of gentlemen and men of the world.

While the 'Andria' has more pathetic situations, and the 'Adelphi' is on the whole more true to human nature, the 'Eunuchus' presents the greatest number of interesting personages. The Thais of that play is the most favourable delineation of the Athenian 'Hetaera' in ancient literature. She has grace and dignity, a consciousness of her charms combined with a proud humility, and not only kindliness of nature, but real goodness of heart. The natural dignity of her nature, tempered by the sense of her position, appears in her rebuke to Chaerea,—

> Non te dignum, Chaerea,
> Fecisti: nam si ego digna hac contumelia
> Sum maxume, at tu indignus qui faceres tamen;[1]

and her kindness is equally manifest in her ready admission of his excuse,

> Non adeo inhumano ingenio sum, Chaerea,
> Neque ita inperita, ut quid amor valeat, nesciam.[2]

Gnatho is a new and more subtly conceived type of the parasite, and in Thraso the 'Miles Gloriosus' does not

---

[1] 'This act was not worthy of you, Chaerea: for even if it is quite fitting that I should receive such an insult, it was not fitting that it should come from you.'

[2] 'I am not so wanting in natural feeling or so unschooled in its ways as not to know what love is capable of.'

transcend the limits of credibility. Parmeno and Phaedria are natural embodiments of the confidential slave and the weak lover. Their relations to one another are brought out with more delicate irony and finer psychological analysis, though with less vigour than those of Pseudolus and Calidorus, or of Ludus and Pistoclerus in the Pseudolus and Bacchides of Plautus. The Davus, Geta, and Syrus of the other plays are tamer and less humourous than the slaves of Plautus; but they play their part with wit and liveliness, and the rôle which they have to perform is not felt to be incompatible with the ordinary conditions of life. Aeschylus, in the Adelphi, shows a higher spirit and more energy of character than most of the other lovers in Plautus or Terence. The contrast between the genial, indulgent, selfish man of the world, and the harder type of character produced by exclusive devotion to business, is well brought out in the Micio and Demea of the Adelphi, and in the Chremes and Menedemus of the Heauton Timorumenos. The two brothers in the 'Phormio,' Demipho and Chremes, are also happily characterised and distinguished from one another; and Phormio is himself a type of the parasite, as distinct from Gnatho, as he is from the Gelasimus or Curculio of Plautus. The character-painting in Terence is altogether free from the tendency to exaggeration and caricature which is the besetting fault of some of the greatest humourists. Yet with all his truth of detail, his careful avoidance of the extreme forms of villainy, roguery, and inhuman hardness, it may be doubted whether the life represented by Terence is not on the whole more purely conventional than that represented by Plautus. His personages seem to move about in a kind of 'Fools' paradise' without the knowledge either of good or evil. All the sentimental virtues seem to flourish spontaneously, even in the hearts of his courtesans: and the only lesson that seems to be suggested is the duty of overcoming the restraints imposed by prudence and conscience on the indulgence of natural inclination.

If we consider the form, substance, and spirit of these six

plays, we find that their merit consists in the art with which the situation is unfolded and the plot developed, the consistency and moderation with which a conventional view of life and various types of character are set before us, and in the large part played in them by the tender and sympathetic emotions. But their great attraction, both to ancient and modern readers, has been their charm of style. The diction of Terence, while it wants the creativeness and exuberance of Plautus, is free from the mannerisms which accompanied these large endowments of the older poet. He does not attempt to emulate his 'numeri innumeri,' but limits himself almost entirely to those metres which suit the natural flow of placid or more animated conversation, viz. the iambic (senarian or septenarian) and the trochaic septenarian. The effect of his metre is to introduce measure, propriety, grace, and point into ordinary speech without impairing its ease and spontaneousness. The natural vivacity and urbanity of his style is equally apparent in dialogue, or in rapid and picturesque narrative of incidents and pathetic situations[1]. He is full of happy often-quoted sayings, such as

> Hinc illae lacrimae. Amantium irae amoris integratiost.
> Quot homines, tot sententiae.
> Homo sum, humani nihil a me alienum puto.
> Tacent: satis laudant.
> Nosse omnia haec salus est adulescentulis.
> Cantilenam eandem canis—laterem lavem,—etc. etc.

Many of these—such as 'ne quid nimis,' 'ad restim res redit mihi' 'auribus teneo lupum,' etc.—are obviously translations from Greek proverbial sayings; and in all his use of language we may trace the influence of a close observation and sympathetic enjoyment of Greek subtlety, reserve, delicate allusiveness, curious felicity in union with direct simplicity. These qualities of style, reproduced in the purest Latin idiom, had a great influence on the familiar style of Horace. Expressions in his Satires and Epistles, and even in his Odes, show how closely he studied the language of

---

[1] E.g. Andria, 115-136; 282-298; Heauton Timorumenos, 273-301.

Terence[1]. It is from a scene in Terence that Horace takes his example of the weakness of passion[2]; and the mode in which he tells how his father trained him to correct his own faults by observing other men must have been suggested by the conversation between Demea and Syrus in the Adelphi[3]:

De.   Denique
Inspicere tamquam in speculum in vitas omnium
Iubeo atque ex aliis sumere exemplum sibi.
'Hoc facito.' *Sy.* Recte sane. *De.* 'Hoc fugito.' *Sy.* Callide.
De. 'Hoc laudist.' *Sy.* Istaec res est. *De.* 'Hoc vitio datur.'[4]

Again, the remonstrance of Micio to Demea,

Si esses homo,
Sineres nunc facere, dum per aetatem licet,

expresses the philosophy of many of his love poems and his drinking songs. The Epicurean sentiment and reflexion borrowed from Menander were congenial to one side of Horace's nature, as the manly independence and serious spirit of Lucilius were to another: and in his own style he has incorporated the conversational urbanity of the one writer no less than the intellectual vigour of the other. But Horace was much richer and more varied in the subjects of his art, as he was larger and more penetrating in his knowledge of the world, and more manly and serious in his view of life, than the comic poet who died so early in his career. It is as the 'puri sermonis amator' that Terence deserves to be ranked high among Latin authors. The limitation of his ambition to the production of a faithful copy of his original enables us better than any other evidence to appreciate the originality and creative force of Plautus. The absence of all moral fibre in his representations of character and his philosophy of life, makes us feel how necessary the Roman 'gravity' was for the

---

[1] The original of such expressions as—'Appone lucro;' 'Dulce est desipere in loco;' 'Rimosa quae deponuntur in aure;' 'Qua parte debacehentur ignes;' 'Cena dubia;' 'Paucorum hominum et mentis bene sanae;' 'Quam sapere et ringi;' 'Quid non ebrietas designat;'—and others, are to be found in Terence.
[2] Eunuch. A. i. 1; cf. Hor. Sat. ii. 3, 260, etc.   [3] 414, etc.
[4] 'Then I bid him look into the lives of men as into a mirror, and to form for himself an example from others.' 'Do this.' *Sy.* 'Quite right.' *De.* 'Avoid this.' *Sy.* 'Cleverly said.' *De.* 'This is honourable.' *Sy.* 'That is it.' *De.* 'This is discreditable.'

creation of a new literature as well as for the conquest and governing of the world.

After the death of Terence the only writer of *palliatae* of any name was Sextus Turpilius, who died about the end of the second century B.C. No new element seems to have been contributed by him to the Roman Stage. After the decline of the Comoedia palliata, the Comoedia togata, which professed to represent the Roman and Italian life of the middle classes, first obtained popular favour. The principal writers of this branch of comedy were T. Quintius Atta and L. Afranius. The latter was regarded as the Roman Menander :—

> Dicitur Afrani toga convenisse Menandro.

The admiration which he expressed for Terence, whom he regarded as the foremost of all the Roman comic poets, is in keeping with this criticism. From the testimony of Quintilian[1] we may infer that the change of scene from Athens to Rome and the provincial towns of Italy did not improve the morality of the Roman stage. A further decline both in intellectual interest and in moral tendency appeared in the resuscitation in a literary form of the Fabulae Atellanae, the chief writers of which were L. Pomponius and Novius. A still further degradation was witnessed in the later days of the Republic and under the Empire in the rise of the 'Mimus,' as a recognised branch of dramatic literature. If the influence of the comic stage, when its chief representatives were Plautus and Terence, is to be regarded as only of a mixed character, it is difficult to associate any idea of intellectual pleasure with the gross buffooneries of the Atellan farce, when it had passed from the spontaneous hilarity of primitive times into the conditions of an artistic performance, and still less with the 'mimi,' which were intended to gratify the lowest propensities of the spectators. The rapid degeneracy of the mass of the people from the characteristic virtues of the older Republic is testified as much by the popularity of such spectacles as by the passionate delight excited by the gladiatorial combats.

[1] Quint. x. 1, 100.

CHAPTER VIII.

EARLY ROMAN SATIRE—C. LUCILIUS, DIED 102 B.C.

POETICAL satire, as a branch of cultivated literature, arose out of the social and political circumstances, and the moral and literary conditions of Roman life in the last half of the second century B.C. The tone by which that form of poetry has been characterised, in ancient and modern times, is derived from the genius and temper of a remarkable man, belonging to that era, and from the spirit in which he regarded the world. C. Lucilius invented satire, by first imparting a definite purpose to an inartistic kind of metrical composition, in which miscellaneous topics had been treated in accordance with the occasional mood or interests of the writer. Although the satire of Lucilius was rude and unfinished, and evidently retained much of the vague general character belonging to the satura of Ennius, yet he was undoubtedly the first Roman writer who used his materials with the aim and in the manner which poetical satire has permanently assumed. The indigenous satura existing at Rome before the rise of regular literature had been merged partly in the Latin comedy of Naevius, Plautus, Caecilius, etc., partly in the metrical miscellanies of Ennius and Pacuvius, which, though not written for the stage, retained the name of the old scenic medley. The new satire differed from Latin comedy in form and style, and in the personal and national aims which it set before itself. The satire of

Lucilius, and even that of Horace, retained many features in common with the desultory medley which Ennius had formed out of the older satura. But the latter was the parent of no permanent form of literary art. The miscellanies of Varro, the most famous work produced on this model, were composed partly in prose and partly in verse, and were never ranked by the Romans among their poetical works. The former, on the other hand, was the parent of the satire of Horace, of Persius, and of Juvenal, and, through that, of the poetical satire of modern times. The spirit of censorious criticism, in which Lucilius treated the politics and morals, the social manners and the literary taste of his age, has become the essential characteristic of that form of literature which derived its name from the old Italian satura.

Of all the forms of Roman poetry, satire was least indebted to the works of the Greeks. Quintilian claims it altogether for his countrymen—'satira tota nostra est.' Horace characterises it as 'Graecis intacti carminis.' While the names by which they are known at once betray the Greek invention of the other great forms of poetic art, the name of satire alone indicates a Roman origin. It is true that Lucilius, like every educated man of his time, was acquainted with the Greek language and literature. It is true also that the critical spirit in Greece had found vent for itself in the works both of the early iambic writers, Archilochus, Simonides of Amorgos, and Hipponax, and of the great authors of the old political comedy of Athens. But Roman satire sprang up and flourished independently of either of those kinds of composition. In national spirit and moral purpose it was unlike the personal lampoons of the Greek satirists. It was perhaps not less personal, but was more ethical; it professed at least to be animated not by private enmity but by public spirit. It embraced also a much greater variety of topics. Horace finds a closer parallel to the satire of Lucilius in the old Athenian comedy. These two kinds of literature have this in common, that they are the expression of public, not of personal feeling. But though animated by a similar spirit, Roman satire was not imitated from Greek comedy. Each was the independent result of freedom of speech and criticism in different ages and countries. Their difference in form arose out of fundamental differences in the character as well as in the genius of the two nations. Although Roman speakers and writers exercised a licence of speech and of personal criticism equal to that which prevailed in the Athenian democracy, and beyond what the spirit of personal honour tolerates in modern times, yet the exposure of public men to ridicule on the stage was utterly repugnant to the instincts of an aristocratic republic in which one of the great bonds of union was respect for outward authority. The tendency of the Roman mind to reduce all things to rule and to express itself in abstract comments on life, rather than to represent human nature in living forms, also favoured the assumption by Lucilius of a mode of literature addressing itself to the understanding of readers, and not to the sympathies of spectators.

The spirit by which satire is animated was native to Italy. The germ out of which it was developed was the *Fescennina licentia*, or, as it is called by Dionysius, the '$\kappa\acute{\epsilon}\rho\tau o\mu os\ \kappa a\grave{\iota}\ \sigma a\tau v\rho\iota\kappa\grave{\eta}\ \pi a\iota\delta\iota\acute{a}$,' peculiar to the Italian people. But in assuming a regular literary form, this native raillery was tempered by the serious spirit and vigorous understanding of Rome, and liberalised by the tastes and ideas derived from a Greek education. The age in which satire arose,—the age of the Gracchi,—was one of social discontent, of political excitement, of intellectual activity, of moral and religious unsettlement: and all these conditions exercised a powerful influence on its character. As addressed not to the imagination but to the practical understanding, it was in a peculiar manner the literary product of a people 'rebus natus agendis.' It combined the practical philosophy of the 'abnormis sapiens,' expressing itself in proverbial sayings, anecdotes, and homely illustrations; the keen perceptions, the criticism, and vivacity of a circle, educated, well-bred, and versed in affairs; the serious purpose of a moral reformer; and the knowledge of life, which results from the mixed study of men and books. Their circumstances, temper, and pursuits, united these various elements, in different proportions, first in Lucilius, and after him in Horace. By writing what interested themselves, in accordance with their own natural bent, they appealed to the practical and social tastes of their countrymen. While the higher poetical imagination was a rare and exceptional gift among Roman authors, and was appreciated only by a limited class of readers, there was in Roman satire a true popular ring and a close adaptation to the national character, understanding, and circumstances. As the most genuine product of actual Roman life, it was, if not so luxuriant, a more vigorous plant than any other species of Roman poetry. It is seen growing up in hardy vigour under the free air of the Republic, attaining to mature perfection amid the rich intellectual life of the Augustan age, and still fresh and vital in the general intellectual languor and corruption of the Empire.

The Roman character of satire is attested also by the fact that other Roman poets and authors, besides those who professed to follow in the footsteps of Lucilius, have exhibited the satiric spirit. The caustic sense of Ennius, the generous scorn of Lucretius, the license of Catullus, attest their affinity, in some elements of character, to the Roman satirists. There may be remarked also in the best modern works of poetical satire,—such as the Absalom and Achitophel, the Prologue to Pope's Satires, the Vanity of Human Wishes,—a conscious or unconscious echo of that vigorous sense and nervous speech, which accompanied the great practical energy of the Romans.

Satire was not only national in its intellectual and moral characteristics, but it played a part in public life at Rome. Even under the Empire, when free speech and comment on the government were no longer possible, the Roman satirists claimed to perform an office similar in spirit to that which the Republic in its best days had devolved on its most honourable magistracy. But the satire of the Republic, besides performing this magisterial office, played an active part in the politics of the day. It combined the freedom of a tribune with the severity of a censor. It held up to public criticism the delinquencies of leading politicians, and of the mass of the people in their elective divisions,—

> Primores populi arripuit populumque tributim.

Nor was it confined to aggressive criticism: it was used also as an instrument of political partisanship, to paint the virtues of Scipio as well as the vices of his antagonists. It thus performed something of the same kind of public office as the political pamphlet of an earlier time, and the newspaper of the present day.

It endeavoured also, by acting on individual character, to effect objects which the Roman State strove to accomplish by direct legislation. The various sumptuary laws of that age, and the enactments made to repress the study of Greek rhetoric and philosophy, emanated from the same spirit which led Lucilius to denounce the increase of luxury and the affectation of Greek manners among his contemporaries. The strong Roman appetites and the novelty of new studies prevailed alike over the artificial restraints of legislative enactments, and over the contemptuous and the earnest teaching of satire. But the influence of satire could reach further than that of censors or sumptuary laws. While it could brand notorious offenders it was able also to unmask hypocritical pretences—

> Detrahere et pellem, nitidus qua quisque per ora
> Cederet, introrsum turpis.

It could stimulate to virtue as well as denounce flagrant offences. It wielded something of the power of the preacher to produce an inward change in the characters of men. By its close contact with real experience and its close adherence to the national standard of virtue, it might educate men for the duties of citizens more effectually than the teaching of Greek rhetoric or philosophy.

But while satire, from one side, is to be regarded as the directest expression of Roman public life, it was, at the same time, the truest exponent of the character, pursuits, and interests of the individual writer. The old definition of it by a Latin grammarian, 'Carmen maledicum et ad carpenda hominum vitia compositum,' is quite inapplicable to those familiar writings of Horace, in which he gives a pleasant account of his habits and mode of life in town and country, or that in which he humorously narrates his various adventures on his journey to Brundisium. The writings of Horace and Lucilius bore a more varied and miscellaneous character than that of the satire of the Empire or of modern times. Horace expresses his opinions and feelings in the form sometimes of a dialogue, sometimes of a familiar epistle, sometimes of a discourse put into the mouth of another, sometimes of a moral disquisition. He makes abundant use of fables, anecdotes, personal portraiture, real and imaginary, autobiography, and self-analysis. The fragments of Lucilius, and the notices about him in ancient authors, prove that in these respects Horace followed in his footsteps. The testimony of the lines—

<blockquote>Ille velut fidis arcana sodalibus olim, etc.,</blockquote>

implies that Lucilius used his satire as a natural vehicle for expressing everything that interested him, in his own life and in the circumstances of his time. In regard to the miscellaneous nature of the topics treated by him, and the frankness of his personal revelations, his truest modern parallel is Montaigne,—the father of the prose essay, which has performed the function of the older Roman satire more completely than even the poetical satire of modern times.

Among the poets of the Republic, whose works have reached us only in fragments, Lucilius is only second in importance to Ennius. Roman Satire owes as much in form, substance, and spirit to him as the Roman epic does to the older poet. While Ennius represents the highest mood of Rome, and first gave expression to that imperial idea which ultimately realised itself in history, Lucilius is the exponent of her ordinary moods, manifested in the streets and the forum, and of those internal dissensions and destructive forces by which her political life was agitated and ultimately overthrown. His personal characteristics and literary position can be inferred with nearly as much certainty as those of Ennius. The most important external evidence from which we form our idea of him is that of Horace and Cicero. But the numerous fragments of his writings bear a strong impress of his personality. From the confirmation which they give to other testimonies, we may endeavour to recover some of the lines and colours of that 'votiva tabula' which the contemporaries of Horace found in his books, and to realise the nature of the work performed by him and of the influence which he exercised over his countrymen.

The time at which he appeared was one of the most critical epochs in Roman history, the end of one great era,—that of the undisputed ascendency of the Senate,—the beginning of the century of revolution which ended with the Battle of Actium. The mind of the nation began then to turn from the monotonous spectacle of military conquest and to busy itself with the conditions of internal well-being. A spirit of discontent with these, similar to that which called forth the legislation of the Gracchi, opened up a new path for Latin literature. It began then to concern itself, not with the national idea of conquest and empire, but with the actual condition of men. It sought for its material, not in the representation which had been fashioned by Greek dramatic art out of the heroic legends of early Greece or the citizen life of her later days, but out of the every day life of the Roman streets, law-courts, public assemblies, dinner-tables, and literary coteries, and out of the baser details of actual experience by which the magnificent ideal of Roman greatness was largely qualified. Though there is considerable difficulty in accepting the dates usually assigned for the birth and death of Lucilius, there is no reason to doubt that his active literary career began about the time of the tribunates of Tib. Gracchus, and continued till nearly the end of the first century B.C. This period is so important and interesting that such glimpses of light as are afforded by the fragments of the contemporary satirist are highly to be prized.

The dates of his birth and death, according to Jerome, were 148 B.C. and 102 B.C. We are told, on the same authority, that he died at Naples and received the honour of a public funeral. The chief difficulty in accepting these dates arises from the statement of Velleius that Lucilius served as an 'eques' under Scipio in the Numantine War[1], and from the fact, attested by Horace and other authorities, of his great intimacy with both Scipio and Laelius[2]. Horace also mentions that he celebrated in his writings the justice and valour of Scipio,—

> Attamen et iustum poteras et scribere fortem
> Scipiadem ut sapiens Lucilius—;

and the parallel there suggested between the relation of Lucilius to the great soldier and statesman of his age, and of Horace to Augustus, would be inappropriate unless the praises there spoken of had been bestowed on Scipio in his life-time. Fragments from one book of the Satires appear to be parts of a letter written by Lucilius to congratulate his friend on the capture of Numantia[3]. One line of Book xxvi,—

> Percrepa pugnam Popilli, facta Corneli cane,

contrasts the defeat of M. Popillius Laenas in 138 B.C. with the subsequent successes of Scipio. In another fragment Lucilius charges Scipio with affectation for pronouncing

---

[1] Vell. Paterc. ii. 9. The service of Lucilius in Spain seems to be confirmed by a line in one of his Satires:—
> 'Publiu' Pavu' mihi [   ] quaestor Hibera
> In terra fuit, lucifugus, nebulo, id genu' sane.'

[2] Hor. Sat. ii. 1. 71-5.

[3] Cf. L. Müller's edition of the Fragments.

the word 'pertaesum' as if it were pertisum[1]. He is also mentioned as one of those whose criticism Lucilius dreaded[2]. These and other passages must have been written in the life-time of Scipio—i.e. before 129 B.C. Thus, if the date assigned for the birth of Lucilius is correct, he must have served in the Numantine War at the age of fourteen or fifteen, he must have been admitted into the most intimate familiarity with the greatest man of the age, and must have composed some books of his Satires, and thus introduced a new form of literature, before the age of nineteen. L. Müller in his edition of the Fragments adduces other considerations for rejecting the dates given by Jerome, such as the allusions to the career of Lupus (whom he supposes to be the same as the Censor of 147 B.C.) and to the war with Viriathus. He holds also that the words of Horace—

> Quo fit ut omnis
> Votiva pateat veluti descripta tabella
> Vita senis—

lose their point, unless *senis* is to be understood in its usual sense. He supposes that the mistake of Jerome arose from a similarity in the names of the Consuls of 148 B.C. and 180 B.C., and would therefore throw the date of the poet's birth more than thirty years further back than that commonly received.

Whatever strength there may be in the other objections urged against accepting the date 148 B.C. as that of the birth of Lucilius, it is difficult to believe that Lucilius should have taken part in the Numantine War, and been admitted to apparently equal intimacy with Scipio before he had attained the age of fifteen. It is still more difficult to suppose that the earliest book or books of his Satires, composed before the death of Scipio, should be the work

---

[1] 'Quo facetior videare et scire plus quam caeteri
Pertisum hominem, non pertaesum dices.'
The comment of Festus shows that these words were addressed by Lucilius to Scipio.

[2] Cic. de Fin. i. 3.

of a boy under nineteen years of age. But with these admissions it is not necessary to throw back the date of the poet's birth so far as is done by Müller. A more probable explanation of the error in the date is suggested by Mr. Munro in a recent number of the Journal of Philology. He supposes that Jerome in copying the words of Suetonius referring to the death and funeral of Lucilius substituted the 'anno aetatis xlvi. for lxiv. or lxvi., and then adapted the year of birth to the 'annus Abrahae which would correspond to this false reading.' Mr. Munro adds, 'Everything would now run smooth. Lucilius when he went with Scipio to Spain, would be in the prime of manhood, thirty-two or thirty-four years of age. Soon after that time he would be writing and publishing his earliest Books, xxvi.–xxix., and then xxx. Some of these at all events would be published before the death of Scipio, when the poet would be thirty-seven or thirty-nine[1].' It may be added against the supposition that Lucilius was born in the year 180 B.C., that, in that case, we should have expected to have found in his numerous fragments allusions to events even earlier than the Censorship of P. Cornelius Lupus or the wars with Viriathus. Moreover the notices of his relation to Scipio and Laelius, as in the 'discincti ludere' of Horace, and in the story told by the Scholiast on that passage, of Laelius coming on them, when the poet was chasing Scipio round the table with a napkin, seem to indicate the familiar footing of a much younger to older men.

His birth-place was Suessa Aurunca in Campania. Juvenal calls him 'Auruncae magnus alumnus.' He belonged to the equestrian order, a fact indicated in the passage in which Horace speaks of himself as 'infra Lucili censum.' The Scholiast on that passage mentions that he was on the mother's side grand-uncle to Pompey—a relationship confirmed by a passage in Velleius, who mentions that the mother of Pompey was named Lucilia.

His satires were written in thirty Books. The remain-

[1] Journal of Philology, vol. viii. 16.

ing fragments amount to about 1100 lines. Most of these are single lines, preserved by grammarians as illustrative of the use of words. The amount and variety of these, if they had no other value, would at least be suggestive of the industry with which grammatical and philological research into their own language was carried on by Roman writers. Some fragments are found in ancient commentaries on the Satires and Epistles of Horace. The longer passages are quoted by Cicero, Gellius, Lactantius, and others. The Books from i. to xx. were written in hexameters; Book xxii., apparently, in elegiacs, a metre which had hitherto been employed only in short epigrams. Of the intervening Books between xxii. and xxvi. there remains only one line[1]. Books xxvi. and xxix., from which a large number of lines have been preserved, were written in trochaics and iambics. The last Book (xxx.) was written in hexameters. From the fact that the trochaic and iambic metres had been chiefly employed by the older writers of saturae, it seems probable that Lucilius made his first attempts in these metres, that he afterwards adopted the hexameter, and that in one or two of his latest books he attempted to write continuously in elegiacs. The allusions in Book xxvi. to the Spanish wars and to the 'exploits of Cornelius,' and the statement of his reasons for coming forward as an author, render it not improbable that this Book was the earliest in order of composition. It was in this Book that he appeared most conspicuously as the censor and critic of the older writers, a position not unlikely to have been assumed, at the very outset of his career, by one who claimed to initiate a change in Roman literature.

The first impression produced by reading these fragments, as they have been arranged by Müller or Lachmann, is one of extreme desultoriness and discursiveness of treatment. The words applied by Horace to Lucilius,—

Garrulus atque piger scribendi ferre laborem,

[1] 'Iucundasque puer qui lamberat ore placentas'
One of many lines imitated and almost reproduced by Horace.

characterise not his style only but his whole mode of composition. Subjects most widely removed from one another seem to have been introduced into the same book. We have no means of determining whether the separate books consisted of one or several miscellaneous pieces. He seems to start off on some new chase on the slightest suggestion, verbal or otherwise, as in the opening of Book v.—

> Quo me habeam pacto, tametsi non quaeri', docebo,
> Quando in eo numero mansti, quo in maxima nunc est
> Pars hominum,
> Ut periise velis quem visere nolueris, cum
> Debueris. Hoc nolueris et debueris te
> Si minu' delectat, quod τεχνίον Isocratium est,
> Ληρῶδέsque simul totum ac συμμειρακιῶδες,
> Non operam perdo.[1]

We cannot accordingly expect to trace in them anything of the unity of purpose, the formal discourse and illustration of a set topic, which characterise the Satires of Persius and Juvenal, nor yet, of the apparently artless, but carefully meditated ease with which Horace, in his Satires, reproduces the manner of cultivated conversation. Lucilius adopts many modes of bringing himself into relations with his reader. Sometimes he speaks of himself by name, and appears to be communing with himself on his own fortunes or feelings. Sometimes he carries on a controversy in the form of dialogue; at other times he addresses the reader directly; or again, he puts a discourse in the mouth of another, as that on the luxury of the table in the mouth of Laelius. He makes frequent use of the epistolary form—a form which in prose and verse became one of the happiest products of Roman literature. He employs fables, quotations, and parodies, to illustrate his subject. He gives a narrative of his travels, and describes scenes and

---

[1] 'I will tell you how I am, though you don't ask me, since you are of the fashion of most men now, and would rather that the man whom you did not choose to visit, when you ought, had died. If you don't like this "nolueris" and "debueris," because it is the trick of Isocrates, and altogether nonsensical and puerile, I don't waste my time on the matter.' This passage illustrates two characteristics of Lucilius—his habit of mixing Greek with Latin words, and the attention he bestowed on technical rules of style.

incidents at which he was present, such as a fight between two gladiators, a rustic feast, and a storm which he encountered in his voyage to Sicily. In other places he plays the part of a moralist, and discourses to a friend on the nature of virtue. More frequently he takes on himself the special office of a censor, and assails the vices of the day by direct denunciation and living examples. In other places he appears as a literary critic and a dictator on questions of grammar and orthography.

In Book i., dedicated to Aelius Stilo the grammarian, a council of the gods was introduced, debating how the Roman State was still to be preserved; and some of the most notorious men of the time were exposed by name to public reprobation. Book iii. contained an account of the author's journey from Rome to the Sicilian Strait, and has been imitated by Horace in his journey to Brundisium. From the line—

> Mantica cantheri costas gravitate premebat[1]—

it appears that some part of the journey was made on horseback, but other lines [2] show that the latter part was made by water, and that a severe storm was encountered on the voyage. In Book iv., imitated by Horace (Sat. ii. 2), and by Persius in his third satire, was included the discourse of Laelius against gluttony. In this book mention was made of the sturgeon which gained notoriety for Gallonius[3]. Book v. contained a letter to a friend of the poet, who had neglected to visit him when ill. Book ix. was composed of a dissertation on questions of grammar, ortho-

---

[1] Imitated by Horace in the lines:—
'Nunc mihi curto
Ire licet mulo, vel, si libet, usque Tarentum,
Mantica cui lumbos onere ulceret, atque eques armos.'

[2] 'Promontorium remis superamu' Minervae.—
Hinc media remis Palinurum pervenio nox.—
Tertius hic mali superat decumanis fluctibus—carchesia summa.'

[3] Hor. Sat. ii. 2. 46:—
'Haud ita pridem
Galloni praeconis erat acipensere mensa
Infamis.'

graphy, and criticism. Book xi. treated of the wars in Spain and Transalpine Gaul, and contained criticisms and anecdotes of various public men. Book xvi. was named 'Collyra,' in honour of the poet's mistress. In other books the castigation of particular vices formed a prominent topic, and some of the latest (probably the earliest in the order of composition), were largely filled with personal explanations and with criticisms of the older poets. But the desultory, discursive, self-communing character seems to have been common to all of them; and it would be contrary to our evidence to speak of any single book as composed on a definite plan, or as treating of a special topic.

The fragments however, when read collectively, bring out the main sources of interest which the Romans found in the writings of Lucilius; first, the interest of a self-portraiture and close personal relation established with the reader[1]: second, the interest of a censorious criticism on politics, morals, and literature[2].

Among the personal indications of the author we note the great freedom and independence of his life and character. In his mode of expressing this freedom and independence he reminds us of Horace, who seems to have imitated him in his view of life as well as in his writings. Thus, Lucilius declares his indifference to public employment, and his unwillingness to change his own position for the business of the Publicani of Asia, just as Horace declares that he would not exchange his leisure for all the wealth of Arabia[3]. Like Horace, he speaks of the joy of escaping from the storms of life into a quiet haven

[1]   'Quo fit ut omnis
 Votiva pateat veluti descripta tabella
 Vita senis.'
[2]   'Secuit Lucilius urbem—
 Primores populi arripuit populumque tributim—
 Non ridet versus Enni gravitate minores—?'
[3] 'Mihi quidem non persuadetur publiceis mutem meos.
 Publicanu' vero ut Asiae fiam scriptuarius
 Pro Lucilio, id ego nolo, et uno hoc non muto omnia.'
Cf. Hor. Ep. i. 7. 36;
       'Nec
 Otia divitias Arabum liberrima muto.'

of repose[1], or inculcates contentment with one's own lot[2] and immunity from envy[3], and the superiority of plain living to luxury[4]. Like Horace, while holding to his independence of life, he put a high value on friendship, and strove to fulfil its duties[5]. Like him, while condemning excess and weakness, he did not conform to any austerer standard of morals than that of the world around him. Like Horace, too, in his later years, he seems to have been something of a valetudinarian[6], and to have had much of the self-consciousness which accompanies that condition. On the whole the impression we get of him is that of an independent, self-reliant character,—of a man living in strong contact with reality, taking all the rubs of life cheerfully[7],—enjoying society, travelling[8], the exercise of his art[9],—a warm friend and partisan, and a bold and uncompromising enemy,—not professing any austerity of life, but knowing and following the course which gave his own nature most satisfaction[10], while, at the same time,

---

[1] 'Quadque te in tranquillum ex saevis transfers tempestatibus.'
[2] 'Nam si quod satis est homini, id satis esse potisset
Hoc sat erat; nam cum hoc non est, qui credimu' porro
Divitias ullas animum mi explere potisse.'
[3] 'Nulli me invidere: non strabonem fieri saepius
Deliciis me istorum.'
[4] 'O lapathe, ut jactare nec es sati cognitu' qui sis—
Quod sumptum atque epulas victu praeponis honesto.'
[5] 'Munifici comesque amicis nostris videamur viri—
Sic amici quaerunt animum, rem parasiti ac ditias.'
Among the friends of Lucilius, besides Scipio and Laelius, were Aelius Stilo, Albinus, and Granius, whom Cicero quotes for his wit.
[6] 'Querquera consequitur capitisque dolores
Infesti mihi.—
Si tam corpu' loco validum ac regione maneret.
Scriptoris quam vera manet sententia cordi.'
[7] 'Verum haec ludus ibi susque omnia deque fuerunt,
Susque et deque fuere, inquam, omnia ludu' iocusque.'
[8] 'Et saepe quod ante
Optasti, freta Messanae, Regina videbis
Moenia.'
[9] 'Quantum haurire animus Musarum ec fontibu' gestit.'
[10] 'Cum sciam nil esse in vita proprium mortali datum
Jam qua tempestate vivo chresin ad me recipio.'
Cf. 'Vitaque mancipio nulli datur, omnibus usu.'

upholding a high standard of public duty and personal honour[1].

This establishment of a personal relation with his readers was one of the most original elements in the Lucilian satire. He was the first of Roman, and one of the first among all, writers, who took the public into his confidence, and gained their ear, without exposing himself to contempt, by making a frank and unreserved display of his inmost and most personal thoughts and feelings. Had his works reached us entire, we should probably have found the same kind of attraction in them, from the sense of familiar intimacy with a man of interesting character and intelligence, which we find in the Epistles of Cicero and the Satires and Epistles of Horace.

His independent social position, and the character of the times in which he lived, enabled him to perform the office of a political satirist with more freedom than any other Roman writer. He belonged to the middle party between the extreme partisans of the aristocracy and of the democracy, the party of Scipio and Laelius, and that to which Cicero, in a later age, naturally inclined. He directed his satire against the corruption, incapacity, and arrogance[2] of the nobles by whom the wars abroad and affairs at home were mismanaged. His service under Scipio, and his admiration of his generalship, made him keenly sensitive to the disgrace incurred by the Roman arms under 'the limping Hostilius and Manius[3],' and in the war against Viriathus. Among those assailed by him on political grounds, L. Hostilius Tubulus, notorious for openly receiving bribes while presiding at a trial for murder, and C. Papirius Carbo, the friend of Tib. Gracchus and the suspected murderer of Scipio, were conspicuous. The more reputable names of Q. Caecilius Metellus Macedonicus and Mucius Scaevola are also mentioned among the objects of his

[1] Cf. Virtus, Albine, etc. Infra, p. 240.
[2] 'Peccare impune rati sunt
   Posse et nobilitate procul propellere iniquos.'
[3] 'Hostiliu' contra
   Pestem permitiemque catax quam et Maniu' nobis.'

satire[1]. Personal motives—and especially his devotion to Scipio[2]—may have stimulated these animosities; but there were instances enough of incapacity in war, profligacy and extortion in the government of the provinces, corruption and favouritism in the administration of justice, venality and ignorance in the electoral bodies, to justify the bold exposure by Lucilius of 'the leading men of the State and of the mass of the people in their tribes.' The personality of his attacks probably made him many enemies; and thus we hear that he was assailed by name on the stage, and was unable to obtain redress, while a writer who had taken a similar liberty with the tragic poet Accius was condemned. But the honour of a public funeral awarded to him at his death would indicate that the final verdict of his contemporaries was that in assuming the censorial function of attaching marks of infamy against the names of eminent men he was actuated, in the main, by worthy motives, and had done good service to the State.

The chief social vices which Lucilius attacks are those which reappear in the pages of the later satirists. They are the two extremes to which the Roman temperament was most prone, rapacity and meanness in gaining money, vulgar ostentation and coarse sensuality in using it[3]. These were opposite results of a sudden influx of wealth among a people trained through many generations to habits of thrift and self-restraint, and, through this accumulated vital force, unaccompanied, as it was, with much capacity for refined enjoyment, animated by a strong craving for the coarser enjoyments of life. The intensity

[1] Cf. Cic. De Or. i. 16:—'Sed ut solebat C. Lucilius saepe dicere, homo tibi (i. e. Scaevolae) subiratus, mihi propter eam causam minus quam volebat familiaris, sed tamen et doctus et perurbanus.'
Hor. Sat. ii. 1. 67:—
'Aut laeso doluere Metello
Famosisque Lupo cooperto versibus?'
Pers. i. 115:—
'Secuit Lucilius urbem
Te Lupe, te Muci.'
[2] 'Fuit autem inter P. Africanum et Q. Metellum sine acerbitate dissensio.'
[3] Cf. 'Diversisque duobus vitiis, avaritia et luxuria civitatem laborare.'—Livy, xxxiv. 4.

and concentrativeness of the Roman temperament also tended to produce those one-sided types of character, which are the favourite objects of satiric portraiture. The parasites and spendthrifts, the misers and money-makers of Horace's Satires and Epistles, Maenius and Avidienus for instance, are among the most strongly marked of his personal sketches. Lucilius witnessed the same tendencies in his time and exposed them with greater freedom. The names which are typical of certain characters in Horace, such as Nomentanus, Pantolabus (probably a nickname) Maenius and Gallonius, had first been taken by Lucilius from the streets and dinner-tables of Rome. This indifference to the claims of personal feeling, in which Lucilius emulates the license of the old Greek comedy, although sanctioned by the approval of Horace in a poet of an earlier age, would probably have been forbidden by the greater urbanity and decorum of the Augustan age.

The excesses of his contemporaries in the way of good living, against which numerous sumptuary laws, (the Lex Fannia and Lex Licinia for instance), enacted in that age, vainly contended, were largely satirised by Lucilius. Such passages as these—

> O Publi, O gurges Galloni, es homo miser, inquit,
> Cenasti in vita numquam bene, quom omnia in ista
> Consumis squilla atque acipensere quum decumano.
> Hoc fit item in cena, dabis ostrea millibu' nummum
> Empta.
> Occidunt, Lupe, saperdae te et iura siluri.
> Vivite lurcones, comedones, vivite ventres.
> Illum sumina ducebant atque altilium lanx
> Hunc pontes Tiberinu' duo inter captu' catillo.
> Purpureo tersit tunc latas gausape mensas, etc.[1]

[1] 'O Publius Gallonius, thou whirlpool of excess; thou art a miserable man, says he; never in thy life hast thou supped well, since thou spendest all thy substance in that lobster of thine and that monstrous sturgeon.'
'This too is the case at dinner, you will give oysters, bought at a thousand sesterces.'
'Sardines and fish-sauce are your death, O Lupus.'
'Long live, ye gluttons, gourmands, belly-gods.'
'One was attracted by sow-teats and a dish of fatted fowls; another by a gourmandising pike caught between the two bridges.'

show the proportions already assumed by a form of sensuality, the beginnings of which may be traced in Plautus and in the publication of the Hedyphagetica of Ennius, but of which the final culmination is to be sought in the ideal of life realised under the Empire, by Apicius, Vitellius, and Elagabalus, and many men of less note.

The other extreme of unceasing activity in getting, and sordid meanness in hoarding money, and the discontent produced among all classes by the restless passion to grow rich, which fills so large a place in the Satires and Epistles of Horace, appears also frequently in the fragments of Lucilius; as, for instance, in the following :—

> Milia dum centum frumenti tolli medimnum,
> Vini mille cadum.—
> Denique uti stulto nihil est satis, omnia cum sint.—
> Rugosi passique senes eadem omnia quaerunt.—
> Mordicus petere aurum e flamma expediat, e caeno cibum.—
> Aquam te in animo habere intercutem.[1]

The following description of a miser seems to have suggested the beginning of one of Catullus' lampoons[2] :—

> Cui neque iumentumst nec servos nec comes ullus,
> Bulgam et quidquid habet nummum secum habet ipse,
> Cum bulga cenat, dormit, lavit; omnis in unast
> Spes homini bulga. Bulga haec devincta lacertost.[3]

In other passages he inculcates the lessons of good sense and moderation in the use of money, or urges, in the person of an objector, that a man is regarded in proportion to the estimate of his means. In his enumeration of the various constituents of virtue, one on which he dwells with

---

'Then he wiped the ample table with a purple cloth.'
The two last passages are reproduced by Horace in the lines:—

> 'Unde datum sentis, lupus hic Tiberinus, an alto
> Captus hiet, pontesne inter iactatus, an amnis
> Ostia sub Tusci?'—Sat. ii. 2. 31.

And

> 'Gausape purpureo mensam pertersit.'—Ib. ii. 8. 11.

[1] Cf. 'Crescit indulgens sibi dirus hydrops,' etc.
[2] 'Furei cui neque servus est neque arca,' etc.
[3] 'Who has neither beast, or slave, or attendant; he carries about him his purse and all his money; with his purse he sleeps, dines, bathes—his whole hopes centre in his purse; this purse is fastened to his arm.'

emphasis, is the right estimation of the value of money. In all his thoughts and expressions on this subject it is easy to see how closely Horace follows on his traces.

The extravagance, airs, and vices of women, are another theme of his satire. But he deals with these topics rather in the spirit of raillery adopted by Plautus, than in that of Juvenal. In one fragment he compares, in terms neither delicate nor complimentary, the pretensions to beauty of the Roman ladies of his time with those of the Homeric heroines. In another he contrasts the care which they take in adorning themselves when expecting the visits of strangers with their indifference as to their appearance when alone with their husbands,—

> Cum tecumist, quidvis satis est: visuri alieni
> Sint homines, spiras, pallam, redimicula promit.[1]

Another fragment—

> Homines ipsi hanc sibi molestiam ultro atque aerumnam offerunt,
> Ducunt uxores, producunt quibus haec faciant liberos,—

indicates the same repugnance to marriage, which is expressed in a fragment of contemporary oratory, quoted by A. Gellius: 'If, Quirites, we could get on at all without wives, we should all keep clear of that nuisance; but since, in the way of nature, life cannot go on comfortably with them, nor at all without them, we ought rather to provide for the continued well-being of the world than for our temporary comfort.' The dislike to incur the responsibilities of family life, which appears so conspicuously among the cultivated classes in the later times of the Republic, was probably, if we are to judge from the testimony and examples of Lucilius and Horace, as much the result of the license allowed to men, as of the extravagant habits or jealous imperiousness of women.

The intellectual, as well as the moral and social peculiarities of the age were noted by Lucilius. One fragment is directed against the terrors of superstition, and shows

---

[1] Cp. the speech of Cato (Livy, xxxiv. 4) in support of the Oppian law:—
'An blandiores in publico quam in privato, et alienis quam vestris estis?'

that Lucilius, like all the older poets, was endowed with that strong secular sense which enabled the educated Romans, notwithstanding the forms and ceremonies of religion encompassing every private and public act, to escape, in all their ordinary relations, from supernatural influences. This passage affords a fair specimen of the continuous style of the author :—

> Terriculas Lamias, Fauni quas Pompiliique
> Instituere Numae, tremit has, hic omnia ponit;
> Ut pueri infantes credunt signa omnia ahena
> Vivere, et esse homines; et sic isti omnia ficta
> Vera putant, credunt signis cor inesse in ahenis;
> Pergula pictorum, veri nihil, omnia ficta.[1]

His attitude to philosophy, like his attitude to superstitious terrors, was not unlike that of Horace. We find mention in his fragments of the 'Socratici charti,' of the 'eidola atque atomus Epicuri' of the four στοιχεῖα of Empedocles, of the 'mutatus Polemon,' spoken of in Horace (Sat. ii. 3, 253), of Aristippus, and of Carneades; but his own wisdom was that of the world and not of the schools. In these lines,—

> Paenula, si quaeris, canteriu', servu', segestre,
> Utilior mihi, quam sapiens;

and—

> Nondum etiam, qui haec omnia habebit,
> Formosus, dives, liber, rex solu' feretur,

we find an anticipation of the tones in which Horace satirised the professors of Stoicism in his own time. The affectation of Greek manners and tastes is ridiculed in the person of Titus Albutius, in a passage which Cicero describes as written 'with much grace and pungent wit[2].'

> Graecum te, Albuci, quam Romanum atque Sabinum,
> Municipem Ponti, Tritanni, Centurionum,

[1] 'These bugbears and goblins from the days of the Fauni and Numa Pompilius fill him with terror; he believes anything of them. As children suppose that statues of brass are real and living men, so they fancy all these delusions to be real: they believe that there is understanding in brazen images: mere painter's blocks, no reality, all a delusion.' Cf. Horace, Ep. ii. 2. 208 :—
> 'Somnia, terrores magicos, miracula, sagas,
> Nocturnos lemures portentaque Thessala rides?'

[2] De Fin. i. 3.

> Praeclarorum hominum ac primorum signiferumque,
> Maluisti dici. Graece ergo praetor Athenis,
> Id quod maluisti, te, cum ad me accedi,' saluto:
> Chaere, inquam, Tite. Lictores turma omni' cohorsque
> Chaere, Tite. Hinc hostis mi, Albucius, hinc inimicus.[1]

We learn from Cicero's account of the orators antecedent to, and contemporary with himself, that this denationalising fastidiousness was a not uncommon result of the new studies. The practice of Lucilius of mixing Greek words and phrases with his Latin style might, at first sight, expose him to a similar criticism. But this mannerism of style, which is condemned by the good sense of Horace, is merely superficial, and does not impair the vigorous nationality of the sentiment expressed by the Roman satirist. Like the similar practice in the Letters of Cicero, it was probably in accordance with the familiar conversational style of men powerfully attracted by the interest and novelty of the new learning, but yet strong enough in their national self-esteem to adhere to Roman standards in all the greater matters of action and sentiment. Lucilius seems however to recognise a deeper mischief than that of mere literary affectation in the general insincerity of character produced by the rhetorical and sophistical arts fostered by the new studies, and finding their sphere of action in the Roman law-courts.

The satire of Lucilius, besides its political, moral, and social function, assumed the part of a literary critic and censor. The testimony of Horace on this point,—

> Nil comis tragici mutat Lucilius Acci?
> Non ridet versul Enni gravitate minores,
> Cum de se loquitur non ut maiore reprensis?

confirmed by that of Gellius[2], is amply borne out by

---

[1] 'You preferred, Albucius, to be called a Greek, rather than a Roman or Sabine, a fellow-countryman of the Centurions, Pontius, Tritannius, excellent, first-rate men, and our standard-bearers. Accordingly, I, as praetor of Athens, when you approach me, greet you, as you wished to be greeted. "Chaere," I say, Titus; my lictors, escort, staff, address you with "Chaere." Hence you are to me a public and private enemy.'

[2] 'Et Pacuvius, et Pacuvio jam sene Accius, clariorque tunc in poematis eorum obtrectandis Lucilius fuit.'

extant fragments. These criticisms formed a large part of the twenty-sixth book, which Müller supposes to have been the earliest of the compositions of Lucilius. Several lines preserved from that book are either quotations or parodies from the old tragedies[1]. We observe in these and other quotations the peculiarities of style, noticed in the two tragic poets, such as their tendencies to alliteration and the use of asyndeta, the strained word-formations of Pacuvius, and the occasional inflation of Accius[2]. We trace the influence of these criticisms in the sneer of Persius,—

> Est nunc Briseis quem venosus liber Acci,
> Sunt quos Pacuviusque et verrucosa moretur
> Antiopa, aerummis cor luctificabile fulta.

The antagonism displayed by Lucilius to the more ambitious style of the tragic and epic poets was perhaps as much due to his own deficiency in poetical imagination, as to his keen critical discernment, the 'stili nasus' or 'emunctae nares' attributed to him by Pliny and Horace.

The criticism of Lucilius was not only aggressive, but also directly didactic. In the ninth book he discussed, at considerable length, disputed questions of orthography; and a passage is quoted from the same book, in which a distinction is drawn out between 'poëma' and 'poësis.' Under the first he ranks—

---

[1] E.g. 'Ego enim contemnificus fieri et fastidire Agamemnona.—
Di monerint meliora, amentiam averruncassint tuam.—
Hic cruciatur fame,
Frigore, inluvie, inperfundie, inhalnite, incuria.—
Nunc ignobilitas his mirum, taetrum, ac monstrificabile—
Dividant, differant, dissipent, distrahant.'

[2] In the same spirit is the following line:—
'Verum tristis contorto aliquo ex Pacuviano exordio.'
And this from another book of Satires:—
'Ransuro tragicus qui carmina perdit Oreste.'
Among the phrases of Ennius at which Lucilius carped was one which Virgil did not disdain to adopt. The passage of the old poet,—
'Hastis longis campus splendet et horret,'—
parodied by the Satirist in the form 'horret et alget,' was justified by being reproduced in the Virgilian phrase,
'Tum late ferreus hastis
Horret ager.'

Epigrammation, vel
Distichum, epistula item quaevis non magna;

under the second, whole poems, such as the Iliad, or the Annals of Ennius. The only interest attaching to these fragments is that, like the didactic works of Accius, they testify to the crude critical effort that accompanied the creative activity of the earlier Roman poets.

As specimens of his continuous style the two following passages may be given. The first exemplifies the serious moral spirit with which ancient satire was animated; the second vividly represents and rebukes one of the most prevalent pursuits of the age—

> Virtus, Albine, est pretium persolvere verum,
> Queis in versamur, queis vivimu' rebu', potesse:
> Virtus est hominis, scire id quod quaeque habeat res.
> Virtus scire homini rectum, utile, quid sit honestum;
> Quae bona, quae mala item, quid inutile, turpe, inhonestum;
> Virtus quaerendae rei finem scire modumque:
> Virtus divitiis pretium persolvere posse:
> Virtus id dare quod re ipsa debetur honori:
> Hostem esse atque inimicum hominum morumque malorum,
> Contra defensorem hominum morumque bonorum,
> Hos magnifacere, his bene velle, his vivere amicum;
> Commoda praeterea patriae sibi prima putare,
> Deinde parentum, tertia jam postremaque nostra[1].

If there is no great originality of thought nor rhetorical grace of expression in this passage, it proves that Lucilius judged of questions of right and wrong from his own point of view. To him, as to Ennius, common sense and a just estimate of life were large ingredients in virtue. To be

---

[1] 'Virtue, Albinus, consists in being able to give their true worth to the things on which we are engaged, among which we live. The virtue of a man is to understand the real meaning of each thing: to understand what is right, useful, honourable for him; what things are good, what bad, what is unprofitable, base, dishonourable; to know the due limit and measure in making money; to give its proper worth to wealth; to assign what is really due to honour; to be a foe and enemy of bad men and bad principles; to stand by good men and good principles; to extol the good, to wish them well, to be their friend through life. Lastly, it is true worth to look on our country's weal as the chief good; next to that, the weal of our parents; third and last, our own weal.'

a good hater as well as a staunch friend, and to choose one's friends and enemies according to their characters, is another quality of his virtuous man. With him, as with the best Romans of every age, love of country, family, and friends, were the primary motives to right action. The next passage, written in language equally plain and forcible, gives a graphic picture of the growing taste for forensic oratory—

> Nunc vero a mane ad noctem, festo atque profesto,
> Toto itidem pariterque die, populusque patresque
> Iactare indu foro se omnes, decedere nusquam,
> Uni se atque eidem studio omnes dedere et arti,
> Verba dare ut caute possint, pugnare dolose,
> Blanditia certare, bonum simulare virum se
> Insidias facere, ut si hostes sint omnibus omnes.[1]

These passages are probably not unfavourable specimens of the author's continuous style. At its best that style appears to be sincere, serious, rapid, and full of vital force, but careless, redundant, and devoid of all rhetorical point and subtle suggestiveness. Even to these passages the censure of Horace applies,—

> At dixi fluere hunc lutulentum.

If we regard these passages as on the ordinary level of his style we cannot hesitate to recognise his immense inferiority to Terence in elegance and finish[2], and to Plautus in rich and humourous exuberance of expression. There is scarcely a trace of imaginative power, or of susceptibility to the grandeur and pathos of human life, or to the beauty and sublimity of Nature in the thousand lines of his remains. We find a few vivid touches, as in this half-line—

> Terra abit in nimbos imbresque,

but we fail to recognise not only the 'disjecti membra

---

[1] 'But now from morning till night, on holiday and work-day, the whole day alike, common people and senators are bustling about within the Forum, never quitting it—all devoting themselves to the same practice and trick of wary word-fencing, fighting craftily, vying with each other in politeness, assuming airs of virtue, plotting against each other as if all were enemies.'

[2] Cp. Mr. Munro's criticism in the Journal of Philology.

poetae,' but even the elements of the rhetorician, or of the ironical humourist—

> Parcentis viribus atque
> Extenuantis eas consulto.

Thus it is difficult to understand what Cicero means when he speaks of the 'Romani veteres atque urbani sales' as being 'salsiores' than those of the true masters of Attic wit, such as were Aristophanes, Plato, and Menander.

But these passages are simple, direct, and clear, compared with many of the single lines or longer passages, already quoted in illustration of the substance of his satire. These leave an impression not only of a total want of the 'limae labor,' but of an abnormal harshness and difficulty, beyond what we find in the fragments of Pacuvius, Accius, or Ennius. The fragments of his trochaics and iambics are much simpler, 'much less depart from the natural order of the words,' than those of his hexameters: a fact which reminds us of the great advance made by Horace in adapting the heroic measure to the familiar experience of life. Lucilius is moreover a great offender against not only the graces but the decencies of language. Lines are found in his fragments as coarse as the coarsest in Catullus or Juvenal: nor could he urge the extenuating plea of having forgotten the respect due to his readers from the necessity of relieving his wounded feelings or of vindicating morality.

Yet it is undoubted that, notwithstanding the most glaring faults and defects in form and style, he was one of the most popular among the Roman poets. The testimony of Cicero, Persius, Juvenal, Quintilian, Tacitus, and Gellius, confirm on this point the more ample testimony of Horace. If, as Mr. Munro thinks, Horace may have expressed, in deference to the prevailing taste of his time, a less qualified admiration for him than he really felt, this only shows how strong a hold his writings had over the reading public in the Augustan age. But Horace shows by no means the same deference to the admirers of Plautus and Ennius. To Lucilius he pays also the sincerer tribute of frequent imitation. He made him his model, in regard both to form and substance, in his satires; and even in his epistles he still acknowledges the guidance of his earliest master. In reading both the Satires and Epistles we are continually coming upon vestiges of Lucilius, in some turn of expression, some personal or illustrative allusion. Similar vestiges are found, imbedded in the harsh and jagged diction of Persius, and though not to the same extent, in the polished rhetoric of Juvenal. Nor was his literary influence confined to Roman satirists. Lucretius, Catullus, and even Virgil, have not disdained to adopt his thoughts or imitate his manner[1].

But if we cannot altogether account for, we may yet partially understand the admiration which his countrymen felt for Lucilius. In every great literature, while there are some works which appeal to the imagination of the whole world, there are others which seem to hit some particular mood of the nation to which their author belongs, and are all the more valued from the prominence they give to this idiosyncracy. Every nation which has had a literature seems to have valued itself on some peculiar humour or vein of observation and feeling, which it regards as specially allotted to itself, over and above its common inheritance of the sense of the ludicrous, which it shares with other races. Those writers who have this last in unusual measure become the favourite humourists of the world. But their own countrymen often prefer those endowed with the narrower domestic type; and of this type Lucilius seems to have been a true representative. The 'antiqua et vernacula festivitas,' attributed to him, seems to have been more

[1] Passages of Lucilius apparently imitated by Lucretius:—
    (1) 'Quantum haurire animus Musarum ec fontibu' gestit.'
    (2) 'Cum sciam nil esse in vita proprium mortali datum
        Jam quae tempestate vivo, chresin ad me recipio.'
    (3) 'Ut pueri infantes credunt signa omnia ahena
        Vivere et esse homines, sic istic omnia ficta
        Vera putant.'

Virgil's 'rex ipse Phanaeus' is said by Servius to be imitated from the Χῖος τε δυναστής of Lucilius. Other imitations are pointed out in Macrobius and in Servius. An apparent imitation by Catullus has been already noticed.

combative and aggressive than genial and sympathetic. The 'Italum acetum' was employed by the Romans as a weapon of controversy with the view of damaging an adversary and making either himself or the cause he represented appear ridiculous and contemptible. The dictum of a modern humourist, that to laugh at a man properly you must first love him, would have seemed to an ancient Roman a contradiction in terms. When Horace writes—

> Ridiculum acri
> Fortius et melius magnas plerumque secat res,

he means that men are more likely to be made better by the fear of contempt than of moral reprobation.

But Lucilius had much more than this power of personal raillery, exercised with the force supplied and under the restraints imposed by an energetic social and political life. He is spoken of not only as 'comis et urbanus,' but also as 'doctus' and 'sapiens.' Even his fragments indicate that he was a man of large knowledge of 'books and men.' Horace testifies to the use which he made of the old comic poets of Athens:—

> Hinc omnis pendet Lucilius, hosce secutus.

His fragments show familiarity with Homer, with the works of the Greek physical and ethical philosophers, with the systems of the rhetoricians, and some acquaintance with the writings of Plato, Archilochus, Euripides, and Aesop. His habit of building up his Latin lines with the help of Greek phrases illustrates the first powerful influence of the new learning before the Roman mind was able thoroughly to assimilate it, but when it was in the highest degree stimulated and fascinated by it. The mind of Lucilius was susceptible to the novelty of the new thoughts and new impressions, but like that of his contemporaries was insensible to the grace and symmetry of Greek art. Terence is the only writer in the ante-Ciceronian period who had the sense of artistic form. But all this foreign learning was, in the mind of Lucilius, subsidiary to the freshest observation and most discerning criticism of his own age. He was a spectator of life more than an actor in it, but he yet had been present at one of the most important military events of the time, and he had lived in the closest intimacy with the greatest soldier and most prudent statesman of his age. His satire had thus none of the limitation and unreality which attaches to the work of a student and recluse, such as Persius was. To the writings of Lucilius more perhaps than to those of any other Roman would the words of Martial apply—

> Hominem pagina nostra sapit.

It is his strong realistic tendency both in expression and thought that seems to explain his antagonism to the older poets who treated of Greek heroes and heroines in language widely removed from that employed either in the forum or in the social meetings of educated men. The popularity of Lucilius among the Romans may thus be explained on much the same grounds as that of Archilochus among the Greeks. He first introduced the literature of the understanding as distinct from that either of the graver emotions or of humorous and sentimental representation. And, while writing with the breadth of view and wealth of illustration derived from learning, he did not, like the poets of later times, write for an exclusive circle of critical readers, but rather, as he himself said, 'for Tarentines, Consentini, and Sicilians[1].' There was nothing about him of the fastidiousness and shyness of a too refined culture. Every line almost of his fragments attests his possession of that quality which, more than any other, secures a wide, if not always a lasting, popularity, great vitality and its natural accompaniment, boldness and confidence of spirit. While he saw clearly, felt keenly, and judged wisely the political and social action of his time, he reproduced it vividly in his pages. Whatever other quality his style may want, it is always alive. And the life with which it is animated is thoroughly healthy. There is a singular sincerity in the ring of his words, the earnest of a mind, absolutely free

[1] Cic. de Fin. i. 3.

from cant and pretence, not lashing itself into fierce indignation as a stimulant to rhetorical effect, nor forcing itself to conform to any impracticable scheme of life, but glowing with a hearty scorn for baseness, and never shrinking from its exposure in whatever rank and under whatever disguise he detected it[1], and ever courageously ' upholding the cause of virtue and of those who were on the side of virtue '—

> Scilicet uni aequus virtuti atque eius amicis.

It was by the rectitude and manliness of his character, as much as by his learning, his quick and true discernment, his keen raillery and vivid portraiture, that he became the favourite of his time and country, and, alone among Roman writers, succeeded in introducing a new form of literature into the world.

---

[1] ' Detrahere et pellem nitidus qua quisque per ora
    Cederet, introrsum turpis.'

CHAPTER IX.

REVIEW OF THE FIRST PERIOD.

THE poetic literature reviewed in the last five chapters is the product of the second century B.C. The latest writers of any importance belonging to the earlier period of the poetry of the Republic were Lucilius and Afranius. Half a century from the death of Lucilius elapsed before the appearance of the poems of Lucretius and Catullus, which come next to be considered. But before passing on to this more familiar ground, a few pages may be devoted to a retrospect of some general characteristics marking the earlier period, and to a consideration of the social and intellectual conditions under which literature first established itself at Rome.

With striking individual varieties of character, the poets whose works have been considered present something of a common aspect, distinct from that of the literary men of later times. They were placed in different circumstances, and lived in a different manner from either the poets who adorned the last days of the Republic or those who flourished in the Augustan age. The spirit animating their works was the result of the forces acting on the national life, and the form and style in which they were composed were determined by the stage of culture which the national mind had reached, and the stage of growth through which the Latin language was passing under the stimulus of that culture.

Like nearly all the literary men of later times, these poets were of provincial or foreign birth and origin. They were thus born under circumstances more favourable to, or at least less likely to repress, the expansion of individual genius, than the public life and private discipline of Rome. Their minds were thus more open to the reception of new influences; and their position as aliens, by cutting them off from an active public career, served to turn their energies to literature. Their provincial birth and Greek education did not, however, check their Roman sympathies, or prevent them from stamping on their writings the impress of a Roman character.

While, like many of the later poets, they came originally as strangers to Rome, unlike them, they seem to have in later years, resided habitually within the city. The taste for country life prevailing in the days of Cicero and of Horace was not developed to any great extent in the times of Ennius or Lucilius. The great Scipio, indeed, retired to spend the last years of his life at Liternum; and Cicero mentions the boyish delight of Laelius and the younger Africanus in escaping from the public business and the crowded streets of Rome to the pleasant sea-shore of Caieta[1]. Accius seems to have possessed a country farm, and Lucilius showed something of a wandering disposition, and possessed the means to gratify it. But most of these writers were men of moderate means; nor had it then become the practice of the patrons of literature to bestow farms or country-houses on their friends. By their circumstances, as well as the general taste of their time, they were thus brought almost exclusively into contact with the life and business of the city; and their works were consequently more distinguished by their strong sense and understanding than by the passionate or contemplative susceptibility which characterises the great eras of Latin literature.

It is remarkable that nearly all the early poets lived to a great age, and maintained their intellectual vigour unabated to their latest years; while of their successors none reached the natural term of human life, and some among

[1] De Orat. ii. 6.

them, like many great modern poets, were cut off prematurely before their promise was fulfilled. The finer sensibility and more passionate agitation of the poetic temperament appear, in some cases, to exhaust prematurely the springs of life ; while, in natures more happily balanced, or formed by more favourable circumstances, the gifts of genius are accompanied by stronger powers of life, and thus maintain the freshness of youth unimpaired till the last. The length of time during which Naevius, Plautus, Ennius, Pacuvius, Accius, and probably Lucilius, exercised their art suggests the inference, either that they were men of firmer fibre than their successors, or that they were braced to a more enduring strength by the action of their age. As the work of men writing in the fulness of their years, the serious poetry of the time appealed to the mature sympathies of manhood ; and even the comic poetry of Plautus deals with the follies of youth in a genial spirit of indulgence, tempered by the sense of their absurdity, such as might naturally be entertained by one who had outlived them.

But perhaps the most important condition determining the original scope of Roman poetry was the predominance in that era of public over personal interests. Like Virgil and Horace, most of the early poets were men born in comparatively a humble station ; yet by their force of intellect and character they became the familiar friends of the foremost men in the State. But while the poets of the Augustan age owed the charm of their existence to the patronage of the great, the earlier poets depended for their success mainly on popular favour. The intimacy subsisting between the leaders of action and of literature during the second century B.C. arose from the mutual attraction of greatness in different spheres. The chief men in the Republic obtained their position by their services to the State, and thus the personal attachment subsisting between them and men of letters was a bond connecting the latter with the public interest. The early poetry of the Republic is not the expression of an educated minority keeping aloof from public life. If it is animated by a strong aristocratic spirit, the reason is that the aristocratic spirit was predominant in the public life of Rome during that century.

In this era, more than in any later age, the poetry of Rome, like that of Greece in its greatest eras, addressed itself to popular and national, not to individual tastes. The crowds that witnessed and applauded the representations of tragedy as well as comedy, afford a sufficient proof that the reproduction of Greek subjects and personages could be appreciated without the accomplishment of a Greek education. The popularity of the poem of Ennius is attested by his own language, as well as by the evidence of later writers. The honour of a public funeral awarded to Lucilius, implies the general appreciation with which his contemporaries enjoyed the verve, sense, and moral strength which secured for his satire the favour of a more refined and critical age.

This general popularity is an argument in favour of the original spirit animating this early literature. It implies the power of embodying some sentiment or idea of national or public interest. Thus Roman tragedy appears to have been received with favour, chiefly in consequence of the grave Roman tone of its maxims, and the Roman bearing of its personages. The epic poetry of the age did not, like the Odyssey, relate a story of personal adventure, but unfolded the annals of the State in continuous order, and appealed to the pride which men felt, as Romans, in their history and destiny. The satire of Lucilius was not intended merely to afford amusement by ridiculing the follies of social life, but played a part in public affairs by political partisanship and antagonism, and maintained the traditional standard of manners and opinions against the inroads of foreign influences. Latin comedy, indeed, was a more purely cosmopolitan product. The plays of Terence especially would affect those that listened to them simply as men and not as Roman citizens. But that of Plautus abounded in the humour congenial to the Italian race, and owed much of its popularity to the strong Roman colouring spread over the Greek outlines of his representations.

The national character of this poetry is attested also by the spirit and character which pervades it. Among all the authors who have been reviewed, Ennius alone possessed in a large measure that peculiar vein of imaginative feeling which is the most impressive element in the great poets of a later age. The susceptibility of his mind to the sentiment that moulded the institutions and inspired the policy of the Imperial Republic, entitles him to rank as the truest representative of the genius of his country, notwithstanding his apparent inferiority to Plautus in creative originality. The glow of moral passion, which is another great characteristic of Latin literature, as it was of the best types of the Latin race, reveals itself in the remains of all the serious writers of the age. The struggle between the old Roman self-respect and the new modes of temptation, is exemplified in the antagonistic influence exercised by the tragic, epic, and satiric poetry on the one hand, and the comedy of Plautus and Terence on the other. The more general popularity of comedy was a symptom of the facility with which the severer standard of life yielded to the new attractions. The graver writers, equally with the writers of comedy, shared in the sceptical spirit, or the religious indifference, which was one of the dissolving forces of social and political life during this age. The strong common sense which characterised all the writers of the time, could not fail to bring them into collision with the irrational formalism of the national religion; while the distaste for speculative philosophy which Ennius and Plautus equally express, and the strong hold which they all have on the immediate interests of life, explain the absence of any, except the most superficial, reflections on the more mysterious influences which in the belief of the great Greek poets moulded human destiny.

The political condition of Rome in the second century B.C. is reflected in the changes through which her literature passed. For nearly two-thirds of that century, Roman history seems to go through a stage of political quiescence, as compared at least with the vigorous life and stormy passions of its earlier and later phases. But under the surface a great change was taking place, both in the government and the social condition of the people, the effects of which made themselves sufficiently manifest during the last century of the existence of the Republic. The outbreak of the long gathering forces of discontent and disorder is as distinctly marked in Roman history, as the outbreak of the revolutionary forces in modern Europe. The year 133 B.C., the date of the first tribunate of Tiberius Gracchus, has the same kind of significance as the year 1789 A.D. Nor is it a mere coincidence that about the same time a great change takes place in the spirit of Roman literature. The comedies of Plautus, written in the first years of the century, while they reflect the political indifference of the mass of the people, are yet indicative of their general spirit of contentment, and their hearty enjoyment of life. The epic of Ennius, written a little later, proclaims the undisputed ascendency of an aristocracy, still moulded by its best traditions, and claiming to lead a united people. The remains of Roman tragedy breathe the high spirit of the governing class, and attest the severer virtue still animating its best representatives. The comedies of Terence seem addressed to the taste of a younger generation of greater refinement, but of a laxer moral fibre than their father's, and of a class becoming separated by more elaborate culture from ordinary Roman citizens. Expressions in his prologues[1], however, show that there was as yet no division between classes arising from political discontent. But in the satire of Lucilius we read the protest of the better Roman spirit against the

---

[1] Adelphi, 18-21:—

'Quom illis placet,
Qui vobis univorsis et populo placent,
Quorum opera in bello, in otio, in negotio
Suo quisque tempore usust sine superbia.'

lawless arrogance of the nobles, their incapacity in war, their corrupt administration of justice, their iniquitous government of the provinces; against the ostentatious luxury of the rich; the avarice of the middle classes; the venality of the mob, and the profligacy of their leaders; and against the insincerity and animosities fostered among the educated classes by the contests of the forum and the law-courts.

In passing from the substance and spirit of this early literature to its form and style, we can see by the rudeness of the more original ventures which the Roman spirit made, how slowly it was educated by imitative effort to high literary accomplishment. The only writer who aimed at perfection of form was Terence, and his success was due to his close adherence to his originals. But as some compensation for their artistic defects, these early writers display much greater productiveness than their literary successors. They were like the settlers in a new country, who are spared the pains of exact cultivation owing to the absence of previous occupation of the soil, and the large extent of ground thus open to their industry. The contrast between the standard aimed at, and the results attained by the sincerest literary force in two different eras of Roman literature, is brought home to the mind by contrasting the rude fragments of the lost works of Ennius, embodying the results of a long, hearty, active, and useful life, with the small volume which still preserves the flower of a few passionate years, as fresh as when the young poet sent it forth :—

Arido modo pumice expolitum.

The style of the early poets was marked by haste, harshness, and redundance, occasionally by verbal conceits and similar errors of taste. That of the writers of comedy, on the other hand, is easy, natural, and elegant. The Latin language seems thus to have adapted itself to the needs of ordinary social life more readily than to the expression of elevated feeling. Though many phrases in the fragments which have been reviewed are boldly and vigorously conceived, few passages are written with continuous ease and smoothness, and the language constantly halts, as if inadequate to the meaning which labours under it. The style has, in general, the merits of directness and sincerity, often of freshness and vigour, but wants altogether the depth and richness of colour, as well as the finish and moderation which we expect in the literature of a people to whom poetry and art are naturally congenial, and associated with many old memories and feelings. Their merits of style, such as the simple force with which they go directly to the heart of a matter, and the grave earnestness of their tone, are qualities characteristic rather of oratory than of poetry. But this colouring of their style is very different from the artificial rhetoric of the literature of the Empire. The oratorical style of the early poets was the natural result of a sympathy with the most practical intellectual instrument of their age. The rhetoric of the Empire was the expression of an artificial life, in which literature was cultivated to beguile the tedium of compulsory inaction, and the highest form of public speaking had sunk from its proud office as the organ of political freedom into a mere exercise of pedants and school-boys[1].

The same impulse in this age which gave birth to the forms of serious poetry, stimulated also the growth of oratory and history. While these different modes of mental accomplishment all acted and reacted on one another, oratory appears to have exercised the most influence on the others. Roman literature is altogether more pervaded by oratorical feeling than that of any other nation, ancient or modern. From the natural deficiency of the Romans in the higher dramatic and speculative genius, the rhetorical element entered largely into their poetry, their history, and their ethical discussions. Cicero identifies the faculties of the orator with those of the historian and the philosopher. His treatise *De Claris Oratoribus* bears witness to the

---

[1] Cf. Juv. x. 167:—
'Ut pueris placeas et declamatio fias.'

energy with which this art was cultivated for more than a century before his own time; and the remains of Ennius and Lucilius confirm this testimony. It was from the impassioned and dignified speech of the forum and senate-house that the Roman language first acquired its capacity of expressing great emotions. All the serious poetry of the age bears traces of this influence. Roman tragedy shows its affinity to oratory in its grave and didactic tone. This affinity is further implied in the political meaning which the audience attached to the sentiments expressed, and which the actor enforced by his voice and manner. It is also attested by the fact that in the time of Cicero, famous actors were employed in teaching the external graces of public speaking. The theatre was a school of elocution as much as a place of dramatic entertainment. Cicero specifies among the qualifications of a speaker, 'Vox tragoedorum, gestus paene summorum actorum.' Although the epic poetry of the time mainly appealed to a different class of sympathies, yet the fragments of speeches in Ennius indicate that kind of rhetorical power which moves an audience by the weight and authority of the speaker. Roman satire could wield other weapons of oratory, such as the fierce invective, the lashing ridicule, the vehement indignation which have often proved the most powerful instruments of debate in modern as well as ancient times.

Historical composition also took its rise at Rome at this period. Although the earliest Roman annalists composed their works in the Greek language, it was not from the desire of imitating the historic art of Greece that this art was first cultivated at Rome. The origin of Roman history may be referred rather to the same impulse which gave birth to the epic poems of Naevius and Ennius. The early annalists were men of action and eminent station, who desired to record the important events in which they themselves had taken part, and to fix them for ever in the annals of their country. History originated at Rome in the impulse to keep alive the record of national life, not, as among the Greeks, in the spell which human story and the wonder of distant lands exercised over the imagination. Its office was not to teach lessons of political wisdom, but to commemorate the services of great men, and to satisfy a Roman's pride in the past, and his trust in the future of his country. The word *annales* suggests a different idea of history from that entertained and exemplified by Herodotus and Thucydides. The purpose of building up the record of unbroken national life was present to, though probably not realised by, the earliest annalists who preserved the line of magistrates, and kept account of the religious observances in the State: in the time of the expansion of Roman power, this purpose directed the attention of men of action to the composition of prose annals, and stimulated the productive genius of Naevius and Ennius: and when, in the Augustan age, the national destiny seemed to be fulfilled, the same purpose inspired the great epic of Virgil, and the 'colossal masterwork of Livy.'

Another form of literature, in which Rome became preeminent, first began in this era,—the writing of familiar letters. It was natural that a correspondence should be maintained among intimate friends and members of an active social circle, separated for years from one another by military service, or employment in the provinces; and the new taste for literature would induce the writers to give form and finish to these compositions, so that they might be interesting not only to the persons addressed, but to all the members of the same circle. The earliest compositions of this kind of which we read, are the familiar letters in verse ('Epistolas versiculis facetis ad familiares missas' Cicero calls them) written to his friends by the brother of Mummius, during the siege of Corinth[1]. That these had some literary value may be inferred from the fact that they survived down to the age of Cicero, and are spoken of in the letters to Atticus, as having often been quoted to him by a member of the family of Mummii. One of the earliest

---

[1] Referred to by Mommsen.

satires of Lucilius appears to have been a letter written to Scipio after the capture of Numantia; and several of his other satires were written in an epistolary form. How happily the later Romans employed this form in prose and verse is sufficiently proved by the letters of Cicero and Pliny, and the metrical Epistles of Horace.

This era also saw the beginning of the critical and grammatical studies which flourished through every period of Roman literature, and continued long after the cessation of all productive originality. This critical effort was a necessary condition of the cultivation of art by the Romans. The perfection of form attained by the great Roman poets of a later time was no exercise of a natural gift, but the result of many previous efforts and failures, and of much reflection on the conditions which had been, with no apparent effort, fulfilled by their Greek masters. Neither did their language acquire the symmetry, precision, and harmony, which make it so effective a vehicle in prose and verse, except as the result of assiduous labour. The natural tendency of the spoken language was to rapid decomposition. This was first arrested by Ennius, who cast the literary language of Rome into forms which became permanent after his time. Among his poetic successors in this era Accius and Lucilius made critical and grammatical studies the subjects of some of their works. Lucilius was a contemporary and friend of the most famous of the early grammarians, Aelius Stilo, the critic to whom is attributed the saying that 'if the muses were to speak in Latin, they would speak in the language of Plautus.' Critical works in trochaic verse were written by Porcius Licinus, and Volcatius Sedigitus, who appear to have been the chief authorities from whom later writers derived their information as to the lives of the early poets. It is characteristic of the want of spontaneousness in Latin literature, as compared with the fresh and varied impulses which the Greek genius obeyed in every stage of its literary development, that reflection on the principles of composition, efforts to form the language into a more certain and uniform vehicle, and, comment on living writers, were carried on concurrently with the creative efforts of the more original minds.

The existing works of the two great writers of Roman comedy have an acknowledged value of their own, but even the fragments of this early literature, originally scattered through the works of many later authors, and collected together and arranged by the industry of modern scholars, are found to possess a peculiar interest. They recall the features of the remarkable men by whom the foundations of Roman literature were laid, and the Latin language was first shaped into a powerful and symmetric organ. They present the Roman mind in its earliest contact with the genius of Greece; and they are almost the sole contemporary witnesses of national character and public feeling in the most vigorous and interesting age of the Republic. They throw also much light on the national sources of inspiration in the later Roman literature. The early poets are seen to be men living the life of citizens in a Republic, appealing rather to popular taste than to the sympathies of a refined and limited society; men of mature years and understanding, animated by a serious purpose and with a strong interest in the affairs of their time; rude and negligent but direct and vigorous in speech,—more remarkable for energy, industry, and common sense, than for the finer gifts and susceptibility of genius. Their poetry springing from their sympathy with national and political life, and from the impulses of the will and the manlier energies, was less rich, varied, and refined than that which flows out of the religious spirit of man, out of his passions and affections, or of his imaginative sense of the life and grandeur of Nature. But in these respects the early poetry was essentially Roman in spirit, in harmony with the strength and sagacity, the sobriety and grave dignity of Rome.

The accomplished art of the last age of the Republic and of the Augustan age owed much of its national and moral nourishment to the vigorous life of this early literature. The earnest enthusiasm of Ennius was inherited by Lucretius,—his patriotic tones were repeated by Virgil. The lofty oratory of the Aeneid sometimes sounds like an echo of the grave and ardent style of early tragedy. The strong sense and knowledge of the world, the frank communicativeness and lively portraiture of Lucilius reappeared in the familiar writings of Horace, while his fierce vehemence and bold invective were reproduced by the vigorous satirist of the Empire.

SECOND PERIOD.

THE CLOSE OF THE REPUBLIC.

LUCRETIUS AND CATULLUS.

CHAPTER X.

TRANSITION FROM LUCILIUS TO LUCRETIUS AND CATULLUS.

AN interval of nearly half a century elapsed between the death of Lucilius and the appearance of the poem of Lucretius. During this period no poetical works of any value were produced at Rome. The only successors of the older tragedians, C. Julius Caesar (Consul B.C. 88) and C. Titius, never obtained a success on the stage approaching to that still accorded to the older dramas. No rival appeared to dispute the popularity enjoyed by Plautus, Caecilius, and Terence, as authors of the Comoedia Palliata; but the literary activity of Afranius and of T. Quintius Atta, the most eminent among the authors of the Fabulae togatae, extended into the early years of the first century B.C. It was during this period also that the Fabula Atellana was raised by L. Pomponius of Bononia and Novius into the rank of regular literature. The tendency to depart more and more from the Greek type of comedy, and to revert to the scenic entertainment native to Italy, is seen in the attempt of Laberius, in the last years of the Republic, to raise the Mimus into the sphere of recognised literary art. The Annalistic epic of Hostius on the Istrian war, and the Annales of Furius, of Antium, a friend of the elder Catulus, perpetuated the traditional influence of Ennius, during the interval between Lucilius and Lucretius. The first attempts to introduce the erotic poetry of Alexandria, in the form of epigrams and short lyrical poems, also belong to this period. The writers of this new kind of poetry,—Valerius Ædituus, Q. Latatius Catulus (the colleague of Marius in his consulship of the year 102 B.C.), and Laevius, the author of Erotopaegnia, have significance only as indicating the direction which Roman poetry followed in the succeeding generation. Cicero in his youth cultivated verse-making, both as a translator of the poem of Aratus, and as the author of an original poem on his townsman Marius. His hexameters show considerable advance in rhythmical smoothness and exactness beyond the previous condition of that metre, as exemplified in the fragments of Ennius and Lucilius: and his translation of Aratus marks a stage in the history of Latin poetry as affording a native model, which Lucretius did not altogether disregard in the structure of his verse and diction[1]. But Cicero is not to be ranked among the poets of Rome. He merely practised verse-making as part of his general literary training. He retained the accomplishment till his latest years, and shows his facility by translating passages from the Greek tragedians in his philosophical works. That he had no true poetical faculty is shown by the indifference with which he regarded the works of the two great poets of his time. This indifference is the more marked from his generous recognition of the oratorical promise and accomplishment of the men of a younger generation. The tragedies of Q. Cicero were mere literary exercises. Though several of the multifarious works of Varro were written in verse, yet the whole cast of his mind was thoroughly prosaic. His tastes and abilities were those of an antiquarian scholar, not of a man of poetic genius and accomplishment.

The period of nearly half a century, from 102 till about 60 B.C., must thus be regarded as altogether barren in genuine poetical result. During this long interval there appeared no successor to carry on the work of developing the poetical side of a national literature, begun by Plautus, Ennius, and Lucilius. The only metrical compositions of this time were either inferior reproductions of the old

[1] Mr. Munro, in his Introduction to Part II of his Commentary on Lucretius, illustrates this relation of the work of the poet to this youthful production of Cicero.

forms or immature anticipations of the products of a later age. The political disturbance of the times between the tribunate of Tib. Gracchus and the first consulship of Crassus and Pompey (B.C. 70) was unfavourable to the cultivation of that poetry which is expressive of national feeling : and the Roman genius for art was as yet too immature to produce the poetry of individual reflexion or personal passion. The state of feeling throughout Italy, before and immediately subsequent to the Social War, alienated from Rome the sympathetic genius of the kindred races from whom her most illustrious authors were drawn in later times. It was in the years of comparative peace, between the horrors of the first civil war and the alarm preceding the outbreak of the second, that a new poet grew apparently unnoticed to maturity, and the silence was at last broken by a voice at once stronger in native vitality and richer in acquired culture from the long repression of Italian genius.

But there is one thing significant in the literary character of this period, otherwise so barren in works of taste and imagination. Those by whom the art of verse was practised are no longer ' Semi-Graeci ' or humble provincials, but Romans of political or social distinction. The chief authors in the interval between the first and second era of Roman poetry are either members of the aristocracy or men of old family belonging to the equestrian order. And this connexion between literature and social rank continues till the close of the Republic. The poets of the Ciceronian age,—Hortensius, Memmius, Lucretius, Catullus, Calvus, Cinna, &c. —either themselves belonged to the governing class, or were men of leisure and independent means, living as equals with the members of that class. This circumstance explains much of the difference in tone between the literature of that age and both the earlier and later literature. The separation in taste and sympathy between the higher classes and the mass of the people which had begun in the days of Terence, grew wider and wider with the growth of culture and with the increasing bitterness of political dissensions. It was only among the rich and educated that poetry could now expect to find an audience; and the poetry written for them appealed, for the most part, to the convictions, tastes, pleasures, and animosities which they shared as members of a class, not, like the best Augustan poetry, to the higher sympathies which they might share as the depositaries of great national traditions. But if this poetry was too exclusively addressed to a class —a class too, though refined by culture, yet living for the most part the life of fashion and pleasure—it had the merit of being the sincere expression of men writing to please themselves and their equals. It was not called upon to make any sacrifice of individual conviction or public sentiment to satisfy popular taste or the requirements of an Imperial master.

But though barren in poetry this interval was far from being barren in other intellectual results. This was the era of the great Roman orators, the successors of Laelius, Carbo, the Gracchi, &c., and the immediate predecessors and contemporaries of Cicero. It was through the care with which public speaking was cultivated that Latin prose was formed into that clear, exact, dignified, and commanding instrument, which served through so many centuries as the universal organ of history, law, philosophy, learning, and religion,—of public discussion and private correspondence. While Latin poetry is quite as much Italian as Roman, both in spirit and manner, Latin prose bears the stamp of the political genius of Rome. It was the deliberate expression of the mind of men practised in affairs, exercised in the deliberations of the Senate, the harangues of the public assemblies, the pleadings of the courts,—of men accustomed to determine and explain questions of law and to draw up edicts binding on all subjects of the State,—trained, moreover, to a sense of literary form by the study of Greek rhetoric, and naturally guided to clearness and dignity of expression by the orderly understanding, the strong hold of reality, and the authoritative bearing which were their birthright as Romans. The effort which obtained its crowning success in the prose style of Cicero left its mark on other forms of literature. History continued to be written by members of the great governing families to serve both as a record of events and a weapon of party warfare. The large and varied correspondence of Cicero shows how general the accomplishment of style had become among educated men. And if this result was, in the main, due to the fervour of mind and temper elicited by the contests of public life, the systematic teaching of grammarians and rhetoricians acted as a corrective of the natural exuberance or carelessness of the rhetorical faculty.

Perfection of style attained in one of the two great branches of a national literature cannot fail to react on the other. It was the peculiarity of Latin literature that this perfection or high accomplishment was reached in prose sooner than in poetry. The contemporaries of Cicero and Caesar, whose genius impelled them to awaken into new life the long silent Muses of Italy, were conscious that the great effort demanded of them was to raise Latin verse to a similar perfection of form, diction, and musical cadence. What Cicero did for Latin prose, in revealing the fertility of its resources, in giving to it more ample volume, and eliciting its capabilities of sonorous rhythmical movement, Lucretius aspires to do for Latin verse. Although Catullus in forming his more elaborate style worked carefully after the manner of his Greek models, yet we may attribute something of the terseness, the idiomatic verve, the studied simplicity of expression in his lighter pieces to the literary taste which he shared with the younger race of orators, who claimed to have substituted Attic elegance for Asiatic exuberance of ornament.

During all this interval, in which native poetry was neglected, the art and thought of Greece were penetrating more deeply into Italy. Cicero, in his defence of Archias, attests the eagerness with which Greek studies were cultivated during the early years of the century; 'Erat Italia tunc plena Graecarum artium ac disciplinarum, studiaque haec et in Latio vehementius tum colebantur quam nunc iisdem in oppidis, et hic Romae propter tranquillitatem reipublicae non neglegebantur.' With the reviving tranquility of the Republic these studies also revived. Learned Greeks continued to flock to Rome and to attach themselves to members of the great houses,—the Luculli, the Metelli, Pompey, &c.; and it became more and more the custom for young men of birth and wealth to travel or spend some years of study among the famous cities of Greece and Asia. This new and closer contact of the Greek with the Roman mind came about, not as the earlier one through dramatic representations, but, in a great measure, through the medium of books, which began now to be accumulated at Rome both in public and private libraries. Probably no other cause produces so great a change in national character and intellect as the awakening of the taste and the creating of facilities for reading. By the diffusion of books, as well as by the instruction of living teachers, the Romans of this generation came under the influence of a new class of writers, whose spirit was more in harmony with the modern world than the old epic and dramatic poets, viz. the exponents of the different philosophic systems and the learned poets of Alexandria. These new influences helped to denationalise Roman thought and literature, to make the individual more conscious of himself, and to stimulate the passions and pleasures of private life. While the endeavour to regulate life in accordance with a system of philosophy tended to isolate men from their fellows, the study of the Alexandrine poets, the cultivation of art for its own sake, the exclusive admiration of a particular manner of writing fostered the spirit of literary coteries as distinct from the spirit of a national literature. But making allowance for all these drawbacks, it is to the Alexandrine culture that the education of the Roman sense of literary beauty is primarily due. Along with this culture, indeed, the taste for other forms of art, which was rapidly developed and largely fed in the last age of the Republic, powerfully cooperated. Lucretius specifies among the 'deliciae vitae'

> Carmina, picturas, et daedala signa;[1]

and, in more than one place, he writes, with sympathetic admiration, of the charm of instrumental music,

> Musaea mele per chordas organici quae
> Mobilibus digitis expergefacta figurant.[2]

The delicate appreciation of the paintings, statues, gems, vases, etc., either brought to Rome as the spoils of conquest, or seen in their original home by educated Romans, travelling for pleasure or employed in the public service, was not without effect in calling forth the ideal of literary form, realised in some of the master-pieces of Catullus. We may suppose too that the cultivation of music had some share in eliciting the lyrical movement in Latin verse from the fact mentioned by Horace, that the songs of Catullus and Calvus were ever in the mouths of the fashionable professors of that art in a later age. If the life of the generation which witnessed the overthrow of the Republic was one of alarm and vicissitude, of political unsettlement and moral unrestraint, it was, at the same time, very rich in its capabilities of sensuous and intellectual enjoyment. The appetite for pleasure was still too fresh to produce that deadening of energy and of feeling, which is most fatal to literary creativeness. The passionate life led by Catullus and his friends may have shortened the days of some of them, and tended to limit the range and to lower the aims of their genius, but it did not dull their vivid sense of beauty, chill their enjoyment of their art, or impair the mastery over its technical details, for which they strove.

As the bent given to philosophical and literary studies developed the inner life and personal tastes of the individual, the political disorganisation of the age tended

---

[1] v. 1451.
[2] ii. 412; cf. also ii. 505-6:—
> Et cycnea mele Phoebeaque daedala chordis
> Carmina consimili ratione oppressa silerent.

These lines point to the union of music and lyrical poetry.

to stimulate new modes of thought and life, which had not, in any former generation, been congenial to the Roman mind. While the work of political destruction was being carried on along with the most strenuous gratification of their passions by one set among the leading men at Rome —such as Catiline and his associates, and, somewhat later, Clodius, Curio, Caelius, Antony, etc.—among men of more sensitive and refined natures the pleasures of the contemplative life began to exercise a novel fascination. The comparative seclusion in which men like Lucullus and Hortensius lived in their later years may, perhaps, be accounted for by other reasons than the mere love of ease and pleasure. It was a symptom of that despair of the Republic which is so often expressed in Cicero's letters, and of the consequent diversion of thought from practical affairs to the questions and interests which concern the individual. In the same way the unsettlement and afterwards the loss of political life at Athens gave a great impulse both to the various philosophical sects on the one hand, and to the literature of the new comedy, which deals exclusively with private life, on the other. In Rome this alienation from politics naturally allied itself, among members of the aristocracy, with the acceptance of the Epicurean philosophy. The slow dissolution of religious belief which had been going on since the first contact of the Roman mind with that of Greece, awoke in Rome, as it had done in Greece, a deeper interest in the ultimate questions of the existence and nature of the gods and of the origin and destiny of the human soul. We see how the contemplation of these questions consoled Cicero when no longer able to exercise his energy and vivid intelligence on public affairs. He discusses them with candour and seriousness of spirit and with a strong leaning to the more hopeful side of the controversy, but scarcely from the point of view which regards their settlement as of supreme importance to human well-being. But they are raised from much greater depths of feeling and inward experience by Lucretius, to whom the life of political warfare and personal ambition was utterly repugnant, and who had dedicated himself, with all the intensity of his passionate and poetical temperament, to the discovery and the teaching of the true meaning of life. The happiest results of his recluse and contemplative life were the revelation of a new delight open to the human spirit through sympathy with the spirit of Nature, and the deepening beyond anything which had yet found expression in literature of the fellow-feeling which unites man not only to humanity but to all sentient existence. The taste, so congenial to the Italian, for country life found in him its first and most powerful poetical interpreter: while the humanity of sentiment, first instilled through the teaching of comedy, and fostered by later literary and ethical study, was enforced with a greatness of heart and imagination which has seldom been equalled in ancient or modern times.

The dissolution of traditional beliefs and of the old loyalty to the State produced very different results on the art and life of the younger poets of that generation. The pursuit of pleasure, and the cultivation, purely for its own sake, of art which drew its chief materials from the life of pleasure became the chief end and aim of their existence. In so far as they turned their thoughts from the passionate pleasures of their own lives and the contemplation of passionate incidents and situations in art, it was to give expression to the personal animosities which they entertained to the leaders of the revolutionary movement. Nor did this animosity spring so much from public spirit as from a repugnance of taste towards the coarser partisans of the popular cause, and from the instinctive sense that the privileges enjoyed by their own caste were not likely to survive any great convulsion of the State. The intensity of their personal feelings of love and hatred, and the limitation of their range of view to the things which gave the most vivid and immediate pleasure to themselves and to others like them, were the sources of both their strength and weakness.

Of the poetry which arose out of these conditions of life and culture, two representatives only are known to us in their works, Lucretius and Catullus. From the testimony of their contemporaries we know them to have been recognised as the greatest of the poets of that age. Lucretius in his own province held an unquestioned pre-eminence. Yet that other minds were occupied with the topics which he alone treated with a masterly hand is proved by the existence of a work, of a somewhat earlier date, by one Egnatius, bearing the title 'De Rerum Natura,' and also by Cicero's notice, in connexion with his mention of Lucretius, of the 'Empedoclea' of Salustius. Varro also is mentioned by ancient writers, in connexion with Empedocles and Lucretius, as the author of a metrical work 'De Rerum Natura[1].' More satisfactory evidence is afforded by the discussions in the 'De Natura Deorum,' the 'Tusculan Questions,' and the 'De Finibus,' of the interest taken by educated men in the class of questions which Lucretius professed to answer. Yet neither the antecedent nor the later attention devoted to these subjects explains the powerful attraction which they had for Lucretius. In him, more than in any other Roman, we recognise a fresh and deep source of poetic thought and feeling appearing in the world. The culture of his age may have suggested or rendered possible the channel which his genius followed, but cannot account for the power and intensity with which it poured itself into that channel. He cannot be said either to sum up the art and thought contemporary with himself, or, like Virgil, to complete that of preceding times. The work done by him, and the influence exercised by him on the poetry of Rome and on the world, are to be explained only by his original and individual force.

Catullus, on the other hand, was the most successful among a band of rival poets with most of whom he lived in intimacy. Among the men older than himself, Hortensius, the orator, and Memmius were known as writers of amatory poetry. His name as a lyric poet is most usually coupled with that of his friend Calvus; and a well-known

[1] Cp. the passages quoted from Quintilian, Lactantius, etc. by W. S. Teuffel. Wagner's Translation, p. 239.

passage of Tacitus[1] brings together his lampoons and those of Bibaculus as being 'referta contumeliis Caesarum.' Among others to whom he was bound by the ties of friendship and common tastes were C. Helvius Cinna, author of an Alexandrine epic, called Zmyrna, and Caecilius, author of a poem on Cybele. Ticidas and Anser, mentioned by Ovid among his own precursors in amatory poetry, also belong to this generation. Among the swarms of poetasters—

> Saecli incommoda, pessimi poetae,—

a countryman of his own, Tanusius Geminus, the author of a long Annalistic epic, is held up by Catullus to especial obloquy under the name of Volusius.

While so much of the literature of that age has perished, we are fortunate in possessing the works of the greatest masters in prose and verse. The poems of Lucretius and Catullus enable us, better perhaps than any other extant Latin works, to appreciate the most opposite capacities and tendencies of the Roman genius. In their force and individuality, they are alike valuable as the last poetic voices of the Republic, and as, perhaps, the most free and sincere voices of Rome. The first is one of the truest representatives of the national strength, majesty, seriousness of spirit, massive constructive energy; the second is the most typical example of the strong vitality and passionate ardour of the Italian temperament and of its vivid susceptibility to the varied beauties of Greek art.

---

[1] Annals, iv. 34.

CHAPTER XI.

LUCRETIUS.—PERSONAL CHARACTERISTICS.

It is in keeping with the isolated and independent position which Lucretius occupies in literature, that so little is known of his life. The two kinds of information available for literary biography,—that afforded by the author himself, and that derived from contemporaries, or from later writers who had access to contemporary testimony,—almost entirely fail us in his case. The form of poetry adopted by him prevented his speaking of himself and telling his own history as Catullus, Horace, Ovid, etc., have done in their lyrical, elegiac, and familiar writings. His work appears to have been first published after his death: nor is there any reason to believe that he attracted the attention of the world in his lifetime. To judge from the silence of his contemporaries, and from the attitude of mind indicated in his poem, the words 'moriens natusque fefellit' might almost be written as his epitaph. Had he been prominent in the social or literary circles of Rome during the years in which he was engaged on the composition of his poem, some traces of him must have been found in the correspondence of Cicero or in the poems of Catullus, which bring the personal life of those years so close to modern readers. It is thus impossible to ascertain on what original authority the sole traditional account of him preserved in the Chronicle of Jerome was based. That account, like similar notices of other Roman writers, came to Jerome in all probability from the lost work of Suetonius, 'de viris illustribus.' But as to the channels through which it passed to Suetonius, we have no information.

The well-known statement of Jerome is to this effect,—
'The poet Lucretius was born in the year 94 B.C. He became mad from the administration of a love-philtre, and after composing, in his lucid intervals, several books which were afterwards corrected by Cicero, he died by his own hand in his forty-fourth year.' The date of his death would thus be 50 B.C. But this date is contradicted by the statement of Donatus in his life of Virgil, that Lucretius died (he says nothing of his supposed suicide) on the day on which Virgil assumed the 'toga virilis,' viz. October 15, 55 B.C. And this date derives confirmation from the fact that the first notice of the poem appears in a letter of Cicero to his brother, written in the beginning of 54 B.C. As the condition in which the poem has reached us confirms the statement that it was left by the author in an unfinished state, it must have been given to the world by some other hand after the poet's death; and, as Mr. Munro observes, we should expect to find that it first attracted notice some three or four months after that event. We must accordingly conclude that here, as in many other cases, Jerome has been careless in his dates, and that Lucretius was either born some years before 94 B.C., or that he died before his forty-fourth year. His most recent Editors, accordingly, assign his birth to the end of the year 99 B.C. or the beginning of 98 B.C. He would thus be some seven or eight years younger than Cicero, a year or two younger than Julius Caesar, and from about twelve to fifteen years older than Catullus and the younger poets of that generation.

But is this story of the poet's liability to fits of derangement, of the cause assigned for these, of his suicide, and of the correction of his poem by Cicero, to be accepted as a meagre and, perhaps, distorted account of certain facts in his history transmitted through some trustworthy channels, or is it to be rejected as an idle fiction which may have assumed shape before the time of Suetonius, and been accepted by him on no other evidence than that of a vague tradition? Though no certain answer can be given to this question, yet some reasons may be assigned for according a hesitating acceptance to the main outlines of the story, or at least for not rejecting it as a transparent fiction.

It may indeed be urged that if this strange and tragical history had been known to the Augustan poets, who, in greater or less degree, acknowledge the spell exercised upon them by the genius of Lucretius, some sympathetic allusion to it would probably have been found in their writings, such as that in Ovid to the early death of Catullus and Calvus. It would seem remarkable that in the only personal reference which Virgil, who had studied his poem profoundly, seems to make to his predecessor, he characterises him merely as 'fortunate in his triumph over supernatural terrors.' But, not to press an argument based on the silence of those who lived near the poet's time, and who, from their recognition of his genius might have been expected to be interested in his fate, the sensational character of the story justifies some suspicion of its authenticity. The mysterious efficacy attributed to a love-philtre is more in accordance with vulgar credulity than with the facts of nature. The supposition that the poem, or any considerable portion of it, was written in the lucid intervals of derangement seems hardly consistent with the evidence of the supreme control of reason through all its processes of thought. The impression both of impiety and melancholy which the poem was likely to produce on ordinary minds, especially after the religious reaction of the Augustan age, might easily have suggested this tale of madness and suicide as a natural consequence of, or fitting retribution for, such absolute separation from the common hopes and fears of mankind[1].

Yet indications in the poem itself have been pointed out which might incline us to accept the story rather as a meagre tradition of some tragic circumstances in the poet's

---

[1] Mr. Wallace in his very interesting account of 'Epicureanism,' just published, writes, in reference to the way in which Epicurus himself was regarded in a later age, 'And the maladies of Epicurus are treated as an anticipatory judgment of Heaven upon him for his alleged impieties.'—*Epicureanism*, p. 46.

history, than as the idle invention of an uncritical age. The unrelieved intensity of thought and feeling, by which more almost than any other work of literature it is characterised, seems indicative of an overstrain of power, which may well have caused the loss or eclipse of what to the poet was the sustaining light and joy of his life[1]. Under such a calamity it would have been quite in accordance with the principles of his philosophy to seek refuge in self-destruction, and to imitate an example which he notes in the case of another speculative thinker, on becoming conscious of failing intellectual power[2]. But this general sense of overstrained tension of thought and feeling is, as was first pointed out by his English Editor, much intensified by references in the poem (as at i. 32; iv. 33, etc.), to the horror produced on the mind by apparitions seen in dreams and waking visions[3]. 'The emphatic repetition,' says Mr. Munro, 'of these horrid visions seen in sickness might seem to confirm what is related of the poet being subject to fits of delirium or disordering sickness of some sort.' He further shows by quotation from Suetonius' 'Life of Caligula,' that such mental conditions were attributed to the administration of a love-philtre. The coincidence in these recorded cases may imply nothing more than the credulity of Suetonius, or of the authorities whom he followed: but it is conceivable that Lucretius may have himself attributed what was either a disorder of his own constitution, or the result of a prolonged overstrain of mind, to the effects of some powerful drug taken by him in ignorance[4].

---

[1] This consideration is urged by De Quincey in one of his essays.
[2] iii. 1039, etc.
[3] iv. 33-38:—
'Atque eadem nobis vigilantibus obvia mentes
Terrificant atque in somnis, cum saepe figuras
Contuimur miras simulacraque luce carentum,
Quae nos horrifice languentis saepe sopore
Excierunt, ne forte animas Acherunte reamur
Effugere aut umbras inter vivos volitare.'
[4] An article, in a recent number of the Fortnightly Review, on 'Hallucina

Thus, while the statement of Jerome admits neither of verification nor refutation, it may be admitted that there are indications in the poem of a great tension of mind, of an extreme vividness of sensibility, of an indifference to life, and, in the later books, of some failure in the power of organising his materials, which incline us rather to accept the story as a meagre and distorted record of tragical events in the poet's life, than as a literary myth which took shape out of the feelings excited by the poem in a later age. Yet this qualified acquiescence in the tradition does not involve the belief that any considerable portion of the poem was written 'per intervalla insaniae,' or that the disorder from which the poet suffered was actually the effect of a love-philtre.

The statement involved in the words 'quos Cicero emendavit,' has also been the subject of much criticism. No one can read the poem without recognising the truth of the conclusion established by Lachmann, and accepted by the most competent Editors of the poem since his time, that the work must have been left by the author in an unfinished state and given to the world by some friend or some person to whom the task of editing it had been entrusted. But there is some difficulty in accepting the statement that this editor was Cicero. His silence on the subject of his editorial labours, when contrasted with the frank communicativeness of his Epistles in regard to anything which for the time interested him, and the slight esteem with which he seems to have regarded the poem and the philosophy which it embodied, justify some hesitation in accepting the authority of Jerome on this point also. He only once mentions the poem in a letter to his brother

---

tion of the Senses,' suggests a possible explanation of the mental condition of Lucretius, during the composition of some part of his work. The writer speaks of the power of calling these hallucinations up as being quite consistent with perfect sanity of mind, but as sometimes inducing madness. He goes on, 'Or, if the person does not go out of his mind, he may be so distressed by the persistence of the apparition which he has created, as to fall into melancholy and despair, and even to commit suicide.' *Fortnightly Review*, Sept. 1878.

Quintus, and in passages of his philosophical works in which he seems to allude to it he expresses himself slightingly and somewhat contemptuously[1]. In the disparaging references to the Latin writers on Greek philosophy before the appearance of his own Tusculan Questions and Academics, he makes no exception in favour of Lucretius. The words in his letter to his brother Quintus are these, 'Lucretii poemata, ut scribis, ita sunt, [non] multis luminibus ingenii, multae tamen artis: sed cum veneris, virum te putabo, si Salustii Empedoclea legeris, hominem non putabo.' In the MS. the *non*, seemingly required by the antithesis, is found neither before the *multis*, nor the *multae*: we are thus left in doubt whether it was the genius or the art of the poem that Cicero denied. A correction of the passage has been suggested[2], in accordance with which Cicero's discernment is vindicated, and the impression that the poem was deficient in art is attributed to Q. Cicero. Those who hesitate to accept this correction may yet agree with the view that if the *non* must be inserted, it is better to insert it before the *multae* than the *multis*. Even as the passage stands, it may be a short summing up of a more detailed criticism of the younger brother[3], to this effect.

[1] E. g. Tusc. Disp. i. 21, especially the sentence—'Quae quidem cogitans soleo saepe admirari non nullorum insolentiam philosophorum qui naturae cognitionem admirantur, eiusque inventori et principi gratias exultantes agunt eumque venerantur ut deum.'

[2] 'Multae tamen artis esse cum inveneris.' Munro's Lucretius, Third Edition, p. 315.

[3] The theory of Lachmann and others that Q. Cicero was the editor may possibly be true. He dabbled in poetry himself, and he was more nearly of the same age as Lucretius, and thus perhaps more likely to have been a friend of his. The fact that Cicero's remark is in answer to one of his might suggest the opinion that the poem had been read by him before it became known to the older brother, and perhaps been sent by him to Cicero. This would explain Cicero's indifference on the subject. He makes a casual reply on a matter more interesting to his correspondent than to himself. But if Q. Cicero was the editor, Jerome must here also have copied his authorities carelessly. In the time of Jerome the familiar name of Cicero must have been understood as applying to the great orator and philosophic writer, not to his comparatively obscure brother. The only certain inference which can be drawn from this mention of the poem is that it had been read, shortly after its appearance, in the beginning of the year 54 B.C., by both brothers. Yet the consideration of the whole case does not lead to the rejection of the distinct statement that

'I agree with you that there is much genius in the poem of Lucretius, and (though this is less apparent) much art.' Cicero certainly admits either the genius or the art of the poem; perhaps both. It is a truer criticism, and more in accordance with Cicero's expressed opinion of all the Epicurean writings, to admit the exceptional genius of the poem while denying its artistic excellence, than to deny the first and admit the last. Thus if his notice of the poem is slight, it is not markedly deficient in appreciation. Mr. Munro succeeds in explaining Cicero's silence on the subject in his other correspondence. It is in his Letters to his oldest and most intimate correspondent, the Epicurean Atticus, that we should expect to find notices of his editorial labours. It was a task on which Atticus might have given most valuable help from his large employment of educated slaves in the copying of manuscripts. Cicero's silence on the subject in the Letters to Atticus is fully explained by the fact that they were both in Rome during the greater part of the time between the death of Lucretius and the publication of his poem. Again, Cicero's strong opposition to the Epicurean doctrines was not incompatible with the closest friendship with many who professed them; and this opposition was not conspicuously declared till some years after this time. Lucretius may have regarded him, as being the greatest master of Latin style who had yet appeared, with an admiration similar to that expressed by Catullus, though about him too Cicero is absolutely silent. There is thus no great difficulty in supposing that the work of even so uncompromising a partisan as Lucretius should have been placed, either by his own request or by the wish of his friends, in the hands of one who was not attracted to it either by strong poetical or philosophical sympathy. The energetic kindliness of Cicero's nature, and his active interest in literature, would have prompted him not to decline the service if he were asked to render it. Thus, although on this point too our

Cicero was the editor as incredible, or even as highly improbable. If it was he, he must have performed his task very perfunctorily.

judgment may well be suspended, we may think with pleasure of the good-will and kindly offices of the most humane and energetic among Roman writers, as exercised in behalf of Lucretius after his untimely death, just as his name is inseparably associated with that of Catullus, owing to some service rendered in life, which called forth the lively expression of the young poet's gratitude.

This is all the direct external evidence available for the personal history of Lucretius. It is remarkable, when compared with the information given in his other notices, that the record of Jerome does not even mention the poet's birth-place. This may be explained on the supposition either that the authorities followed by Jerome knew very little about him, or that, if he were born at Rome, there would not be the same motive for giving prominence to the place of his birth, as in the case of poets and men of letters who brought honour to the less famous districts of Italy. While Lucretius applies the word *patria* to the Roman State ('patriai tempore iniquo'), and the adjective *patrius* to the Latin language, these words are used by other Roman poets,—Ennius and Virgil for instance,—in reference to their own provincial homes. The Gentile name Lucretius was one eminently Roman, nor is there ground for believing that, like the equally ancient and noble name borne by the other great poet of the age, it had become common in other parts of Italy. The name suggests the inference that Lucretius was descended from one of the most ancient patrician houses of Rome, but one, as is pointed out by Mr. Munro, more famous in the legendary than in the later annals of the Republic. Some members of the same house are mentioned in the letters of Cicero among the partisans of Pompey: and possibly the Lucretius Ofella, who was one of the victims of Sulla's tyranny, may have been connected with the poet. As the position indicated by the whole tone of the poem is that of a man living in easy circumstances, and of one, who, though repelled by it, was yet familiar with the life of pleasure and luxury, he must have belonged either to a senatorian family, or to one of the richer equestrian families, the members of which, if not engaged in financial and commercial affairs, often lived the life of country gentlemen on their estates and employed their leisure in the cultivation of literature. The tone of the dedication to Memmius, a member of a noble plebeian house, and of the occasional addresses to him in the body of the poem, is not that of a client to a patron, but of an equal to an equal:—

> Sed tua me virtus tamen et sperata voluptas
> Suavis amicitiae—.

While Lucretius pays the tribute of admiration to the literary accomplishment of his friend, and to the active part which he played in politics, he yet addresses him with the authority of a master. In a society constituted as that of Rome was in the last age of the Republic this tone could only be assumed to a member of the governing class by a social equal. Memmius combined the pursuits of a politician, a man of letters, and a man of pleasure; and in none of these capacities does he seem to have been worthy of the affection and admiration of Lucretius. But as he filled the office of Praetor in the year 58 B.C.[1] it may be inferred that he and the poet were about the same age, and thus the original bond between them may probably have been that of early education and literary sympathies. That Memmius retained a taste for poetry amid the pursuits and pleasures of his profligate career is shown by the fact that he was the author of a volume of amatory poems, and also by his taking with him, in the year 57 B.C., the poets Helvius Cinna and Catullus, on his staff to Bithynia. The keen discernment of the younger poet, sharpened by personal animosity, formed a truer estimate of his chief, than that expressed by the philosophic enthusiast. But at the time in which the words—

> Nec Memmi clara propago
> Talibus in rebus communi deesse saluti—

were written, even Cicero regarded him as one of the

---

[1] At that time he would be about forty-one years of age—the same age as Lucretius, if, as is most probable, he was born in 99 B.C.

bulwarks of the senatorian cause against Clodius and his influential supporters. And neither the scandal of his private or of his public life prevented his being in later years among the orator's correspondents.

This relation to Memmius is the only additional fact which an examination of the poem brings into light. Nothing is learned from it of the poet's parentage, his education, his favourite places of residence, of his career, of his good or evil fortune. There were eminent Epicurean teachers at Athens and Rome (Patro, Phaedrus, Philodemus, etc.) during his youth and manhood, but it is useless to ask what influence of teachers or personal experience induced him to become so passionate a devotee of the doctrines of Epicurus. Yet though no direct reference to his circumstances is found in his writings, we may yet mark indirect traces of the impression produced upon him by the age in which his youth and manhood were passed; we seem to catch some glimpses of his habitual pursuits and tastes, to gain some real insight into his being, to apprehend the attitude in which he stood to the great teachers of the past, and to know the man by knowing the objects in life which most deeply interested him. Nothing, we may well believe, was further from his wish or intention than to leave behind him any record of himself. No Roman poet has so entirely sunk himself and the remembrance of his own fortunes in absorption in his subject. But his strong personal force and individuality have penetrated deeply into all his representation, his reasoning, and his exhortation. From the beginning to the end of the poem we feel that we are listening to a living voice speaking to us with the direct impressiveness of personal experience and conviction. No writer ever used words more clearly or more sincerely: no one shows a greater scorn for the rhetorical artifices which disguise the lack of meaning or insinuate a false conclusion by fine-sounding phrases:—

Quae belle tangere possunt
Auris et lepido quae sunt fucata sonore.[1]

---

[1] i. 643-4; cf. οὔτε ὡς λογογράφοι ξυνέθεσαν ἐπὶ τὸ προσαγωγότερον τῇ ἀκροάσει ἢ ἀληθέστερον.—Thuc. i. 21.

The union of an original and independent personality with the utmost sincerity of thought and speech is a characteristic in which Lucretius resembles Thucydides. It is this which gives to the works of both, notwithstanding their studied self-suppression, the vivid interest of a direct personal revelation.

The tone of many passages in the poem clearly indicates that Lucretius, though taking no personal part in the active politics of his age, was profoundly moved by the effects which they produced on human happiness and character. Thus the lines at iii. 70-74—

> Sanguine civili rem conflant, etc.—

recall the thought and spectacle of crime and bloodshed vividly presented to him in the impressible years of his youth[1]. Other passages are an immediate reflexion of the anarchy and alarm of the times in which the poem was written. Thus the opening lines of the second book, which contrast the security of the contemplative life with the strife of political and military ambition, seem to be suggested by the action of what is sometimes called the first triumvirate. The lines—

> Si non forte tuas legiones per loca campi, etc.—

have been noted[2] as a probable allusion to the position actually taken up by Julius Caesar outside of Rome in the opening months of the year 58 B.C. Some earlier lines of the same passage—

> Certare ingenio, contendere nobilitate,
> Noctes atque dies niti praestante labore
> Ad summas emergere opes rerumque potiri,—

have a resemblance to words directly applied by Cicero to Caesar[3], and are certainly more applicable to him than

---

[1] The lines (v. 999)—
> 'At non multa virum sub signis milia ducta
> Una dies dabat exitio,' etc.—

might well be a reminiscence of the great massacre at the Colline gate.

[2] Cp. Munro, Note II, p. 413. Third Edition.

[3] 'Si jam violentior aliqua in re C. Caesar fuisset, si eum magnitudo contentionis, studium gloriae, praestans animus, excellens nobilitas aliquo impulisset.' In. Vatinium 6.

to any other of the poet's contemporaries. The political reflexions in the poem, as for instance that at v. 1123, seem, in almost all cases, to be forced from him by the memory of the first civil war, or the vague dread of that which was impending. It is not from any effeminate recoil from danger, but rather from horror of the turbulence, disorder, and crimes against the sanctities of human life, involved in the strife of ambition, that Lucretius preaches the lessons of political quietism. And while his humanity of feeling makes him shrink from the prospect of evil days, like those which he well remembered, again awaiting his country, his capacity for pure and simple pleasures makes him equally shrink from the spectacle of prodigal luxury which Rome then presented in a degree never before witnessed in the world.

Thus the first general impression of Lucretius which we form from his poem is that of one who, from a strong distaste to the life of action and social pleasure, deliberately chose the life of contemplation,—the 'fallentis semita vitae.' Some illustrations of his argument—as, for instance, a description of the state of mental tension produced by witnessing public games and spectacles for many days in succession[1], of the reflexion of the colours cast on the stage by the awnings of the theatre[2], of the works of art adorning the houses of the great[3], etc.—imply that he had not always been a stranger to the enjoyments of city life, and that they attracted him by a certain fascination of pomp and novelty. His pictures of the follies of the 'jeunesse dorée,' (at iv. 1121, etc.), and of sated luxury (at iii. 1060, etc.), show that he had been a witness of the conditions of life out of which they were engendered. At iv. 784, in speaking of the power of the mind to call up images, he specifies 'conventus hominum, pompam, convivia, pugnas.' But such illustrations are rare when compared with those which speak of a life passed in the open air, and of intimate familiarity with many aspects of Nature.

---

[1] iv. 973, etc.   [2] iv. 75, etc.   [3] ii. 24, etc.

The vivid minuteness with which outward things are described, as well as the occasional use of such words as *vidi*[1], show that though a few of the sights observed by him may have been drawn from the physics of Epicurus[2], the great mass of them had either been originally observed by himself or at least had been verified in his own experience. He was endowed not only with the poet's susceptibility to the beauty and movement of the outward world, but also with the observing faculty and curiosity of a naturalist: and by both impulses he was more attracted to the solitudes of Nature than to the haunts of men. Many bright illustrations of his argument tell of hours spent by the sea shore. Thus he notes minutely the effect of the exhalations from the salt water in wearing away rocks and walls (i. 336; iv. 220), the invisible influence of the sea-air in producing moisture in clothes (i. 305; vi. 472), or a salt taste in the mouth (iv. 222), the varied forms of shells paving the shore (ii. 374), the sudden change of colour when the winds raise the white crest of the waves (ii. 765), the appearance of sky and water produced by a black storm-cloud passing over the sea (vi. 256). Other passages show his familiarity with inland scenes,—with the violent rush of rivers in flood (i. 280, etc.), or their stately flow through fresh meadows (ii. 362), or their ceaseless unperceived action in eating away their banks (v. 256);—or again, with all the processes of husbandry, the growth of plants and trees, the ways of flocks and herds in their pastures, and the sounds and sights of the pathless woods. While he anticipates Virgil in his Italian love of peaceful landscape, he shows some foretaste of the modern passion for the mountains,—as (at ii. 331) where he speaks of 'some spot among the lofty hills,' commanding a distant view of a wide expanse of plain, and (at iv. 575) where he recalls the memory of wanderings among mountain solitudes—

> Palantis comites cum montis inter opacos
> Quaerimus et magna dispersos voce ciemus,—

[1] In places where he is not drawing from his own observation, he uses such expressions as *memorant*; e.g. iii. 642.   [2] E.g. iv. 353, etc.

and (at vi. 469) where he notices the more powerful action of the wind on the movements of the clouds at high altitudes—

> Nam loca declarat sursum ventosa patere
> Res ipsa et sensus, montis cum ascendimus altos.

Even some of the metaphorical phrases in which he figures forth the pursuit of truth seem to be taken from mountain adventure[1]. The mention of companionship in some of these wanderings, and in other scenes in which the charm of Nature is represented as enhancing the enjoyment of a simple meal—

> Propter aquae rivum sub ramis arbonis altae,—

enable us to think of him as, although isolated in his thoughts from other men, yet not separated from them in the daily intercourse of life by any unsocial austerity. Such separation would have been quite opposed both to the teaching and the example of his master. Some remembrance of active adventure is suggested by illustrations of his philosophy drawn from the experience of a sea-voyage (iv. 387, etc., 432), of riding through a rapid stream (iv. 420), of watching the action of dogs tracking their game through woods and over mountains (i. 404), or renewing the memories of the chase in their dreams (v. 991, etc.). The lines (at ii. 40, etc., and 323, etc.) show that his imagination had been moved by witnessing the evolutions of armies, not indeed in actual warfare, but in the pomp and pageantry of martial spectacles,—'belli simulacra cientes.' These and many other indirect indications afford some glimpses of his habitual manner of life and of the pursuits that gave him most lively pleasure: but they do not give us any special knowledge of the particular districts of Italy in which he lived, or of the scenes in foreign lands which he may have visited. The poem tells us nothing immediately of the trials or passions of his life, though of both he seems to bear the scars. But as

---

[1] e.g. 'Ardua dum metuunt amittunt vera viai'
and 'Avia Pieridum peragro loca.'

passages in which he reveals the deep secrets of human passion and suffering prove him to have been a man of strong, ardent, and vividly susceptible temperament, so the numerous illustrations drawn from the repertory of his personal observation tell of an eye trained to take delight in the outward face of Nature as well as of a mind unwearied in its search into her hidden laws. One great charm of his work is that it breathes of the open air more than of the library. If, in dealing with the problems of human life, his strain—

> 'Is fraught too deep with pain,'

yet to him too might be applied the lines written of one who, though not comparable to him in intellectual and imaginative power, yet, in his spiritual isolation from the world, seems almost like his modern counterpart—

> 'And thou hast pleasures too to share
> With those who come to thee,
> Balms floating on thy mountain air
> And healing sights to see.'[1]

But we may trust with even more confidence to the indications of his inner than of his outward life. The spirit and purpose which impelled Lucretius to expound his philosophy can be understood without any collateral knowledge of his history. The dominant impulse of his being is the ardent desire to emancipate human life from the fears and passions by which it is marred and degraded. He has more of the zeal of a religious reformer than any other ancient thinker, except one who in all his ways of life was most unlike him, the Athenian Socrates. The speculative enthusiasm which bears him along through his argument is altogether subsidiary to the furtherance of his practical purpose. Even the poetical power to which the work owes its immortality was valued chiefly as a pleasing means of instilling the unpalatable medicine of his philosophy[2] into the minds and hearts of unwilling hearers. It is the constant presence of this practical purpose, and the profound sense which he has of the actual misery and

---

[1] Obermann, by M. Arnold.   [2] i. 935-50.

degradation of human life, and of the peace and dignity which are attainable by man, that impart to his words the peculiar tone of impassioned earnestness to which there is no parallel in ancient literature.

Among his personal characteristics none is more prominent than his consciousness both of the greatness of the work on which he was engaged, and of his own power to cope with it. The passage in which his high self-confidence is most powerfully proclaimed (i. 920, etc.), has been imitated both by Virgil and Milton. The sense of novelty, adventure, and high aspiration expressed in the lines—

> Avia Pieridum peragro loca nullius ante
> Trita solo—

moved Virgil less powerfully in speaking of his humbler theme—

> Sed me Parnassi deserta per ardera dulcis
> Raptat amor;

and inspired the English poet in his great invocation :—

> I thence
> Invoke thy aid to my adventurous song,
> That with no middle flight intends to soar
> Above the Aonian mount, while it pursues
> Things unattempted yet in prose and rhyme.

The sense of difficulty and the joy of overcoming it meet us with a keen bracing effect in many passages of the poem. He speaks disdainfully of those enquirers who fall into error by shrinking from the more adventurous paths that lead to truth—

> Ardua dum metuunt amittunt vera viai.

Without disowning the passion for fame,—'laudis spes magna,'—so powerful an incentive to the Roman temperament, he is more inspired and supported in his arduous task by 'the sweet love of the Muses.' The delight in the exercise of his art and the joyful energy sustained through the long processes of gathering and arranging his materials appear in such passages as iii. 419-20 :—

> Conquisita diu dulcique reperta labore
> Digna tua pergam disponere carmina cura :

and again at ii. 730—

> Nunc age dicta meo dulci quaesita labore
> Percipe.

U

The thoroughness and devotion of a student tell their own tale in such expressions as the 'studio disposta fideli,' and the 'noctes vigilare serenas' in the dedication to Memmius, and in the more enthusiastic acknowledgment of the source from which he drew his philosophy at iii. 29, etc.—

> Tuisque ex, inclute, chartis,
> Floriferis ut apes in saltibus omnia libant,
> Omnia nos itidem depascimur aurea dicta.

The absorbing interest with which he carried on the work of enquiry and of composition appears in illustrations of his argument drawn from his own pursuits; as where (ii. 979) in arguing that, if the atoms have the properties of sense, those of which man is compounded must have the intellectual attributes of man, he says,—

> Multaque de rerum mixtura dicere callent
> Et sibi proporro quae sint primordia quaerunt;[1]

and, again (at iv. 969), in explaining how men in their dreams seem to carry on the pursuits to which they are most devoted, how lawyers seem to plead their causes, generals to fight their battles over again, sailors to battle with the elements, he adds these lines:—

> Nos agere hoc autem et naturam quaerere rerum
> Semper et inventam patriis exponere chartis.[2]

His frequent use of the sacrificial phrase 'Hoc age,' affords evidence of the religious earnestness with which he had devoted himself to his task.

The feeling animating him through all his great adventure,—through the wastest flats as well as the most commanding heights over which it leads him,—is something different from the delight of a poet in his art, of a scholar in his books, of a philosopher in his thought, of a naturalist

---

[1] 'And can discourse much on the combination of things; and enquire moreover, what are their own first elements.'

[2] 'While I seem ever to be plying this task earnestly, to be enquiring into Nature, and explaining my discoveries in writings in my native tongue.' This is one of those passages which seem to indicate an unhealthy overstrain which may have been the precursor of the final disturbance of 'his power to shape.'

in his observation. All of these modes of feeling are combined with the passion of his whole moral and intellectual being, aroused by the contemplation of the greatest of all themes—'maiestas cognita rerum'—and concentrated on the greatest of practical ends, the emancipation and elevation of human life. The life of contemplation which he alone among the Romans deliberately chose and realised he carried out with Roman energy and fortitude. It was with him no life of indolent musing, but one of thought and study, varied and braced by original observation. It was a life, also, of strenuous literary effort employed in giving clearness to obscure materials, and in eliciting poetical charm from a language to which the musical cadences of verse had been hitherto almost unknown. Above all, it was the life of one who, while feeling the spell of Nature more profoundly than any poet who had gone before him, did not in that new rapture forget

'The human heart by which we live.'

His high intellectual confidence, based on his firm trust in his master, shows itself in a spirit of intolerance towards the school which was the chief antagonist of Epicureanism at Rome. His argument is a vigorous protest against philosophical error and scepticism, as well as against popular ignorance and superstition. His polemical attitude is seen in the frequent use of such expressions as 'vinco,' 'dede manus,' etc., addressed to an imaginary opponent. Discussion of topics, not apparently necessary to his main argument, is raised with the object of carrying the war into the enemy's camp. Such frequently recurring expressions as 'ut quidam fingunt,' 'perdelirum esse videtur,' etc., are invariably aimed at the Stoics[1]. Of other early philosophers, even when dissenting from their opinions, he speaks in terms of admiration and reverence: but Heraclitus, whose physical explanation of the universe was adopted by the Stoics, is described in terms of disparage-

---

[1] Cp. Munro's notes on the passages where these expressions occur.

ment, levelled as much against his later followers as against himself, as—

> Clarus ob obscuram linguam magis inter inanis
> Quamde gravis inter Graios qui vera requirunt.

The traditional opposition between Democritus and Heraclitus lived after them. Adherence to the doctrine of 'atoms and the void,' and to that of 'the pure fiery element,' became the symbol of a radical divergence in the whole view of human life.

While there is frequent allusion to the Stoics in the poem, there is no direct mention either of them or of their chief teachers, Zeno, Chrysippus, or Cleanthes. Neither do the greater names of Socrates, Plato, or Aristotle appear in it, though one or two passages clearly imply some familiarity with the writings of Plato[1]. But among the moral teachers of antiquity he acknowledges Epicurus only. The whole enthusiasm of his temperament breaks out in admiration of him. He alone is the true interpreter of Nature and conqueror of superstition (i. 75); the reformer 'who has made pure the human heart' (vi. 24); the 'guide out of the storms and darkness of life into calm and light' (iii. 1; v. 11, 12); the 'sun who at his rising extinguished all the lesser stars' (iii. 1044). He is to be ranked even as a God on account of his great services to man, in teaching him the mastery over his fears and passions:—

> Deus ille fuit, deus, inclute Memmi.[2]

He speaks of his master throughout not only with the affection of a disciple, but with an emotion akin to religious ecstasy[3]. His admiration for him springs from a deeper source of spiritual sentiment than that of Ennius for Scipio,

---

[1] E.g. ii. 77, etc. Augescunt aliae gentes etc., suggested by a passage in the Laws:—γεννῶντας τε καὶ ἐκτρέφοντας παῖδας, καθάπερ λαμπάδα τὸν βίον παραδιδόντας ἄλλοις ἐξ ἄλλων — and the lines which recur several times, etc. 'Nam veluti pueri trepidant,' which Mr. Munro aptly compares with the words in the Phaedo (77), ἴσως ἔνι τις καὶ ἐν ἡμῖν παῖς, ὅστις τὰ τοιαῦτα φοβεῖται.

[2] v. 8.

[3] Cf. 'His ibi me rebus quaedam divina voluptas
Percipit adque horror.'

or of Virgil for Augustus. Though Epicurus inspired much affection in his lifetime, and though other great writers after Lucretius,—such as Seneca, Juvenal, and Lucian,—vindicate his name from the dishonour which the perversion of his doctrines brought upon it, yet even the most favourable criticism of his life and teaching must find it difficult to sympathise with the idolatry of Lucretius. Yet his error, if it be one, springs from a generous source. He attributes his own imaginative interest in Nature to a philosopher who examined the phenomena of the outward world merely to find a basis for the destruction of all religious belief. He saturates with his own deep human feeling a moral system which professes to secure human happiness by emptying life of its most sacred associations, most passionate longings, and profoundest affections.

There was a truer affinity of nature between Lucretius and another philosopher whom he names with the warmest feelings of love and veneration—Empedocles of Agrigentum—the most famous of the early physiological poets of Greece. He flourished during the fifth century B.C., and was the author of a didactic poem on Nature, of which some fragments still remain, sufficient to indicate the nature of the work and the character of the man. These fragments prove that Lucretius had carefully studied the older poem, and adopted it as his model in using a poetical form and diction to expound his philosophical system. He declares, indeed, his opposition to the doctrine of Empedocles, which traced the origin of all things to four original elements; but he adopted into his own system many both of his expressions and of his philosophical ideas. The line in which the Roman poet enunciates his first principle,—

Nullam rem e nilo gigni divinitus unquam,

was obviously taken from the lines of the old poem περὶ φύσεως—

ἐκ τοῦ γὰρ μὴ ἐόντος ἀμήχανόν ἐστι γενέσθαι
τό τ' ἐὸν ἐξόλλυσθαι ἀνήνυστον καὶ ἄπρηκτον.

Speaking of Sicily as a rich and wonderful land, Lucretius

pays his tribute of love and admiration to his illustrious predecessor in these lines,—

> Nil tamen hoc habuisse viro praeclarius in se
> Nec sanctum magis et mirum carumque videtur.
> Carmina quin etiam divini pectoris eius
> Vociferantur et exponunt praeclara reperta,
> Ut vix humana videatur stirpe creatus.[1]

There is a close agreement between the two poetical philosophers in their imaginative mode of conceiving Nature. They both represented the principle of beauty and life in the universe under the symbol of the Goddess of Love—'Κύπρι βασίλεια ;' 'alma Venus, genetrix.' They both explain the unceasing process of decay and renovation in the world by an image drawn from the most impressive spectacle of human life—a mighty battle, waged through all time between opposing forces. The burden and the mystery of life seem to weigh heavily on both, and to mould their very language to a deep, monotonous solemnity of tone. But along with this affinity of temperament there is also a marked difference in their modes of thought and feeling. The view of Nature in the philosophy of Empedocles appears to be just emerging out of the anthropomorphic fancies of an earlier time: the first rays of knowledge are seen trying to pierce through the clouds of the dawn of enquiry: the dreams and sorrows of religious mysticism accompany the awakened energies of the reason. His mournful tone is the voice of the intellectual spirit lamenting its former home, and baffled in its eager desire to comprehend 'the whole.' Lucretius, on the other hand, saw the outward world as it looks in the light of day, neither glorified by the mystic colours of religion, nor concealed by the shadows of mythology. He was moved neither by the passionate longing of the soul, nor by the 'divine despair' of the intellect; but he felt profoundly

---

[1] 'But nought greater than this man does it seem to have possessed, nor aught more holy, more wonderful, or more dear. Yea, too, strains of divine genius proclaim aloud and make known his great discoveries, so that he seems scarcely to be of mortal race.'—i. 729-33.

the sorrows of the heart, and was weighed down by the ever-present consciousness of the misery and wretchedness in the world. The complaint of the first is one which has been uttered from time to time by some solitary thinker in modern as in ancient days :—

> παῦρον δὲ ζωῆς ἀβίου μέρος ἀθρήσαντες
> ὠκύμοροι, καπνοῖο δίκην ἀρθέντες ἀπέπταν
> αὐτὸ μόνον πεισθέντες, ὅτῳ προσέκυρσεν ἕκαστος,
> παντοσ' ἐλαυνόμενοι· τὸ δ' οὖλον ἐπεύχεται εὑρεῖν
> αὕτως. οὔτ' ἐπιδερκτὰ τάδ' ἀνδράσιν οὔτ' ἐπάκουστα
> οὔτε νόῳ περιληπτά.[1]

The other gives a real and expressive utterance to that 'thought of inexhaustible melancholy,' which has weighed on every human heart :—

> Miscetur funere vagor
> Quem pueri tollunt visentis luminis oras:
> Nec nox ulla diem neque noctem aurora secutast
> Quae non audierit mixtos vagitibus aegris
> Ploratus mortis comites et funeris atri.[2]

Besides Epicurus and Empedocles Lucretius mentions Democritus and Anaxagoras, and speaks even of those whom he confutes as 'making many happy discoveries by divine inspiration,' and as 'uttering their responses from the shrine of their own hearts with more holiness and truth than the Pythia from the tripod and laurel of Apollo.' The reverence which other men felt in presence of the ceremonies of religion he feels in presence of the majesty of Nature; and to the interpreters of her meaning he ascribes the holiness claimed by the ministers of religion. Thus, to a doctrine of Democritus he applies the words 'sancta viri sententia.' The divinest faculty in man

---

[1] 'When they have gazed for a few years of a life that is indeed no life, speedily fulfilling their doom, they vanish away like a smoke, convinced of that only which each hath met in his own experience, as they were buffeted about to and fro. Vainly doth each boast to have discovered the whole. The eye cannot behold it, nor the ear hear it, nor the mind of man comprehend it.'

[2] 'With death there is ever blending the wail of infants newly born into the light. And no night hath ever followed day, no morning dawned on night, but hath heard the mingled sounds of feeble infant wailings and of lamentations that follow the dead and the black funeral train.'—ii. 576-80.

is that by which truth is discovered. The highest office of poetry is to clothe the discoveries of thought with the charm of graceful expression and musical verse[1].

Of other Greek authors, Homer and Euripides are those of whom we find most traces in the poem. To the first he awards a high preeminence above all other poets,—

> Adde repertores doctrinarum atque leporum,
> Adde Heliconiadum comites; quorum unus Homerus
> Sceptra potitus eadem aliis sopitu' quietest[2].

The passages in which Lucretius imitates him show how clearly he recognised his exact vision of outward things, and his true appreciation of the moral strength and dignity of man. The frequent imitations of Euripides[3] show that while he felt the spell of his pathos, he was also attracted by the poetic mould into which the tragic poet has cast the physical speculations of Anaxagoras. Allusion is made in tones of indifference or disparagement to other poets of Greece, as having, in common with the painters of former times, given shape and substance to the superstitious fancies of mankind. It is characteristic of his powerful and independent genius, that, unlike the younger poets of his generation, he adheres to the older writers of the great days of Greece, and acknowledges no debt to the Alexandrine School. Although amply furnished with the knowledge necessary for the performance of his task, he is a poet of original genius much more than of learning and culture: and he is thus more drawn to those who acted on him by a kindred power, than by those who might have served him as models of poetic form or repertories of poetic illustration. The strength of his understanding attracted him to some of the great prose-writers of Greece, by whom that quality is most conspicuously displayed; notably to Thucydides, whom he has closely followed in his account of the 'Plague at Athens,' and, as has been shown by Mr. Munro, to Hippocrates. The kind of attraction which the last of these has for him confirms the

---

[1] i. 943-50.   [2] iii. 1036-38.   [3] Cf. notes ii. of Mr. Munro's edition.

criticism of Goethe, that Lucretius shows the observing faculty of a physician, as well as of a poet.

The diction and rhythm of the poem, as well as the more direct tribute of personal acknowledgment[1], prove that he was an admiring student of his own countryman Ennius, to whom in some qualities of his temperament and genius he bore a certain resemblance. Many lines, phrases, and archaic words in Lucretius, such as—

> Per gentis Italas hominum quae clara clueret,—
> Lumina sis oculis etiam bonus Ancu' reliquit,—
> inde super terras fluit agmine dulci,—

multa munita virum vi; caerula caeli Templa; Acherusia templa; luminis oras; famul infimus; induperator; Graius homo, etc.—

have a clear ring of the older poet. The few allusions to Roman history in the poem, as, for instance, the line—

> Scipiadas, belli fulmen, Carthaginis horror,—

the specification at iii. 833 of the second Punic War as a momentous crisis in human affairs,—the description at v. 1226 of a great naval disaster, such as happened in the first Punic War,—the introduction there of elephants into the picture of the pomp and circumstance of war,—suggest the inference that, just as events and personages of the earlier history of England live in the imaginations of many English readers from their representation in the historical plays of Shakspeare, so the past history of his country lived for Lucretius in the representation of Ennius. But of the national pride by which the older poet was animated, the work of Lucretius bears only scanty traces. The feeling which moved him to identify the puissant energy pervading the universe with 'the mother of the Aeneadae,' and the motive of his prayer for peace addressed to that Power,—

> Nam neque nos agere hoc patriai tempore iniquo,—

seem indeed to spring from sources of patriotic affection, perhaps all the deeper because not too loudly proclaimed.

---

[1] i. 117, etc.

But in the body of the poem his illustrations are taken as frequently from Greek as from Roman story, from the strangeness of foreign lands as from the beauty of Italian scenes. The Georgics of Virgil, in the whole conception of Nature as a living power, and in many special features, owe much to the imaginative thought of Lucretius; but nothing can be more unlike the spirit of the older poet than the episodes in which Virgil pours forth all his Roman feeling and his love of Italy. The height from which Lucretius contemplates all human history, as 'a procession of the nations handing on the torch of life from one to another,' is wide apart from that from which Virgil beholds all the nations of the world doing homage to the majesty of Rome. The poem of Lucretius breathes the spirit of a man, apparently indifferent to the ordinary sources of pleasure and of pride among his countrymen. Living in an era, the most momentous in its action on the future history of the world, he was only repelled by its turbulent activity. The contemplation of the infinite and eternal mass and order of Nature made the issues of that age and the imperial greatness of his country appear to him as transient as the events of the old Trojan and Theban wars. To him, as to the modern poet, whose imagination most nearly resembles his, the thought of more enduring things had

> 'Power to make
> Our noisy years seem moments in the being
> Of the eternal silence.'

But while by his silence on the subject of national glory and his ardent speculative enthusiasm Lucretius seems to be more of a Greek than of a Roman, yet no Roman writer possessed in larger measure the moral temper of the great Republic. He is a truer type of the strong character and commanding genius of his country than even Virgil or Horace. He has the Roman conquering energy, the Roman reverence for the majesty of law, the Roman gift for introducing order into a confused world, the Roman power of impressing his authority on the minds of men. In his fortitude, his superiority to human weakness, his seriousness of spirit, his dignity of bearing, he seems to embody the great Roman qualities 'constantia' and 'gravitas.' If in the force and sincerity of his own nature he reminds us of the earliest Roman writer of genius, in these last qualities, the acquired and inherited virtues of his race, he reminds us of the last representative writer, whose tone is worthy of the 'Senatus populusque Romanus.' But Lucretius is much more than a type of the strong Roman qualities. He combines a poetic freshness of feeling, a love of simple living, an independence of the world, with a tenderness and breadth of sympathy, and a power of sounding into the depths of human sorrow, such as only a very few among the ancients—Homer, Sophocles, Virgil, —and not many among the poets or thinkers of the modern world have displayed. In no quality does he rise further above the standard of his age than in his absolute sincerity and his unswerving devotion to truth[1]. He combines in himself some of the rarest elements in the Greek and the Roman temperament,—the Greek ardour of speculation, the Roman's firm hold of reality. A poet of the age of Julius Cæsar, he is animated by the spirit of an early Greek enquirer. He unites the speculative passion of the dawn of ancient science with the minute observation of its meridian; and he applies the imaginative conceptions formed in the first application of abstract thought to the universe to interpret the living beauty of the world.

[1] Mr. Froude, in his 'Julius Cæsar,' says, 'The age was saturated with cant.' Perhaps, to that condition of his age we, in part, owe one of the sincerest protests against cant, and unreality of every kind, ever written. Both speculatively and practically Cicero appears at a great disadvantage when compared with Lucretius in these respects.

CHAPTER XII.

THE PHILOSOPHY OF LUCRETIUS.

THE peculiarity of the poem of Lucretius, that which makes it unique in literature, is the fact that it is a long sustained argument in verse. The prosaic title of the poem, 'De rerum natura,'—a translation of the Greek περὶ φύσεως,—indicates that the method of exposition was adopted, not primarily with the view of affecting the imagination, but with that of communicating truth in a reasoned system. In the lines, in which the poet most confidently asserts his genius, he professes to fulfil the three distinct offices of a philosophical teacher, a moral reformer, and a poet,—

> Primum quod magnis doceo de rebus et artis
> Religionum animum nodis exsolvere pergo,
> Deinde quod obscura de re tam lucida pango
> Carmina, musaeo contingens cuncta lepore.[1]

We have, accordingly, to examine the poem in three different aspects:—

I. as the exposition of a system of speculative philosophy.

II. as an attempt to emancipate and reform human life.

III. as a work of poetical art and genius.

But these three aspects, though they may be considered separately, are not really independent of one another. The speculative ideas on which the system of philosophy is ultimately based impart confidence and elevation to the moral

---

[1] 'First, by reason of the greatness of my argument, and because I set the mind free from the close-drawn bonds of superstition; and next because, on so dark a theme, I compose such lucid verse, touching every point with the grace of poesy.'—i. 931-34.

teaching, and new meaning and imaginative grandeur to the interpretation of Nature and of human life, on which the permanent value of the poem depends. Thus, although the philosophical argument, which forms as it were the skeleton of the work, is in many places barren and uninteresting, yet it is necessary to master it before we can form a true estimate of the personality of the poet, of the main passion and labour of his life, of the full meaning of his thought, and the full compass of his poetic genius. Moreover, the study of the argument is interesting on its own account. In no other work are the strength and the weakness of ancient physical philosophy so apparent. If the poem of Lucretius adds nothing to the knowledge of scientific facts, it throws a powerful light on one phase of the ancient mind. It is a witness of the eager imagination and of the searching thought of that early time, which endeavoured, by the force of individual thinkers and the intuitions of genius, to solve a problem which is perhaps beyond the reach of the human faculties, and to explain, at a single glance, secrets of Nature which have only slowly been revealed to the patient labours and combined investigations of many generations of enquirers.

I.—EXAMINATION OF THE ARGUMENT.

I. The philosophical system expounded in the poem is the atomic theory of Democritus[1], in the form in which it was accepted by Epicurus, and made the basis of his moral and religious doctrines. Lucretius lays no claim to original discovery as a philosopher : he professes only to explain, in his native language, 'Graiorum obscura reperta.' His originality consists, not in any expansion or modification of the Epicurean doctrine, but in the new life which he has imparted to its exposition, and in the poetical power with which he has applied it to reveal the secret of the life of Nature and of man's true position in the world. After enunciating the first principles of the atomic philo-

[1] Of Leucippus, with whose name the theory is also associated, very little is known.

sophy, he discusses in the last four books of the poem some special applications of that doctrine, which formed part of the physical system of Epicurus. But the extent to which he carries these discussions is limited by the practical purpose which he has in view. The impelling motive of all his labour is the impulse to purify human life, and, especially, to emancipate it from the terrors of superstition. The source of these terrors is traced to the general ignorance of certain facts in Nature,—ignorance, namely, of the constitution and condition of our souls and bodies, of the means by which the world came into existence and is still maintained, and lastly, of the causes of many natural phenomena, which are attributed to the direct agency of the gods. With the view of establishing knowledge in the room of ignorance on these questions, it is necessary, in the first place, to give a full account of the original principles of being: and to this enquiry the two first books of the poem are devoted. Had his purpose been merely speculative, the subject of the fifth book,—viz. the origin of the world, of life, and of human society,—would naturally have been treated immediately after the exposition of these first principles. But the order of treatment is determined by the immediate object of attacking the chief stronghold of superstition: and, accordingly, the third and fourth books contain an examination of the nature of the soul, a proof of its non-existence after death, and an explanation of the origin of the belief in a future state. In the fifth and sixth books an attempt is made to show that the creation and preservation of the world, the origin and progress of human society, and the phenomena of thunder, tempests, volcanoes, and the like, are the results of natural laws, without Divine intervention. Although he sometimes carries his argument into greater detail than is necessary for his purpose, and addresses himself to the reform of other evils to which the human heart is liable, yet his whole treatment of his subject is determined by the thought of the irreconcilable opposition between the truths of Nature and the falsehood of the ancient religions. The key-note to the argument is contained in the lines, which recur as a kind of prelude to the successive stages on which it enters, in the first, second, third, and sixth books :—

> Hunc igitur terrorem animi tenebrasque necessest
> Non radii solis neque lucida tela diei
> Discutiant, sed naturae species ratioque.[1]

The action of the poem might be described as the gradual defeat of the ancient dominion of superstition by the new knowledge of Nature. This meaning seems to be symbolised in its magnificent introduction, where the genial, all-pervading Power—the source of order, beauty, and delight in the world and in the heart of man,—and the grim phantom of superstition —

> Horribili super aspectu mortalibus instans,—

the cause of ignorance, degradation, and misery,—are vividly personified and presented in close contrast with one another. The thought, thus symbolised, pervades the poem. The processes of Nature are explained not chiefly for the purpose of satisfying the love of knowledge (although this end is incidentally attained), but as the means of establishing light in the room of darkness, peace in the room of terror, faith in the laws and the facts of the universe in the room of a base dependence on capricious and tyrannical Powers.

What then was this philosophy which supplied to Lucretius an answer to the perplexities of existence? The object contemplated by all the early systems of ontology was the discovery of the original substance or substances out of which all existing things were created, and which alone remained permanent amid the changing aspects of the visible world. Various systems, of a semi-physical, semi-metaphysical character, were founded on the answers given by the earliest enquirers to this question. In the first book of the poem several of these theories are discussed. Lucretius following Epicurus, adopts the answer given by Democritus to this question, that the original substances were the

---

[1] 'This terror of the soul, therefore, and this darkness must be dispelled, not by the rays of the sun or the bright shafts of day, but by the outward aspect and harmonious plan of nature.'—i. 146–48.

'atoms and the void'—ἄτομα καὶ κενόν. After the invocation and the address to Memmius, and the representation of the universal tyranny exercised by superstition until its power was overcome by Epicurus, and after a summary of the various topics to be treated in order to banish this influence from the world, he lays down this principle as the starting-point of his argument,—that no existing thing is formed out of nothing by divine agency—

> Nullam rem e nilo gigni divinitus unquam.

The apprehension of this principle—a principle common to all the ontological systems of antiquity—is the first step in the enquiry, as to what are the original substances out of which all creation comes into being and is maintained. The proof of this principle is the manifest order and causation recognisable in the world. If things could arise out of nothing, all existence would be confused and capricious. The regularity of Nature subsists—

> Materies quia rebus reddita certast
> Gignundis e qua constat quid possit oriri.

The complement of this first principle is the proposition that no thing is annihilated, but all existences are resolved into their ultimate elements. As the first is a necessary inference from the existence of universal order, the second is proved by the perpetuity of creation and the observed transformation of things into one another.

The original substances out of which all things are produced, and into which they are ultimately resolved, are found to be certain primordial particles of matter or atoms, which are called by various names— 'materies,' 'genitalia corpora,' 'semina rerum,' 'corpora prima.' Some of these names, it may be observed, are expressive not only of their primordial character, but also of a germinative or productive power. The objection that these atoms are invisible to our senses is met by showing that there are many invisible forces acting in Nature, the effects of which prove that they must be bodies,—

> Corporibus caecis igitur natura gerit res.

In addition to bodily substance there must also be vacuum

or space; otherwise there could be no motion in the universe, and without motion nothing could come into being. The existence of matter is proved by our senses, of vacuum by the necessity of there being space for matter to move in, and also by the varying density of bodies. But besides body and vacuum there is no other absolute substance—

> Ergo praeter inane et corpora tertia per se
> Nulla potest rerum in numero natura relinqui.[1]

All material bodies are either elemental substances or compounded out of a union of these substances. The elemental substances are indestructible and indivisible. This is proved by the necessities of thought (i. 498, etc.) and of Nature. If there were no ultimate limit to the divisibility of these substances, if there were not something immutable underlying all phenomena, there could be no law or order in the world. The existence and ultimate constitution of the atoms is thus enunciated—

> Sunt igitur solida primordia simplicitate
> Quae minimis stipata cohaerent partibus arte,
> Non ex illarum conventu conciliata,
> Sed magis aeterna pollentia simplicitate,
> Unde neque avelli quicquam neque deminui jam
> Concedit natura reservans semina rebus.[2]

At this stage in the argument, from line 635 to 920 of Book I, the first principles of other philosophies, and particularly of the systems of Heraclitus, Empedocles, and Anaxagoras, are discussed at considerable length, and shown to be inconsistent with the actual appearance of things and with the principles already established.

A new departure is made at line 920, and it is shown that the atoms must be infinite in number, and space infinite in extent;—the contrary supposition being both

---

[1] i. 445-56.

[2] 'The original atoms are, therefore, of solid singleness, composed of the smallest particles in close and compact union, not kept together by any meeting of these particles, but rather powerful by their eternal singleness, from which nature allows no loss by violence or decay, storing them as the seeds of all things.'—i. 609-14.

inconceivable and incompatible with the origin, preservation, and renewal of all existing things. It is shown also that the existing order of things has not come into being through design, but by infinite experiments through infinite time. The doctrine that all things tend to a centre is denied, and the book concludes with the imaginative presentation of the thought that, if matter were not infinite, the whole visible fabric of the world would perish in a moment, 'and leave not a rack behind.'

The second book opens with an impressive passage, in which the security and charm of the contemplative life is contrasted with the restless anxieties and alarms of the life of worldly ambition. The argument then proceeds to explain the process by which these atoms, primordial, indestructible, and infinite in number, combine together in infinite space, so as to carry on the birth, growth, and decay of all things. While the sum of things always remains the same, there is constant change in all phenomena. This is explicable only on the supposition of the original elements being in eternal motion. The atoms are borne through space, either by their own weight, or by contact with one another, with a rapidity of motion far beyond that of any visible bodies. All motion is naturally in a downward direction and in parallel lines, but to account for the contact of the atoms with one another it must be supposed that in their movements they make a slight declension from the straight line at uncertain intervals. This liability to declension is the sole thing to break the chain of necessity—'quod fati foedera rumpat.' It is through this liability in the primal elements that volition in living beings becomes possible.

As the sum of matter in the universe is constant, so the motions of the atoms always have been and always will be the same[1]. All things are in ceaseless motion, although they may present to our senses the appearance of perfect rest.

It is necessary further to assume the existence of other

[1] ii. 297-302.

properties in the atoms, in order to account for the variety in Nature, and the individuality of existing things. They have original differences in form; some are smooth, others round, others rough, others hooked, &c. These varieties in form are not infinite, but limited in number.

As the diversity in the world depends on the diversity of these forms, the order and regularity of Nature imply that there is a limit to these varieties. But while they are limited, the individuals of each kind are infinite, otherwise the primordial atoms would be finite in number, and there could be no cohesion among atoms of the same kind, in the vast and chaotic sea of matter—

> Unde ubi qua vi et quo pacto congressa coibunt
> Materiae tanto in pelago turbaque aliena?[1]

The motions which tend to the support and the destruction of created things are balanced by one another: there must be an equilibrium in these opposing forces—

> Sic aequo geritur certamine principiorum
> Ex infinito contractum tempore bellum.[2]

Death and birth succeed one another, as now the vitalising, now the destructive forces gain the upper hand.

Further, the great diversity in Nature is to be accounted for by diversity, not only in the original forms of matter, but also in their modes of combination. No existing thing is composed solely of one kind of atoms. The greater the variety of forces and powers which anything displays, the greater is the variety of the elements out of which it was originally composed. Of all visible objects the earth contains the greatest number of elements; therefore it has justly obtained the name of the universal mother. There is however a limit to the modes in which atoms can combine with one another: each nature appropriates elements suitable to its being and rejects those unsuitable. All existing things differ from one another in consequence of the difference in their elements and in their modes of combination. The different modes of combination give rise to many of the secondary properties of matter, which are

[1] ii. 549. [2] ii. 575-76

not in the original elements. Colour, for instance, is not one of the original properties of atoms: for all colour is changeable, and all change implies the death of what previously existed. Moreover, colour depends on light, and the atoms never come forth into the light. The atoms are also devoid of heat and cold, of sound, taste, and smell. All these properties must be kept distinct from the original elements—

> Immortalia si volumus subiungere rebus
> Fundamenta quibus nitatur summa salutis;
> Ne tibi res redeant ad nilum funditus omnes.[1]

Further, although they are the origin of all living and sentient things, the atoms themselves are devoid of sense and life, otherwise they would be liable to death. All living things are merely results of the constant changes in the primordial elements contained in the heavens and the earth. Hence the heaven is addressed as the father, the earth as the mother, of all things that have life.

Finally, from the infinity of space and matter, it may be inferred that there are infinite other worlds and systems beside our own. Many elements were added from the infinite universe to our system before it reached maturity: and many indications prove that the period of growth is now past, and that we are living in the old age of the world.

The sum of the first two books, in which the principles of the atomic philosophy are methodically unfolded and illustrated, is, accordingly, to this effect:—that all things have their origin in, and are sustained by, the various combinations and motions of solid elemental atoms, infinite in number, various in form, but not infinite in the variety of their forms,—not perceptible to our senses, and themselves devoid of sense, of colour, and of all the secondary properties of matter. These atoms, by virtue of their ultimate conditions, are capable only of certain combinations with one another. These combinations have been

---

[1] 'If we are to suppose the existence of an eternal substance, at the basis of all things, on which the safety of the whole universe rests, lest you find creation resolved into nonentity.'—ii. 862–64.

brought about by perpetual motion, through infinite space and through all eternity. As the order of things now existing has come into being, so it must one day perish. Only the atoms will permanently remain, moving unceasingly through space, and forming new combinations with one another.

These first principles being established, the way is made clear for the true explanation, according to natural laws, of those phenomena which give rise to and maintain the terrors of superstition.

The third book treats of the nature of the mind, and of the vital principle. As it is by the fear of death, and of eternal torment after death, that human life is most disturbed, it is necessary to explain the nature of the soul, and to show that it perishes in death along with the body.

The mind and the vital principle are parts of the man as much as the hands, feet, or any other members. The mind is the directing principle, seated in the centre of the breast. The vital principle is diffused over the whole body, obedient to and in close sympathy with the mind. The power which the mind has in moving the body proves its own corporeal nature, as motion cannot take place without touch, nor touch without the presence of a bodily substance.

The soul (including both the mind and vital principle) is, therefore, material, formed of the finest or minutest atoms, as is proved by the extreme rapidity of its movement, and by the fact that there is nothing lost in appearance or weight immediately after death:—

> Quod simul atque hominem leti secura quies est
> Indepta atque animi natura animaeque recessit,
> Nil ibi libatum de toto corpore cernas
> Ad speciem, nil ad pondus: mors omnia praestat
> Vitalem praeter sensum calidumque vaporem.[1]

Four distinct elements enter into the composition of the

---

[1] 'So soon as the deep rest of death hath fallen upon a man, and the mind and the life have departed from him, there is no loss in his whole frame to be perceived, either in appearance or in weight. Death still presents everything that was before, except the vital sense and the warm heat.'—iii. 211–15.

soul—heat, wind, calm air, and a finer essence 'quasi anima animai.' The variety of disposition in men and animals depends on the proportion in which these elements are mixed.

The soul is the guardian of the body, inseparably united with it, as the odour is with frankincense; nor can the soul be disconnected from the body without its own destruction. This intimate union of soul and body is proved by many facts. They are born, they grow, and they decay together. The mind is liable to disease, like the body. Its affections are often dependent on bodily conditions. The difficulties of imagining the state of the soul as existing independently of the body are next urged; and the book concludes with a long passage of sustained elevation of feeling, in which the folly and the weakness of fearing death are passionately insisted upon.

The fourth book, which treats of the images which all objects cast off from themselves, and, in connexion with that subject, of the senses generally, and of the passion of love, is intimately connected with the preceding book. If there is no life after death, what is the origin of the universal belief in the existence of the souls of the departed? Images cast off from the surface of bodies, and borne incessantly through space without force or feeling, appearing to the living sometimes in sleep and sometimes in waking visions, have suggested the belief in the ghosts of the dead, and in many of the portents of ancient mythology. The rapid formation and motion of these images and their great number are explained by various analogies. Some apparent deceptions of the senses are next mentioned and explained. These deceptions are shown to be not in the senses, but in our minds not rightly interpreting their intimations. There is no error in the action of the senses. They are our 'prima fides'—the foundation of all knowledge and of all conduct—

> Non modo enim ratio ruat omnis, vita quoque ipsa
> Concidat extemplo, nisi credere sensibus ausis.[1]

[1] 'For, not only would all reason come to nought, even life itself would immediately be overthrown, unless you dare to trust the senses.'—iv. 507–8.

THE PHILOSOPHY OF LUCRETIUS. 311

Images that are too fine to act on the senses sometimes directly affect the soul itself. Discordant images unite together in the air, and present the appearance of Centaurs, Scyllas, and the like. In sleep, images of the dead—

> Morte obita quorum tellus amplectitur ossa,[1]—

appear, and give rise to the belief in the existence of ghosts. The mind sees in dreams the objects in which it is most interested, because, although all kinds of images are present, it can discern only those of which it is expectant.

Several other questions are discussed in connexion with the doctrine of the 'simulacra.' The final cause of the senses and the appetites is denied, and, by implication, the argument from design founded on the belief in final causes. The use of everything is discovered through experience. We do not receive the sense of sight in order that we may see, but having got the sense of sight, we use it—

> Nil ideo quoniam natumst in corpore ut uti
> Possemus, sed quod natumst id procreat usum.[2]

There follows an account of sleep, and of the condition of the mind during that state; and the book concludes with a physical account of the passion of love, which is dependent on the action of the simulacra on the mind. Love is shown also to arise from natural causes, and not to be engendered by divine influence. The fatal consequences of yielding to the passion are then enforced with much poetical and satirical power.

The object of the fifth book is to explain the formation of our system—of earth, sea, sky, sun, and moon,—the origin of life upon the earth, and the advance of human nature from a savage state to the arts and usages of civilisation. The purpose of these discussions is to show that all our system was produced and is maintained by natural agency,

---

[1] i. 135.
[2] 'Since nothing in our body has been produced in order that we might be able to put it to use, but what has been produced creates its own use.'—iv. 834-35.

that it is neither itself divine nor created by divine power, and that, as it has come into existence, so it must one day perish.

As the parts of our system,—earth, water, air, and heat, —are perishable, and constantly passing through processes of decay and renovation, the system must have had a beginning, and will have an end. There must at last be an end of the long war between the contending elements.

The world came into existence as the result not of design, but of every variety of combination in the elemental atoms throughout infinite time. Originally all were confused together. Gradually those that had mutual affinities combined and separated themselves from the rest. The earthy particles sank to the centre. The elemental particles of the empyrean (aether ignifer) formed the 'moenia mundi.' The sun and moon were formed out of the particles that were neither heavy enough to combine with the earth, nor light enough to ascend to the highest heaven. Finally, the liquid particles separated from the earth and formed the sea. Highest above all is the empyrean, entirely separated from the storms of the lower air, and moving round with its stars by its own impetus. The earth is at rest in the centre of our system, supported by the air, as our body is by the vital principle. The movements of the stars and of the sun and moon through the heavens are next explained; then the origin of vegetable and animal life on the earth, and the beginning and progress of human society.

First plants and trees, afterwards men and animals, were produced from the earth in the early and vigorous prime of the world. Many of the animals originally produced afterwards became extinct. Those only were capable of continuation which had either some faculty of self-preservation against others, or were useful to man, and so shared his protection. The existence of monsters such as Scylla, the Centaurs, the Chimaera, is shown to be impossible according to the natural laws of production.

The earliest condition of man was one of savage vigour

and power of endurance, but liable to danger and destruction from many causes. The first humanising influence is traced to domestic union and the affection inspired by children—

> Et Venus inminuit viris puerique parentum
> Blanditiis facile ingenium fregere superbum.[1]

The origin of language is next explained, then that of civil society, of religion, and of the arts,—the general conclusion being that all progress is the result of natural experience, not of divine guidance.

The last source of superstition is our ignorance of the causes of natural phenomena—

> Praesertim rebus in illis
> Quae supera caput aetheriis cernuntur in oris.[2]

Hence the sixth book is devoted to the explanation of thunderstorms, tempests, volcanoes, earthquakes, and the like,—phenomena which are generally attributed to the direct agency of the gods. The whole work terminates with an account of the Plague at Athens, closely following that given by Thucydides.

The first question which arises after a review of the whole argument is that suggested by the statement of Jerome, and brought into prominence since the publication of Lachmann's edition of Lucretius, viz. whether there is good reason for believing that the poem was left by the author in an unfinished state. In answering this question, it is to be observed, on the one hand, that there is no incompleteness in the fulfilment of the original plan of the work, unless from one or two hints[3] we conclude that the poet intended giving a fuller account of the blessed state of the Gods than that given at iii. 17-24. He announces at i. 54, etc., and again at i. 127, etc., the design of the poem as embracing the first principles of natural philosophy, and the application of these principles to

---

[1] 'And love impaired their strength, and children, by their coaxing ways, easily broke down the proud temper of their fathers.'—v. 1017-18.
[2] vi. 60-1.   [3] E.g. i. 54; v. 154.

certain special subjects, viz. the nature of soul and body, the origin of the belief in ghosts, the natural causes of creation, and the meaning of certain celestial phenomena.

The practical purpose of the poem—the overthrow of superstition—limits the argument to these subjects of discussion. They are severally mentioned where the argument is resumed in Books iii, iv, v, and vi, as those matters which require a clear explanation from the poet. All the topics enunciated in the opening statement are discussed with the utmost fulness. The great strongholds of superstition are attacked and overthrown in regular succession. In the introduction to the sixth book, the lines (91-95)

> Tu mihi supremae praescribta ad candida calcis, etc.

clearly show that the poet considered himself approaching the end of his task.

But, on the other hand, an examination of the poem in detail leads to the conclusion that it did not receive its author's final touch. The continuity of the argument is occasionally broken in all the books except the first. In the fourth, fifth, and sixth, especially, these breaks are very frequent, and there are more frequent instances in them of repetition and careless workmanship. They extend also to a greater length than the earlier books, which would naturally be the case if they had not received the author's final revision. The poem throughout gives the impression of great fulness of matter—

> Usque adeo largos haustus e fontibu' magnis
> Lingua meo suavis diti de pectore fundet;—

and in the composition of these later books, new suggestions seem to have been constantly occurring to the poet as new materials were added to his stores of knowledge: and the first draft of his argument has not been recast so as to incorporate and harmonise them with it. The passages containing these new materials appear to have been fitted into the place which they now occupy in the work, not always very judiciously, either by Cicero or some other editor.

It was also part of the author's design to enunciate his deepest thoughts on the Gods, on Nature, and on human life in more highly finished digressions from the main argument. Such passages are, in general, introduced at the beginning and the end of the different books. They seem to bring out the more catholic interest which underlies the special subject of the poem. Some of these passages are highly finished, and were evidently fixed by the poet in the places which he designed them to occupy. Such are, especially, the introductions to the first, second, and third books, and the concluding passages of the second and third. But the repetition of a passage of the first book as the introduction to the fourth, the long break in the continuity of the introduction to the fifth, the unfinished style of that to the sixth, and the abrupt and episodical conclusion to the whole poem (when contrasted with its elaborately artistic introduction), show that the same cause which marred the symmetry of his argument deprived it of the finished execution of a work of art. Yet these books—especially the fifth—are as rich in poetical feeling and substance as the earlier ones. The eye and hand of the master are as powerful as in the first enthusiasm with which he dedicated himself to his task, but they are less certain in their action. Whether his powers became intermittent owing to the attacks of illness, or whether his habit was to work roughly in the first instance and to perfect his work by subsequent revision, which in the case of his latest labours was prevented by death, must remain uncertain. It is a noticeable result of the vastness of the tasks which Roman genius set before itself, that two such works as the didactic poem of Lucretius and the Aeneid of Virgil were left unfinished by their authors, and given to the world in a more or less imperfect condition by other hands.

The poem, though incomplete in regard to the arrangement of its materials and artistic finish, presents a full and clear view of the philosophy accepted and expounded by Lucretius. What, then, is the intellectual interest and value of the work, considered as a great argument, in which the plan of Nature is explained, and the position of man in relation to that plan is determined? Is it true, as an illustrious modern critic[1] has said, that 'the greatest didactic poem in any language was written in defence of the silliest and meanest of all systems of natural and moral philosophy?' Is this work a mere maze of ingeniously woven error, enriched with a few brilliant colours which have not yet faded with the lapse of time? or is it a great monument of the ancient mind, marking indeed its limitations, but at the same time perpetuating the memory of its native strength and energy? Has all the meaning of this controversy between science in its infancy and the pagan mythology in its decrepitude passed away, as from the vantage-ground of nineteen centuries the blindness and the ignorance of both combatants are apparent? Or, may we not rather discern that amid all the confusion of this dim νυκτομαχία a great cause was at issue; that truths the most vital to human wellbeing were involved on both sides; and that some positions were then gained which are not now abandoned?

In estimating the strength and the weakness of the system expounded by Lucretius, it is necessary to distinguish between the exposition of the principles of the atomic philosophy, contained in the first two books, and the explanation of natural phenomena contained in the remaining books. The first, notwithstanding some arbitrary and unverifiable assumptions, represents a real and important stage in the progress of enquiry; the second, although containing many striking observations and immediate inferences from the facts and processes of Nature, is, from the point of view of modern science, to be regarded mainly, as a curious page from the records of human error. Whatever may be said of the Epicurean additions to the system, it seems to be admitted that the original hypothesis of Democritus has been more pregnant in results, and has more affinity with the most advanced physical speculations

[1] Macaulay.

of modern times, than the doctrines of all the other philosophers of antiquity. But even amid the mass of unwarranted assumptions and erroneous explanations contained in the later books, the topics discussed—such as the relation of the mind to the body, the mode by which sensible impressions are conveyed to the mind, the processes by which our globe assumed its present form, the origin of life, the evolution of humanity from its lowest to its higher stages of development, the origin of spiritual beliefs, of the humaner sentiments, of language, etc.—possess the interest of being kindred to those on which speculative activity is most employed in the present day. If the study of Lucretius forces upon our minds the arbitrary assumptions, the inadequate method, and the false conclusions of ancient science, it enables us to appreciate the disinterested greatness of its aims, and the enlightened curiosity which sought to solve the vastest problems.

It might be said, generally, that the argument of Lucretius was an attempt to give a philosophical description of Nature before the advent of physical science. But, as a means of throwing light on the inadequacy of such speculations, it may be well to consider in detail some of those points where the argument most obviously fails in premises, method, and results.

The ancient as well as the modern enquirer into the truth of things was confronted with the question of the origin of all our knowledge. Is knowledge obtained originally through the exercise of the reason or the senses, or through their combined and inseparable action? To this question Lucretius distinctly answers, that the senses are the foundation of all our knowledge[1]. They are our 'prima fides'; the basis not only of all sound inference, but of all human conduct. The very conception of the meaning of true and false is derived from the senses :—

> Invenies primis ab sensibus esse creatam
> Notitiam veri neque sensus posse refelli.[2]

[1] E. g. i. 694. [2] iv. 478-79.

But besides the direct action of outward things on the senses, he admits the power of certain images to make themselves immediately present to the mind (iv. 722–822), and also a certain immediate apprehension or intuition of the mind (iniectus animi) into things beyond the cognisance of sense[1]. Thus there is no actual inconsistency with his principles in claiming the power of understanding the properties and configuration of the atoms, which are represented as lying below the reach of our senses—

> Omnis enim longe nostris ab sensibus infra
> Primorum natura iacet.

But of the mode of operation of this 'intuition of the mind' there is no criterion. The doctrine of the properties, shapes, motions, etc. of the atoms is a creation of the imagination, suggested by certain analogies from sensible things, but incapable of being verified by the senses, which he regards as the only sure foundations of knowledge.

But even on the supposition that the existence and properties of the atoms had been satisfactorily established, no adequate explanation is offered of their relation to the facts of existence. The same difficulty is encountered at the outset of this as of all other ancient systems of ontology, viz. how to pass from the eternal and immutable forms of the atoms to the variety and transitory nature of sensible objects. This is the very difficulty which Lucretius himself urges against the system of Heraclitus,—

> Nam cur tam variae res possint esse requiro,
> Ex uno si sunt igni puroque creatae.

The order of Nature now subsisting is declared to be the result of the manifold combination of the atoms through infinite time and space, but the intermediate stages by which this process was effected are assumed rather than investigated. We seem to pass 'per saltum' from the chaos of lifeless elements to the perfect order and manifold life of our system. This wide chasm seems as little capable

---

[1] 'In quae corpora si nullus tibi forte videtur
Posse animi iniectus fieri, procul avius erras.'—ii. 739-40.

of being bridged by the help of the atoms of Democritus, as by the watery element of Thales or the fiery element of Heraclitus. But in Lucretius this difficulty is partially concealed, by a poetical element in his conception, really inconsistent with the mechanical materialism on which his philosophy professes to be based.—It is to be observed that while the Greek word ἄτομα implies merely the notion of individual existences, the words used by Lucretius, 'semina,' 'genitalia corpora,' really indicate a creative capacity in these existences. In conceiving their power of carrying on and sustaining the order of Nature, his imagination is thus aided by the analogy of the growth of plants and living beings. A secret faculty in the atoms, distinct from their other properties, is assumed. Thus he says—

> At primordia gignundis in rebus oportet
> Naturam clandestinam caecamque adhibere.[1]

In his statement of the doctrine of the *Clinamen*, or slight declension in the motion of the atoms, so as 'to break the chain of fate,' he attributes to them a power analogous to volition in living beings. This doctrine is suggested by the necessity of explaining contingency in Nature and freedom in the movements of sentient beings. We are, as in all attempts to account for creation, forced back on the thought of an ultimate unexplained power in virtue of which things have been created and are maintained in being.

The Lucretian hypothesis of the atoms, even if it were accepted as the most reasonable explanation of the original constitution of matter, is, by itself, altogether inadequate as a key to the secret of Nature. It cannot be shown either how these atoms succeeded in arranging themselves in order, or how from their negative properties all positive life has been produced. The explanation of physical phenomena given in the four last books, as to the nature of our bodies and souls,—as to the action of outward things on

---

[1] 'But it is necessary that the atoms, in the act of creation, should exercise some secret, invisible faculty.'—i. 778-79.

the senses,—the origin and existence of the sun and moon, the earth and the living beings upon it, etc., although professedly deduced from the principles established in the first two books, are really reached independently. They are either immediate inferences from the obvious intimations of sense, or they are the suggestions of analogy.

The weakness as well as the strength of ancient science lay in its perception of analogies. The mind of Lucretius was both under the influence of earlier analogical conceptions, and also shows great boldness and originality in the logical and poetical apprehension of 'those same footsteps of Nature, treading on diverse subjects or matters.' But, in common with the earlier enquirers of Greece, he trusts too implicitly to their guidance through all his daring adventure. He seems to believe that the hidden properties of things are as open to discovery through this 'lux sublustris' of the imagination, as through the 'lucida tela' of the reason.

To take one prominent instance of this influence, it is remarkable how, in his explanation of our mundane system, he is both consciously and unconsciously guided by the analogy of the human body. Even Lucretius, living in the very meridian of ancient science, cannot in imagination absolutely emancipate himself from the associations of mythology. He is indeed conscious of the inconsistency of attributing life and sense to the earth: yet not only does he speak poetically of Earth being the creative mother, Aether the fructifying father of all things, but his whole conception of the creation of the world is derived from a supposed likeness between the properties of our terrestrial and celestial systems, and those of living beings. Thus we read—

> Undique quandoquidem per caulas aetheris omnis
> Et quasi per magni circum spiracula mundi
> Exitus introitusque elementis redditus extat.[1]

---

[1] 'Since on all sides, through all the pores of aether, and, as it were, all round through the breathing-places of the mighty world, a free exit and entrance is given to the atoms.'—vi. 492-94.

Of the growth of plants and herbage it is said—

> Ut pluma atque pili primum saetaeque creantur
> Quadripedum membris et corpore pennipotentum,
> Sic nova tum tellus herbas virgultaque primum
> Sustulit, inde loci mortalia saecla creavit.[1]

From v. 535 to 563 the power of the air in supporting the earth 'in media mundi regione' is compared with the power which the delicate vital principle has in supporting the human body. Again, the gathering together of the waters of the sea is thus represented—

> Tam magis expressus salsus de corpore sudor
> Augebat mare manando camposque natantis.[2]

And finally, though it would be easy to multiply such quotations, the striking account, at the end of the second book, of the growth and the decay of our world is drawn directly from the obvious appearances of the growth and decay of the human body; e.g.—

> Quoniam nec venae perpetiuntur
> Quod satis est neque quantum opus est natura ministrat.[3]

As a necessary result of a system of natural philosophy based on assumptions, largely illustrated indeed, but not corroborated by the observation of phenomena, with no verification of experiment or ascertainment of special laws, there is throughout the poem the utmost hardihood of assertion and inference on many points, on which modern science clearly proves this system to have been as much in error as it was possible to be. It is strange to note how inadequate an idea Lucretius had of the vastness and complexity of the problem which he professed to solve. He has no real conception of the progressive advance of knowledge, and of the necessity of

---

[1] 'As feathers, and hair, and bristles are first formed on the limbs of beasts and the bodies of birds, so the young earth then first bore herbs and plants, afterwards gave birth to the generations of living things.'—v. 788-91.

[2] 'So more and more, the sweat oozing from the salt body, increased the sea and the moving watery plains by its flow.'—v. 487-88.

[3] 'Since neither its veins can support adequate nourishment, nor does Nature supply what is needful.'—ii. 1141-42.

patiently building on humble foundations. The striking lines—

> Namque alid ex alio clarescet nec tibi caeca
> Nox iter eripiet quin ultima naturai
> Pervideas: ita res accendent lumina rebus,[1]

look rather like an unconscious prophecy of the future progress of science than an account of the process of enquiry exhibited in the book.

A few out of many erroneous assertions about physical facts, in regard to some of which the opinions of Lucretius are behind the science even of his own time, may be noticed. Thus, at i. 1052, the existence of the Antipodes is denied. Again, in Book iii. the mind is stated to be a material substance, seated in the centre of the breast, composed of very minute particles, the relative proportions of which determine the characters both of men and animals. Lucretius shows a close and subtle observation of facts that establish the interdependence of mind and body, but no suspicion of that interdependence being connected with the functions of the brain and nervous system. His whole account of the *mundus*, of the earth at rest in the centre, and of the rolling vault of heaven, with its sun and moon and stars—'trembling fires in the vault'— all no larger than they appear to our eyes, is given without any notion of the inadequacy of his data to bear out his conclusions. The science which satisfied Epicurus was on astronomical and meteorological questions behind that attained by the mathematicians of Alexandria: and thus some of the conclusions enunciated by Virgil in the Georgics are nearer the truth than those accepted by Lucretius. While enlarging on the variety and subtlety in the combinations of his imaginary atoms, he has no adequate idea of the variety and subtlety in the real forces of Nature. His observation of the outward and visible appearances of things is accurate and vivid: there is

---

[1] 'For one thing will grow clear after another: nor shall the darkness of night make thee lose thy way, before thou seest, to the full, the furthest secrets of Nature: so shall all things throw light one on the other.'—i. 1115-17.

often great ingenuity as well as a true apprehension of logical conditions in his processes of reasoning both from ideas and from phenomena: yet most of his conclusions as to the facts of Nature, which are not immediately perceptible to the senses, are mere fanciful explanations, indicating, indeed, a lively curiosity, but no real understanding of the true conditions of the enquiry. The root of his error lies in his not feeling how little can be known of the processes and facts of Nature by ordinary observation, without the resources of experiment and of scientific method built upon experiment.

The weak points of this philosophy, the mistaken aim and incomplete method of enquiry, the real ignorance of facts disguised under an appearance of systematic treatment, the unproductiveness of the results for any practical accession to man's power over Nature, are quite obvious to any modern reader, who, without any special study of physical science, cannot help being familiar with information which is now universally diffused, but which was beyond the reach of the most ardent enquirers and original thinkers of antiquity. But the amount of information possessed by different ages, or by different men, is no criterion of their relative intellectual power. The mental force of a strong and adventurous thinker may be recognised struggling even through these mists of error. The weakness of the system, interpreted by Lucretius, is the necessary weakness of the childhood of knowledge. But along with the weakness and the ignorance there are also the keen feeling, the clear eye, and the buoyant fancies of early years,—the germs and the promise of a strong maturity.

The full light in which ancient poetry, history, and mental philosophy can still be read, makes us apt to forget that a great part even of the intellectual life of antiquity has left scarcely any record of itself. Of one aspect of this intellectual life Lucretius is the most complete exponent. The genius of Plato and Aristotle has been estimated, perhaps, as justly in modern as in ancient times. But the great intellectual life of such men as Democritus, Empedocles, or Anaxagoras, escapes our notice in the more familiar studies of classical literature. The work of Lucretius reminds us of the intensity of thought and feeling, the clearness and minuteness of observation, with which the earliest enquiries into Nature were carried on. In some respects the general ignorance of the times enhances our sense of the greatness of individual philosophers. Each new attempt to understand the world was an original act of creative power. The intellectual strength and enthusiasm displayed by the poet himself may be regarded as some measure of the strength of the masters, who filled his mind with affection and astonishment.

The history of the physical science of the ancients cannot, indeed, be regarded as so interesting or important as that of their metaphysical philosophy. And this is so, not only on account of the comparative scantiness of their real acquisitions in the one as compared with the ideas and method which they have contributed to the other, and with the masterpieces which they have added to its literature; but still more on this account, that in physical knowledge new discovery supplants the place of previous error or ignorance, and can be understood without reference to what has been supplanted; whereas the power and meaning of philosophical ideas is unintelligible, apart from the knowledge of their origin and development. The history of physical science in ancient times affords satisfaction to a natural curiosity, but is not an indispensable branch of scientific study. The history of ancient mental philosophy, on the other hand,—the source not only of most of our metaphysical ideas and terms, but of many of the most familiar thoughts and words in daily use,—is the basis of all speculative study. Yet among the various kinds of interest which this poem has for different classes of modern readers this is not to be forgotten, that it enables a student of science to estimate the actual discoveries, and, still more, the prognostications of discovery attained by the irregular methods of early enquiry. The school of philosophy to which Lucretius belonged was distinguished above other schools for the attention which it gave to the facts of Nature. Though he himself makes no claim to original discovery, he yet shows a philosophical grasp of the whole system which he adopted, and a rigorous study of its details. He does not, like Virgil, merely reproduce some general results of ancient physics, to enhance the poetical conception of Nature: as he is not satisfied with those general results about human life and the origin of man, which amused a meditative poet and practical epicurean like Horace. He was a real student both of the plan of Nature and of man's relation to it. Out of the stores of his abundant information the modern reader may best learn not only the errors but also the happy guesses and pregnant suggestions of ancient science.

To the general reader there is another aspect, in which it is interesting to compare these germs of physical knowledge with some tendencies of scientific enquiry in modern times. The questions, vitally affecting the position of man in the world, which are discussed or raised by Lucretius in the course of his argument, are parallel to certain questions which have risen into prominence in connexion with the increasing study of Nature. Most conspicuous among these is the relation of physical enquiry to religious belief. Expressions such as this,

> Impia te rationis inire elementa viamque
> Indugredi sceleris,

show that scientific enquiry had to encounter the same prejudice in ancient as in modern times. The insufficiency and audacity of human reason were reprobated by the antagonists of Lucretius as they often are in the present day. Ancient religion denounced those who investigated the origin of sun, earth, and sky, as

> Immortalia mortali sermone notantes.[1]

The views of Lucretius as to the natural origin of life, and

---

[1] 'Dishonouring immortal things by mortal words.'—v. 121.

the progressive advance of man from the rudest condition by the exercise of his senses and accumulated experience,—his denial of final causes universally, and specially in the human faculties,—his resolution of our knowledge into the intimations of sense,—his materialism and consequent denial of immortality,—and his utilitarianism in morals,—all present striking parallels to the opinions of one of the great schools of modern thought. At v. 875 there is a passage concerning the preservation and destruction of species, originally suggested by Empedocles,—which shows that the idea of the struggle for existence and of the survival of those species best fitted for the conditions of that struggle was familiar to ancient thinkers. It is there observed that those species alone have escaped destruction which possess some natural weapon of defence, or which are useful to man. Of others that could neither live by themselves nor were maintained by human protection, it is said—

>Scilicet haec aliis praedae lucroque iacebant
>Indupedita suis fatalibus omnia vinclis,
>Donec ad interitum genus id natura redegit.[1]

The attempt to trace the origin of all supernatural belief to the impressions made by dreams, the explanation given of the first manifestation of the humaner sentiments, of the beginning of language, and of the whole condition of 'primitive man,' are in conformity with the teaching of the most popular exponent of the doctrine of evolution in the present day.

But altogether apart from the truth and falsehood, the right and wrong tendencies of his system of philosophy, our feeling of personal interest in the poet is strengthened by noting the power of reasoning, observation, and expression put forth by him through the whole course of his argument. The pervading characteristic of Lucretius is

---

[1] 'They, doubtless, became the prey and the gain of others, unable to break through the bonds of fate by which they were confined, until Nature caused that species to disappear.'—v. 875–77.

Mr. Wallace (Epicureanism, p. 114) in commenting on this passage adds, 'Of course in this there is no implication of the peculiarly Darwinian doctrine of descent, or development of kind from kind, with structure modified and complicated to meet changing circumstances.'

the 'vivida vis animi.' The freshness of feeling and vividness of apprehension denoted by the words,

> Mente vigenti
> Avia Pieridum peragro loca,

are as remarkable in the processes of his intellect as of his imagination.

The passionate intensity of his nature has left its impress on the enunciation of his physical as well as of his moral doctrines. He has a thoroughly logical grasp of his subject as a whole. He shows the capacity of unfolding it and marshalling all his arguments in symmetrical order, and of arranging in due subordination vast masses of details. Vigour in acquiring and tenacity in retaining the knowledge of facts are combined with a high organising faculty. He has also, beyond any other Roman writer, a power of analysing and comprehending abstract ideas, such as that of the infinite, of space and time, of causation and the like, and of keeping the consequences involved in these ideas present to his mind through long-sustained processes of reasoning. He alone among his countrymen possessed, if not the faculty of original speculation, the genuine philosophic impulse, and the powers of mind demanded for abstruse and systematic thinking.

This vigour of understanding is displayed in many processes of deductive reasoning, in the power of seizing some general principle underlying diverse phenomena, in the use of analogies by which he illustrates the argument and advances from known to unknown causes and from things within the cognisance of our senses to those beyond their range, and in the clearness and variety of his observation.

His system cannot be called either purely inductive or purely deductive, though it is more of the former than of the latter. He argues with great force both from a large and varied mass of facts to general laws and from general principles to facts involved in them. The best examples of his power of following abstract ideas into their consequences may be found in the first two books, where he establishes the existence of vacuum, the infinity of space and of the atoms, the limitations of the form of the atoms and the like. The reasoning at i. 298–328 where the existence of invisible bodies is established affords a good instance of his power of recognising a common principle involved in a great number and variety of phenomena.

The vigour with which he reasons from known to unknown facts and causes may be judged most fairly by his arguments on the progress of society, where he is more on an equality with modern speculation. He discards, altogether, as might be expected, the fancies concerning a heroic or a golden age, and assumes as his data the facts of human nature as observed in his own day. The grounds from which he starts, his method of reasoning, and the nature of his conclusions remind a reader of the positive tendencies of Thucydides, as they are displayed in the introduction to his history. The importance of personal qualities, such as beauty, strength, and power of mind, in the earliest stage of civil society, the influence of accumulated wealth at a later period, the causes of the establishment and overthrow of tyrannies and of the rise of commonwealths in their room, are all set forth with a degree of strong sense and historical sagacity, such as no other Roman writer has shown in similar investigations. The inferiority even of Tacitus in his occasional digressions into the philosophy of history is very marked. On such topics, where the data were accessible to the natural faculties of observation and inference, and where conclusions were sought which, without aiming at definite certainty, should yet be true in the main, the reader of Lucretius has no sense of that wasted ingenuity which he often feels in following the investigations into some of the primary conditions of the atoms, the component elements of the soul, the process by which the world was formed, or the causes of electric or volcanic phenomena.

Lucretius makes a copious, and often a very happy use, of analogies, both in the illustration of his philosophy, and in passages of the highest poetical power. Some of the most striking of the former kind have already been noticed as sources of error, or at least of disguising ignorance, in his reasoning, viz., those founded on the supposed parallel between the world and the human body; others again are employed with force and ingenuity in support of various positions in his argument. Among these may be mentioned his comparison of the effect of various combinations of the same letters in forming different words, with that of the various combinations of similar atoms in forming different objects in nature. So too the ceaseless motion of the atoms is brought visibly before the imagination by the analogy of the motes dancing in the sunbeam. There is something striking in the comparison of the human body immediately after death to wine 'cum Bacchi flos evanuit,' and again, in that of the relation of body and soul to the relation of frankincense and its odour—

> E thuris glaebis evellere odorem
> Haud facile est quin intereat natura quoque eius.[1]

But this faculty of his understanding is in general so united with the imaginative feeling through which he discerns the vital indentity of the most diverse manifestations of some common principle, that it can best be illustrated in connexion with the poetical, as distinct from the logical, merits of the work.

So also it is difficult to separate his faculty of clear, exact, and vivid observation from his poetical perception of the life and beauty of Nature. His powers of observation were, however, stimulated and directed by scientific as well as poetic interest in phenomena. From the wide scope of his philosophy he was led to examine the greatest variety of facts, physical as well as moral. His sense of the immensity of the universe led him to contemplate the largest and widest operations of Nature, —such as the movements of the heavenly bodies, the recurrence of the seasons, the forces of great storms, volcanoes, etc.; while, again, the theory of the invisible atoms drew his attention to the minutest processes of Nature, in

[1] iii. 327-28.

so far as they can be perceived or inferred without the appliances of modern science. Thus, for instance, in a long passage beginning—

> Denique fluctifrago suspensae in litore vestes,[1]

he shows by an accumulation of instances that there are many invisible bodies, the existence of which is inferred from visible effects. In other places he draws attention to the class of facts which have been the basis of the modern science of geology,—such as the mark of rivers slowly wearing away their banks,—of walls on the seashore mouldering from the long-continued effects of the exhalations from the sea,—of the fall of great rocks from the mountains under the wear and tear of ages.

Again, the argument is frequently illustrated by observation of the habits of various animals. In these passages Lucretius shows the curiosity of a naturalist, as well as the sympathetic feeling and insight of a poet. How graphic, for instance, is his description of dogs following up the scent of their game—

> Errant saepe canes itaque et vestigia quaerunt.[2]

How happily their characteristics are struck off in the line—

> At levisomna canum fido cum pectore corda.[3]

The various cries and habits of birds are often observed and described, as—

> Et validis cycni torrentibus ex Heliconis
> Cum liquidam tollunt lugubri voce querellam;[4]

and again—

> Parvus ut est cycni melior canor ille gruum quam
> Clamor in aetheriis dispersus nubibus austri.[5]

The description of sea-birds,

---

[1] i. 305.
[2] iv. 705.
[3] 'Dogs, lightly sleeping, with faithful heart.'—v. 864.
[4] 'When from the strong torrents of Helicon the swans raise their liquid wailing with doleful voice.'—iv. 547-48.
[5] 'As the low note of the swan is sweeter than the cry of the cranes, far-scattered among the south-wind's skiey clouds.'—iv. 181-82.

> Mergique marinis
> Fluctibus in salso victum vitamque petentes,[1]

recalls the vivid and natural life of those that haunted the isle of Calypso—

> τανύγλωσσοί τε κορῶναι
> εἰνάλιαι τῇσίν τε θαλάσσια ἔργα μέμηλεν.[2]

His lively personal observation and active interest in the casual objects presented to his eyes in the course of his walks are seen in such passages as—

> Cum lubrica serpens
> Exuit in spinis vestem; nam saepe videmus
> Illorum spoliis vepres volitantibus auctas.

There is also much truth and liveliness of observation in his notices of psychological and physiological facts; as in those passages where he establishes the connexion between mind and body, and in his account of the senses. With what a graphic touch does he paint the outward effects of death[4], the decay of the faculties with age, and the madness that overtakes the mind—

> Adde furorem animi proprium atque oblivia rerum,
> Adde quod in nigras lethargi mergitur undas;[5]

the bodily waste, produced by long-continuous speaking—

> Perpetuus sermo nigrai noctis ad umbram
> Aurorae perductus ab exoriente nitore;[6]

the reflex action of the senses, produced by the nervous strain of witnessing games and spectacles for many days in succession; the insensibility to the pain of the severest wounds in the excitement of battle! In his account of the plague of Athens, in which he enters into much greater detail than Thucydides, he displays the minute observation

---

[1] 'And gulls among the sea-waves, seeking their food and pastime in the brine.'—v. 1079-80.   [2] Od. vi. 66.

[3] 'And likewise, when the lithe serpent casts its skin among the thorns; for often we notice the briers, with their light airy spoils hanging to them.'—iv. 60-2.   [4] iii. 213-15.

[5] 'Consider, too, the special madness of the mind, and forgetfulness of things; consider its sinking into the black waves of lethargy.'—iii. 828-29.

[6] 'Unbroken speech prolonged from the first light of dawn till the shadows of the dark night.'—iv. 537-38.

of a physician, as well as the profound thought of a moralist.

The 'vivida vis' of his understanding is apparent also in the clearness and consecutiveness of his philosophical style. His complaint of 'the poverty of his native tongue' is directed against the capacities of the Latin language for scientific, not for poetical expression—

> Nunc et Anaxagorae scrutemur Homoeomerian
> Quam Grai memorant nec nostra dicere lingua
> Concedit nobis patrii sermonis egestas.[1]

That language, which gives admirable expression to the dictates of common sense and to the dignified emotions which inspire the conduct of great affairs, is ill adapted both for the expression of abstract ideas and for maintaining a long process of connected argument. Lucretius has occasionally to meet the first difficulty by the adoption of Graecisms, and the second by some sacrifice of artistic elegance. Thus he uses *omne* for τὸ πᾶν (II. 1108), *esse*, again, for τὸ εἶναι, and the like. Something of a formal and technical character appears in the links by which his argument is kept together, as in the constantly recurring use of certain connecting particles, such as the 'etenim,' 'quippe ubi,' 'quod genus,' 'amplius hoc,' 'huc accedit,' and the like. Virgil has retained some of the most striking of these connecting formulae, such as 'contemplator item,' 'nonne vides,' etc; but, as was natural in a poem setting forth precepts and not proofs, he uses them much more sparingly and with more careful selection. As used by Lucretius, they add to our sense of the vividness of the book, of the constant personal address of the author, and of his ardent polemical tone. They also keep the framework of the argument more compact and distinct: but they bring into greater prominence the artistic mistake of conducting an abstract discussion in verse. The very merits of the work considered as an argument,—its

---

[1] 'Now, too, let us examine the "Homoeomeria" of Anaxagoras, as the Greeks call it, though the poverty of our native speech does not admit of its being named in our language.'—i. 830-33.

clearness, fullness, and consecutiveness,—detract from the pleasure which a work of art naturally produces. But the style cannot be too highly praised for its logical coherence and lucid illustration. The meaning of Lucretius can never be mistaken from any ambiguity in his language. There are difficulties arising from the uncertainty of the text, difficulties also from our unfamiliarity with his method and principles, or with the objects he describes, but none from confusion in his ideas or his reasoning, or from a vague or unreal use of words.

II.—THE SPECULATIVE IDEAS IN LUCRETIUS.

But it is in his grasp of speculative ideas, and in his application of them to interpret the living world, that the greatness of Lucretius as an imaginative thinker is most apparent. The substantial truth of all the ancient philosophies lay in the ideas which they attempted to express and embody, not in the symbols by which these ideas were successively represented. Lucretius has a place among the few adventurous thinkers of antiquity who attained to high eminences of contemplation, which were hidden from the mass of their contemporaries, and which, in the breadth of view afforded by them, are not far below the higher levels of our modern conceptions of Nature and human life. And there came to him, as to the earlier race of thinkers, that which comes so rarely to modern enquiry, the fresh and poetical sense of surprise and keen curiosity, as at the first discovery of a new country, or the first unfolding of some illimitable prospect.

(1) In the philosophy of Lucretius the world is conceived as absolutely under the government of law. The starting-point of his system—

> Nullam rem e nilo gigni divinitus unquam,

is an inference from the recognition of this condition. There is no need to prove its truth: it is openly revealed in all the processes of Nature. This fact of universal order is indeed supposed to result from the eternal and immutable properties of the atoms and from the original limitation in their varieties: but the idea of law is prior to, and the condition of, all the principles enunciated in the first two books, in regard to the nature and properties of matter. In no ancient writer do we find the certainty and universality of law more emphatically and unmistakably expressed than in Lucretius. This is the final appeal in all controversy. The superiority of Epicurus is proclaimed on the ground of his having discovered the fixed and certain limitations of all existence—

> Unde refert nobis victor quid possit oriri,
> Quid nequeat, finita potestas denique cuique
> Quanam sit ratione atque alte terminus haerens.[1]

Following on his steps the poet himself professes to teach—

> Quo quaeque creata
> Foedere sint, in eo quam sit durare necessum,
> Nec validas valeant aevi rescindere leges.[2]

In another place he says—

> Et quid quaeque queant per foedera naturai
> Quid porro nequeant, sancitum quandoquidem extat.[3]

All knowledge and speculative confidence are declared to rest on this truth—

> Certum ac dispositumst ubi quicquit crescat et insit.[4]

Superstition, the great enemy of truth, is said to be the result of ignorance of 'what may be and what may not be.' This is the thought which underlies and gives cogency to the whole argument. The subject of the poem is 'maiestas cognita rerum,'—the revelation of the majesty and order of

---

[1] 'Whence returning victorious he brings back to us tidings of what may and what may not come into existence: on what principle, in fine, the power of each thing is determined and the deeply-fixed limit of its being.'—i. 75-77.

[2] 'According to what condition all things have been created, what necessity there is that they abide by it, and how they may not annul the mighty laws of the ages.'—v. 56-58.

[3] 'Since it is absolutely decreed, what each thing can and what it cannot do, by the conditions of nature.'—i. 586.

[4] 'It is fixed and ordered where each thing may grow and exist.'—iii. 787.

the universe. The doctrine proclaimed by Lucretius was, that creation was no result of a capricious or benevolent exercise of power, but of certain processes extending through infinite time, by means of which the atoms have at length been able to combine and work together in accordance with their ultimate conditions. The conception of these ultimate conditions and of their relations to one another involves some more vital agency than that of blind chance or an iron fatalism.[1] The 'foedera naturai' are opposed to the 'foedera fati.' The idea of law in Nature, as understood by Lucretius, is not merely that of invariable sequence or concomitance of phenomena. It implies at least the further idea of a 'secreta facultas' in the original elements. This idea is not, necessarily, inconsistent with that of a creative will determining the original conditions of the elemental substances. If the ultimate principles of Lucretius were incompatible with a belief in the popular religions of antiquity, his mode of conceiving the operation of law in the universe is not irreconcileable with the conceptions of modern Theism.

The idea of law not only supports the whole fabric of his physical philosophy, but moulds his convictions on human life and imparts to his poetry that contemplative elevation by which it is pervaded. It is from this ground that he makes his most powerful assault on the strongholds of superstition. Nature is thus declared to be free from the arbitrary and capricious agency of the gods:—

> Libera continuo dominis privata superbis.[2]

Man also is under the same law, and is made free by his knowledge and acceptance of this condition. A sense of security is thus gained for human life; a sense of elevation above its weakness and passions, and the courage to bear its inevitable evils[3]. This absolute reliance on law does not act upon his mind with the depressing influence of fatalism. Although the fortunes of life and the phases of individual character are said to be the results of the

---

[1] ii. 254.   [2] ii. 1091.   [3] vi. 32.

infinite combinations of blind atoms, yet man is made free by knowledge and the use of his reason. Notwithstanding the original constitution of his nature, arising out of influences over which there is no control, he still has it in his power to live a life worthy of the gods:—

> Illud in his rebus videor firmare potesse,
> Usque adeo naturarum vestigia linqui
> Parvola, quae nequeat ratio depellere nobis
> Ut nil inpediat dignam dis degere vitam.[1]

From these high places of his philosophy,—'the "templa serena" well-bulwarked by the learning of the wise'[2] he derives not only a sense of certainty in thought and security in life, but also his wide contemplative view, and his profound feeling of the majesty of the universe. The idea of universal law enables him to apprehend in all the processes of Nature a presence which awakens reverence and enforces obedience. This idea imparts unity of tone to the whole poem, informs its language, and seems to mould the very rhythm of its verse.

(2) But a closer view brings another aspect of the world into light; viz., the interdependence of all things on one another. There is not only fixed order, but there is also infinite mobility in Nature. The sum of all things remains unchanged, though all individual existences decay and perish. So too the sum of force remains the same[3]. There is no rest anywere; all things are continually changing and passing into one another; decay and renovation form the very life and being of all things. Nothing is ever lost. 'Nature repairs one thing from another, and allows of no birth except through the death of something else':—

> Haud igitur penitus pereunt quaecumque videntur,
> Quando alid ex alio reficit natura nec ullam
> Rem gigni patitur nisi morte adiuta aliena?[4]

---

[1] 'This, in these circumstances, I think I can establish, that such faint traces of our native elements are left beyond the powers of our reason to dispel, that nothing prevents us from leading a life worthy of the gods.'—iii. 319-22.
[2] ii. 8.   [3] ii. 297-99.   [4] i. 262-64.

As the 'ever-during peace' at the heart of all things is supposed to result from the eternal and immutable properties of the atoms, this 'endless agitation' arises out of their unceasing motion through infinite space. There are two kinds of motion,—the one tending to the renewal,—the other, to the destruction of things as they now exist. The maintenance of our whole system depends on the equilibrium of these opposing forces—

> Sic aequo geritur certamine principiorum
> Ex infinito contractum tempore bellum.[1]

There is thus seen to be not only absolute order, but also infinite change in the processes of Nature. Decay and renovation, death and life, support the existing creation in unceasing harmony. The imagination represents this process under the impressive symbol of an endless battle, in which now one side now the other gains some position, but neither, as yet, can become master of the field—

> Nunc hinc nunc illic superant vitalia rerum,
> Et superantur item.[2]

This symbol is the poetical form of the old philosophical distinction of αὔξησις and φθορά. It is another form of the ἔρις and φιλία which to the imagination of Empedocles appeared to pervade the universe. The idea of a constant battle imparts to the infinite and all-pervading movement of Nature the interest and the life of human passion on the grandest and widest sphere of action. The greatness of the thought makes each particular object in Nature pregnant with a deeper meaning, associates trivial and ordinary phenomena with a sense of imaginative wonder, and throws an august solemnity around the familiar aspects of human life. The passage in which this principle is most powerfully announced at ii. 575, &c., swells into deeper and grander tones, as the real human pathos involved in this strife of elements is made manifest. This struggle of life and decay is no mere war of abstractions: it is the daily and hourly process of existence.

[1] ii. 573-74.   [2] ii. 575-76.

Birth and death are the fulfilment of this law. 'The old order changeth, yielding place to new'—

> Cedit enim rerum novitate extrusa vetustas.[1]

'New nations wax strong, while the old are waning away; the generations of living things are changed within a brief space, and, like the runners in a race, pass on the torch of life'—

> Augescunt aliae gentes, aliae minuuntur,
> Inque brevi spatio mutantur saecla animantum
> Et quasi cursores vitai lampada tradunt.[2]

Man also must resign himself to the universal law, and accept his life not as a thing to be possessed for ever, but only to be used for a time—

> Sic alid ex alio numquam desistet oriri
> Vitaque mancipio nulli datur, omnibus usu.[3]

Under this law of universal decay and restoration, we see the rains of heaven lost in the earth, but passing into new life in the fruits from which all living things are supported—

> Hinc alitur porro nostrum genus atque ferarum,
> Hinc laetas urbes pueris florere videmus
> Frondiferasque novis avibus canere undique silvas.[4]

Or we see the waters of a river lost in the sea and returning through the earth to their original source, and again flowing in a fresh stream along the channel first formed for them—

> Inde super terras fluit agmine dulci
> Qua via secta semel liquido pede detulit undas.[5]

Under the same law the earth is seen to be the parent of all things and their tomb (v. 259); the sea, which loses its substance through evaporation and the subsidence of

---

[1] iii. 964.   [2] ii. 77–79.
[3] 'So one thing shall never cease being born from another, and life is given to no man as a possession, to all for use.'—iii. 970–71.
[4] 'Hence, moreover, the race of man and the beasts of the forest are fed; hence we see cities glad with the flower of their children, and the leafy woods on all sides loud with the song of young birds.'—i. 254–56.
[5] v. 271–72.

its waters, is found to be ever renewed by its native sources and the abundant tribute of rivers (v. 267; i. 231; vi. 608); the air is ever giving away and receiving back its substance; the sun ('liquidi fons luminis'), moon, and stars, are ever losing and ever renewing their light. The day on which the 'long-sustained mass and fabric of the world' will pass away, leaving only void space and the viewless atoms, is destined to come suddenly through the termination of this long balanced warfare :—

> Denique tantopere inter se cum maxima mundi
> Pugnent membra, pio nequaquam concita bello,
> Nonne vides aliquam longi certaminis ollis
> Posse dari finem? vel cum sol et vapor omnis
> Omnibus epotis umoribus exsuperarint;
> Quod facere intendunt, neque adhuc conata patrantur.[1]

(3.) It is to be observed, also, how vividly Lucretius realises and how steadfastly he keeps before his mind the ideas of the eternity and infinity of the primordial atoms and of space. These conceptions support him in his antagonism to the popular religion, and deepen the feeling with which he contemplates human life and Nature. Our world of earth, sea, and sky is only one among infinite other systems. It stands to the universe in much the same proportion as any single man to the whole earth—

> Et videas caelum summai totius unum
> Quam sit parvula pars et quam multesima constet
> Nec tota pars, homo terrai quota totius unus.[2]

It was the glory of Epicurus that he first passed beyond the empyrean that bounds our world—

> Atque omne immensum peragravit mente animoque.[3]

---

[1] 'Finally, since the vast members of the world, engaged in no holy warfare, so mightily contend with one another, see'st thou not that some end may be assigned to their long conflict, either when the sun and every mode of heat, having drunk up all the moisture, shall have gained the day, which they are ever tending to do, but do not yet accomplish?' etc.—v. 380-85.

[2] 'And that you may see how very small a part one firmament is of the whole sum of things, how small a fraction it is, not even so much in proportion as a single man is to the whole earth.'—vi. 650-52.

[3] 'And traversed the whole boundless region of space, in mind and spirit.'—i. 74.

The immensity of the universe is incompatible with the constant agency and interference of the gods,—

> Quis regere immensi summam, quis habere profundi
> Indu manu validas potis est moderanter habenas.[1]

This negative idea is, at least, a step in advance towards a higher conception of the attributes of Deity. The infinity and complexity of the universe protest against the limited and divided powers, as the natural feelings of human nature protest against the moral qualities attributed to the gods of the Pagan mythology.

The power of these conceptions is also seen in the poet's deep sense of the littleness of human life. Such pathetic expressions of the shortness and triviality of each man's mortal span, as that,—

> Degitur hoc aevi quodcumquest,[2]

are called forth by the ever-present thought of the Infinite and the Eternal. But this thought, if associated with a feeling of the pathos of human life does not lead Lucretius into cynicism or despair. It rather elevates him and fortifies him to suppress all personal complaint in the presence of ideas so stupendous. His imagination expands in contemplating the objects either of thought or of sight, which produce the impression of immensity,—such as the vast expanse of earth, sea and sky,—or of great duration,—such as the 'aeterni sidera mundi' or the 'validas aevi vires.' Thus, as much of the majesty of his poetry may be connected with his contemplative sense of law, much of its pervading life with his sense of the mobility of Nature, so the sublimity of many passages may be resolved into the influence of the ideas of immensity, both of time and space, on his imagination.

(4.) Another aspect of things vividly realised by Lucretius is that of their individuality. It was in the atomic philosophy, that the thought of 'the individual' first rose into prominence. The meaning of the word 'atom' is simply 'individual.' The sense of each separate existence is not

---

[1] 'Who can order the infinite mass? who can hold with a guiding hand the mighty reins of immensity?'—ii. 1095-96.   [2] ii. 16.

merged in the conception of law, of change, or of the immensity of the universe. The atoms are not only infinite in number, they are also varied in kind and powerful in solid singleness,—'solida pollentia simplicitate.' From their variety and individuality the variety and individuality in Nature emerge. No two classes and no two single objects are exactly alike. Between any two of the birds that gladden the sea-shore, the river banks, or the woods, there is some difference in outward appearance—

> Invenies tamen inter se differre figuris.[1]

Each individual of a flock is different from every other, and by this difference only can the mother recognise her offspring. This sense of individuality intensifies the pathos of many passages in the poem. By regarding each being as having an existence of its own, the poet enters with sympathy into the feelings of all sentient existence,—of dumb animals as well as of human creatures. The freshness and distinctness of all his pictures from Nature are the result of an eye trained by his philosophy to see each thing not only as part of the universal life, but as existing in and for itself.

(5.) The thought, also, of the infinite subtlety of combination in the elements and forces of the world acts powerfully on his imagination. The individuality of things depends on the fact that no two are composed of exactly the same elements, combined in the same way. The infinity of the elements, the immensity of the spaces in which they meet, and the infinite possibilities in their modes of combination result in the endless variety of beauty and wonder which the world presents to the eye. The epithet 'daedala,' by which this subtlety is expressed is applied not only to Nature, but to the earth as the sphere in which the elements are most largely mixed, and the creative forces most powerfully active. The varied loveliness of the world,—the 'varii lepores,' by which the eye is gratified and relieved,— are the result of the variety in the elements and the infinite

[1] ii. 348.

subtlety in their modes of combination. Their invisibility and inscrutable action enhance the imaginative sense of the power and beauty resulting from these causes.

(6.) The abstract properties of the atoms, discussed in the first two books, so far from being arbitrary assumptions, without any relation to actual existence, are thus found to be the conditions which explain the order, life, immensity, individuality, and subtlety manifested in the universe. These conceptions, which bridge the chasm between the particles of lifeless matter and the living world, unite in the more general conception of Nature. What then is involved in this conception—the dominant conception of the poem in its philosophical as well as its imaginative aspects? Something more than the subsidiary conceptions mentioned above. There is, in the first place, all that is involved in the unity of an organic whole. But to this whole the imagination of the poet seems, in some passages, to attach attributes scarcely reconcileable with the mechanical principles of his philosophy. In emancipating himself from the religious traditions of antiquity, Lucretius did not altogether escape from the power of an idea, so deeply rooted in the thought of past ages, as to seem to be an integral element of human consciousness. It is against the limitations which the ancient mythology imposed on the idea of Divine agency, rather than against the idea itself, as it is understood in modern times, that his philosophy protests. To Nature his imagination attributes not only life, but creative and regulative power. There would be more truth in calling this conception pantheistic than atheistic. But the sense of will, freedom, individual life, is so strong in Lucretius, that we think of the 'natura daedala rerum' rather as a personal power, with attributes in some respects analogous to those of man, than as a being in whose existence all other life is merged. Though this figurative attribution of personal qualities to great natural forces cannot be pressed as evidence of philosophical belief, yet as it shows, on the one hand, an unconscious survival of the state of mind which gave birth to mythology, so it seems to be the unconscious awakening of a spiritual conception of a creative and sustaining power in the universe.

This new and more vital conception which supersedes the old mythological modes of thought is not altogether independent of them. Lucretius still interprets the world by analogies and illustrations which attach personal attributes to different phases and forces of Nature. Thus he speaks of Aether as the fructifying father, of Earth as the great mother of all living things. But the survival of the mythological conception of the universe, blended indeed with other modes of imaginative thought, appears most conspicuously in the famous invocation to the poem,—

> Aeneadum genetrix, hominum divomque voluptas,
> Alma Venus.

The mysterious power there addressed is identified with the Alma Venus of Italian worship,—the abstract conception of the life-giving impulse, the operations of which are most visible in the new birth of the early spring,—and with the Aphrodite of Greek art and poetry,—the concrete and passionate conception of the beauty and charm which most fascinate the senses. But if nothing more was meant in the opening lines of the poem than a fanciful appeal to one of the Deities of the popular belief, it might with justice be said that some of the finest poetry in Lucretius directly contradicted his sincerest convictions. But the language in which she is addressed clearly proves that the ' Alma Venus ' of the invocation is not an independent capricious power, separate from the orderly action of Nature. She is emphatically addressed as a Power, present through all the world,—

> Caeli subter labentia signa
> Quae mare navigerum quae terras frugiferentis
> Concelebras.

She is not only omnipresent, but all-creative,—

> Per te quoniam genus omne animantum
> Concipitur,—

and all-regulative—

> Quae quoniam rerum naturam sola gubernas, &c.

Thus under the name, and with some of the attributes of the Goddess of Mythology, the genial force of Nature,—'Natura Naturans' as distinct from the 'rerum summa,' or 'Natura Naturata,'—is apprehended as a living, all-pervading energy, the cause of all life, joy, beauty, and order in the world, the cause too of all grace and accomplishment in man. To this mysterious Power, from which all joy and loveliness are silently emanating, the poet, (remembering at the same time that the friend to whom he dedicates his poem claims especially to be under the protection of that Goddess with whom she is identified), prays for inspiration,—

> Quo magis aeternum da dictis, diva leporem.[1]

Here, as in earlier invocations of the Muse, there is a recognition of the truth that the feeling, the imagery, and the words of the poet come to him in a way which he does not understand,—

> ἡμεῖς δὲ κλέος οἶον ἀκούομεν, οὐδέ τι ἴδμεν,—

and by the gift of a Power which he cannot command. Like Goethe, Lucretius seems to feel that his thoughts and feelings pass into form and musical expression under the influence of the same vital movement which in early spring fills the world with new life and beauty. But still true to his philosophy, and remembering the Empedoclean thought[2], which recurs with impressive solemnity in his argument, that this life-giving energy is inseparably united with a destructive energy, and seeing at the same time before his imagination the figures and colouring of some great masterpiece of Greek art, he embodies his conception in a passionately wrought picture of the loves of Aphrodite and Ares, and concludes with a prayer that the gracious Power whom he invokes would prevail on the fierce God of War to grant a time of peace to his country.

---

[1] i. 28.

[2] Lucretius, in other places where he introduces pictures or stories from the ancient mythology, as at ii. 600, etc., iii. 978, etc., iv. 584, etc., treats them as symbolising some facts of Nature or human life. Occasionally, as at v. 14, etc., he deals with them in the spirit of Euhemerism. He never uses them, as Virgil, Horace, or Ovid do, merely as materials for artistic representation.

If to regard this passage as merely an artistic ornament of the poem would be unjust to the sincerity of Lucretius as a thinker, to regard it merely as a piece of elaborate symbolism would be still more unjust to his genius as a poet. It is a truth both of thought and of imaginative feeling that there is a pervading and puissant energy in the world, manifesting itself most powerfully in animate and inanimate creation, when the deadness of winter gives place to the genial warmth of spring,—

> Tibi rident aequora ponti
> Placatumque nitet diffuso lumine caelum ;—

manifesting itself also in the human spirit in the form of genius, calling into life new feelings and fancies of the poet, and shaping them into forms of imperishable beauty. Whether consistently or inconsistently with the ultimate tenets of his philosophy, the poet, in this invocation, seems to recognise, behind these manifestations of unconscious energy, the presence of a conscious Being with which his own spirit can hold communion, and from which it draws inspiration. With similar inconsistency or consistency a modern physicist speaks of 'the impression of joy given in the unfolding of leaf and the spreading of plant as irresistibly suggesting the thought of a great Being conscious of this joy.'

But this puissant and joy-giving energy, personified in the 'Alma Venus genetrix,' is only one of the aspects which the 'Natura daedala rerum' of Lucretius presents to man. She seems to stand to him rather in the position of a task-mistress than of a beneficent Being, ministering to his wants. The Gods receive all things from her bounty,—

> Omnia suppeditat porro Natura,[1]—

and the lower animals who 'wage no foolish strife with her' have their wants also abundantly satisfied :—

> Quando omnibus omnia large
> Tellus ipsa parit Naturaque daedala rerum.[2]

But to man she is the cause of evil as well as of good;

---

[1] iii. 23.   [2] v. 233-4.

of shipwrecks, earthquakes, pestilence, and untimely death, as well as of all beauty and delight. Sometimes he seems to hear her speaking to him in the tones of stern reproof,—

> Denique si vocem rerum Natura repente, etc.[1]

Again he sees her rising up before him like the old Nemesis of Greek religion, and trampling with secret irony on the pride and pomp of human affairs,—

> Usque adeo res humanas vis abdita quaedam
> Opterit et pulchros fascis saevasque secures
> Proculcare ac ludibrio sibi habere videtur.[2]

It is this large conception of Nature which seems to bring the abstract doctrines of Lucretius into harmony with his poetical feelings and his human sensibilities. The poetry of the living world is thus breathed into the dry bones of the Atomic system of Democritus. The unity which the mind strains to grasp in contemplating the universe is thus made compatible with the perception of individual life in everything. The pathos and dignity of human life are enhanced by the recognition of our dependence on this great Power above and around us. The contemplation of this Power affects the imagination with a sense of awe, wonder, and majesty. But with this contemplative emotion a still deeper feeling seems to mingle. Throughout the poem there is heard a deep undertone of solemnity as from one awakening to the apprehension of a great invisible Power,—'a concealed omnipotence,'—in the world. As the imagination of Lucretius is immeasurably more poetical, so is his spirit immeasurably more reverential than that of Epicurus. If by the analysis of his understanding he seems to take all mystery and sanctity out of the universe, he restores them again by the synthesis of his imagination. If his work seems in some places to 'teach a truth he could not learn,' this is to be explained partly by the fact that he sometimes leaves the beaten road of Epicureanism for the higher and less defined tracks,—'avia loca,'—along which the mystic enthusiasm of Empedocles had borne him.

[1] ii. 931, etc.   [2] v. 1233-5.

But partly it may be explained by the fact that the poetic imagination, which was in him the predominant faculty, asserts its right to be heard after the logical understanding has said its last word. The imagination which recognises infinite life and order in the world unconsciously assumes the existence of a creative and governing Power, behind the visible framework of things. Even the germ of such a thought was more elevating than the popular idolatry and superstition. The recognition of the majesty of Nature enables Lucretius to contemplate life with a sense both of solemnity and security, while it imparts a more elevated feeling to his enjoyment of the beauty of the world. The belief which he taught and by which he lived is neither atheistic nor pantheistic; it is not definite enough to be theistic. It was like the twilight between the beliefs that were passing away, and that which rose on the world after his time,—

$$\tilde{\eta}\mu o\varsigma\ \delta'\ o\tilde{\upsilon}\tau'\ \mathring{\alpha}\rho\ \pi\omega\ \mathring{\eta}\acute{\omega}\varsigma,\ \mathring{\epsilon}\tau\iota\ \delta'\ \mathring{\alpha}\mu\phi\iota\lambda\acute{\upsilon}\kappa\eta\ \nu\acute{\upsilon}\xi.$$

CHAPTER XIII.

THE RELIGIOUS ATTITUDE AND MORAL TEACHING OF LUCRETIUS.

LUCRETIUS does not enforce his moral teaching on the systematic plan on which his physical philosophy is discussed. His view of human life is sometimes presented as it arises in the regular course of the argument, at other times in highly finished digressions, interspersed throughout the work with the view apparently of breaking its severe monotony. These passages might be compared to the lyrical odes in a Greek drama. They afford relief to the strained attention, and suggest the close and permanent human interest involved in what is apparently special, abstract, and remote. There is no necessary connexion between the atomic theory of philosophy, and that view of the end and objects of life which Lucretius derived from Epicurus. Although the moral attitude of Epicurus was, in some respects, anticipated by Democritus, Epicureanism really started from independent sources, viz., from the later development of the ethical teaching of Socrates, and from the personal circumstances and disposition of Epicurus. By the ordinary Epicurean his philosophy was valued chiefly as affording a basis for the denial of the doctrines of Divine Providence and of the immortality of the soul. But there is a wide difference between ordinary Epicureanism and that solemn view of human life which was revealed to the world in the poem of Lucretius. The power which his speculative philosophy exercised over his mind was one cause of this difference. Although there is no necessary connexion between his philosophical convictions and his ethical doctrines, yet the elevation of feeling which he has imparted to the least elevated of all the moral systems of antiquity may be in part accounted for by the influence of ideas derived from the philosophy of Democritus.

Epicureanism, in its original form, was the expression of a character as unlike as possible to that of Lucretius. It arose in a state of society and under circumstances widely different from the social and political condition of the last phase of the Roman Republic. It was a doctrine suited to the easy social life which succeeded to the great political career, the energetic ambition, and the creative genius which ennobled the great age of Athenian liberty. It was essentially the philosophy of the ῥεῖα ζώοντες, who found in refined and regulated pleasure, in friendliness and sociability, a compensation for the loss of political existence, and of the sacred associations and ideal glories of their ancestral religion. Human life, stripped of its solemn meaning and high practical interest, was supposed to be understood and realised, and brought under the control of a comfortable and intelligible philosophy. Pleasure was the obvious end of existence; the highest aim of knowledge was to ascertain the conditions under which most enjoyment could be secured; the triumph of the will was to conform to these conditions. All violent emotion, all care and anxiety, whatever impaired the capacity of enjoyment or fostered artificial desire, was to be controlled or resisted, as inimical to the tranquillity of the soul. The philosophers of the garden taught and acted on the practical truth, that pleasure depended on the mind more than on external things; that a simple life tended more to happiness than luxury[1]; that excess of every kind was followed by reaction. They inculcated political quiescence as well as the abnegation of personal ambition. As death was 'the end of all,' life was to be temperately enjoyed while

---

[1] Cf. Juv. xiv. 319:—
'Quantum Epicure tibi parvis suffecit in hortis.'

it lasted, and resigned, when necessary, with cheerful composure.

Such a philosophy would scarcely be thought capable of having given birth to any form of serious and elevated poetry. Its natural fruit was the refined, cheerful, and witty new comedy of Athens. Yet the genius of Lucretius and of Horace expressed these doctrines in tones of dignity and beauty, which have been denied to more ennobling truths. The philosophy of pleasure thus makes its appeal to the poetical susceptibility, as well as to the ordinary temperament of men. It might have been thought also that no philosophy would have been less attractive to the dignity of the nobler type, or to the coarser texture of the common type of Roman character. Yet among the Romans of the last age of the Republic, Epicureanism was a formidable rival to the more congenial system of Stoicism, and was professed by men of pure character and intellectual tastes as well as by men like the Piso Caesoninus, of whom both Cicero and Catullus have left so unflattering a portrait. These two systems, although antagonistic in their view and aim, yet had this common adaptation to the Roman character, that they held out a definite plan of life, and laid down precepts by which that life might be attained. The strength of will and singleness of aim, characteristic of the Romans, their love of rule and impatience of speculative suspense, inclined and enabled them to embrace the teaching of those schools whose tenets were most definite and most readily applicable to human conduct. To a Greek philosopher the interest of conforming his life to any system arose in a great measure from the freedom and exercise thereby afforded to his intellect. Thus Epicurus, in denying the power of luxury to give happiness, says,—'These are not the things which form the life of pleasure,'—'ἀλλὰ νήφων λογισμὸς καὶ τὰς αἰτίας ἐξερευνῶν πάσης αἱρέσεως καὶ φυγῆς καὶ τὰς δόξας ἐξελαύνων, ἀφ' ὧν πλεῖστος τὰς ψυχὰς καταλαμβάνει θόρυβος[1].' To a

---

[1] 'But the sober exercise of reason, investigating the causes why we choose

Roman, on the other hand, such a scheme of life was recommended by the new power which was thus imparted to the will. Greek philosophy has sometimes been reproached as the cause of the corruption of Roman character and the decay of Roman religion. But it would be more true to say that, to the higher natures at least, philosophy supplied the place of the ancient principles of duty, which had long since decayed with the decay of patriotism and religion. The idea of regulating life by an ideal standard afforded a broader aim and a more humane and liberal sphere of action to that self-control and constancy of will, out of which, in combination with absolute devotion to the State, the ancient Roman virtue had been formed. But still it is true that the principles of Epicureanism were difficult to reconcile with some of the conditions, both good and bad, of Roman character. While fostering the humaner feelings and more social tastes, and so softening the primitive rudeness and austerity, these doctrines tended to discourage national and political spirit, by withdrawing the energies of the will from outward activity to the regulation of the inner life. The attitude both of Stoicism and Epicureanism was one of resistance on the part of the will to outward influences;—the one system striving to attain entire independence of circumstances, the other to regulate life in accordance with them, so as to secure the utmost positive enjoyment, and the utmost exemption from pain. The political passions of the last age of the Republic inclined men of thought and leisure to that philosophy which seemed best fitted to meet and satisfy—

'The longing for confirmed tranquillity
Inward and outward.'

But while Epicureanism was a natural refuge from the passions of a revolutionary era, Stoicism was a fortress of inward strength to the few who, at the fall of the Republic, resisted the manifest tendency of things, and, in

or avoid anything, and banishing those opinions which cause the greatest trouble in the soul.'

a later age, to those who strove to maintain the dignity of Roman citizens under the degradation of the early Empire.

But the profession of Epicureanism, in the last age of the Republic, was not confined to men like Atticus and Lucretius who stood aloof from public life. The existence of Cassius, who acted and suffered for the same cause as the Stoic Cato, shows that political apathy, although theoretically required by this philosophy, was not essential to a Roman Epicurean. Lucretius, though animated by an ardent spirit of proselytism, does not desire that Memmius should forget his duties as a citizen and statesman. The denial of the Divine interference in human affairs and of the doctrine of a future state was the essential bond of agreement among the adherents of Epicureanism. The religious unsettlement of the age assumed in them a positive form. They were the Sadducees of Rome, who escaped from the perplexity as well as from the most elevating influences of life, by moulding their feelings and conduct on the firm conviction, that while man was master of his happiness in this world, he had nothing either to hope or fear after death.

It seems a strange result of the moral confusion of that time to find the enthusiasm of Lucretius springing from this denial of what from the days of Plato have been regarded as the highest hopes of mankind. No writer of antiquity was more profoundly impressed by the serious import and mystery of life. Yet he appears as the unhesitating advocate of all the tenets of this philosophy, and denies the foundations of religious belief with a zeal more like religious earnestness than the spirit of any other writer of antiquity. Without conscious deviation from the teaching of his master, he reproduces the calm unimpassioned doctrines of Epicurus, in a new type,—earnest, austere, and ennobled; enforcing them not for the sake of ease or for the love of pleasure, but in the cause of truth and human dignity. Pleasure is indeed recognised by him as the universal law or condition of existence—'dux vitae dia voluptas,'—the great instrument of Nature through which all life is created and maintained. But the real object of his teaching is to obtain not active pleasure, but peace and a 'pure heart.' 'For life,' he says, 'may go on without corn or wine, but not without a pure heart—

> At bene non poterat sine puro pectore vivi.

All that Nature craves is that the body should be free from actual pain, and that the mind, undisturbed by fear and anxiety, should be open to the influence of natural enjoyment—'

> Nonne videre
> Nil aliud sibi naturam latrare, nisi ut, cui
> Corpore seiunctus dolor absit, mente fruatur
> Iucundo sensu cura semotu' metuque?[1]

Although in different places he indicates a genuine appreciation of the charms of art,—in the form of music, paintings, statues, etc.,—yet he expresses or implies an independence of all the adventitious stimulants to enjoyment. The only needful pleasure is that which Nature herself bestows on a mind free from care, passion, violent emotion, restless discontent, and slothful apathy.

Although no new principle or maxim of conduct appears in his teaching, the view of human life presented by Lucretius was really something new in the world. A strong and deep flood of serious thought and feeling was for the first time poured into the shallow channel of Epicureanism. The spirit in which Lucretius contemplated the world was different from that of any other man of antiquity; especially different from that of his master in philosophy. To the one human life was a pleasant sojourn, which should be temperately enjoyed and gracefully terminated at the appointed time: to the other it was the more sombre and tragic side of the august spectacle which all Nature presents to the contemplative mind. Moderation in enjoyment was the practical lesson of the one: fortitude and renunciation were the demands which the other made of all who would live worthily.

[1] ii. 16-19.

This difference in the spirit, rather than the letter, of their philosophy is to be attributed in some degree to this, that Lucretius was a Roman of the antique type of Ennius, born with the passionate heart of a poet, and inheriting the resolute endurance of the great patrician families. Partly too, as was said before, the effect of the speculative philosophy which he embraced was to deepen and strengthen that mood of imaginative contemplation, which he shares, not with any of his countrymen, but with a few great thinkers of the world. It is his philosophical enthusiasm which distinguishes the teaching of Lucretius from the meditative and practical wisdom which has made Horace the favourite Epicurean teacher and companion of modern times. Partly too, as was said in a former chapter, this new aspect of Epicureanism in Lucretius may be attributed to the reaction of his nature from the confusion of the times in which he lived.

It is not indeed possible to learn whether the passions of his age first drove him to Epicureanism, or whether the doctrines of that philosophy, adopted on speculative grounds, may not rather have led him to regard his age in the spirit of contemplative isolation, which he has described in the well-known passage—

Suave, mari magno turbantibus aequora ventis, etc.

His philosophy may have been forced on him by personal experience, or the intimations of experience may have assumed their form and colour from the nature of his philosophy. But the memories of his youth and the experience of things witnessed in his manhood did undoubtedly colour all his thoughts and feelings on human life. Some of the forms of evil against which he contends had never been so prominently displayed before. Yet all these considerations afford only a partial explanation of the character of his practical philosophy. There were other Roman Epicureans, contemporary with him and later, and none are known to have been in any way like him. Although his nature was made of the strong Roman fibre; although his mind had been deeply imbued with the spirit of Greek philosophy; although his view of life was necessarily coloured by the action of his times; yet all these considerations go but a little way to explain his attitude of mind and the work which he accomplished in the world. Over all these considerations this predominates, that he was a man of great original and individual force, and one who in power and sincerity of thought and feeling rose higher than any other above the level of his age and country.

The moral teaching of the poem was rather an active protest against various forms of evil than the proclamation of a positive good. The happiness which the philosophic life promised is described in vague outline, like the delineation given of the calm and passionless existence of the Gods. Epicureanism appears here in antagonism to the prejudice and ignorance, the weakness and the passions of human nature, rather than in its hold of any positive good. Hence it is that the tones of Lucretius might in many places be mistaken for those of a Stoic rather than an Epicurean. In their resistance to the common forms of evil these systems were at one. Perhaps, too, in the positive good at which he aimed, the spirit of Lucretius was more that of a Stoic than he imagined. His sense of human dignity was much more powerful than his regard for human enjoyment. Yet his philosophy enabled him, along with the strength of Stoicism, to cherish humaner sympathies. While his earnest temper, his scorn of weakness, his superiority to pleasure were in harmony with the militant rather than the quiescent attitude of each of these philosophies, his humanity and tenderness of feeling and the enjoyment which he derived from Nature and art were more in harmony with the better side of Epicureanism than with the formal teaching of the Porch.

The evils of life, for the cure of which Lucretius considers his philosophy available, appeared to him to spring not out of man's relation to Nature, but out of the weakness of his reason and the corruption of his heart.

The great service of Epicurus consisted not only in revealing the laws of Nature, but in laying his finger on the secret cause of man's unhappiness. Observing the insufficiency of all external goods to bestow peace and contentment, he saw that the evil lay in the vessel into which these blessings were poured:—

> Intellegit ibi vitium vas efficere ipsum
> Omniaque illius vitio corrumpier intus,
> Quae conlata foris et commoda cumque venirent;
> Partim quod fluxum pertusumque esse videbat,
> Ut nulla posset ratione explerier umquam;
> Partim quod taetro quasi conspurcare sapore
> Omnia cernebat, quaecumque receperat, intus.[1]

The evils which vitiate our happiness are the cowardice which dares not accept the blessings of life, the weakness which repines at what is inevitable, the restless desires which cannot enjoy the present and crave for what is beyond their reach, the apathy and insensibility to natural enjoyment, which are the necessary consequence of luxurious indulgence. Thus the aim of his moral teaching was to purify the heart from superstition, from the fear of death, from the passions of ambition and of love, from all artificial pleasures and desires.

The greatest of these evils and the mainspring of all human misery is superstition. It is this which surrounds life with the gloom of death—

> Omnia suffundens mortis nigrore.[2]

Against the arbitrary and cruel power, supposed to be exercised by the Gods, Lucretius proclaimed internecine war. The fear of this power is denounced, not as a restraint on natural inclination, but as a base and intolerable burden, degrading life, confounding all genuine feeling, corrupting our ideas of what is holiest and most divine. The pathetic story of the sacrifice of Iphigenia

---

[1] 'Thereupon he perceived that the vessel itself caused the evil, and that all external gains and blessings whatsoever were vitiated within through its fault, partly because he saw that it was so unsound and leaky that it could never be filled in any way, partly because he discerned that it tainted inwardly everything which it had received as it were with a nauseous flavour.'—vi. 17-23.

[2] ii. 39.

is told to enforce the antagonism between the exactions of religious belief and the most sacred human affections. Every line of the poem is indirectly a protest against the religious errors of antiquity. At occasional intervals this protest is directly uttered, sometimes with indignant irony, at other times with the profoundest pathos. The first feeling breaks forth in the passage at vi. 380, etc., where he argues against the fancies which attribute thunder to the capricious anger of the Gods. 'Why is it,' he asks, 'that the bolts pass over the guilty and often strike the innocent? Why are they idly spent on desert places? Is this done by the Gods merely in the way of practice and exercise for their arms? Why is it that Jupiter never hurls his bolts in a clear sky? Does he descend into the clouds in order that his aim may be surer? Why does he cast his bolts into the sea? What charge has he against the waves and the waste of waters?

> Quid undas
> Arguit et liquidam molem camposque natantis.[1]

Why is it that he often destroys and disfigures his own temples and images?'

Elsewhere, however, he is moved by a feeling deeper than scorn,—a feeling of true reverence, springing from a high ideal of the attitude which it became man to maintain in presence of a superior nature. There is no passage in the poem in which he speaks more from the depths of his heart than in the lines—

> O genus infelix humanum, talia divis
> Cum tribuit facta atque iras adiunxit acerbas!
> Quantos tum gemitus ipsi sibi, quantaque nobis
> Volnera, quas lacrimas peperere minoribu' nostris!
> Nec pietas ullast velatum saepe videri
> Vertier ad lapidem atque omnis accedere ad aras
> Nec procumbere humi prostratum et pandere palmas
> Ante deum delubra nec aras sanguine multo
> Spargere quadrupedum nec votis nectere vota,
> Sed mage pacata posse omnia mente tueri.[2]

---
[1] vi. 404–5.
[2] 'O miserable race of man when they imputed to the Gods such acts as these, and ascribed to them also angry passions. What sorrow did they then

The terrors of the popular mythology are denounced as a violation of the majesty of the Gods, as well as the cause of infinite evil to ourselves,—not indeed because any thought or act of ours has the power to rouse the Divine anger, but from the effect that these feelings have on our own minds. 'No longer can we approach the temples of the Gods with a quiet heart, nor receive into our minds the intimations of the Divine nature in peace—'

> Nec delubra deum placido cum pectore adibis,
> Nec de corpore quae sancto simulacra feruntur
> In mentes hominum divinae nuntia formae
> Suscipere haec animi tranquilla pace valebis.[1]

This passage and others in the poem imply that Lucretius both believed in the existence of Gods, and conceived of them as revealing themselves through direct impressions to the mind of man, and filling it with solemn awe and peace. But the account which he gives of their eternal existence is vague and poetical, and might almost be regarded as a symbolical expression of what seemed to him most holy and divine in man. The highest aim of man is to 'lead a life worthy of the Gods': the essential attribute of the divine life is 'peace.' The Gods are said to consist of the finest and purest essence, to be exempt from death, decay, and wasting passions, to be supplied with all things by the liberal bounty of Nature, and to dwell for ever in untroubled serenity above the darkness and the storms of our world. Their abode in the spaces betwixt different worlds—(the 'intermundia' as they are called by Cicero),—is described in words almost literally translated from the description of the Heaven of the Odyssey—

> Apparet divum numen sedesque quietae
> Quas neque concutiunt venti nec nubila nimbis

prepare for themselves, what deep wounds for us, what tears for our descendants. For there is no holiness in being often seen, turning round with head veiled, in presence of a stone, and in drawing nigh to every altar; nor in lying prostrate in the dust, and uplifting the hands before the temples of the Gods: nor in sprinkling altars with the blood of beasts, and in ever fastening up new votive offerings, but rather in being able to look at all things with a mind at peace.'—v. 1194-1203.

[1] vi. 75-78.

> Aspergunt neque nix acri concreta pruina
> Cana cadens violat semperque innubilus aether
> Integit, et large diffuso lumine rident.[1]

'They reveal themselves to man in dreams and waking visions by images of ampler size and more august aspect than that of our mortal condition. Fear and ignorance have assigned to these unchanging forms the functions of creating and governing the world, and out of this fear have arisen all over the earth temples and altars, along with the festivals and the solemn rites of superstition. But the Gods are neither the arbitrary tyrants nor the beneficent guardians of the world. Why should they have done anything for the benefit of man? How can he add to or detract from their eternal happiness? Shall we suppose them weary of their existence, and infected with a human passion for change?—

> At, credo, in tenebris vita ac maerore iacebat,
> Donec diluxit rerum genitalis origo.

Whence could they have obtained the idea of creation, whence gathered the secret powers of matter—

> Si non ipsa dedit specimen natura creandi?'

Against the old argument from final causes he opposes that drawn from the imperfections of the world, such as the waste of Nature's resources on vast tracts of mountain and forest, on desolate marshes, rocks, and seas,—the enmity to man of other occupants of the earth,—the malign influences of climate and the seasons,—the feebleness of infancy,—the devastations of disease,—the untimeliness of early death[2].

While his belief in the Gods is thus expressed in vague outline and poetical symbolism, yet it is clear that as he recognised a secret, orderly, and omnipotent power in

---

[1] 'The holy presence of the Gods becomes visible, and their peaceful dwelling-places, which neither the winds beat upon, nor the clouds bedew with rain; nor does snow, gathered in flakes by keen frost, and falling white, invade them; ever the cloudless ether enfolds them, and they are radiant with far-spread light.'—iii. 18-22.

[2] v. 145-225.

Nature, so also he recognised the ideal of a purer and serener life than that of earthly existence. These two elements in all true religion, a reverential acknowledgment of a universal power and order, and a sense of a diviner life with which man may have communion, were part of the being of Lucretius. His denial of supernatural beliefs extended not only to all the fables and false conceptions of ancient mythology, but to the doctrine of a Divine Providence recompensing men, here or hereafter, according to their actions. The intensity of his nature led him to identify all religion with the cruel or childish fables of the popular faith. The certainty with which he grasped the truth of the laws and order of Nature was incompatible with the only conception he could form of a Divine action on the world. His deep sense of human rights and deep sympathy with human feeling rebelled against a belief in Powers exercising a capricious tyranny over the world, and exacting human sacrifice as a propitiation of their offended majesty. His reverence for truth and his sense of the power and mystery of Nature led him to scorn the virtue attributed to an idolatrous and formal worship. This attitude of religious isolation, not more from his own time than from the subsequent course of thought, in a man of unusual sincerity and earnestness of feeling, is certainly among the most impressive phenomena of ancient literature. The spirit in which he denies the beliefs of the world is far from resembling the triumph of a cold philosophy over the religious associations of mankind. He is moved even to a kind of poetical sympathy with some of the ceremonies and symbols of Paganism. A sense of religious awe,—a sympathetic recognition of the power of religious emotion over the hearts of men,—is expressed, for instance, in the lines which describe the procession of Cybele through the great cities and nations of the world. While guarding himself against the pollution of a base idolatry, he yet acknowledges not only the power of religious associations to entwine themselves with human affections, but the intrinsic power of the truths symbolised in that worship; viz., the truth of the majesty of Nature, and of the duties arising from the elemental affections to parents and country. In regard to all his religious impressions his intensity of feeling and imagination seems to place him on a solitary height, nearly as far apart from the followers of his own school as from their adversaries[1].

The same strength of heart and mind characterises that passage of sustained and impassioned feeling, in which Lucretius encounters the thought of eternal death. The vast spiritual difference between the Roman poet and the Greek philosopher is apparent when we contrast the cold, unsympathetic language of the epistle to Menœceus with the fervent and profoundly human tones of the third book of the poem of Lucretius. Epicurus escapes from the fear of death through a placid indifference of feeling, an easy contentment with the comforts of this life, a sense of relief in getting rid of 'the longing for immortality' (τὸν τῆς ἀθανασίας πόθον). Lucretius, while realising the full pathos and solemnity of the thought of death, preaches submission to the inexorable decree of Nature with a stern consistency and a proud fortitude combating the suggestions of human weakness.

The whole of the third book is devoted to this part of his subject, and the argument of the fourth is to a great extent supplementary to that of the third book. The physical doctrine enunciated and illustrated in the first

[1] The feelings with which Lucretius contemplates the solemn procession of Cybele may be illustrated by the following passage, quoted by Mr. Morley in his Life of Diderot, vol. ii. p. 65 : 'Absurd rigorists do not know the effect of external ceremonies on the people : they can never have seen the enthusiasm of the multitude at the procession of the Fête Dieu, an enthusiasm that sometimes even gains me. I have never seen that long file of priests in their vestments, those young acolytes clad in their white robes, with broad blue sashes engirdling their waists, and casting flowers on the ground before the Holy Sacrament, the crowd, as it goes before and follows after them, hushed in religious silence, and so many with their faces bent reverently to the ground : I have never heard the grave and pathetic chant, as it is led by the priests and fervently responded to by an infinity of voices of men, of women. of girls, of little children, without my inmost heart being stirred, and tears coming into my eyes. There is in it something, I know not what, that is grand, solemn, sombre, and mournful.'

half of the third book is the materiality of the soul and its indissoluble connexion with the body. The practical consequence of this doctrine, viz., that death is nothing to us, is there enforced in a long passage[1] of sustained power and solemnity of feeling. First, we are made to realise the entire unconsciousness in death throughout all eternity. "As it was before we were born, so shall it be hereafter. As we felt no trouble in the past at the clash of conflict between Roman and Carthaginian, when all the world shook with alarm, so nothing can touch us or move us then—

> Non si terra mari miscebitur et mare caelo.[2]

It is but the trick of our fancy which suggests the thought of any kind of suffering after all consciousness has ceased—

> Nec radicitus e vita se tollit et eicit
> Sed facit esse sui quiddam super inscius ipse.[3]

Men feel that the sadness of death lies in the separation from wife, and children, and home; in the extinction which a single day has brought to all the blessings and the gains of a lifetime. But they forget that along with these blessings is extinguished all desire and longing for them. So, too, men 'spice their fair banquets with the dust of death.' They say, 'our joy is but for a season; it will soon be past, nor ever again be recalled,'—as if forsooth any want or any desire can haunt that sleep from which there is no awaking—

> Nec quisquam expergitus exstat,
> Frigida quem semel est vitai pausa secuta.[4]

Nature herself might utter this reproof to all weak complaining: 'Thou fool, if thy life hath given thee joy, and all its blessings have not been poured into a leaky vessel, why dost thou not leave the feast like a satisfied guest, and take thy rest contentedly? But if all has hitherto been to thee vanity and vexation of spirit, why seek to add

---

[1] From 830 till the end. [2] iii. 842.
[3] iii. 877-8. [4] iii. 929-30.

to thy trouble? I can devise or frame no new pleasure for thee. "There is no new thing under the sun"—"eadem sunt omnia semper."' To the weak complaint of age, Nature would speak with sterner voice : 'Away hence with thy tears and thy complainings. It is because, unable to enjoy the present, thou art ever weakly longing for what is absent, that death has come on thee unsatisfied.' 'This would be, indeed, a just charge and reproof. For the old order is ever yielding place to new; and life is given to no man in possession, to all men for use. The time before we were born is a mirror to us of what the future shall be. Is there any gloom or horror there? Is there not a deeper rest than any sleep?'

'The terrors of the unseen world are but the hell which fools make for themselves out of their passions[1]. The torments of Tantalus, of Tityus, of Sisyphus, and the Danaides, are but symbols of the blind cowardice and superstition, of the craving passions, of the ever-foiled and ever-renewed ambition, of the thankless discontent with the natural joy and beauty of the world, which curse and degrade our mortal existence. The stories of Cerberus and the Furies, and of the tortures of the damned are creations of a guilty conscience, or the projections into futurity of the experiences of earthly punishment.'

Other consolations are suggested by the thoughts of those who have gone before us. Echoing the stern irony of Achilles—

ἀλλά, φίλος, θάνε καὶ σύ· τίη ὀλοφύρεαι οὕτως;
κάτθανε καὶ Πάτροκλος, ὅπερ σέο πολλὸν ἀμείνων[2]—

he reminds us that better and greater men than we have died,—kings and soldiers, poets and philosophers, the mightiest equally with the humblest. In the spirit, and partly too in the words of Ennius, he enforces the thought that 'Scipio, the thunderbolt of war, the terror of Carthage, gave his bones to the earth as if he were

---

[1] Hic Acherusia fit stultorum denique vita.
[2] Iliad, xxi. 106-7.

the meanest slave.' 'Why, then, should one whose life is half a sleep, who is the prey of weak fears and restless discontent, complain that he too is subject to the common law? What is this wretched love of life, which makes us tremble at every danger? Death cannot be avoided; no new pleasure can be forged out by longer living. This evil of our lot is not inflicted by Nature, but by our own craving hearts, which cannot enjoy, and are yet ever thirsting for longer life[1].'

The power of the whole of this passage depends partly on the vividness of feeling and conception with which the thought is realised, partly on the august and solemn associations with which it is surrounded. Such graphic touches as these—

>Frigida quem semel est vitai pausa secuta;[2]—
>Cum summo gelidi cubat aequore saxi;[3]—
>Urgerive superne obtritum pondere terrae,[4]—

and again, the life, truth, and tenderness of the picture presented in the lines—

>Iam iam non domus accipiet te laeta, neque uxor
>Optima nec dulces occurrent oscula nati
>Praeripere et tacita pectus dulcedine tangent,[5]

bring home to the mind, in startling distinctness, the old familiar contrast between the 'cold obstruction' of the grave and 'the warm precincts of the cheerful day.' But the horror and pain of the thought of death are lost in a feeling of august resignation to the universal law. Though the fact is made present to our minds in its sternest reality, yet it is encompassed with the pomp and majesty of great associations. It suggests the thought of the most momentous crisis in history—

>Ad confligendum venientibus undique Poenis,[6]

---

[1] iii. 830-1094. [2] iii. 930.
[3] iii. 892. [4] iii. 893.
[5] 'Soon shall thy home receive thee no more with glad welcome, nor thy true wife, nor thy dear children run to snatch thy first kiss, touching thy heart with silent gladness.'—iii. 894-96.
[6] iii. 833.

of the regal state of kings and emperors—

> Inde alii multi reges rerumque potentes
> Occiderunt, magnis qui gentibus imperitarunt,[1]

of the simpler and more impressive grandeur of the great men of old, such as the 'good Ancus,' the mighty Scipio, Homer, 'peerless among poets,' the sage Democritus, Epicurus, 'the sun among all the lesser luminaries.' Lastly, we are reminded of the universal law of Nature, that the death of the old is the condition of the life of the new—

> Sic alid ex alio nunquam desistet oriri.[2]

Even if the spirit of the poet cannot be said to rise buoyantly above the depressing and paralysing influence of this conviction, yet he draws a higher lesson from it than the maxim of 'Eat and drink, for to-morrow we die.' He understands the epicurean precept of 'carpe diem' in a sense more befitting to human dignity. The lesson which he teaches is the need of conquering all weakness, sloth, and irresolution in life. This life is all that we have through eternity; let it not be wasted in unsatisfied desires, insensibility to present and regrets for absent good, or restless disquiet for the future; let us understand ourselves and our position here, bear and enjoy whatever is allotted to us during our few years of existence. We are masters of ourselves and of our fortunes, so far at least as to rise clearly above the degradation of ignorance and misery.

The practical use of the study of Nature, according to Lucretius, is, first, to inspire confidence in the room of an ignorant and superstitious fear of supernatural power; and, secondly, to show what man really needs, and so to clear the heart from all artificial desires and passions. All that is wanted for happiness in this world is a mind free from error, and a heart neither incapable of natural enjoyment (fluxum pertusumque) nor vitiated by false appetite[3]. Of

---

[1] iii. 1027-8.   [2] iii. 970.
[3] Compare the metaphorical expressions at vi. 20-4.

the errors to which man is liable superstition and the fear of death are the most deeply seated. Of the artificial desires and passions, on the other hand, the most destructive are the love of power and of riches, and the sensual appetite for pleasure. In the opening lines of the second book the strife of ambition, the rivalries of rank and intellect in the warfare of politics are contrasted with the serene life of philosophy, as darkness, error, and danger with light, certainty, and peace—

> Sed nil dulcius est, bene quam munita tenere
> Edita doctrina sapientum templa serena,
> Despicere unde queas alios passimque videre
> Errare atque viam palantis quaerere vitae,
> Certare ingenio, contendere nobilitate,
> Noctes atque dies niti praestante labore
> Ad summas emergere oper rerumque potiri.[1]

Yet to be the master of armies and of navies, or to be clothed in gold and purple gives not that exemption from the real terrors and anxieties of life which the power of reason only can bestow—

> Quod si ridicula haec ludibriaque esse videmus,
> Re veraque metus hominum curaeque sequaces
> Nec metuunt sonitus armorum nec fera tela,
> Audacterque inter reges rerumque potentis
> Versantur neque fulgorem reverentur ab auro
> Nec clarum vestis splendorem purpureai,
> Quid dubitas quin omni' sit haec rationi' potestas?
> Omnis cum in tenebris praesertim vita laboret.[2]

The desire of power and station leads to the shame and

---

[1] 'But there is no greater joy than to hold high aloft the tranquil abodes well bulwarked by the learning of the wise, whence thou mayest look down on other men, and see them wandering every way, and lost in error, seeking the road of life; mayest mark the strife of genius, the rivalries of rank, the struggle night and day with surpassing effort to reach the highest place, and be master of the State.'—ii. 48-54.

[2] 'But if we see that all this is but folly and a mockery, and, in real truth, the fears of men and their dogging cares dread not the clash of arms nor the fierce weapons of warfare, and boldly mix with kings and potentates, nor fear the splendour of gold or the bright glare of purple robes, canst thou doubt that it is the force of reason on which all this depends, especially since all our life is in darkness and tribulation?'—ii. 48-55.

misery of baffled hopes, of which the toil of Sisyphus is the type, and also to the guilt which deluges the world in blood, and violates the most sacred ties of Nature[1]. While failure in the struggle is degradation, success is often only the prelude to the most sudden downfall. Weary with bloodshed, and with forcing their way up the hostile and narrow road of ambition[2], men reach the summit of their hopes only to be hurled down by envy as by a thunderbolt[3]. They are slaves to ambition, merely because they cannot distinguish the true from the false, because they cannot judge of things as they really are, apart from the estimate which the world puts upon them—

> Quandoquidem sapiunt alieno ex ore petuntque
> Res ex auditis potius quam sensibus ipsis.[4]

The love of riches and of luxurious living, which had begun to corrupt the Roman character in the age of Lucilius, had increased to gigantic dimensions in the last age of the Republic. By no aspect of his age was Lucretius more repelled than by this. No doctrine is enforced in the poem with more sincerity of conviction than that of the happiness and dignity of plain and natural living, the vanity of all the appliances of wealth, and their inability to give real enjoyment either to body or mind. In a well-known passage at the beginning of the second book he adapts an ideal description from Homer's account of the palace of Alcinous to the costly magnificence and splendour of Roman banquets, with which he contrasts the pleasure of gratifying simple tastes, in fine weather, among the beauties of Nature—

> Praesertim cum tempestas adridet et anni
> Tempora conspergunt viridantis floribus herbas.[5]

With fervid sincerity he announces the truth that 'to the

---

[1] iii. 70.   [2] v. 1131.   [3] v. 1125.
[4] 'Since they take their wisdom from the lips of others, and pursue their object in accordance rather with what they hear than with what they really feel.'—v. 1133-34.   [5] ii. 33.

man who would govern his life by reason plain living and a contented spirit are great riches'—

> Quod siquis vera vitam ratione gubernet,
> Divitiae grandes homini sunt vivere parce
> Aequo animo.[1]

Moderation, independence, and self-control are the virtues which Horace derives from his philosophy. He knew how to enjoy both the luxury of the city and the simple fare of the country. Lucretius is more alive to the dangers of pampering the body and enervating the mind. He is more active in his resistance to the common forms of indulgence: he shows more truly simple tastes, stronger capacity of natural enjoyment. He is vividly sensible of the apathy and *ennui* produced by the luxury and inaction of his age. Others among the Roman poets, with more or less sincerity and consistency, appear to long for a return to more natural ways, and paint their ideals of the purity and simplicity of country life. But no writer of antiquity is less of an idealist than Lucretius: there is no writer, ancient or modern, whose words are more truthful and unvarnished. There is no romance or self-deception in what he longs for. There may be some anticipation of the spirit of Rousseau in Virgil, and still more in Tibullus, but none whatever in Lucretius. The privations and rude misery of savage life are painted in as sombre colours as the satiety and discontent of his own age. It would be difficult to name any writer, ancient or modern, by whom the lesson of 'plain living and high thinking' was more worthily inculcated.

The passion of love, which, in its more violent phases, was seen to be a prominent motive in the comedy of Plautus, became a very powerful influence in actual life during the last years of the Republic and the early years of the Empire. Extreme license in the pursuit of pleasure was common among men and women of the highest rank: but, over and above this, the poetry of Catullus and of the elegiac poets of the Augustan age shows that in the

[1] v. 1117-19.

case of young men of fashion and literary accomplishment (and these were often combined) intrigue and temporary *liaisons* had become the absorbing interest and occupation of life. With these claims of passion and sentiment, apparently so alien to the ancient strength and dignity of the Roman character, Lucretius felt no sympathy. No writer has shown a profounder reverence for human affection. In his eyes the crowning guilt of superstition is the cruel violation of natural ties exacted by it: the chief bitterness of death is the thought of eternal separation from wife and children: the first civilising influence acting on the world is traced to the power of the blandishments of children over the savage pride of strength. The pathos of the famous passage, at Book ii. 350, attests his sympathy with the sorrow caused by the disruption of natural ties, even in the lower animals. Other casual expressions, as in that line of profound feeling—

> Aeternumque daret matri sub pectore volnus;[1]—

or such pictures, as that at iii. 469, of friends and relatives surrounding the bed of one who has sunk into a deep lethargy—

> Ad vitam qui revocantes
> Circumstant lacrimis rorantes ora genasque,[2]—

show how strong and real was his regard for the great elemental affections of human nature. But, on the other hand, he is austerely indifferent to the follies and the idealising fancies of lovers. With satirical and not fastidious realism he strips passion of all romance, and exhibits it as a bondage fatal alike to character and independence, to peace of mind and to self-respect. But it is the weakness, not the immorality of licentious passion which he condemns. And it would be altogether an anachronism to attribute to a writer of that age sentiments on this subject in harmony either with the austere virtue of the primitive Romans, or with the moral standard of modern times. It is not the indulgence of inclination, but its excess and perversion,

[1] ii. 638. [2] iii. 468-9.

by which the happiness and dignity of life are placed in another's power, which he condemns.

In order to perceive the limitation of the view of the evils of human life and of their remedy presented by Lucretius, it is not necessary to contrast it with the higher aspects of moral and religious thought in modern times. It is clear that owing to some idiosyncrasy, the result perhaps of some accident of his early years, and fostered by seclusion in later years from the common ways of life, he greatly exaggerates the influence of the terrors of the ancient religion over the world. There is little trace, either in the literature [1] or in the sepulchral inscriptions of the Romans, of that 'fear of Acheron '—

> Funditus humanam qui vitam turbat ab imo
> Omnia suffendens mortis nigrore neque ullam
> Esse voluptatem liquidam puramque reliquit.

The answer of Cicero to the exaggerated pretensions of Epicureanism seems to express the common sense of his age, 'Where can you find an old woman fatuous enough to believe what you forsooth would have believed, if you had not studied physical science' [2]? The passionate protest of Lucretius seems more applicable to times of religious persecution, and to extreme forms of fanaticism in modern times, than to the tolerant spirit and the not unkindly super-

---

[1] A passage in the Captivi of Plautus (995-7), shows that these terrors did appeal to the imagination in ancient times, and thus might powerfully affect the happiness of persons of specially impressible natures, although they do not seem to have often interfered with the actual enjoyment of life,—

> 'Vidi ego multa saepe picta quae Acherunti fierent
> Cruciamenta: verum enimvero nulla adaequest Acheruns
> Atque ubi ego fui in lapicidinis.'

Mr. Wallace in his 'Epicureanism' (p. 109) writes, 'Whatever may have been the case in earlier ages of Greece, there is no doubt that in the age of Epicurus, the doctrine of a judgment to come, and of a hell where sinners were punished for their crimes, made a large part of the vulgar creed.... Orphic and other religious sects had enhanced the terrors of the world below,' &c. Cicero, however, is a better witness than Lucretius of the actual state of opinion among his educated contemporaries. The exaggerated sense entertained by Lucretius of the influence of such terrors among the class for whom his poem was written is a confirmation of his having acted on the maxim 'λάθε βιώσας.'

[2] Tusc. Disp. i. 21.

stition of the Greek and Roman world, as they are known in its literature. But if the experience of the modern world gives a still more startling significance to the words—

> Tantum religio potuit suadere malorum,—

that experience also enables us better to understand the blindness of Lucretius to the purifying and consoling power which even ancient religion was capable of exercising. Though not insensible to the poetical charm of some of the old mythological fancies, and to the solemnising effect of impressive ceremonials, he can see only the baser influences of fear in man's whole attitude to a supernatural Power. His ordinary acuteness of mind seems to desert him in that passage[1] where he resolves the passions of ambition and avarice into the fear of death, and that again into the dread of eternal punishment.

The limitation of his philosophy is also apparent in his want of sympathy with the active duties and pursuits of life. He can see only different modes of evil in the busy interests of the world. War, politics, commerce, appeared to him a mere struggle of personal passion with a view to personal aggrandisement. A life of peace, not of energetic action, was his ideal. In eternal peace he placed the supreme happiness of the Gods: a state of peaceful contemplation—

> Sed mage pacata posse omnia mente tueri—

he regards as the only true religion for man: the 'mute and uncomplaining' peace of the grave reconciles him to the thought of everlasting death. The inadequacy of his philosophy may thus be traced partly to his vivid impressibility of imagination, which made him too exclusively sensible of the awe produced on man's spirit by the mystery of the universe, partly to his defective sympathy with the active interests and duties of life. Partly, too, the bent of his mind towards material observation and enquiry had some share in determining his convictions. In dwelling on the outward appearances of decay and death, he seems to have

[1] iii. 59, etc.

shut his eyes to those inward conditions of the human spirit which to Plato, Cicero, and Virgil appeared the witnesses of immortality. The inability to form the definite conception of a God without human limitations, as well as his strong sense of the imperfection of the world, forced upon him the absolute denial of any Divine providence over human affairs.

Yet a modern reader, without accepting the conclusions of his philosophy, may sympathise with much of his spirit. In his firm faith in the laws which govern the universe, he will recognise a great position established, as essential to the progress of religious as of scientific thought. He will see, in the earnest intensity of his feeling and the sincerity of his expression, a spirit akin to the purer kinds of religious fervour in modern times. In no other writer, ancient or modern, will he find a profounder sense of human dignity, of the supreme claims of affection, of the superiority of a natural to a conventional life. From the direct exhortation and the indirect teaching of Lucretius, he may learn such lessons as these,—that it is man's first business to know and obey the laws of his being,—that the sphere of his happiest activity is to be found in contemplation rather than in action,—that his well-being consists in valuing rightly the real blessings of life rather than in following the illusions of fancy or of custom,—in reverencing the sanctity of family life,—and in cherishing a kindly sympathy with all living things. If there was nothing especially new in the views which he enunciated, the power of realising the common conditions of life, the passionate effort not only to rise himself above human weakness, but to redeem the whole race of man from the curse of ignorance, and the force of imaginative sympathy with which he executed this part of his task were, perhaps, something altogether new in the world.

The same 'vivida vis' with which he observes natural phenomena characterises his insight into human character and passion. He penetrates below the surface of life with the searching insight of a great satirist, and sees more clearly into the hearts of men, and has a more subtle perception of the secret springs of their unhappiness, than any of his countrymen. The aim of his satire is not to make men seem objects of ridicule or scorn, but to restore them to the dignity which they had forfeited through weakness and ignorance. The observation of Horace is wider and more varied, but it ranges much more over the surface of life. He has neither the same sense of the mystery of our being, nor the same sympathy with the common conditions of mankind.

The power of truthful moral painting which Lucretius exercises is seen in that passage in which he reveals the secret of the 'amari aliquit' 'amid the very flowers of love,'—

> Aut cum conscius ipse animus se forte remordet
> Desidiose agere aetatem lustrisque perire,
> Aut quod in ambiguo verbum iaculata reliquit
> Quod cupido adfixum cordi vivescit ut ignis,
> Aut nimium iactare oculos aliumve tueri
> Quod putat in voltuque videt vestigia risus:[1]

and in that in which he describes the satiety and restlessness which are the avenging nemesis of an opulent and luxurious society,—

> Exit saepe foras magnis ex aedibus ille,
> Esse domi quem pertaesumst, subitoque revertit,
> Quippe foris nilo melius qui sentiat esse.
> Currit agens mannos ad villam praecipitanter,
> Auxilium tectis quasi ferre ardentibus instans;
> Oscitat extemplo, tetigit cum limina villae,
> Aut abit in somnum gravis atque oblivia quaerit,
> Aut etiam properans urbem petit atque revisit.[2]

---

[1] 'Either when his mind is stung with the consciousness that he is wasting his life in sloth, and ruining himself in wantonness; or because from the shafts of her wit she has left in him some word of double meaning, which seizes on his passionate heart and burns there like a fire; or because he fancies that she casts about her eyes too much or gazes at another, and marks the traces of a smile on her countenance.'—iv. 1135-40.

[2] 'Oft-times, weary of home, the lord of some spacious mansion issues forth abroad, and suddenly returns, feeling that it is no better with him abroad. Driving his horses, he speeds in hot haste to his country house, as if his house were on fire and he was hurrying to bring assistance. Straightway he begins to yawn, so soon as he has reached his threshold, or sinks heavily into sleep and seeks forgetfulness, or even with all haste returns to the city.'—iii. 1060-67.

There is always poetry and pathos in the satire of Lucretius. There is no trace in him of the malice or the love of detraction which is seldom wholly absent from satiric writing. The futility of human effort is the burden of his complaint[1]: and this (as has been pointed out by M. Martha) is the explanation of the pathetic recurrence of the word 'nequicquam' in so many passages of his poem. His scorn and indignation are shown only in exposing the impostures which men mistake for truths. There is thus infinite compassion for the common lot of man blended with the irony of the passage in which he represents the aged husbandman complaining of the general decay of piety as the cause of the failure of the earth to respond to his labours. His direct and realistic power of expression enhances his power as a moral painter and teacher. Though the writings of Horace supply many more quotations applicable to various situations in life, and expressed in equally apposite language, yet such lines as these in the older poet seem to come from the heart of one ever 'sounding a deeper and more perilous way' over the sea of human life, than suited the more worldly wisdom of Horace,—

> Tantum religio potuit suadere malorum.—[2]
> Cur non ut plenus vitae conviva recedis?—[3]
> Vitaque mancipio nulli datur omnibus usu.—[4]
> Surgit amari aliquid quod in ipsis floribus angat.—[5]
> Nam verae voces tum demum pectore ab imo
> Eiciuntur et eripitur persona, manet res.—[6]
> Divitiae grandes homini sunt vivere parce
> Aequo animo.[7]

Many other lines and expressions of similar force will occur to every reader familiar with Lucretius. As his ordinary style brings the outward aspects of the world vividly before

---

[1] E. g. v. 1430-34:—
  'Ergo hominum genus incassum frustraque laborat
  Semper et in curis consumit inanibus aevom,
  Nimirum quia non cognovit quae sit habendi
  Finis et omnino quoad crescat vera voluptas.'

[2] i. 101. [3] iii. 938. [4] iii. 971. [5] iv. 1134. [6] iii. 57-8. [7] v. 1116.

the mind, so the language in which his moral teaching is enforced, or the result of his moral observation is expressed, stamps powerfully on the mind important and permanent truths of human nature. His thoughts are uttered sometimes with the impressive dignity of Roman oratory, sometimes with the nervous energy, not without flashes of the vigorous wit, of Roman satire. There are occasionally to be heard also higher and deeper tones than those familiar to classical poetry. His burning zeal and indignation against idolatry, and the scorn with which he exposes the impotence of false gods—

> Cur etiam loca sola petunt frustraque laborant?
> An tum bracchia consuescunt firmantque lacertos?[1]—

show some affinity of spirit to the prophets of another race and an earlier time. The 'grandeur of desolation' uttered in the reproof of Nature,—

> Nam tibi praeterea quod machiner inveniamque,
> Quod placeat, nil est: eadem sunt omnia semper,[2]—

recalls the old words of the Preacher—'The thing that hath been, it is that which shall be; and that which is done, is that which shall be done: and there is no new thing under the sun.'

---

[1] vi. 396-7.   [2] iii. 944-5.

CHAPTER XIV.

THE LITERARY ART AND GENIUS OF LUCRETIUS.

It remains to consider the poem of Lucretius as a work of literary art and genius. Much indeed of what may be said on the subject of his genius has necessarily been anticipated in the chapters devoted to the consideration of his personal characteristics, his speculative philosophy, and his moral teaching. The 'multa lumina ingenii' are most conspicuous in those passages of his poem which best illustrate the range and distinctness of his observation, the grandeur and truth of his philosophical conceptions, the passionate sympathy with which he strove to elevate and purify human life. But, at the same time, the most manifest defects of the poem, considered as a work of art, spring from the same source as its greatness considered as a work of genius, viz., the diversity and conflicting aims of the faculties employed on its production. Although, perhaps, from a Roman point of view, the practical purpose which reduces the mass of miscellaneous details to unity, and the success with which he encounters the difficulties both of matter and language, might entitle the poem to be regarded as a work 'multae artis,' yet, when tested by the canons either of Greek or of modern taste, it fails in the most essential conditions of art,—the choice of subject and the form of construction. The title of the poem is indeed taken from a Greek model, the poem of Empedocles, 'περὶ φύσεως': and the form of a personal address to Memmius, in which Lucretius has embodied his teaching, was suggested by the personal address of the older poet to the 'son of Anchytus.' But although Aristotle acknowledges the poetical genius of Empedocles by applying to him the epithet Ὁμηρικός, he denies to his composition the title of a poem. The work of Empedocles and the kindred works of Xenophanes and Parmenides are inspired not by the passion of art but by the enthusiasm of discovery. They are to be regarded rather as philosophical rhapsodies than as purely didactic poems, like either the 'Works and Days' of Hesiod or the writings of the Alexandrine School. They were written in hexameter verse partly because that was the most familiar vehicle of expression in the first half of the fifth century, B.C., and partly because it was the vehicle most suited to the imaginative conceptions of Nature which arose out of the old mythologies. But in the time of Lucretius a prose vehicle was more suited than any form of verse for the communication of knowledge in a systematic form. The conception of Nature was no longer mystical or purely imaginative as it had been in the age of Empedocles. Thus the task which Lucretius had to perform was both vaster and more complex than that of the early φυσιόλογοι. He had to combine in one whole the prosaic results of later scientific observation and analysis with the imaginative fancies of the dawn of ancient enquiry. He professes to make both conducive to the practical purpose of emancipating and elevating human life; but a great part of his argument is as remote from all human interest as it is from the ascertained truths of science.

All life and Nature were to his spirit full of imaginative wonder, but they were believed also to be susceptible of a rationalistic explanation. And the greater part of the work is devoted to give this explanation. This large infusion of a prosaic content necessarily detracts from the artistic excellence and the sustained interest of the poem. Lucretius speaks of the difficulty which he had to encounter in gaining the ear of his countrymen, in the lines,—

> Quoniam haec ratio plerumque videtur
> Tristior esse quibus non est tractata, retroque
> Volgus abhorret ab hac.[1]

[1] i. 943-45.

And the unattractiveness of much of his theme is not diminished when the real discoveries of science have shewn how illusory are his processes of investigation, and how false are many of his conclusions. He has made his poetry ancillary to his science, instead of compelling, as Virgil, Dante, and Milton have done, a subject, susceptible of purely artistic treatment, to assimilate the stores of his knowledge. His theme—'maiestas cognita rerum,'—is too vast and complex to be brought within the compass and proportions of a single work of art. The processes of minute observation and reasoning employed in establishing his conclusions are alien from the movement of the imagination. The connecting links of the argument are suggestive of the labour of the workman, not of the finished perfection of the work. And while some of the ideas of science may be so applied to the interpretation of the outward world, as to act on the imaginative emotions with greater power than any mere description of the forms and colours of external things, yet the pleasure with which processes of investigation are pursued is quite distinct from the pleasure derived from poetic intuition into the secret life of Nature and man. If it be the condition of a great poem to produce the purest and noblest pleasure by its whole conception and execution, the poem of Lucretius fails to satisfy this condition. It is, in spite of its design and proportions,—in spite of the fact that long parts of the work neither interest the feelings nor satisfy the reason, that the poem still speaks with impressive power to the modern world.

And while the whole conception of the work, as regards both matter and method of treatment, necessarily involves a large interfusion of prosaic materials with the finer product of his genius, it must be added that there is considerable inequality of execution even in its more inspired passages. A few consecutive passages show indeed the finest sense of harmony, and are finished in a style not much inferior to that of Virgil. Such, for instance, are the opening lines :—

> Aeneadum genetrix, hominum divomque voluptas, etc.;—

and again the lines in the introduction to Book iii :—

> Apparet divum numen scdesque quietae, etc.

But long passages seem rather to revert to the roughness of Ennius than to approach the smooth and varied cadences of Virgil. Though the imaginative effect of single expressions is generally more forcible than in any Latin poet, yet the composition of long paragraphs is apt to overflow into prosaic detail, or to display the qualities of logical consecutiveness or close adherence to fact rather than those of skilled accomplishment and conformity with the principles of beauty. In common with the older race of Roman poets he exhibits that straining after verbal effects by means of alliteration, assonances, asyndeta, etc., which marks the ruder stages of literary development. The Latin language, although beginning to feel the quickening of a new life, had not yet been formed into its more exquisite modulations, nor learned the power of suggesting delicate shades of meaning and the new strength derivable from the reserved use of its resources. All these causes,—the vast and miscellaneous range, and the abstruse character of his subject, the dryness and futility of much of the argument, the frequent subordination of poetry to science, the inadequacy of the Latin language as a vehicle of thought and its imperfect development as an organ of poetry,—prevented the poem from ever obtaining great popularity in ancient times, and have denied to it in modern times anything like the large influence which has been enjoyed in different ages and countries by Virgil, Horace, and Ovid. Even the more ardent admirers of the poem are tempted to pass from one to another of the higher ranges and more commanding summits, which swell gradually or rise abruptly out of the general level over which he leads them, rather than to follow him through all the windings of his argument.

Yet it is only after the poem has been mastered in its details that we realise its full effect on the imagination.

It is only then that we understand the complete greatness of the man, as a thinker, a teacher, and a poet. The most familiar beauties reveal a deeper meaning when they are seen to be not mere resting places in the toilsome march of his argument, but rather commanding positions, successively reached, from which the widest contemplative views of the realms of Nature and human life are laid open to us. As we follow closely in his footsteps, through all his processes of observation, analysis, and reasoning, we feel, that he too, like the older Greeks, is borne along by a strong enthusiasm,—the philosophical ἔρως of Plato,—different from, but akin to, the impulses of poetry. That marvellous intensity of feeling in conjunction with the operations of the intellect, which the Greeks regarded as a kind of divine possession, and which Lucretius, by the use of such phrases as 'divinitus invenientes,' ascribes to the earliest enquirers, animates all his interpretation of the facts and laws of Nature. The speculative passion imparts life to the argumentative processes which are addressed to the understanding, while it adds a fresher glory or more impressive solemnity to those aspects of the subject by which the imagination is most powerfully moved.

Again, although his rhythm, even at its best, falls far short of the intricate harmony and variety of Virgil, and, in its more level passages, scarcely aims at pleasing the ear at all, yet there is a kind of grandeur and dignity even in its monotony, varied, as that is, by deeper and more majestic tones whenever his spirit is stirred by impulses of awe, wonder, and delight. There is always a sense of life and onward movement in the flow of his verse. Often there is a kind of cumulative force revealing a more powerful emotion of heart and imagination as his thoughts and images press on one another in close and ordered sequence. Thus, for instance, the effect of the lines describing the religious impressions produced on the early inhabitants of the world by the grand and awful aspects of Nature, depends, not on any harmonious variation of sounds, but on the swelling and culminating power with which the whole passage breaks on the ear,—

> In caeloque deum sedes et templa locarunt,
> Per caelum volvi quia nox et luna videtur,
> Luna dies et nox et noctis signa severa
> Noctivagaeque faces caeli flammaeque volantes,
> Nubila sol imbres nix venti fulmina grando
> Et rapidi fremitus et murmura magna minarum.[1]

In many passages it may be noticed how much is added to the rhythmical effect by the force or weight of the concluding line, as at iii. 870–893, by the rugged grandeur of the line,—

> Urgerive superne obtritum pondere terrae,—

at ii. 569–580, by the sad and solemn movement of the close,—

> Ploratus mortis comites et funeris atri,—

and at i. 101, by the line of cardinal significance, which ends a passage of most finished power and beauty,—

> Tantum religio potuit suadere malorum.

The music of Lucretius is altogether his own. As he was the first among his countrymen who contemplated in a reverential spirit the majesty of Nature and the more solemn meaning of life, so he was the first to call out the full rhythmical majesty and deep organ-tones of the Latin language, to embody in sound the spiritual emotions stirred by that contemplation.

The poetical style of Lucretius is, like his rhythm, a true and powerful symbol of his genius. Though his diction is much less studied than that of Virgil, yet his large use of alliterations, assonances, asyndeta[2], etc., shows that he consciously aimed at producing certain effects by recog-

---

[1] 'And they placed the dwelling-places and mansions of the gods in the heavens, because it is through the heavens that the night and the moon are seen to sweep—the moon, the day, and night, and the stern constellations of night, the torches of heaven wandering through the night, and flying meteors, the clouds, the sun, the rains, the snow, the winds, lightning, hail, the rapid rattle, the threatening peals and murmurs of the thunder.'—v. 1188–93.

[2] Cf. Munro, Introduction, ii. pp. 311, etc.

nised rhetorical means. The attraction which the artifices of rhetoric had for his mind is as noticeable in his style as a similar attraction is in the speeches of Thucydides. But neither Lucretius nor Thucydides can be called the slave of rhetorical forms. In both writers recourse is had to them for the legitimate purpose of emphasising thought, not for that of disguising its insufficiency. The use of such phrases, for instance, as 'sed casta inceste,' 'immortalia mortali sermone notantes,' 'mors immortalis,' etc., is no mere play of words, but rather the tersest phrase in which an impressive antithesis of thought can be presented. The mannerisms of his style, if they show that he was not altogether emancipated from archaic rudeness, afford evidence also of the prolific fertility of his genius. The amplitude and unchecked volume of his diction flow out of the mental conditions, described in the lines,—

> Usque adeo largos haustus e fontibu' magnis
> Lingua meo suavis diti de pectore fundet.

And he had not only the 'suavis lingua diti de pectore;' he had also the 'daedala lingua,'—the formative energy which shapes words into new forms and combinations. The frequent ἅπαξ λεγόμενα in his poem and his abundant use of compound words, such as *fluctifragus, montivagus, altitonans*, etc., most of which fell into disuse in the Augustan age, were products of the same creative force which enabled Plautus and Ennius to add largely to the resources of the Latin tongue. In him, more than in any Latin poet before or after him, we meet with phrases too full of imaginative life to be in perfect keeping with the more sober tones and tamer spirit of the national literature. Thus his language never became trite and hackneyed, and, as we read him, no medium of after-associations is interposed between his mind and our own.

But it is not in individual phrases, however fresh and powerful, but in continuous passages, that the power of his style is best seen. The processes of his mind are characterised by continuity, consistency, and a kind of gathering intensity of movement. The periods of Virgil delight us by their intricate harmony; those of Lucretius impress us by their continuous and hurrying impetus. The long drawn out charm of the one is indicative of the deep love which induced him to linger over every detail of his subject: the force and grandeur of the other are the outward signs of the inward wonder and enthusiasm by which his spirit was borne rapidly along. Virgil's movement displays the majesty of grace and serenity; that of Lucretius the majesty of power, and largeness of mind.

Thus although the poetical style of Lucretius shows the traces of labour and premeditation, and of occasional imitation both of foreign and native models, it is more than that of any other Latin poet, the immediate creation of his own genius. The 'ingenuei fontis,' by which his imagination was so abundantly fed, found many spontaneous outlets, and were not checked in their speed or stained in their purity by the artificial channels in which he sometimes forced them to flow. If the loving labour, so prodigally bestowed upon the task of finding words and rhythm[1] adequate to his great theme, explains some peculiarities of his diction, the qualities which have made the work immortal are due to his noble singleness of heart and sincerity of nature, and to the openness and sensibility with which his imagination received impressions, the penetrative force with which it saw into the heart of things, and the creative energy with which it shaped what it received and discerned into vivid pictures and symbols.

He has, in the first place, the freshness of feeling, the living sense of the wonder of the world, which is a great charm in the older poets of all great literatures,—in Homer, Dante, Chaucer;—and this sense he communicates by words used in their simplest and directest meaning. The life which animates and gladdens the familiar face of earth, sea, and sky,—of river, wood, field, and hill-side,—is

[1] Cf. 'Quaerentem dictis quibus et quo carmine demum
  Clara tuae possim praepandere lumina menti
  Res quibus occultas penitus convisere possis.'
         i. 143–5.

vividly and immediately reproduced in such lines as these:—

> Caeli subter labentia signa
> Quae mare navigerum quae terras frugiferentis
> Concelebras.[1]

> Denique per maria ac montis fluviosque rapacis
> Frondiferasque domos avium camposque virentis.[2]

> Frondiferasque novis avibus canere undique silvas.[3]

> Nam saepe in colli tondentes pabula laeta
> Lanigerae reptant pecudes quo quamque vocantes
> Invitant herbae gemmantes rore recenti.[4]

> Nec tenerae salices atque herbae rore vigentis
> Fluminaque illa queunt summis labentia ripis.[5]

So, too, he makes us realise, with a quickening and expanding emotion, which seems to bring us nearer to the core of Nature, the majesty of the sea breaking on a great expanse of shore,—the solemn stillness of midnight,—the invisible agency by which the clouds form the pageantry of the sky,—the active noiseless energy by which rivers wear away their banks,—by the use of words that seem exactly equivalent to the thing which they describe,—

> Quam fluitans circum magnis anfractibus aequor
> Ionium glaucis aspargit virus ab undis.[6]

> Severa silentia noctis
> Undique cum constent.[7]

> Ut nubes facile interdum concrescere in alto
> Cernimus et mundi speciem violare serenam
> Aera mulcentes motu.[8]

> Pars etiam glebarum ad diluviem revocatur
> Imbribus et ripas radentia flumina rodunt.[9]

The changing face of Nature is to his spirit so full of power and wonder, that it needs no poetical adornment, but is left to tell its own tale in the plainest language. If words are a true index of feeling, it would be difficult to name any poet by whom the living presence and full being of Nature were more immediately apprehended, nor has any

---

[1] i. 2-4.   [2] i. 17-18.   [3] i. 256.
[4] ii. 317-19.   [5] ii. 362-63.   [6] i. 718-19.
[7] iv. 460-61.   [8] iv. 136-38.   [9] v. 255-56.

one caught with more fidelity the intimations of her hidden life, as they betray themselves in her outward features and motions.

With similar fidelity and directness of language he communicates to his reader the spell of awe and wonder by which his own spirit is possessed in presence of the impressive facts of human life. No subtlety of reflection nor grandeur of illustrative imagery could enhance the effect of the thought of the dead produced by the austere plainness of the words,—

> Morte obita quorum tellus amplectitur ossa,

and,

> Ossa dedit terrae proinde ac famul infimus esset.

By no pomp of description could a deeper sense of religious solemnity be created than by the lines describing the silent influence of the procession of Cybele on the minds of her devotees,—

> Ergo cum primum magnas invecta per urbis
> Munificat tacita mortalis muta salute.[1]

The undying pain of a great sorrow,—the paralysis of all human effort in the face of new and terrible agencies of death,—the blessedness and pathos of the purest human affections,—the ecstatic delight derived from the revelation of great truths—imprint themselves permanently on the imagination through the august simplicity of the phrases,—

> Aeternumque daret matri sub pectore volnus,[2]—
>
> tacito mussabat medicina timore,[3]—
>
> tacita pectus dulcedine tangent,[4]—
>
> His ibi me rebus quaedam divina voluptas
> Percipit adque horror.[5]—

His language has the further power of producing a vague sense of sublimity, where the cause of the feeling is too vast or undefined to be distinctly conceived or visibly presented to the mind. The very sound of his words seems sometimes to be a kind of echo of the voices by which

---

[1] ii. 624-25.   [2] ii. 639.   [3] vi. 1179.
[4] iii. 896.   [5] iii. 28-30.

Nature produces a strange awe upon the imagination. Such, for instance, are these lines and phrases—

> Altitonans Volturnus et auster fulmine pollens.[1]
> Nec fulmina nec minitanti
> Murmure compressit caelum.[2]
> Murmura magna minarum,[3] etc.

The sublimity of vagueness and vastness is present in the language of these lines—

> Impendent atrae formidinis ora superne.[4]
> Sustentata ruet moles et machina mundi.[5]
> Aut cecidisse urbis magno vexamine mundi.[6]
> Non si terra mari miscebitur et mare caelo.[7]

While no other ancient poet brings before the mind more forcibly and immediately the living presence of the outward world and the solemn meaning of familiar things, there is none whose language seems to respond so sensitively to the vague suggestions of an invisible and awful Power omnipresent in the universe.

The creative power of imagination which gives new life to words and thoughts is also present in many vivid and picturesque expressions, either scattered through the main argument, or shining in brilliant combinations in the more elaborate parts of the work. By this more imaginative use of language, the poet can illustrate his ideas by subtle analogies, or embody them in visible symbols, or endow the objects he describes with the personal attributes of will and energy. Thus, for instance, the penetrating subtlety of the mind in exploring the secrets of Nature becomes a visible force in the curious felicity of the expression (i. 408), 'caecasque latebras insinuare omnis.' The freedom and boundless range of the imagination is suggested with picturesque effect in the familiar expression—

> Avia Pieridum peragro loca nullius ante
> Trita solo;[8]

while the calm serenity of the contemplative mind is symbolised in such figurative expressions as ' sapientum templa

[1] v. 745.   [2] i. 68–9.   [3] v. 1193.   [4] vi. 254.
[5] v. 96.   [6] v. 340.   [7] iii. 842.   [8] i. 926-27.

serena;' 'humanum in pectus templaque mentis;' and the stormy tumult of the passions and the perilous errors of life become vividly present to the imagination by means of the analogies pictured in the lines—

and
Volvere curarum tristis in pectore fluctus,[1]

Errare atque viam palantis quaerere vitae.[2]

What life and energy again are imparted to external things and abstract conceptions by such expressions as these:—'flammai flore coorto;' 'avido complexu quem tenet aether;' 'caeli tegit impetus ingens;' 'circum tremere aethera signis;' 'semina quae magnum iaculando contulit omne;' 'vagos imbris tempestatesque volantes;' 'concussaeque cadunt urbes dubiaeque minantur;' 'simulacraque fessa fatisci;' 'sol lumine conserit arva;' 'lucida tela diei;' 'placidi pellacia ponti;' 'vivant labentes aetheris ignes;' 'leti sub dentibus ipsis;' 'leti praeclusa est ianua caelo,' etc.

A similar power of imagination is shown in his more elaborate use of analogies, in his symbolical representation of ideas, and in his power of painting scenes from Nature and from human life. Few great poets have been more sparing in the use of mere poetical ornament. The grandest imagery which he strikes out, and the finest pictures which he paints are immediately suggested by his subject. The earnestness of his speculative and practical purpose restrains all exuberance of fancy. Thus his imaginative analogies are more often latent in single expressions than drawn out at length. But the few which he has elaborated, 'stand out with the solidity of the finest sculpture[3],' to embody some deep or powerful thought for all time. They are suggested not by outward resemblance, but by an identity which the imagination discerns in the innermost meaning of the objects compared with one another. The strong emotion attending on the presence of some great thought calls up before the inward

---

[1] vi. 34.   [2] ii. 10.
[3] Prevost Paradol, *Nouveaux Essais de Politique et de Littérature.*

eye some scene or action, which, if actually witnessed, would produce a similar effect upon the mind. Thus the thought of the chaotic confusion which the universe would present, on the supposition that the original atoms were limited in number, calls up the image of the most impressive and awful devastation, wrought by Nature upon the works of man.

> Sed quasi naufragiis magnis multisque coortis
> Disiectare solet magnum mare transtra guberna
> Antemnas proram malos tonsasque natantis,
> Per terrarum omnis oras fluitantia aplustra
> Ut videantur et indicium mortalibus edant,
> Infidi maris insidias virisque dolumque
> Ut vitare velint, neve ullo tempore credant,
> Subdola cum ridet placidi pellacia ponti,
> Sic tibi si finita semel primordia quaedam
> Constitues, aevom debebunt sparsa per omnem
> Disiectare aestus diversi materiari,
> Numquam in concilium ut possint compulsa coire
> Nec remorari in concilio nec crescere adaucta.[1]

It is through the penetrating intuition of his imagination into the deepest meaning of the two phenomena, and his sensibility to the pathos and the strangeness involved in each of them, that he sees the birth of every child into the world under the well-known image of the shipwrecked sailor—'saevis proiectus ab undis.' Other analogies, suggested rather than elaborately drawn out, express an inward or spiritual, not an outward or bodily resemblance. Or rather the thing illustrated is a thought or a mental act, the illustration a scene or action, visible to the eye, suggestive of the same power in Nature, and calculated to rouse the same emotions in the mind. Thus he compares the life transmitted in succession through the nations

[1] 'But as when there have been at the same time many and mighty shipwrecks, the mighty sea is wont to drive in all directions the rowers' benches, rudders, sailyards, prows, masts, and floating oars, so that along all the coasts of land there may be seen the tossing flag-posts of ships, to warn mortals that they shun the wiles, and force, and craft of the faithless sea, nor ever trust the treacherous alluring smile of the calm ocean; so if once you will suppose any finite number of elements, you will find that the many surging forces of matter must disperse and drive them apart through all time, so that they never can meet and gather into union, nor stay in union and wax in increase.'—ii. 552-64.

of the world to the torch passed on by the runners in the torch-race; or he illustrates his calm contemplation of the struggles of life from the heights of his Epicurean philosophy, by the vision of the dangers of the sea, as seen from some commanding position on the land.

Although his subject did not afford much scope for the exercise of the idealising faculty of a poetical artist, yet there are some passages in the poem conceived with the finest pictorial power. Such, for instance, is the representation of the sacrifice of Iphigenia, suggested indeed, in some of its features, by an earlier poet, but executed with original power. There are also one or two pictures from the ancient mythology, as that of Venus and Mars in the invocation to the poem, and that of Pan—

> Pinea semiferi capitis velamina quassans,[1]—

showing that he might have rivalled Catullus and Ovid as a poet of creative fancy, had he not felt himself more powerfully called to interpret the laws and facts of Nature. By this power of imagination he presents that superstition against which all the weight of his argument is directed, not as an abstraction, but as a real palpably existing Power of evil—

> Quae caput a caeli regionibus ostendebat
> Horribili super aspectu mortalibus instans.[2]

So, too, in his vivid account of the orderly procession of the seasons, he invests the freshness and the beauty of spring with the charm of personal and human associations in the lines—

> It ver et Venus, et veris praenuntius ante
> Pennatus graditur zephyrus, vestigia propter
> Flora quibus mater praespargens ante viai
> Cuncta coloribus egregiis et odoribus opplet.[3]

But it is in describing actual scenes and actual aspects

---

[1] iv. 587. [2] i. 64-5.
[3] 'Spring advances and Venus, and before them goes the harbinger of Spring, the winged Zephyr; and near their path, Mother Flora, scattering her treasures before her, fills all the way with glorious colours and fragrance.'—v. 737-40.

of human life that Lucretius chiefly employs his power of poetical conception and expression. He looks upon the world with an eye which discerns beneath the outward appearances of things the presence of Nature in her attributes both of majesty and of genial all-penetrating life,—as at once the 'Magna mater' and the 'alma mater' of all living things[1]. She appears to his imagination not as an abstraction, or a vast aggregate of forces and laws, but as a living Power, whose processes are on an infinitely grander scale, but are yet analogous to the active and moral energies of man. He shows the same sympathy with this life of Nature, the same vivid sense of wonder and delight in her familiar aspects, the same imaginative perception of her secret agency, which led the early Greek mind to people the world with the living forms of the old mythology, and which have been felt anew by the great poets of the present century. All natural life is thus endowed with a poetical interest, as being a new manifestation of the creative energy, which is the fountain of all beauty and delight in the world.

The minutest phenomena and the most gigantic forces, the changes of decay and renovation in all outward things, the growth of plants and trees, the habits of beasts rioting in a wild liberty over the mountains,—

> Quod in magnis bacchatur montibu' passim,[2]—

or tended by the care and ministering to the wants of man; the life and enjoyment of the birds that gladden the early morning with their song by woods and river-banks, or that seek their food and pastime among the sea-waves;—these, and numberless other phenomena, are all contemplated and described by an eye quickened

---

[1] Cp. 'Keats has, above all, a sense of what is pleasurable and open in the life of Nature; for him she is the *Alma Parens*: his expression has, therefore, more than Guérin's, something genial, outward, and sensuous. Guérin has above all a sense of what there is adorable and secret in the life of Nature; for him she is the *Magna Parens*; his expression has, therefore, more than Keats', something mystic, inward, and profound.' *Essays in Criticism*, by M. Arnold, p. 130. *Third Edition*.

[2] v. 824.

by the poetical sense of manifold and inexhaustible energy in the world.

It is not so much the beauty of form and colour, as the appearance of force and life which he reproduces. He has not, like Catullus, the pure delight of an artist in painting outward scenes. He does not express, like Virgil, the charm of old associations attaching to famous places. It is the association of great laws, not of great memories, which moves him in contemplating the outward world. Neither has he invested any particular place with the attraction which Horace has given to his Sabine home, and Catullus to Sirmio. But no ancient or modern poet has expressed more happily the natural enjoyment of beholding the changing life and familiar face of the world. No other writer makes us feel with more reality the quickening of the spirit, produced by the sunrise or the advent of spring, by living in fine weather or looking on fair and peaceful landscapes. The freshness of the feeling with which outward scenes inspire him is one of the great charms of the poem, especially as a relief to the pervading gravity of his thought. More than any poet, except Wordsworth, he seems to derive a pure and healthy joy from the common sights and sounds of animate and inanimate Nature. No distempered fancies or regrets, no vague longings for some unattainable rapture, coloured the natural aspect which the world presented to his eyes and mind.

In the descriptions of Lucretius, as in those of Homer, there is always some active movement and change represented as passing before the eye. What power and energy there are, for instance, in that of a river-flood,—(like one of equal force and truth in Burns's 'Brigs of Ayr,')—

> Nec validi possunt pontes venientis aquai
> Vim subitam tolerare: ita magno turbidus imbri
> Molibus incurrit validis cum viribus amnis.[1]

How naturally is the pure and sparkling life of brooks and

---

[1] 'Nor can the strong bridges endure the sudden force of the rushing water: in such wise, swollen by heavy rain, the stream with mighty force dashes upon the piers.'—i. 285-87.

springs brought before the mind in the passage at v. 269[1], already quoted,—and again, in these lines—

> Denique nota vagi silvestria templa tenebant
> Nympharum, quibus e scibant umori' fluenta
> Lubrica proluvie larga lavere umida saxa,
> Umida saxa, super viridi stillantia musco,
> Et partim plano scatere atque erumpere campo.[2]

In this representation of the sea-shore—

> Concharumque genus parili ratione videmus
> Pingere telluris gremium, qua mollibus undis
> Litoris incurvi bibulam pavit aequor harenam,[3]—

there is the same suggestion of quiet ceaseless movement, as in a line of the Odyssey representing the same phase of Nature—

> λαῖγγας πότι χέρσον ἀποπλύνεσπε θάλασσα.

There is the same sense of active life in all his pictures of the early morning; as, for instance,—

> Primum aurora novo cum spargit lumine terras
> Et variae volucres nemora avia pervolitantes
> Aera per tenerum liquidis loca vocibus opplent,
> Quam subito soleat sol ortus tempore tali
> Convestire sua perfundens omnia luce,
> Omnibus in promptu manifestumque esse videmus.[4]

And again,—

> Aurea cum primum gemmantis rore per herbas
> Matutina rubent radiati lumina solis
> Exhalantque lacus nebulam fluviique perennes,
> Ipsaque ut interdum tellus fumare videtur;

---

[1] 'Percolatur enim virus,' etc.

[2] 'Finally, in their wandering they made their dwelling in the familiar woodland grottoes of the nymphs, from which they marked the rills of water laving the dripping rocks, made slippery with their abundant flow,—dripping rocks, with drops oozing out above the green moss,—and gushing forth and forcing their way over the level plain.'—v. 944-52.

[3] 'And in like manner we see shells paint the lap of the earth, where with its soft waves the sea beats on the porous sand of the winding shore.'—ii. 374-76.

[4] 'When the dawn first sheds its new light over the earth, and birds of every kind, flying over the pathless woods through the delicate air, fill all the land with their clear notes, the suddenness with which the risen sun then clothes and steeps the world in his light, is clear and evident to all men.'—ii. 144-49.

> Omnia quae sursum cum conciliantur, in alto
> Corpore concreto subtexunt nubila caelum.[1]

Two other passages (at iv. 136 and vi. 190), in which the movements and shifting pageantry of the clouds are described, may be compared with a more elaborate passage in the Excursion, in which Wordsworth has represented a similar spectacle[2] wrought by 'earthly Nature,'—

> 'Upon the dark materials of the storm.'

Nowhere does he present pictures of pure repose. The philosophical idea of ceaseless motion and change animates to his eye every aspect of the world. Every separate description in the poem possesses the charm of freshness and faithfulness, and of relevance to the great ideas of his philosophy. His living enjoyment in the outward world, and his sympathy with all existence, both fed and were fed by his trust in speculative ideas. The poetical descriptions which adorn and illustrate his argument are like the sublime and beautiful scenes which refresh and reward the adventurous discoverer of distant lands.

Some passages, illustrative of philosophical principles, blend the movements of animal and human life with descriptions of natural scenery. The lines at ii. 352-366, describing the cow searching for her calf, which has been sacrificed at the altar, combine many characteristics of the poetical style of Lucretius. There is the literal—almost too minute faithfulness of reproduction—as in the line—

> Noscit humi pedibus vestigia pressa bisulcis;[3]—

the active life of the whole representation, too full of movement for a picture, yet flashing the objects on the inward eye with graphic pictorial power; the ever fresh

---

[1] 'Just as when first the morning beams of the bright sun glow all golden through the grass gemmed with dew, and a mist arises from meres and flowing streams; and as even the earth itself is sometimes seen to steam; then all these vapours gather together above, and taking shape, as clouds on high, weave a canopy beneath the sky.'—v. 460-66.

[2] Excursion, Book ii:—
> 'The appearance, instantaneously disclosed,' etc.

[3] ii. 356.

charm of some familiar scene, called up by the lines already referred to,—

> Nec tenerae salices atque herbae rore vigentes
> Fluminaque illa queunt summis labentia ripis;—

the pathos and respect for every mode of natural feeling denoted in such expressions as 'desiderio perfixa iuvenci'; and, lastly, the power of investing the most common things with the majesty of the laws which they express and illustrate. This passage is adduced as a proof and illustration of the varieties in form of the primordial atoms. In a passage, immediately preceding, the perpetual motion of the atoms, going on beneath an appearance of absolute rest, is illustrated by two pictures, one taken from the jubilant life of the animal creation—

> Nam saepe in colli tondentes pabula laeta,[1] etc.;

the other taken from the pomp of human affairs, and the gay pageantry of armies—

> Praeterea magnae legiones cum loca cursu
> Camporum complent belli simulacra cientes,
> Fulgor ibi ad caelum se tollit totaque circum
> Aere renidescit tellus supterque virum vi
> Excitur pedibus sonitus clamoreque montes
> Icti reiectant voces ad sidera mundi
> Et circumvolitant equites mediosque repente
> Tramittunt valido quatientes impete campos.[2]

The truth and fulness of life in this passage are immediately perceived, but the element of sublimity is added by the thought in the two lines with which the passage concludes, which reduces the whole of this moving and sounding pageant to stillness and silence—

> Et tamen est quidam locus altis montibus unde
> Stare videntur et in campis consistere fulgor.[3]

---

[1] ii. 317.

[2] 'Besides when mighty legions fill the plains with their rapid movement, raising the pageantry of warfare, the splendour rises up to heaven, and all the land around is bright with the glitter of brass, and beneath from the mighty host of men the sound of their tramp arises, and the mountains, struck by their shouting, re-echo their voices to the stars of heaven, and the horsemen hurry to and fro on either flank, and suddenly charge across the plains, shaking them with their impetuous onset.'—ii. 323-30.

[3] 'And yet there is some place in the lofty mountains whence they appear to be all still, and to rest as a bright gleam upon the plains.'—ii. 331-32.

As Lucretius was the first poet who revealed the majesty and wonder of the Natural world, so he restored the sense of awe and mystery, felt by the earlier Greek poets, to the contemplation of human life. In dealing with the problem of human destiny, he has sounded deeper than any of the other ancient poets of Italy: but others have sympathised with a greater variety of the moods of life, and have allowed its lights and shadows to play more easily over their poetry. The thought both of the dignity and the littleness of our mortal state is ever present to the mind of Lucretius. His imagination is involuntarily moved by the pomp and grandeur of affairs, while his strong sense of reality keeps ever before him the conviction of the vanity of outward state, the weariness of luxurious living, and the miseries of ambition. Thus his imaginative recognition of the pomp and circumstance of war brings out by the force of contrast his deeper conviction of the littleness and impotence of man in the presence of the great forces of Nature—

> Summa etiam cum vis violenti per mare venti
> Induperatorem classis super aequora verrit
> Cum validis pariter legionibus atque elephantis,
> Non divom pacem votis adit ac prece quaesit
> Ventorum pavidus paces animasque secundas, etc.[1]

If his reason acknowledges only inward strength as the attribute of human dignity, yet his imagination feels the outward spell that swayed the Roman genius, through the symbols of power and authority, through great spectacles, and in impressive ceremonials.

But it is with more heart-felt sympathy, and with not less imaginative emotion, that he recognises the deep wonder and the infinite pathos of human life. There is perhaps no passage in any poet which reveals more truthfully that union of feelings in meditating on the

---

[1] 'When, too, the utmost force of a violent gale is sweeping the admiral of some fleet over the seas, along with his mighty legions and elephants, does he not court the protection of the Gods with vows, and in his terror pray for a calm to the storm, and for favouring gales?'—v. 1226–30.

strangeness and sadness of our mortal destiny than the well-known passage describing the birth of every infant into the world—

> Tum porro puer, ut saevis proiectus ab undis
> Navita, nudus humi iacet, infans, indigus omni
> Vitali auxilio, cum primum in luminis oras
> Nixibus ex alvo matris natura profudit,
> Vagituque locum lugubri complet, ut aecumst
> Cui tantum in vita restet transire malorum.[1]

With what truth and naiveté is the complaint of the husbandman over his ineffectual labour and scanty returns echoed!—

> Iamque caput quassans grandis suspirat arator
> Crebrius incassum manuum cecidisse labores,
> Et cum tempora temporibus praesentia confert
> Praeteritis, laudat fortunas saepe parentis
> Et crepat, anticum genus ut pietate repletum
> Perfacile angustis tolerarit finibus aevom,
> Cum minor esset agri multo modus ante viritim.[2]

His feeling is profoundly solemn, as well as infinitely tender. Above all the tumult of life, he hears incessantly the funeral dirge over some one departed, and the infant wail of a new-comer into the troubles of the world,

> mixtos vagitibus aegris
> Ploratus mortis comites et funeris atri.[3]

His tone can, indeed, be stern and indignant, as well as tender and melancholy: it is never morbid or effeminate. His tenderness is that of a thoroughly masculine nature. Some signs of the same mood may be discovered in the fragments of Ennius; but the feeling of Lucretius springs

---

[1] 'Moreover, the babe, like a sailor cast ashore by the cruel waves, lies naked on the ground, speechless, in need of every aid to life, when first nature has cast him forth by great throes from his mother's womb; and he fills the air with his piteous wail, as befits one whose doom it is to pass through so much misery in life.'—v. 222-27.

[2] 'And now, shaking his head, the aged peasant laments, with a sigh, that the toil of his hands has often come to naught; and, as he compares the present with the past time, he extols the fortune of his father, and harps on this theme, how the good old race, full of piety, bore the burden of their life very easily within narrow bounds, when the portion of land for each man was far less than now.'—ii. 1164-70.

[3] ii. 569-70.

from a more sympathetic heart and a more contemplative imagination.

His imagination, which depicts so forcibly the intimations of experience, is able to bear him beyond the known and familiar regions of life. As it enables him to pass—

extra flammantia moenia mundi—

and to behold the dawn of creation, and even the blank desolation which will follow on the overthrow of our system, so it has enabled him to realise with vivid feeling the primeval condition of man upon the world. Yet even in these daring enterprises of his fancy he adheres strictly to the conclusions of his philosophical system, and shows that sincerity and truthful adherence to fact are as inseparable from the operations of his creative faculty as of his understanding and moral nature.

His excellencies are so different from those of Virgil that the question need not be entertained, whether the rank of the greatest of Roman poets is or is not to be awarded to him. If each nation must be considered the best judge of its own poets, it will be admitted that Lucretius would have found few Roman voices to support his claim to the first or even the second place. The strongest support which he could have received would have been Virgil's willing acknowledgment of the powerful spell which the genius of his predecessor had exercised over him. Both the artistic defects and the profound feeling and imaginative originality of his work were calculated to alienate both popular favour and critical opinion in the Rome of the Empire. The poem has a much deeper significance for modern than it had for ancient times. Lucretius stands alone as the great contemplative poet of antiquity. He has proclaimed with more power than any other the majesty of Nature's laws, and has interpreted with a truer and deeper insight the meaning of her manifold life. Few, if any among his countrymen, felt so strongly the mystery of man's being, or have indicated so passionate a sympathy with the real sorrows of life, and so ardent a desire to raise man to his proper dignity, and to support him in bearing his inevitable burden. If he has, in large measure, the antique simplicity and grandeur of character, he has much also in common with the spirit and genius of modern times. He contemplates human life with a profound feeling, like that of Pascal, and with a speculative elevation like that of Spinoza. The loftier tones of his poetry and the sustained effort of mind which bears him through his long argument remind us of Milton. His sympathy with Nature, at once fresh and large, is more in harmony with the feeling of the great poets of the present century than with the general sentiment of ancient poetry. In the union of poetical feeling with scientific passion he has anticipated the most elevated mode of the study of Nature, of which the world has as yet seen only a few great examples. His powers of observation, thought, feeling, and imagination, are characterised by a remarkable vitality and sincerity. His strong intellectual and poetical faculty is united with some of the rarest moral qualities,— fortitude, seriousness of spirit, love of truth, manly tenderness of heart. And if it seems that his great powers of heart, understanding, and genius led him to accept and to teach a philosophy, paralysing to the highest human hope and energy, it is to be remembered that he lived at a time when the truest minds may well have despaired of the Divine government of the world, and must have honestly felt that it was well to be rid, at any cost, of the burden of Pagan superstition.

CHAPTER XV.

CATULLUS.

LUCRETIUS and Catullus were regarded by their contemporaries as the greatest poets of the last age of the Republic[1]. They alone represent the poetry of that time to the modern world. Although born into the same social rank, and acted upon by the dissolving influences, the intellectual stimulus, and the political agitation of the same time, no poets could be named of a more distinct type of genius and character. The first has left behind him only the record of his impersonal contemplation. His life was passed more in communion with Nature than in contact with the world: his experiences of happiness or sorrow entered into his art solely as affording materials for his abstract thought. The second has stamped upon his pages the lasting impression of the deepest joy and pain of his life, as well as of the lightest cares and fancies that occupied the passing hour. Intensely social in his temper and tastes, he lived habitually the life of the great city and the provincial town, observing and sharing in all their pleasures, distractions, and animosities, and only escaping, from time to time, for a brief interval to his country houses on the Lago di Garda and in the neighbourhood of Tivoli. He seems to have had no other aim in life than that of passionately enjoying his youth in the pleasures of love, in friendly intercourse with men of his own rank and age,

---

[1] Cf. 'L. Julium Calidum, quem post Lucretii Catullique mortem multo elegantissimum poetam nostram tulisse aetatem vere videor posse contendere.' —Corn. Nep. Vit. A.t. 12.

in the practice of his art, and the study of the older poets, by whom that art was nourished. All his poems, with the exception of three or four works of creative fancy and one or two translations, have for their subject some personal incident, feeling, or character. Nearly all have some immediate relation to himself, and give expression to his love or hatred, his admiration or scorn, his happiness or misery. There is nearly as little in them of reflection on human life as of meditative communion with Nature; but, as individual men and women excited in him intense affection or passion, so certain beautiful places and beautiful objects in Nature charmed his fancy and sank into his heart. He shows himself, spiritually and intellectually, the child of his age in his ardent vitality, in the license of his life and satire, in the fierceness of his antipathies; and also in his eager reception of the spirit of Greek art, his delight in the poets of Greece and the tales of the Greek mythology, in his striving after form and grace in composition, and in the enthusiasm with which he anticipates the joy of travelling among 'the famous cities of Asia.' In all our thoughts of him he is present to our imagination as the 'young Catullus'—

> hedera iuvenalia vinctus
> Tempora.

More than any great ancient, and than any great modern poet, with the exception, perhaps, of Keats, he affords the measure of what youth can do, and what it fails to do, in poetry. Although the exact age at which he died is disputed, yet the evidence of his poems shows that he did not outlive the boyish heart, the frank trusting simplicity, the ardent feelings and passions, the careless unreflecting spirit of early youth. In character he was even younger than in actual age. Nearly all his work was done between the years 60 and 54 B.C.; and most of it, apparently, with little effort. Born with the keenest capacities of pleasure and of pain, he never learned to regulate them: nor were they, seemingly, united with such enduring vital power as to carry him past the perilous stage of his career, so as to enable him with maturer power and more concentrated industry to employ his genius and accomplishment on works of larger scope, more capable of withstanding the shocks and chances of time, than the small volume which, by a fortunate accident, has preserved the flower and bloom of his life, and the record of all the 'sweet and bitter' which he experienced at the hands of that Power—

> Quae dulcem curis miscet amaritiem.

The ultimate preservation of his poems depended on a single copy, which, after being lost to the world for four centuries, was re-discovered in Verona, the poet's birthplace, during the fourteenth century. As that copy was again lost, the text has to be determined from the conflicting testimony of later copies, only two of which are considered by the latest critics to be of independent value. There is thus much more uncertainty, and much greater latitude for conjecture, as to the actual words of Catullus, than in the case of almost any other Roman poet. As lines not found in this volume are attributed to him by ancient authors, and as he appears to allude to the composition of love poems in his first youth[1] which must have been written before the earliest of the Lesbia-poems, it may be inferred that we do not possess all that he wrote. It has been generally assumed that the dedicatory lines to Cornelius Nepos, with which the volume opens, were prefixed by the poet to the collected edition of his poems which we now possess; but Mr. Ellis has shown that that poem may more probably have been prefixed to a smaller and earlier collection. The lines—

> Namque tu solebas
> Meas esse aliquid putare nugas, etc.—

imply that earlier poems of Catullus were well known for

---

[1] 'Multa satis lusi.'—lxviii^a. 17. The context shows that the 'lusi,'—like Horace's 'lusit Anacreon,'—refers to the composition of amatory poetry founded on his own experience. It was for this kind of poetry that Manlius had applied to him, and he pleads his grief as an excuse for his inability to write any at that time, although he had written much in his earliest youth.

D d

some time before the writing of this dedication; and allusions in more than one of the poems[1] prove that the poems of an earlier date must have been in circulation before those in which these allusions occur were written. It may be concluded that, as he wrote his poems from his earliest youth till his death, he gave them to the world at various stages of his career. The attention which he attracted from men eminent in social rank and literature,—such as Hortensius, Manlius Torquatus, Memmius, etc.,—shows that his genius was soon recognised: and his eager craving for sympathy and appreciation would naturally prompt him to bring his various writings immediately before the eyes of his contemporaries. It seems likely, therefore, that this final collection was made either by the poet himself shortly before, or by some of his many literary friends shortly after his death, from several shorter collections already in circulation; that some poems were omitted which were not thought worthy of preservation, and that some may have then been added which had not previously been given to the world. It would be difficult to believe that poems expressive of the most passionate love and the bitterest scorn of the same person could have appeared for the first time in the same collection.

This collection consists of about 116 poems[2], written in various metres, and varying in length from epigrams of only two lines to an 'epyllion' which extends to 408 lines. The poems numbered from i to lx, are short lyrical or satiric pieces, written in the phalaecian, glyconic, or iambic metres, and devoted almost entirely to subjects of personal interest. The middle of the volume is occupied by the longer poems—numbered lxi to lxviii[b]—of a more purely artistic and mostly an impersonal character, written in the glyconic, galliambic, hexameter, and elegiac metres.

---

[1] E. g. xvi. 12; liv. 6.

[2] Three poems formerly attributed to Catullus,—those between xvii and xxi,—are now omitted from all editions. On the other hand, one poem, lxviii must certainly be divided into two, and possibly some lines now attached to others are parts of separate poems.

The latter part of the volume is entirely occupied by epigrammatic or other short pieces in elegiac metre, varying in length from two to twenty-six lines. Many of the epigrams refer to the persons who are the subject of the short lyric and iambic pieces. There is no attempt to arrange the poems in anything like chronological order. Thus, among the first twelve poems, ii, iii, v, vii, ix, xii, are probably to be assigned to the years 61 and 60 B.C., while iv, x, xi, certainly belong to the three last years of the poet's life. It is difficult to imagine on what principle the juxtaposition of certain poems was determined. Perhaps, in some cases, it may have been on the mere mechanical one of filling up the pages symmetrically by poems of suitable length. Sometimes we find poems of the same character, or referring to the same person, grouped together, and yet varied by the insertion of one or two pieces related to the larger group by contrast rather than similarity of tone. Thus the passionate exaltation of the earlier Lesbia-poems is first relieved by a poem (iv) written in another metre, and appealing to a much calmer class of feelings, and next varied by one (vi) written in the same metre, and suggested by a friend's amour, which in its meanness and obscurity serves as a foil to the glory and brightness of the good fortune enjoyed by the poet. Yet this clue does not carry us far in determining the principle, if indeed there was any principle, on which either the short lyrical poems or the elegiac epigrams were arranged. These various poems were written under the influence of every mood to which he was liable; and, like other passionate lyrical poets, he was susceptible of the most opposite moods. The most trivial incident might give rise to them equally with the greatest joy or the greatest sorrow of his life. As he felt a strong need to express, and had a happy facility in expressing his purest and brightest feelings, so he felt no shame in indulging, and knew no restraint in expressing, his coarsest propensities and bitterest resentments: and he evidently regarded his worst moods no less than his best as legitimate material for his art. Thus pieces more coarse than almost anything in literature are interspersed among others of the sunniest brightness and purity. The feelings with which we linger over the exquisite beauty of the 'Sirmio,' and are stirred by the noble inspiration of the 'Hymn to Diana,' receive a rude shock from the two intervening poems, characterised by a want of reticence and reserve not often paralleled in the literature or the speech of civilised nations. In a poet of modern times a similar collocation might be supposed indicative of a cynical bitterness of spirit—of a mind mocking its own purest impulses. But Catullus is too genuine and sincere a man, too natural in his enjoyments, and too healthy in all his moods, to be taken as an example of this distempered type of genius. The place occupied by some poems in the series may be regarded rather as a confirmation of Horace's dictum—

> In longum tamen aevum
> Manserunt hodieque manent vestigia ruris.

As Catullus had a larger share than any other Roman poet of the Italian vigour and ardent sensuous temperament, so, too, the coarser fibre, associated with that temperament, was especially conspicuous in him: nor was this element in his nature much restrained by the urbanity and culture on which he and his intimate associates prided themselves.

These poems, however, whether good or bad, serious or trivial, are all written with such transparent sincerity that they bring the poet before us almost as if he were our contemporary. They make him known to us in many different moods,—in joy and grief, in the ecstasy and the despair of love, in the frank outpouring of affection and the enjoyment of social intercourse, in the bitterness of his scorn and animosity, in the license of his coarser indulgences. They enable us to start with him on his travels; to enjoy with him the beauty of his home on the Italian lakes; to pass with him from the life of letters and idle pleasure and the brilliant intellectual society of Rome to the more homely but not more virtuous ways and the more commonplace people of his native province; to join with him in ridiculing some affectation of an acquaintance, or to feel the contagion of his admiration for genius or wit in man, grace in woman, or beauty in Nature. In the glimpses of him which we get in the familiar round of his daily life, we seem to catch the very turn of his conversation[1], to hear his laugh at some absurd incident[2], to see his face brighten as he welcomes a friend from a distant land[3], to mark the quick ebullition of anger at some slight or rudeness[4], or to be witnesses of his passionate tears as something recalls to him the memory of his lost happiness, or makes him feel his present desolation[5]. His impressible nature realises with extraordinary vividness of pleasure and pain experiences which by most people are scarcely noticed. To be rightly appreciated, his poems must be read with immediate reference to the circumstances and situations which gave rise to them. We must take them up with our feelings attuned to the mood in which they were written. Hence, before attempting to criticise them, we must try, by the help of internal and any available external evidence, to determine the successive stages of his personal and literary career, and so to get some idea of the social relations and the state of feeling of which they were the expression.

There is some uncertainty as to the exact date of his birth and death. The statement of Jerome is that he was born at Verona in the year 87 B.C., and that he died at Rome, at the age of thirty, in the year 57 B.C. But this last date is contradicted by allusions in the poems to events and circumstances, such as the expeditions of Caesar across the Rhine and into Britain, the second Consulship of Pompey, the preparations for the Eastern expedition of Crassus, which belong to a later date. The latest incident which Catullus mentions is the speech of his friend Calvus, delivered in August 54 B.C. against Vatinius[6]. A line in

---

[1] x. 6.
[2] xvii. 7; liii. 1; lvi. 1.
[3] ix.
[4] xxv, xl, xlii, etc.
[5] Cf. viii, xxxviii, lxv, etc.
[6] liii.

the poem, immediately preceding that containing the allusion to the speech of Calvus,—

Per consulatum perierat Vatinius,—

was, till the appearance of Schwabe's 'Quaestiones Catullianae,' accepted as a proof that Catullus had actually witnessed the Consulship of Vatinius in 47 B.C. But it has been satisfactorily shown that that line refers to the boasts in which Vatinius used to indulge after the conference at Luca, or after his own election to the Praetorship, and not to their actual fulfilment at a later time. There is thus no evidence that Catullus survived the year 54 B.C.; and some expressions in some of his later poems, as, for instance,—

Malest Cornifici tuo Catullo,—

and—

Quid est Catulle? quid moraris emori?

are thought to indicate the anticipation of approaching death. But if 54 B.C. is to be accepted as the year of his death, one of Jerome's two other statements, viz., that he was born in the year 87 B.C. and that he died at the age of thirty, must be wrong. Most critics and commentators hold that the first date is right, and that the mistake lies in the words 'xxx. aetatis anno.' Mr. Munro, with more probability, believes the error to lie in the 87 B.C., and that Jerome, 'as so often happens with him, has blundered somewhat in transferring to his complicated era, the Consulships by which Suetonius would have dated.' He argues further, that the phrase ' iuvenalia tempora,' in the passage quoted above from Ovid and written by him at the age of twenty-five, is more applicable to one who died at the age of thirty than of thirty-three. A further argument for believing that the 'xxx. aetatis anno' is right, and the date 87 B.C. consequently wrong, is that the age at which a person died was more easily ascertained than the date at which he was born, owing to the common practice of recording the former in sepulchral inscriptions. It is easy to see how a mistake might have occurred in substituting the first of the four successive Consulships of Cinna (87

B.C.) for the last in 84 B.C.; but it is not so obvious how the substitution of xxx. for xxxiii. could have taken place. The only ground for assuming that the date of 87 B.C. is more likely to be right, is that thereby the disparity of age between Catullus and his mistress Clodia, who must have been born in 95 or 94 B.C., is somewhat lessened. But when we remember that she was actually twelve years older than M. Caelius Rufus, who succeeded Catullus as her lover, and that Cicero in his defence of Caelius speaks of her as supporting from her own means the extravagance of her youthful ('adulescentis') lovers [1], there is no more difficulty in supposing that she was ten than that she was seven years older than Catullus. Moreover, the brotherly friendship in which Catullus lived with Calvus, and his earlier intimate relations with Caelius and Gellius, who were all born in or about the year 82 B.C., seem to indicate that he was nearer to them in age than he would have been if born in 87 B.C. Between the age of twenty and thirty a difference of five years is not frequent among very intimate associates, who live together on a footing of perfect freedom. Again, the expression of the feelings both of love and friendship in the earlier poems of Catullus—written about the year 61 or 60 B.C.—seems more like that of a youth of twenty-three or four, than of twenty-six or seven, especially when we remember that, by his own confession, he had entered at a precociously early age on his career both of pleasure and of poetry. The date 84 B.C. accordingly seems to fit the recorded facts of his life and the peculiar character of his poetry better than that of 87 B.C.; and there seems to be more opening for a mistake in assigning the particular date of the poet's birth and death, than in recording the number of years which he lived.

It seems, therefore, most probable that he was born in the

---

[1] Cf. 'quae etiam aleret adulescentis et parsimoniam patrum suis sumptibus sustentaret.' Cic. Pro M. Caelio, 16, 38. Gellius, another of her lovers, was probably about the same age, or a year or two younger than Caelius. Cf. Schwabe, p. 112, etc.

year 84 B.C., and that he died at the age of thirty, either late in 54 B.C. or early in 53 B.C. The much less important, but still more disputed question as to his 'praenomen,' appears now to be conclusively settled, in accordance with the evidence of Jerome and Apuleius, in favour of Gaius, and against Quintus. In the large number of places in which he speaks of himself, he invariably calls himself 'Catullus'; and in the best MSS. his book is called 'Catulli Veronensis liber.' His Gentile name Valerius is confirmed by Suetonius in his life of Julius Caesar; and the evidence of inscriptions shows that that name was not uncommon in the district near Verona. How it happened that a branch of this patrician Roman house was settled in Cisalpine Gaul we do not know; but that the family of Catullus was one of high consideration in his native district, and maintained relations with the great families of Rome, is indicated by the intimate footing on which Julius Caesar lived with his father, and also by the fact that the poet was received as a friend into the best houses of Rome,—such as that of Hortensius, Manlius Torquatus, Metellus Celer,—shortly after his arrival there. Although some humorous complaints of money difficulties—the natural consequences of his fashionable pleasures—occur in his poems [1], yet from the fact of his possessing, in his father's lifetime, a country house on Lake Benacus and a farm on the borders of the Sabine and the Tiburtine territories, and of his having bought and manned a yacht in which he made the voyage from Bithynia to the mouth of the Po, it may be inferred that he belonged to a wealthy senatorian or equestrian family. One or two expressions, such as 'se atque suos omnes,' and again, 'te cum tota gente, Catulle, tua' [2] seem to speak of a large connexion of kinsmen: but we only know of one other member of his own family, his brother, whose early death in the Troad is mentioned with very genuine feeling in several of his poems. The statement of Jerome that he was born at Verona is confirmed by Ovid and Martial, and by the poet

---

[1] Cf. x, xiii, xxvi, xli, ciii.   [2] lviii. 3 ; lxxix. 2.

himself. He speaks of the 'Transpadani' as his own people ('ut meos quoque attingam'); he addresses Brixia (the modern Brescia), as—

> Veronae, mater amata meae;

he speaks of one of his fellow-townsmen, as—

> Quendam municipem meum.

Besides spending his early youth there, we find him, on three different occasions, retiring thither from Rome, and making a considerable stay there; first, at the time of his brother's death, apparently at the very height of his *liaison* with Clodia; next, immediately after his return from Bithynia; and again in the winter of 55–54 B.C., when his interview and reconciliation with Julius Caesar took place. We find him inviting his friend, the poet Caecilius, to come and visit him from the newly established colony of Como. He had his friends and confidants among the youth of Verona, and he records his intrigues both with the married women and courtesans of the place[1]. He took a lively interest in the humorous scandals of the Province, and he has made them the subjects of several of his poems,— e.g. xvii and lxvii. Although his life was too full of social excitement and human relations to make him dwell much on natural beauty, yet the pure feeling expressed in the Sirmio—

> Salve, o venusta Sirmio, atque ero gaude;
> Gaudete vosque o vividae[2] lacus undae—

shows that he derived keen enjoyment from the familiar loveliness of that 'ocellus' of 'all isles and capes': and in the illustrative imagery of his more artistic poems we seem to find traces of the impression made unconsciously on his imagination by the mountain scenery of Northern Italy[3].

---

[1] Cf. cx, xli.   [2] Reading suggested by Mr. Munro.
[3] E.g. lxiv. 240–41 :—
> 'Ceu pulsae ventorum flamine nubes,
> Aerium nivei montis liquere cacumen.'

And this most characteristic feature of Alpine scenery.—lxviii[b]. 17, etc. :—
> 'Qualis in aerii perlucens vertice montis
> Rivos muscoso, prosilit e lapide,' etc.

His native district afforded scope for the culture, which was the serious charm of his life, as well as for the pleasures which formed a large part of it. It was in the youth of Catullus that the power of Greek studies was first felt by the impressionable race, half-Italian, half-Celtic, of Cisalpine Gaul, which still remained outside of Italy, and is called by him 'Provincia.' Among the men of letters belonging to the last age of the Republic, Cornelius Nepos, Quintilius Varus, Furius Bibaculus, Cornificius, and Caecilius, most of whom were among the intimate friends of Catullus, came from, or resided in, the North of Italy. In the poem already mentioned he speaks of the mistress of Caecilius as being—

> Sapphica puella
> Musa doctior,—

an indication that, not only in Rome but even in the northern province, the finest literary taste and culture was shared by women. Catullus shows in the earlier stage of his poetic career his familiarity both with the 'Muse of Sappho,' and with the more laboured art of Callimachus. His special literary butt, Tanusius Geminus, whose poems are ridiculed under the title of 'Annales Volusi,' was also his 'Conterraneus.' The strength of the impulse first given to literary study in this age is marked also by the eminent names from the North of Italy, which belong to the next generation, those of Virgil, Cornelius Gallus, Aemilius Macer, Livy, etc. There is no indication that Catullus left his native district in order to complete his education, nor have we any sure sign of his presence at Rome before the year 61 B.C.[1]. He tells us that he began his career both as an amatory poet and as a man of pleasure in his earliest youth,—

---

[1] The epigram on Cominius (cviii.) was probably written at Rome, as he was not of sufficient importance to have made an impression on the people of Verona. The accusation of C. Cornelius, which excited odium against him, was made in 65 B.C. But it does not follow that the poem was written by Catullus at that time. He may have become acquainted with him later, and avenged some private pique by reference to the unpopularity formerly excited by him. There is no direct reference to the trial of Cornelius in the poem, which appears among others referring to a much later date.

> Tempore quo primum vestis mihi tradita pura'st,
> Iucundum cum aetas florida ver ageret,
> Multa satis lusi: non est dea nescia nostri,
> Quae dulcem curis miscet amaritiem.[1]

The early poems there referred to probably gained him his first reputation and attracted that notice of Cornelius Nepos, which is gratefully acknowledged in the dedication,—

> Quoi dono lepidum novum libellum.

One or two of those which we still possess—the 'Ianua,' for instance, the 'O colonia quae cupis ponte ludere magno,' possibly also the 'Vesper adest: invenes consurgite'—may have been written before Catullus settled in Rome, and before his genius was fully awakened by his passion for Lesbia: but the great majority belong to a later date; and if he did write many love poems before leaving Verona, in the pleasant spring-time of his life, nearly all, if not all, of them were omitted from the final collection. Even the 'Aufilena poems,' which are based on an intrigue carried on at Verona, are shown to be subsequent to the *liaison* with Clodia by the lines in c.—

> Cui faveam potius? Caeli, tibi, nam tua nobis
> Per facta exhibitas't unica amicitia,
> Cum vesana meas torreret flamma medullas.

This last line can only refer to the one all-absorbing passion of the poet's life. His own relations to Aufilena, in whose affections he seems to have tried to supplant his friend Quintius, were subsequent to the composition of that poem. It is not unlikely, as Westphal suggests, that the Veronese bride, 'viridissimo nupta flore puella' of the 17th poem, in whom Catullus evidently took a lively interest, may have been this Aufilena, at an earlier stage of her career.

The event which first revealed the full power of his genius, and which made both the supreme happiness and supreme misery of his life, was his passion for 'Lesbia.' After the elaborate discussions of the question by Schwabe, Munro, Ellis and others, it can no longer be doubted that the lady

[1] lxviii. 15-18.

addressed under that name was the notorious Clodia, the βοῶπις who appears so prominently in the second book of Cicero's Letters to Atticus, and the 'Medea Palatina' whose crimes, fascination, and profligacy stand out so distinctly in the defence of Caelius. We learn first from Ovid that 'Lesbia' was a feigned name; and the application of that name is easily intelligible from the admiration which Catullus felt, and which his mistress probably shared, for the 'Lesbian poetess,' whose passionate words he addressed to his mistress when he was first dazzled by her exceeding charm and beauty. Apuleius tells us further that the real name of 'Lesbia' was Clodia; and the truth of his statement is confirmed by his mention in the same place of other Roman ladies, who were celebrated by their poet-lovers,—Ticidas, Tibullus, and Propertius,—under disguised names. The statement made there that the real name of the Cynthia of Propertius was Hostia, is confirmed by the line in one of his elegies,

> Splendidaque a docto fama refulget avo.[1]

The fact that this Clodia was the sister of P. Clodius Pulcher is also indicated, and her supposed relations to her brother are hinted at in the 79th poem of Catullus,

> Lesbius est pulcher: quidni? quem Lesbia malit
> Quam te cum tota gente, Catulle, tua.

The play on the word *pulcher* might be illustrated by many parallel allusions in Cicero's Letters to Atticus. The gratitude expressed by Catullus to Allius[2], a man of rank and position, for having made arrangements to enable him to meet his mistress in secret, clearly shows that she could not have belonged to the class of *libertinae*, in whose case no such precautions could have been necessary: and the language of Catullus in the first period of his *liaison*—

> Ille mi par esse deo videtur;

and again

> Quo mea se molli candida diva pedem
> Intulit,

---

[1] In the 'docto avo' we have an allusion to the author of the 'Istrian War.'
[2] lxviii[b].

is like the rapture of a lover acknowledging the gracious condescension of a superior, as well as the delight of passion returned. Of the two kinds of lovers, those who 'allow themselves to be loved' and are flattered by this tribute to their superiority, and those who are carried out of themselves by their idealising admiration of the object of their love, Catullus, in his earlier and happier time, unquestionably belonged to the latter. Such a feeling, on the part of a young provincial poet, although primarily inspired by charms of person and manner, would naturally be enhanced by the thought that the lady whom he loved belonged to one of the oldest and highest patrician houses, and was the wife of one of the greatest nobles of Rome, who was either actual Consul, or Consul designate, at the time when she first returned the poet's passion. The subsequent course of their *liaison* affords further corroboration of her identity with the famous Clodia. The rival against whom the poet's anger is most fierce and bitter, is addressed by him as Rufus,[1]—the cognomen of M. Caelius, who became the lover of Clodia in the latter part of the year 59, and was defended by Cicero in a prosecution instigated by her in the early part of 56 B.C. The speech of Cicero amply confirms the charges of Catullus as to the multiplicity of her later lovers. As, therefore, there seems no reason to doubt, and the strongest reason to accept the statement of Apuleius that the real name of Lesbia was Clodia; as the Lesbia of Catullus was, like her, evidently a lady of rank and of great accomplishment[2]; as there was no other Clodia of the family of Clodius Pulcher at Rome, except the wife of Metellus Celer, to whom the statements made in the poems of Catullus could apply; and as these statements closely agree with all that Cicero says of her,—there is no reasonable ground for doubting their identity. If it is urged,

---

[1] The *Caelius* addressed in some of the poems is not M. Caelius Rufus, but a Veronese friend and confidant of Catullus—

'Flos Veronensum . . . iuvenum.'

Caesar, Bell. Civ. i. 2. mentions M. Caelius Rufus simply as M. Rufus.

[2] Among other indications the vow of Lesbia (xxxvi.) throws light on her literary taste and accomplishment.

on the other side, that a lady of the rank and station of Clodia cannot have sunk so low, as some of the later poems of Catullus imply, it may be said that all that Catullus in his jealous wrath imputed to her need not have been true, and also that other Roman ladies of as high rank and position, both in the last age of the Republic and in the early Empire, did sink as low [1].

That the intrigue was carried on and had even reached its second stage—that of the 'amantium irae'—in the lifetime of Metellus, appears from the 83rd poem,

> Lesbia mi praesente viro mala plurima dicit, etc.

Metellus was governor of the Province of Gallia Cisalpina in 62 B.C., and he must have returned to Rome early in 61 to stand for the Consulship. Catullus may have become known to Clodia in his absence, and the earliest poem addressed to her, the translation from Sappho, which is expressive of passionate and even distant admiration rather than of secure possession, may belong to the time of her husband's absence. But in the 68th poem, which recalls most vividly the early days of their love, when they met in secret at the house provided by Allius, the lines, in which the poet excuses her faithlessness to himself—

> Sed furtiva dedit mira munuscula nocte,
> Ipsius ex ipso dempta viri gremio [2]—

clearly imply that these meetings occurred after the return

---

[1] On the whole question compare Mr. Munro's Criticisms and Elucidations, etc., pp. 194–202.

It has been argued on the other side that public opinion would not have tolerated the publicity given to an adulterous intrigue, especially one with a Roman matron so high in rank as the wife of Metellus Celer. But the state of public opinion in the last years of the Republic is not to be gauged either by that of an earlier time, or by that existing during the stricter censorship of the Augustan régime. Catullus himself (cxiii.) testifies to what is known from other sources, the extreme laxity with which the marriage tie was regarded in the interval between 'the first and second consulships of Pompey.' Perhaps, however, if Metellus Celer had survived Catullus, the Lesbia-poems might never have been publicly given to the world. After his death Clodia by her manner of life forfeited all claim to the immunities of a Roman matron.

[2] lxviii[b]. 105–6.

of Metellus to Rome. The earlier love poems to Lesbia —those on her pet sparrow, the 'Vivamus, mea Lesbia, atque amemus,' and the 'Quaeris quot mihi basiationes,' —in all of which the feeling expressed is one at once of passionate admiration and of perfect security, — belong probably to the year 60, or to the latter part of the year 61 B.C. To this period may, in all probability, be assigned some of the poet's brightest and happiest efforts,—the Epithalamium in honour of the marriage of Manlius and Vinia Aurunculeia,[1] and the poems ix, xii, xiii, commemorative of his friendship with Veranius and Fabullus. The words in the last of these—

> Nam unguentum dabo, quod meae puellae
> Donarunt Veneres Cupidinesque—

show that they were written in the heyday of his passion. The lines in the poem, welcoming Veranius,—

> Visam te incolumem audiamque Hiberum
> Narrantem loca, facta, nationes—

seem to speak of some adventures encountered in Spain: and from the fact that three years later the two friends, who are always coupled together as inseparables by Catullus, went together on the staff of Calpurnius Piso, the father-in-law of Caesar, to his Province of Macedonia, it seems a not unwarranted conjecture[2] that they were similarly engaged at this earlier time, and had gone to Spain in the train of Julius Caesar, and had returned with him to Rome in the middle of the year 60 B.C. The twelfth poem, which is interesting as a testimony to the honour and good taste of Asinius Pollio, then a boy of sixteen,

---

[1] The poem lxviii:—
    'Quod mihi fortuna casuque oppressus acerbo'—
was addressed to Manlius just after Catullus had heard of his brother's death, i.e. probably late in the year 60, or early in the year 59 B.C. Manlius was himself suffering then from a great and sudden sorrow. The expressions in lines 1, 5, 6, 'casu acerbo,' 'sancta Venus,' 'desertum in lecto caelibe,' make it at least highly probable that this sorrow was the premature death of his young bride. If this generally accepted opinion is true the Epithalamium must have been written some time before 59 B.C.

[2] That of Westphal.

was written somewhat earlier, while Veranius and Fabullus were still in Spain.

The first hint of any rift in the loves of Catullus and Clodia is contained in the 68th poem, written in the form of a letter to Manlius—

> Quare, quod scribis Veronae turpe Catullo, etc.

Catullus had retired to Verona on hearing of the death of his brother, and he was for a time so overwhelmed with grief as to become indifferent both to poetry and love. He is as sincere and unreserved in the expression of his grief as of his former happiness, and as completely absorbed by it. He writes to Hortensius, enclosing, in fulfilment of an old promise, a translation of the 'Coma Berenices' of Callimachus, but at the same time expressing his loss of all interest in poetry owing to his recent affliction,—

> Etsi me adsiduo confectum cura dolore
> Sevocat a doctis, Ortale, virginibus, etc.

In his letter to Manlius, in which he excuses himself on the same ground for not sending any poetry of his own, and for not complying with his request to send him some volumes of Greek poetry, on the ground that his collection of books was at Rome, he notices, with a feeling almost of hopeless indifference, a hint conveyed to him by Manlius, of his mistress' faithlessness.[1] In the poem written somewhat later to Allius,—

> Non possum reticere deae qua me Allius in re, etc.—

in which his grief is still fresh but more subdued, and in which the full tide of his old passion, as well as his old delight in his art, returns to him, he speaks lightly of her occasional infidelities,—

> Quae tamen etsi uno non est contenta Catullo
> Rara verecundae furta feremus erae.

---

[1] There is some uncertainty both as to the reading and interpretation of the lines (lxviii. 15–19). The most generally accepted view is that Manlius had written to let Catullus know that several fashionable rivals were supplanting him in his absence. Mr. Munro supposes that the letter was written from Baiae, and that the *hic* is so to be explained. Another view of the passage is that Manlius had, without any reference to Clodia, merely rallied Catullus on leading a dull and lonely life at Verona, a place quite unsuitable for the pleasures of a man of fashion.

If he can no longer be her only lover, he still hopes to be the most favoured. But he soon finds even this privilege denied to him. His love-poetry henceforth assumes a different sound. For a time, indeed, his reproaches are uttered in a tone of sadness not unmixed with tenderness. Afterwards, even though his passion from time to time revives with its old vehemence, and he again becomes the slave of Lesbia's caprice, his tone becomes angry, hard, and scornful. Finally, the evidence of her shameless life and innumerable infidelities with Caelius, Gellius, Egnatius, and 'three hundred others,' enables him utterly to renounce her. The earlier of the poems, both of anger and reconciliation, may probably have been written in the lifetime of Metellus, i.e. in 60 or in the beginning of 59 B.C. But later in that year Metellus died, suspected of being poisoned by his wife, who, on the ground of that suspicion was named by Caelius Rufus, after his passion had merged in a hatred equal to that of Catullus, by the terrible *oxymoron* of 'Clytemnestra quadrantaria.' Her widowhood gained for her absolute license in the indulgence of her propensities, and the first use she made of her liberty was to receive Caelius Rufus into her house on the Palatine. What her ultimate fate was we do not know, but the language of Cicero, Caelius, and Catullus show that she could inspire as deadly hatred as passionate admiration, and that the 'Juno-like' charm of her beauty, the grace and fascination of her presence, the intellectual accomplishment which made poets and orators for a time her slaves, did not save her from sinking into the lowest degradation.

The poems representing the second and third stage— that in which passion and scorn strive with one another— of the relations to 'Lesbia,' and containing the savage attacks on his rivals, belong to the years 59 and 58 B.C.: nor do there appear to be any other poems of importance referable to this latter date. One or two poems, in which his final renunciation is made with much scornful emphasis, belong to a later date after his return from Bithynia. He went there early in the year 57 B.C., on the staff of the

Propraetor Memmius, and remained till the spring of the following year. The immediate motive for this step may have been his wish to escape from his fatal entanglement, but the chances of bettering his fortunes, the congenial society of his friend the poet Helvius Cinna and other members of the staff, and the attraction of visiting the famous seats of the old Greek civilization, were also powerful inducements to a man who combined a strong social and pleasure-loving nature with the enthusiasm of a poet and a scholar. His severance from his recent associations and from the animosities they engendered was favourable to his happiness and his poetry. He did not indeed improve his fortunes, owing, as he says, to the poverty of the province and the meanness of his chief. He detested Memmius, and has recorded his detestation in the hearty terms of abuse of which he was a master; and he expresses his joy in quitting, in the following spring, the dull monotony of the Phrygian plains and the hot climate of Nicaea. But he had great enjoyment in his association with his comrades on the Praetor's staff—

O dulces comitum valete coetus.—

He was attracted to one of them, Helvius Cinna, by warm admiration for his poetic accomplishment, as well as by friendship[1]; and the time spent by them together was probably lightened by the practice of their art, and the study of the Alexandrine poets. Although the fame of Cinna did not become so great as that of Catullus or Calvus, he seems to have been regarded by the poets of that school in the light of a master[2]; and it is probably owing to the example of his Zmyrna, so highly lauded in the 95th poem of Catullus, that Catullus composed his Epithalamium of Peleus and Thetis, and Calvus composed his Io. A still more remarkable poem of Catullus, the Attis, the subject of which, so remote not only from Roman but even Greek life, is identified with the Phrygian highlands and the seats of the worship of Cybele, probably owes its inspira-

---

[1] Cf. poems x. 30, etc., and xcv.
[2] Cf. Munro's Criticisms and Elucidations of Catullus, p. 214.

tion as well as its local colouring to the poet's sojourn in this district. The mention of the 'Catagraphi Thyni' in a later poem is suggestive of the interest which he took in the novel aspects of Eastern life opened up to him in the province. But it is in the poems which are written in the year 56 B.C., that we chiefly note the happy effect of the poet's absence from Rome, and of his emancipation from his passion. Some of these poems,—more especially xlvi, ci, xxxi, and iv,—are among the happiest and purest products of his genius. They bring him before us eagerly preparing to start on his journey 'among the famous cities of Asia,'—making his pious pilgrimage to his brother's tomb in the Troad,—greeting his beloved Sirmio and the bright waters of the Lago di Garda on his first return home, and recalling sometime later to his guests by the shores of the lake the memories of the places visited, and of the gallant bearing of his pinnace, 'tot per impotentia freta,' on his homeward voyage. Some of the poems written from Verona—those referring to his intrigue or perhaps his disappointment with Aufilena, and the invitation to Caecilius (xxxv), were probably written about this time, before his return to Rome. The 'Aufilena' poems belong certainly to a time later than his passion for Lesbia; and during a still later visit to Verona—that during which he met and was reconciled to Julius Caesar—Catullus is found engaged in love-affairs in which Mamurra was his rival. As the invitation to Caecilius was written after the foundation of Como (B.C. 59), it could not have been sent by Catullus during his earlier sojourns at Verona: and 'the ideas' which he wished to interchange with the poet who was then engaged in writing a poem on Cybele—'Dindymi domina,'—to which Catullus pointedly refers, may well have been those suggested by his eastern sojourn, and embodied in the Attis. But soon afterwards we find him back in Rome, and the lively and most natural piece of 'genre-painting' contained in x—

Varus me meus ad suos amores
Visum duxerat e foro otiosum—

bears the freshest impress of his recent Bithynian experiences. Poems xxviii and xlviii, inspired by his hatred of Memmius and his sympathy with the treatment, like to that which he had himself experienced, which his friends Veranius and Fabullus had met with at the hands of their chief Piso, probably belong to a later time, after the return of Piso from his province in 55 B.C. Some critics have found the motive of the famous lines addressed to Cicero—

> Disertissime Romuli nepotum
> Quot sunt quotque fuere, Marce Tulli—

in the speech delivered in the early part of 56 B.C., in defence of Caelius, of which, from the prominence given in it to the vices of Clodia, Catullus must have heard soon after his return to Rome. But the words of the poem hardly justify this inference. Catullus was not interested in the vindication of Caelius, who had proved false to him as a friend, and supplanted him as a rival. And he was himself so perfect a master of vituperation that he did not need to thank Cicero for his having done that office for him in regard to Clodia. Yet the reference to Cicero's eloquence, and to his supremacy in the law courts,—

> Tanto pessimus omnium poeta
> Quanto tu optimus omnium patronus—

seems to point to some exercise of Cicero's special talent as an advocate, for which Catullus was grateful. The great orator and the great poet, who speaks so modestly of himself in the contrast he draws between them, may have been brought together in many ways. They had common friends and acquaintances—Hortensius, Manlius Torquatus, Sestius, Licinius Calvus, Memmius, etc.; and they heartily hated the same persons, Clodia, Vatinius, Piso, and others. The intimate associates of Catullus shared the political views and sympathies of the orator. Cicero, too, was naturally attracted to young men of promise and genius,— if they did not belong too prominently to the 'grex Catilinae';—and, like Dr. Johnson in his relations to Beauclerk and Boswell, he may have valued their society more for their intellectual vivacity than their moral virtues.

The poems written in the two last years of the poet's life do not indicate any emancipation from the coarser passions and the fierce animosities of the period immediately preceding the Bithynian journey. To this later time may be assigned the famous lampoons on Julius Caesar and Mamurra, the poems referring to some of his Veronese amours, those addressed to Juventius, and the reckless, half-bantering, half-savage assaults on 'Furius and Aurelius,' who were both the butts of his wit and the sharers of his least reputable pleasures. They seem to have been needy men, though of some social standing [1], probably of the class of 'Scurrae,' who preyed on his purse and made loud professions of devotion to him, while they abused his confidence and his character behind his back. Some of the poems of his last years, however, are indicative of a more genial frame of mind and of happier relations with the world. It was at this time that he enjoyed the intimate friendship of Licinius Calvus [2], to whom he was united by similarity of taste and of genius, as well as by sympathy in their personal and political dislikes. Four poems—one certainly among the very last written by Catullus—are inspired by this friendship, and all clearly prove that at least this source o happiness was unalloyed by any taint of bitterness. Two other poems, the final repudiation of Lesbia, and the bright picture of the loves of Acme and Septimius, which, by their allusions to the invasion of Britain, and to the excitement preceding the Parthian expedition of Crassus, show unmistakeably that they belong to the last year of his life, afford conclusive evidence that neither the exhausting passions, the rancorous feuds, nor the deeper sorrows of his life had in any way impaired the vigour of his imagination or his exquisite sense of beauty. Perhaps

---

[1] Cf. xxiv. 7:—
 'Qui? non est homo bellus? inquies. Est.'

[2] Two of the four poems connected with Calvus allude to his antagonism to Vatinius, which went on actively between the years 56 and 54 B.C. In none of them is there any allusion to Lesbia, who was never out of Catullus' thoughts or his verse till after his Bithynian journey.

the latest verses addressed by Catullus to any of his friends are those lines of tender complaint to Cornificius, in which he begs of him some little word of consolation—

> Maestius lacrimis Simonideis.

The lines—
> Malest, me hercule. et est laboriose,
> Et magis magis in dies et horas—

might well have been drawn from him by the rapid advance of his fatal illness, and the phrase 'lacrimis Simonideis' is suggestive of the anticipation of death rather than of the misery of unfortunate love[1]. Yet, if we are to regard Catullus as himself responsible for the final arrangement of his poems, and if we suppose that there was any principle in their arrangement, the position of the poem between those two utterly incongruous in tone, 'Salax taberna,' and 'Egnatius quod candidos habet dentes,'—both directed against his rivals in the last stage of his *liaison* with Lesbia,—leaves some doubt as to whether the poem may not belong to the period of his fatal passion.

The length as well as the diction, rhythm, and structure of the 64th poem—

> Peliaco quondam prognatae, etc.—

shows that it was a work of much greater labour and thought than any of those which sprang spontaneously out of the passion or sentiment of the moment. Probably in the composition of this, which he must have regarded as the most serious and ambitious effort of his Muse, Catullus may have acted on the principle which he commends so warmly in his lines on the Zmyrna of Cinna—

> Zymrna mei Cinnae nonam post denique messem
> Quam coepta'st nonamque edita post hiemem,—

and have kept it by him for years, elaborating the unfamiliar poetic diction in which it is expressed, and enlarging its original plan by the insertion of the long Ariadne Episode. It is the only poem of Catullus which produces the impression of the slow and reflective processes

---

[1] Horace contrasts the 'dirge of Simonides' ('Ceae retractes munera neniae') with the lighter poetry of love.

of art as distinct from the rapidly shaping power of immediate inspiration. From this circumstance alone we should regard it as a work on which his maturest faculty was employed. But it has been shown [1] that throughout the poem, and more especially in the episode of Ariadne, there are clear indications that Catullus had read and imitated the poem of Lucretius, which appeared about the end of 55 or the beginning of 54 B.C. We may therefore conclude that in the year 54 B.C.—the last of his life—Catullus was still engaged either in the original composition of his longest poem, or in giving to it the finishing touches. The concluding lines of the poem—

> Sed postquam tellus scelere est imbuta nefando, etc.—

which are written in a more serious spirit, and with a graver judgment on human life than anything else he has left, perhaps indicate the path which his maturer genius might have struck out for itself, if he had ever risen from the careless freedom of early youth to the reflective habits and steady labour of riper years.

But although longer life might have brought to Catullus a still higher rank among the poets of the world, the chief charm of the poems actually written by him arises from the strength and depth of his personal feelings, and the force, freshness, and grace with which he has expressed them. Other Roman poets have produced works of more elaborate composition, and have shown themselves greater interpreters of Nature and of human life : none have expressed so directly and truthfully the great elemental affections, or have uttered with such vital sincerity the happiness or the pain of the passing hour. He presents his own simple experience and emotions, uncoloured by idealising fancy or reflexion, and the world accepts this as among the truest of all records of human feeling. The 'spirat adhuc amor' is especially true of all the poems inspired by his love for Lesbia. It is by the union of the utmost fire of passion with a heart capable of the utmost

---

[2] Cf. Munro's Lucretius, p. 468, third edition.

constancy of feeling that he transcends all other poets of love. We pass with him through every stage of his passion, from the first rapture of admiration and the first happiness of possession, to the biting words of scorn in which he announces to Lesbia his final renunciation of her. We witness the whole 'pageant of his bleeding heart,' from the fresh pain of the wound on first fully realising her unworthiness, through the various stages of superficial reconcilement,—the 'amoris integratio' following on the 'amantium irae[1],'—on to the state of torture described by him in the words 'Odi et amo[2],' till at last he obtains his emancipation by the growth of a savage rancour and loathing in the place of the passionate love which had tried so long to sustain itself 'like a wild flower at the edge of the meadow[3].' Among the many poems, written through nearly the whole of his poetical career, and called forth by this, the most vital experience of his life, those of most charm and power are the two on the 'Sparrow of Lesbia' (ii and iii) written in tones of playful tenderness, not without some touch of the luxury of melancholy which accompanies and enhances passion;—the two, v and vii,

>Vivamus, mea Lesbia, atque amemus,

and

>Quaeris, quot mihi basiationes, etc.,—

written in the very height of his short-lived happiness, in the wildest tumult and most reckless abandonment of passion, when the immediate joy is felt as the only thing of any moment in life;—the 8th poem—

>Miser, Catulle, desinas ineptire—

in which he recalls the bright days of the past—

>Fulsere quondam candidi tibi soles,—

and steels his heart against useless regret:—and another

---

[1] lxxii. 5-8:—
>'Nunc te cognovi: quare etsi impensius uror,
>   Multo mi tamen es vilior et levior.
>Qui potis est? inquis. Quia amantem iniuria talis
>   Cogit amare magis, set bene velle minus.'

[2] lxxxv. 1.   [3] xi. 23.

poem written in a different metre, in the same mood, and apparently after the wounds, which had been partially healed, had broken out afresh,—

> Si qua recordanti benefacta priora voluptas, etc.;[1]

in which he prays for a deliverance from his passion as from a foul disease, or a kind of madness;—and lastly, the final renunciation (xi),—

> Furi et Aureli comites Catullo,—

in which scornful irony is combined with an imaginative power and creative force of expression which he has only equalled or surpassed in one or two other of his greatest works,—such as the 'Attis' and the Epithalamium of Manlius. Other tales of love told by poets have been more beautiful in their course, or more pathetic in their issue; none have been told with more truthful realism, or more desperate intensity of feeling.

The fame of Catullus, as alone among ancient poets of love, rivalling the traditional glory of Sappho, does not rest only on those poems which record the varying vicissitudes of his own experience. His longer and more artistic poems are all concerned with some phase of this passion, either in its more beautiful and pathetic aspects, or in its perversion and corruption. Thus he not only selects from Greek legends the story of the desertion of Ariadne, of the brief union of Protesilaus and Laodamia, of the glory and blessedness of Peleus and Thetis, but he makes the tragic deed of Attis, instigated by the fanatical hatred of love,— 'Veneris nimio odio,'—the subject of his art. Others of his poems are inspired by sympathy with the happiness of his friends in the enjoyment of their love, and with their sorrow when that love is interrupted by death. The most charming of all his longer poems is the Epithalamium which celebrates the union of Manlius with his bride. No truer picture of the passionate devotion of lovers has ever been painted than that presented in the few playful and tender but burning lines of the ' Acme and Septimius.' His own

[1] lxxvi.

experience did not teach him the lessons of cynicism. At
the close as at the beginning of his career, he finds in the
union of passion with truth and constancy the most real
source of happiness. The elegiac lines in which he com-
forts his friend Calvus for the loss of Quintilia bear witness
to the strength and delicacy of his friendship, and, along
with others of his poems, make us feel that the life of
pleasure in that age was not only brightened by genius
and culture, but also elevated by pure affection and un-
selfish sympathy,—

> Si quicquam mutis gratum acceptumque sepulchris
>   Accidere a nostro Calve dolore potest,
> Quo desiderio veteres renovamus amores
>   Atque olim missas flemus amicitias
> Certe non tanto mors immatura dolori est
>   Quintiliae, quantum gaudet amore tuo.[1]

The most attractive feature in the character of Catullus
is the warmth of his affection. No ancient poet has left
so pleasant a record of the genial intercourse of friends,
or has given such proof of his own dependence on human
attachment and of his readiness to meet all the claims
which others have on such attachment. In his gayest
hours and his greatest sorrow, amid his pleasures and his
studies, he shows his thoughtful consideration for others,
his grateful recollection of past kindness, and his own
extreme need of sympathy. Perhaps he expects too much
from friendship, and, in addressing his comrades, is too
ready to assume that whatever gives momentary pleasure
or pain to 'their own Catullus' must be of equal import-
ance to them. No poet makes such use of terms of
endearment and affectionate diminutives in writing both
to and of his friends, and of himself in his relation to them.

[1] 'Calvus, if those now silent in the tomb
  Can feel the touch of pleasure in our tears
For those we loved, who perished in their bloom,
  And the departed friends of former years:
Oh then, full surely thy Quintilia's woe,
  For the untimely fate that bade ye part,
Will fade before the bliss she feels to know
  How very dear she is unto thy heart.'—Martin.

But if he expected much from the sympathy of his associates, he possessed in no ordinary measure the capacity of feeling with and of heartily loving and admiring them. He often expresses honest and delicate appreciation of the works, or of the wit, taste, and genius of his friends. The dedication of his volume to Cornelius Nepos, the lines addressed to Cicero, the invitation to Caecilius—

> Poetae tenero, meo sodali
> Velim Caecilio papyre dicas,—

the poem in which he recalls to Licinius Calvus a day passed together in witty talk and the interchange of verses over their wine, the contrast which he draws between the doom of speedy oblivion which he pronounces on the 'Annals of Volusius,' and the immortality which he confidently anticipates for the 'Zmyrna' of Cinna,—all show that, though fastidious in his judgments, he was without a single touch of literary jealousy, and that he felt a generous pride in the fame and accomplishments of men of established reputation as well as of his own younger compeers. Nor was his affection limited by literary sympathy. Of none of his associates does he write more heartily than of Veranius and Fabullus, young men, apparently enjoying their youth, and trying to better their fortunes by serving on the staff of some Praetor or Proconsul in his province. The language of affection could not be uttered with more cordiality, simplicity, and grace than in the poem of ten or eleven lines welcoming Veranius on his return from Spain,—

> Venistine domum ad tuos Penates
> Fratresque unanimos anumque matrem?
> Venisti. O mihi nuntii beati.

There is not a word in the poem wasted; not one that does not come straight and strong from the heart. The 'Invitation to Fabullus' is in a lighter strain, and is written with the freedom and humour which he could use to add a charm to his friendly intercourse[1], and a sting to his less

[1] Compare also his humourous notice of the compliment which he heard in the crowd paid to the speech of Calvus against Vatinius—
'Dii magni, salaputium disertum.'

congenial relations. Yet through the playful banter of this poem his delicate and kindly nature betrays itself in the words 'venuste noster,' and in those lines of true feeling,—

> Sed contra accipies meros amores
> Seu quid suavius elegantiusve.

His affection for both comes out incidentally in his remonstrance with Marrucinus Asinius[1] for having filched after dinner, 'in ioco atque vino,' one of his napkins, which he valued as memorials of the friends who had sent them to him, and which he endows with some share of the love he felt for them,—

> Haec amem necessest
> Ut Veraniolum meum et Fabullum.

The lampoons on Piso and his favourites, Porcius and Socration, show that those who wronged his friends could rouse in him as generous indignation as those who wronged himself.

Other poems express the pain and disappointment of a very sensitive nature, which expects more active and disinterested sympathy from others than ordinary men care either to give or to receive. Of this sort are his complaint to Cornificius[2],—

> Malest, Cornifici, tuo Catullo—

and the affectionate reproach which he addresses to Alphenus (xxx):—

> Certe tute iubebas animam tradere, inique, me
> Inducens in amorem, quasi tuta omnia mi forent.
> Inde nunc retrahis te ac tua dicta omnia factaque
> Ventos irrita ferre ac nebulas aerias sinis.

These, and other poems, show that Catullus was quick to feel any coldness or neglect on the part of his friends, and exceedingly dependent for his happiness on their sympathy. But the tone of these poems is quite different from the resentment which he feels and expresses against those from whom he had experienced malice or treachery. It does great injustice to his noblest qualities, to think of him as

[1] xii.   [2] xxxviii.

one who wantonly attacked or lightly turned against his friends. No instance of such levity of feeling can be adduced from his writings. It has been conclusively shown[1] that in the third line of the 95th poem there can be no reference to Hortensius, who, under the name of Hortalus, is addressed by Catullus in his 65th poem with courteous consideration: and if 'Furius and Aurelius' are to be regarded, on the strength of the opening lines of the 11th poem, as having ever ranked among his devoted friends, then the poem, instead of being a magnificent outburst of scornful irony, becomes a mere specimen of bathos. Nothing, on the other hand, can be more in keeping with the feeling of contemptuous tolerance which Catullus expresses in his other poems relating to them, than the pointed contrast between their hollow professions of enthusiasm and the degrading office which he assigns to them,—

> Pauca nuntiate meae puellae
> Non bona dicta.

Catullus could pass from friendship or love to a state of permanent enmity and hatred, when he believed that those in whom he had trusted had acted falsely and heartlessly towards him: and then he did not spare them. But the duties of loyal friendship and affection are to him a kind of religion. Perfidy and falsehood are regarded by him not only as the worst offences against honour in man, but as sins against the Gods. He lays claim to a good conscience and to the character of piety, on the ground that he had neither failed in acts of kindness or violated his word or his oath in any of his human dealings;—

> Si qua recordanti benefacta priora voluptas
> Est homini, cum se cogitat esse pium,
> Nec sanctam violasse fidem, nec foedere in ullo
> Divum ad fallendos numine abusum homines, etc.[2]

That he possessed no ordinary share of 'piety,' in the

---

[1] Mr. Munro, in his Elucidations (pp. 209, etc.), shows that the whole point of the poem consists in the contrast drawn between the 'Zmyrna' of Cinna and the 'Annals of Volusius.' Baehrens admits the reading 'Hortensius' into the text, but adds in a note on the word, *vox corrupta est*.

[2] lxxvi. 1-4.

Roman sense of the word, appears from the poems which express his grief for his brother's death. He died in the Troad; and we have seen how, some years after the event, Catullus turned aside from his pleasant voyage among the Isles of Greece and coasts of Asia, to visit his tomb and to offer upon it the customary funeral gifts. His words in reference to this great sorrow, in all the poems in which he speaks of it, are full of deep and simple human feeling. He does not venture to comfort himself with the hope which he suggests to Calvus, in the lines on the death of Quintilia, of a conscious existence after death; but he resolves that his love shall still endure even after the eternal separation from its object. Yet while yielding to the first shock of this affliction, so as to become for the time indifferent to the passion which had swayed his life, and to the delight which he had taken in the works of ancient poets and the exercise of his art, he does not allow himself to forget what was due to living friends. It is characteristic of his frank affectionate nature, that, while dead to his old interests in life and literature, he finds his chief comfort in unburthening his heart to his friends and in writing to them words of delicate consideration. He cannot bear that, even in a trifling matter, Hortalus should find him forgetful of a promise: and he longs to lighten the sorrow of his friend Manlius, who had written to him in some sudden affliction, —probably the loss of the bride in whose honour Catullus had, a short time previously, composed his great Nuptial Ode. Though all other feelings were dead, and neither love could distract nor poetry heal his grief, his heart was alive to the memory of former kindness[1], to the natural craving for sympathy, and to the duty of thinking of others.

Another, and less admirable, side of the nature of Catullus is reflected in his short satirical poems. These have nothing in common with the ethical and reflective satire of Lucilius and Horace: and although the objects of some

---

[1] Cf. lxviii. 12:—
'Neu me odisse putes hospitis officium.'

of them are the most prominent personages in the State, yet their motive cannot, in any case, be called purely political. They are like the lampoons of Archilochus and the early Greek Iambic writers, purely personal in their object. They are either the virulent expression of his antipathies, jealousies, and rancours, or they are inspired by his lively sense of the ridiculous and by his extreme fastidiousness of taste. The most famous, most incisive, and least justifiable of these lampoons are the attacks on Julius Caesar, especially that contained in the 29th poem,—

> Quis hoc potest videre, quis potest pati,
> Nisi impudicus et vorax et aleo, etc.—

and in the less vigorous but much more offensive 57th poem.

Catullus in these poems expresses the animosity which the 'boni' generally entertained towards the chiefs of the popular party: and his intimacy at this time with Calvus, who was a member of the Senatorian party, and who lampooned Caesar and Pompey in the same spirit, may have given some political edge to his Satire. He was moved also by a feeling of disgust towards the habits and manners of some of Caesar's instruments and creatures,—such as Vatinius, Libo, Mamurra, etc. But the chief motive both of the 29th and the 57th,—the two poems which Suetonius regarded as attaching an 'everlasting stigma' to the name of Caesar—is the jealousy of Mamurra,—the object also of many separate satires,—who, through the favour of the Proconsul and the fortune which he thereby acquired, was a successful rival of Catullus in his provincial love affairs. The indignation of Cicero was roused against the riches of Mamurra on political grounds: that of Catullus on the ground that they gave their possessor an unfair advantage in the race of pleasure:—

> Et ille nunc superbus et superfluens
> Perambulabit omnium cubilia, etc.

Suetonius tells the story, confirmed by the lines in a later poem of Catullus—

> Irascere iterum meis iambis
> Inmerentibus, unice imperator,—

that Caesar, while staying at his father's house at Verona, accepted the poet's apology for his libellous verses, and admitted him the same day to his dinner-table. Had he attached the meaning to the imputations contained in them, which Suetonius did two hundred years afterwards, even his magnanimous clemency could not well have tolerated them. But, as Cicero tells us in his defence of Caelius, such charges were in those days regarded as a mere 'façon de parler,' which if made coarsely were regarded as 'rudeness' ('petulantia'), if done wittily, as 'polite banter' ('urbanitas'). Caesar must have looked upon the imputations of the 57th poem as a mere angry ebullition of boyish petulance: and he showed the same disregard for imputations made by Calvus, which, though as unfounded, were not so absolutely incredible and unmeaning. His clemency to Catullus met with a return similar to that which it met with at a later time from other recipients of his generosity. Catullus, though the 'truest friend,' was certainly not the 'noblest foe.' The coarseness of his attack may be partly palliated by the manners of the age: but the spirit in which he returns to the attack in the 54th poem leaves a more serious stain on his character. He was too completely in the wrong to be able frankly to forgive Caesar for his gracious and magnanimous treatment.

Many of his personal satires are directed against the licentiousness of the men and women with whom he quarrelled. Notwithstanding the evidence of his own frequent confessions, he lays a claim to purity of life in the phrase, 'si vitam puriter egi[1],' and in his strange apology for the freedom of his verses,—

> Nam castum esse decet pium poetam
> Ipsum, versiculos nihil necesse est.[2]

He is absolutely unrestrained both in regard to the imputations which he makes, and to the choice of the language in which he conveys them; and in these imputations he spares neither rank nor sex. It is one of the strangest paradoxes to find a poet like Catullus, endowed with the

---

[1] lxxvi. 19.   [2] xvi. 5-6.

purest sense of beauty, and yet capable of turning all his vigorous force of expression to the vilest uses. He is coarser in his language than any of the older poets, and than any of those of the Augustan age. In the time of the former the traditional severity of the old Roman life,—'tetrica ac tristis disciplina Sabinorum,'—had not altogether lost its influence. In the Augustan age, if there was as much immorality as in the age preceding it, there was more outward decorum. The licentiousness of that age expresses itself in tones of refinement; it associates itself with sentimentalism in literature; it was reduced to system and carried out as the serious business of life. The coarseness of Catullus is symptomatic rather of more recklessness than of greater corruption in society. Impurity is less destructive to human nature when it vents itself in bantering or virulent abuse, than when it clings to the imagination, associates itself with the sense of beauty, and expresses itself in the language of passion. Though, in his nobler poetry, Catullus is ardent and impassioned, he is much more free from this taint than Ovid or Propertius. The errors of his life did not deaden his sensibility, harden his heart, or corrupt his imagination. It is only in his careless moods, when he looks on life in the spirit of a humourist, or in moods of bitterness when his antipathies are roused, or in fits of savage indignation against some violation of natural feeling or some prosperous villainy, that he disregards the restraints imposed by the better instincts of men on the use of language.

Many of his Satires, however, are written in a more genial vein, and are not much disfigured by coarseness or indelicacy of expression. As he especially valued good taste and courtesy, wit, and liveliness of mind in his associates, so he is intolerant of all mean and sordid ways of living, of all stupidity, affectation, and pedantry. The pieces in which these characteristics are exposed are marked by keen observation, a lively sense of absurdity, and sometimes by a boisterous spirit of fun. They are expressed with vigour and directness; but they want the subtle irony which pervades the Satires, Epistles, and Odes of Horace. Among the best of his lighter satires is the poem numbered xvii :—

> O Colonia, quae cupis ponte ludere magno,—

which has some touches of graceful poetry as well as of humourous extravagance. It is directed against the dullness and stolid indifference of one of his fellow-townsmen, who, being married to a young and beautiful girl,—

> Quoi cum sit viridissimo nupta flore puella
> (Et puella tenellulo delicatior haedo,
> Asservanda nigerrimis diligentius uvis),—

was utterly careless of her, and insensible to the perils to which she was exposed. To rouse him from his sloth and stupor, Catullus asks to have him thrown head over heels—

> Munus hoc mihi maximi da, Colonia, risus—

from a ricketty old bridge into the deepest and dirtiest part of the quagmire over which it was built. In another piece Catullus laughs at the affectation of one of his rivals, Egnatius,—a black-bearded fop from the Celtiberian wilds,—who had a trick of perpetually smiling in order to show the whiteness of his teeth;—a trick which did not desert him at a criminal trial, during the most pathetic part of the speech for the defence, or when he stood beside a weeping mother at the funeral pyre of her only son. In another of his elegiac pieces he gives expression to the relief felt on the departure for the East of a bore who afflicted the ears of the polite world by a superfluous use of his aspirates—

> Chommoda dicebat, si quando commoda vellet
> Dicere, et insidias Arrius hinsidias, etc.[1]

Just as the ears of men had recovered from this infliction—

> Subito affertur nuntius horribilis,
> Ionios fluctus, postquam illuc Arrius isset,
> Iam non Ionios esse, sed Hionios.

[1] lxxxiv.

Like fastidious and irritable poets of other times (Horace, Pope, Byron, etc.), Catullus waged internecine war against pedants, literary pretenders, and poetasters. He remonstrates in a vein of humorous exaggeration with his friend Licinius Calvus, for palming off on him as a gift on the Saturnalia (corresponding to our Christmas presents) a collection of the works of these 'miscreants,' (impiorum) originally sent to him by some pedantic grammarian, in acknowledgment of his services as an advocate—

> Dii magni, horribilem ac sacrum libellum.

In the 36th poem he represents Lesbia as offering a holocaust to Venus of the work of 'the worst of all poets,' 'The Annals of Volusius,' in quittance of a vow on her reconcilement with Catullus. In another, addressed to Varus, probably the fastidious critic whom Horace quotes in the 'Ars Poetica[1],' he exposes the absurdity of one of their friends, who, though in other respects a man of sense, wit, and agreeable manners, entertained the delusion that he was a poet, and was never so happy as when he had surrounded himself with the newest and finest literary materials, and was plying his uncongenial occupation. In another he records the nemesis, in the form of a severe cough, which overtook him for allowing himself to be seduced by the hopes of a good dinner to read (or perhaps listen to the reading of) a speech of Cicero's friend and client Sestius,—

> Plenam veneni et pestilentiae.

About one half of the shorter poems, and more than half of the epigrams, are to be classed among his personal lampoons or light satiric pieces. Many of these show Catullus to us on that side of his character, which it is least pleasant or profitable to dwell on. He could not indeed write anything which did not bear the stamp of the vital force and sincerity of his nature: but even his vigour of

---

[1] Hor. A. P. 437–38:—
  'Quintilio si quid recitares, Corrige, sodes,
  Hoc aiebat et hoc.'—

expression does not compensate for the survival in literature of the feelings and relations which are most ignoble in actual life. Yet some of these satiric pieces have an interest which amply justifies their preservation. The greatest of all his lampoons, the 29th, has an historical as well as a literary value. Tacitus, as well as Suetonius, refers to it. It is not only a masterpiece of terse invective, but, like the 11th, it is a powerful specimen of imaginative irony. The momentous events of a most momentous era—the Eastern conquests of Pompey, the first Spanish campaign of Caesar, the subjugation of Gaul, the invasion of Britain, the revolutionary measures of 'father-in-law and son-in-law,'—are all made to look as if they had had no other object or result than that of pampering the appetites of a worthless favourite. Other lampoons, such as those against Memmius and Piso, have also an historical interest. They testify to the republican freedom of speech, which was soon to be silenced for ever. They enable us to understand how strong a social and political weapon the power of epigram was in ancient Rome,—a power which continued to be exercised, though no longer with republican freedom, under the Empire. The pen of the poet was employed in the warfare of parties as fiercely as the tongue of the orator; and although Catullus did not spare partisans of the Senate, such as Memmius, yet all his associations and tastes combined to turn his hostility chiefly against the popular leaders and their tools. The more genial satiric pieces, again, are chiefly interesting as throwing light on the social and literary life of Rome and the provincial towns of Italy. They give us an idea of the lighter talk, the criticism, and merriment of the younger men in the world of letters and fashion during the last age of the Republic. If they are not master-pieces of humour, they are full of gaiety, animal spirits, shrewd observation, and not very unkindly comment on men and manners.

Besides the poems which show Catullus in various relations of love, affection, animosity, and humorous criticism, there are still a few of the shorter pieces which have a personal interest. He had the purest capacity of enjoying simple pleasures; and some of his most delightful poems are vivid records of happy experiences procured to him by this youthful freshness of feeling. Three of these are especially beautiful,—the dedication of his yacht to Castor and Pollux,—the lines written immediately before quitting Bithynia,—

> Iam ver egelidos refert tepores,—

and the famous lines on Sirmio. They all belong to the same period of his life, and all show how happy and serene his spirit became, when it was untroubled by the passions and rancours of city life. The lines on his yacht—

> Phaselus ille quem videtis, hospites,—

express with much vivacity the feelings of affectionate pride which a strong and kindly nature lavishes not only on living friends, but on inanimate objects, associated with the memory of past happiness and adventure. His fancy endows it with a kind of life from the earliest time when, under the form of a clump of trees, it 'rustled its leaves' on Cytorus, till it obtained its rest in a peaceful age on the fair waters of Benacus. The 46th poem is inspired by the new sense of life which comes to early youth with the first approach of spring, and by the eager flutter of anticipation—

> Iam mens praetrepidans avet vagari,
> Iam laeti studio pedes vigescunt—

with which a cultivated mind forecasts the pleasure of travelling among famous and beautiful scenes. But perhaps the most perfect of his smaller pieces is that in which the love of home and of Nature, the sense of rest and security after toil and danger, the glee of a boy and the strong happiness of a man unite to form the charm of the lines on Sirmio, of which it is as impossible to analyse the secret as it is to reproduce in another tongue the language in which it is expressed.

Catullus is one of the great poets of the world, not so much through gifts of imagination—though with these he was well endowed—as through his singleness of nature, his vivid impressibility, and his keen perception. He received the gifts of the passing hour so happily, that, to produce pure and lasting poetry, it was enough for him to utter in natural words something of the fulness of his heart. His interests, though limited in range, were all genuine and human. His poems inspired by personal feeling seem to come from him without any effort. He says, on every occasion, exactly what he wanted to say, in clear, forcible, spontaneous language. There are, indeed, even in his simplest poems, a few strokes of imaginative expression, as, for instance,—

> Aut quam sidera multa, cum tacet nox,
> Furtivos hominum vident amores,[1]—

and this, written with the feeling and with the application which Burns makes of the same image,—

> Velut prati
> Ultimi flos, praetereunte postquam
> Tactus aratro est;[2]—

and these two touches of tenderness and beauty, which appear in a poem otherwise characterised by a tone of careless drollery,—

> Nec sapit pueri instar
> Bimuli, tremula patris dormientis in ulna,—

and—

> Et puella tenellulo delicatior haedo,
> Adservanda nigerrimis diligentius uvis.[3]

But the great charm of the style in these shorter poems is its simple directness, and its popular idiomatic ring. There is nothing, apparently, studied about it, no ornament or involution, no otiose epithets, no subtle allusiveness. Yet it shows the happiest selection, not only of the most appropriate, but of the most exquisite words. To no style, in prose or verse, in any language, could the words 'simplex munditiis' be with more propriety applied. It has all the ease of refined and vigorous conversation, combined with the grace of consummate art. Though this perfection

---

[1] vii. 7–8.   [2] xi. 22–24.   [3] xvii. 12–13 and 15–16.

of expression could not have been attained without study and labour, yet it bears no trace of them.

In these smaller poems he shows himself as great a master of metre as of language. The more sustained power which he has over the flow of his verse, is best exemplified by the skylark ring of his great Nuptial Ode, by the hurrying agitation of the Attis, and the stately calm of the Peleus and Thetis, giving place to a more impassioned movement in the 'Ariadne' episode. But in his shorter poems, also, he shows the true gift of the ἀοιδός—the power of using musical language as a symbol of the changing impulses of feeling. Thus the delicate playfulness and tenderness of his phalaecians,—the lingering long-drawn out sweetness, and the calm subdued sadness of the scazon, as exemplified in the 'Sirmio,' and the

> Miser Catulle desinas ineptire,—

the 'bright speed' of the pure iambic, so happily answering to the subject of the 'phaselus,' and its bold impetus as it is employed in the attack on Julius Caesar,—the irregular but sonorous grandeur of his Sapphic [1],—the majesty which in the Hymn to Diana blends with the buoyant movement of the glyconic,—all attest that the words and melody of the poems were born together with the feeling and meaning animating them. Although his elegiac poems are not written with the smoothness and fluency which was attained by the Augustan poets, yet those among them which record his graver and sadder moods have a plaintive force and natural pathos, which their roughness seems to enhance. If his epigrammatic pieces, written in that metre, want the polish and point to which his brilliant disciple attained under the Empire, we may believe that Catullus experienced the difficulty which Lucilius found, and which Horace at last successfully overcame, of adapting a metre originally framed for the expression of serious feeling to the more prosaic interests and experiences of life.

---

[1] E.g. 'Litus ut longe resonante Eoa
    Tunditur unda.'

The language of Catullus in these shorter poems is his own, or, where not his own, is drawn from such wells of Latin undefiled as Plautus and Terence. His metres are happy applications of those invented or largely used by the earlier lyric poets of Greece,—Sappho, Anacreon, Archilochus,—and the later Phalaecus. For the form of some of his longer poems he has taken, and not with the happiest result, the Alexandrine poets for his models. But in these shorter poems, so far as he has had any models, he has tried to emulate the perfection attained in the older and purer era of Greek inspiration. But it is not through imitation that he has attained a perfection of form like to theirs. It is owing to the singleness and strength of his feeling and impression, that these poems are so exquisite in their unity and simplicity. Catullus does not care to present the gem of his own thought in an alien setting, as Horace, in his earlier Odes at least, has often done. It is one of the surest notes of his lyrical genius that, while more modest in his general self-estimate than any of the great Roman poets, he trusts more implicitly than any of them to his own judgment and inspiration to find the most fitting and telling medium for the communication of his thought. Thus he presents only what is essential, unencumbered with any associations from older poetry. The form is indeed so perfect that we scarcely think of it. We feel only that nothing mars or interrupts the revelation of the poet's heart and soul. We apprehend, as perhaps we never apprehended before, some one single feeling of great potency and great human influence in a poem of some ten or twenty lines, every word of which adds something to the whole impression. Thus, for instance, in the poems—

  Vivamus, mea Lesbia, atque amemus,—
  Acmen Septimius suos amores,—
  Verani, omnibus e meis amicis,—
  Iam ver egelidos refert tepores,—
  Paene insularum Sirmio insularumque,—
  Miser Catulle, desinas ineptire,—

we apprehend through a perfectly pure medium, and by a single intuition, the highest pitch of the passionate love of man and woman, the perfect beauty and joy of self-forgetful friendship, the eager enthusiasm for travel and adventure, the deep delight of returning to a beautiful and well-loved home, the 'sorrow's crown of sorrows' in 'remembering happier things.' We may see, too, in a totally different sphere of experience, how Catullus instinctively seizes the moment of supreme intensity of emotion, and utters what is vitally characteristic of it. He is not, in any sense, one of the Anacreontic singers of the pleasures of wine, of whom Horace is the typical example in ancient times. Neither was he one, who, like Burns, habitually forgot, in the excitement of good fellowship, the perils of Bacchanalian merriment. Yet even the drinking songs of the Scottish poet scarcely realise with more vivacity the moment of mad elevation when a revel is at its height, than Catullus has done in the song of seven short lines—

> Minister vetuli puer Falerni
> Inger mi calices amariores, etc.

The 'Hymn to Diana' occupies an intermediate place between the poems founded on personal feelings and the longer and more purely artistic pieces. Like the first it seems unconsciously, or at least without leaving any trace of conscious purpose, to have conformed to the conditions of the purest art. It is, like them, a perfect whole, one of those, to quote Mr. Munro, '"cunningest patterns" of excellence, such as Latium never saw before or after, Alcaeus, Sappho, and the rest then and only then having met their match'[1]. It resembles some of the longer poems in being a creation of sympathetic imagination, not an immediate expression of personal feeling. It must have been written for some public occasion; and the selection of Catullus to compose it would imply that he was recognised as the greatest lyrical poet in his lifetime, and that it was written after his reputation was established. It is a poem not only of pure artistic excellence, but of imaginative conception,

---

[1] 'Criticisms and Elucidations, etc.' p. 73.

like that exemplified in the 'Attis' and the 'Epithalamium of Peleus and Thetis.' The 'Diana' of Catullus is not a vague abstraction or conventional figure, as the Gods and Goddesses in the Odes of Horace are apt to be. The mythology of Greece received a new life from his imagination. In this poem he shows too, what he hardly indicates elsewhere[1], that he could identify himself in sympathy with the national feeling and religion of Rome. The Goddess addressed is a living Power, blending in her countenance the human and picturesque aspects of the Greek Artemis with the more spiritual and beneficent attributes of the Roman Diana. Yet no confusion or incongruity arises from the union into one concrete representation of these originally diverse elements. She lives to the imagination as a Power who, in the fresh morning of the world, had roamed in freedom over the mountains, the woods, the secret dells, and the river-banks of earth[2],—and now from a far away sphere watched over women in travail, increased the store of the husbandman, and was the especial guardian of the descendants of Romulus.

This poem affords a natural transition to the longer and more purely artistic pieces in the centre of the volume. Yet with some even of these a personal element is interfused. The hymn in honour of the nuptials of Manlius, is, like the short poem on the loves of Acme and Septimius, inspired by the poet's sympathy with the happiness of a friend. The 68th poem attempts to weave into one texture his own love of Lesbia, and the romance of Laodamia and Protesilaus. But in general these poems bring before us a new side of the art of Catullus. In one way indeed they add to our knowledge of his personal tastes.

---

[1] The pride of Roman nationality, is perhaps, unconsciously betrayed in such phrases as 'Romuli nepotum,' in the lines addressed to Cicero.

[2] xxxiv. 7-12:—

'Quam mater prope Deliam
Deposivit olivam,
Montium domina ut fores
Silvarumque virentium
Saltuumque reconditorum
Amniumque sonantum.'

The larger place given in them to ornament and illustration lets us know what objects in Nature afforded him most delight. His life was too full of human interest to allow him to devote his art to the celebration of Nature: yet he could not have been the poet he was if he had not been susceptible to her influence. And this susceptibility, indicated in occasional touches in the shorter poems, finds greater scope in the poems of impersonal art which still remain to be considered.

Among the more purely artistic pieces none is more beautiful than the Nuptial Ode in celebration of the marriage of his friend Manlius, a member of the great house of the Torquati, and one of the most accomplished men of his time, with Vinia Aurunculeia. In this poem Catullus pours forth the fulness of his heart

'In profuse strains of unpremeditated art.'

It is marked by the excellence of his shorter pieces and by poetical beauty of another order. Resembling his shorter poems in being called forth by an event within his own experience, it breathes the same spirit of affection and of sympathy with beauty and passion. It is written with the same gaiety of heart, blending indeed with a graver sense of happiness. The feeling of the hour does not merely express itself in graceful language: it awakens the active power of imagination, clothes itself in radiant imagery, and rises into the completeness and sustained melody of the highest lyrical art. The tone of the whole poem is one of joy, changing from the rapture of expectation in the opening lines to the more tranquil happiness of the close. The passion is ardent, but, on the whole, free from grossness or effeminate sentiment. Even where, in accordance with the Roman marriage customs, he abandons himself for a few stanzas to the spirit of raillery and banter—

Ne diu taceat procax
Fescennina locutio [1]—

he remembers the respect due to the innocence of the

[1] lxi. 122-46.

bride. Thoughts of her are associated with the purest objects in Nature,—with ivy clinging round a tree, or branches of myrtle,—

> Quos Hamadryades deae
> Ludicrum sibi roscido
> Nutriunt humore,—

or with a hyacinth growing in some rich man's garden. Like the eager lover of beauty among our own poets, he sees in other flowers—

> Alba parthenice velut
> Luteumve papaver—

the symbol of maidens—

> 'Whom youth makes so fair and passion so pale.'

The grace of trees and the bloom of flowers were prized by him among the fairest things in Nature. The charm in woman which most moves his imagination is virgin innocence unfolding into love, or passion ennobled by truth and constancy of affection. So too, in the Epithalamium of Peleus and Thetis, he compares Ariadne in her maidenhood to the myrtle trees growing on the banks of Eurotas, and to the bloom of vernal flowers :—

> Quales Eurotae progignunt flumina myrtos
> Aurave distinctos educit verna colores.[1]

In this Ode he expresses not merely, as in the Acme and Septimius, his sympathy with the joy of the hour. He recognises in marriage a greater good than in the love for a mistress. He associates it with thoughts of the power and security of the household, of the pure happiness of parental love, of the continuance of a time-honoured name, and of the birth of new defenders of the State.

The charm of the poem does not arise from its tone of feeling and its clear ringing melody alone. The bright spirit of the day awakens the inward eye which creates pictures and images of beauty in harmony with itself. The poet sees Hymenaeus coming from the distant rocks of Helicon, robed in saffron, and wreathed with fragrant

[1] lxiv. 89–90.

amaracus, in radiant power and glory, chanting the song with his ringing voice, beating the ground with his foot, shaking the pine-torch in his hand. As the doors of the house are opened, and the bride is expected by the singers outside, by one vivid flash of imagination he reveals all their eager excitement—

> Viden ut faces
> Splendidas quatiunt comas?

The two pictures, further on in the poem, of a peaceful old age prolonged to the utmost limit of human life—

> Usque dum tremulum movens
> Cana tempus anilitas
> Omnia omnibus annuit.—

and of infancy, awakening into consciousness and affection,—

> Torquatus volo parvulus
> Matris e gremio suae
> Porrigens teneras manus,
> Dulce rideat ad patrem
> Semihiante labello.
>
> Sit suo similis patri
> Manlio et facile insciis
> Noscitetur ab omnibus,
> Et pudicitiam suae
> Matris indicet ore.[1]

are drawn with the truest and most delicate hand.

The whole conception and execution of this poem, as also of the Attis and of the Epithalamium of Peleus and Thetis, leave no doubt that Catullus was richly endowed with the

---

[1] 'Soon my eyes shall see, mayhap,
Young Torquatus on the lap
Of his mother, as he stands
Stretching out his tiny hands,
And his little lips the while
Half-open on his father's smile.

'And oh! may he in all be like
Manlius his sire, and strike
Strangers when the boy they meet
As his father's counterfeit,
And his face the index be,
Of his mother's chastity.'—Martin.

vision and the faculty of genius, as well as with impassioned feeling and the gift of musical expression.

The poem which immediately follows is also an Epithalamium, intended to be sung by young men and maidens, in alternate parts. It is written in hexameter verse, and in rhythm, thought, and feeling resembles some of the golden fragments from the Epithalamia of Sappho. The whole poem sounds like a song in a rich idyl. Its charm consists in its calm and mellow tone, in the dramatic truth with which the feelings and thoughts natural to the young men and maidens are alternately expressed, and especially in the beauty of its two famous similes. In the first of these a flower is again the symbol of the bloom and innocence of maidenhood, growing up apart and safe from all rude contact. The idea in the concluding lines of the simile—

> Idem cum tenui carptus defloruit ungui,
> Nulli illum pueri, nullae optavere puellae,—

may probably have been suggested by a passage in Sappho, of which these two lines remain,

> οἴαν τὰν ὑάκινθον ἐν ὤρεσι ποίμενες ἄνδρες
> πόσσι καταστείβοισι, χάμαι δέ τε πόρφυρον ἄνθος.

In the second simile, which is supposed to be spoken by the young men, the vine growing upon a bare field, scarcely rising above the ground, unheeded and untended, is compared to the maid who

> 'Grows, lives, and dies in single blessedness;'

while the same vine, when wedded to the elm, is regarded as the symbol of the usefulness, dignity, and happiness which await the bride.

The absence of all personal allusion in this poem, and its resemblance in tone and rhythm to some fragments of the Lesbian poetess, might suggest the idea that it was translated, or at least imitated, from the Greek. But, on the other hand, from its harmony with the kind of subject and imagery in which Catullus most delights, and from the close observation of Italian Nature, shown in such lines as this—

> Iam iam contingit summum radice flagellum,—

it seems more probable that it was an adaptation of the style of his great model to some occasion within his own experience, than that it was a mere exercise in translation, like his 'Coma Berenices.'

The 'Attis' is the most original of all his poems. As a work of pure imagination, it is the most remarkable poetical creation in the Latin language. In this poem Catullus throws himself, with marvellous power, into a character and situation utterly alien to common experience, and pours an intense flood of human feeling and passion into a legend of strange Oriental fanaticism. The effect of the piece is, in a great measure, produced by the startling vividness of its language and imagery, and by the impetuous rush of its metre. Though the poem may have been partly founded on Greek materials, yet Catullus has treated the subject in a thoroughly original manner. It is difficult to believe that any translation could produce that impression of genuine creative power, which is forced upon every reader of the Attis. There is nothing at all like the spirit of this poem in extant Greek literature. No other writer has presented so life-like an image of the frantic exultation and fierce self-sacrificing spirit of an inhuman fanaticism; and of the horror and sense of desolation which the natural man, more especially a Greek or Roman, would feel in the midst of the wild and strange scenes described in the poem, when first awaking to the consciousness of his voluntary bondage, and of the forfeiture of his country and parents, and the free social life of former days. A few touches in the poem—as, for instance, the expressions, 'niveis manibus,' 'roseis labellis,' and 'Ego gymnasii fui flos,'—all introduced incidentally,—force upon the mind the contrast between the tender youth and beauty of Attis and the fierce power of the passion that possesses him. The false excitement and noisy tumult of the evening deepen the sense of the terrible reality and blank despair of the morning.

The effect of the whole drama of human passion and agony is intensified by the vividness of all its pictorial environment;—by the vision of the wild surging seas, through which the swift ship and its mad crew were borne, and of the gloom and horror of the woods that hid the sounding rites of the goddess, and the tall columns of her temple. With what a powerful and rapid touch he paints the aspect of sky, earth, and sea in the early morning—

> Sed ubi oris aurei Sol radiantibus oculis
> Lustravit aethera album, sola dura, mare ferum,
> Pepulitque noctis umbras vegetis sonipedibus.

Everything is seen in those sharply-defined forms, which imprint themselves on the brain in moments of intense excitement or agony.

These three poems are composed with the unity and simplicity of the purest art. Like the shorter poems they have taken shape under the influence of one powerful motive; and the feeling with which they were conceived is sustained at its height through the whole composition. It is more difficult to find any single motive which combines into unity the original nucleus of the Epithalamium of Peleus and Thetis with the long episode of the desertion of Ariadne, which interrupts the continuity of the 64th poem. The form of art to which it belongs is the 'Epyllion' or heroic idyl, of which several specimens are found among the poems of Theocritus. This form was due to the invention of the Alexandrians; and Catullus in the selection of his subject and in his manner of treating it takes up the position of an imitator. But there is no reason to suppose that he is reproducing, still less translating, any particular work of these poets, or that his contemporaries—Cinna, Calvus, and Cornificius,—merely reproduced some Alexandrine original in their Zmyrna, Io, and Glaucus. A comparison of the imagery of this poem with that of the earlier Epithalamia, and a consideration of the passionate beauty with which the subject of love and marriage is treated, favour the conclusion that the style and substance of the poem are the workmanship of Catullus. It may be doubted whether any Alexandrine poet, except perhaps Apollonius, whom Catullus in this poem [1] often imitates, but does not translate, had sufficient imagination to produce the original which Catullus is supposed to have copied. But the plan of the poem may have been suggested by some Alexandrine model. The more complicated structure of the 68th poem is fashioned after a particular style of Greek art: and on entering upon a new and larger adventure, Catullus may have trusted to the guidance of those whom he regarded as his masters. The Alexandrians studied pictorial representation of outward scenes and of passionate situations, and works of tapestry on which such representations were wrought were common among their 'deliciae vitae[2].' Thus, the mode in which the story of Ariadne is told is one likely to have occurred to an Alexandrine poet. It would be also in keeping with the over-subtlety of a class of poets who owed more to learning than to inspiration, to combine apparently incongruous parts into one whole by some obscure link of connexion. Thus Catullus may have intended, in imitation of Callimachus or some other Alexandrian, to paint two pictures of the love of an immortal for a mortal,—the love of Thetis for Peleus, and of Bacchus for Ariadne,— and to heighten the effect of each by the contrast presented in the pendent picture. The original good fortune and the unbroken happiness of Peleus are more vividly realised by the contrast presented to the imagination in the betrayal and passionate agitation of Ariadne. The thought of the crowds of mortals and immortals who come together to celebrate the marriage of the Thessalian prince brings into greater relief the utter loneliness of Ariadne, when first discovered by 'Bacchus and his crew.' Or the original unifying motive of both pictures might be sought in the

---

[1] Cf. Mr. Ellis' notes on the poem.
[2] Cf. Plaut. Pseud. 147 :—
   'Neque Alexandrina beluata conchyliata tapetia.'
Mr. Ellis, in his Commentary on Catullus, p. 226, mentions that both the marriage of Peleus and Thetis, and the legend of Ariadne, were common subjects of ancient art. He points out also that the idea of the quilt on which the Ariadne story was represented was borrowed from Apollonius, i. 730-66.

concluding lines, written in a graver tone than anything else in Catullus; and it might be supposed that he intended by the two pictures of divine favour granted to mortals (in one of which retribution is exacted for what he regards as the greatest sin in actual life—a violation of good faith) to enforce the lesson that it is owing to the sins of the latter time that the Gods have withdrawn their gracious presence from the earth. The thought contained in the lines

> Sed postquam tellus scelerest imbuta nefando, etc.,

is pure and noble, and purely and nobly expressed. These lines reveal a genuine and unexpected vein of reverence in the nature of Catullus. The sins which he specifies as alienating the Gods from men are those most rife in his own time, with which he has dealt in a more realistic fashion in his satiric epigrams. All this may, perhaps, be said. But on the other hand, Catullus is the least didactic of poets. He is also the least abstract and reflective. We cannot suppose (in the case of such a writer) all the concrete passionate life of the poem taking shape in his imagination in order to embody any idea however noble. The idea was the afterthought, not the creative germ. Nor can we think that the conception of the whole poem existed in his mind before, or independently of, the separate conception of its parts. He was attracted to both subjects by the charm which the Greek mythology and the bright spectacle of the heroic age had for his imagination, by their harmony with the feelings and passions with which he had most sympathy in real life, and by the scope which they afforded to his peculiar power as a pictorial artist. The device of the tapestry, by which the tale of Ariadne is told, was especially favourable to the exercise of this gift. He looked back upon an ideal vision of the golden morning of the world, when men were so stately and noble, and women so fair and true, that even the blessed Gods and Goddesses deigned to visit them, and to unite with them in marriage. The original motive of the two poems appears to be purely imaginative. If there was any intention to give artificial unity to the poem, by pointing the contrast between a love calm and happy from the beginning, and one at first passionate and afterwards betrayed, or between the holiness and nobleness of an ideal past, and the sin and baseness of the actual present, that intention was probably not present to the mind of the poet when he first contemplated his subject, but came to him in the course of its development.

It may be said, therefore, that if any principle of unity is aimed at in the poem, it is one so artificial as rather to detract from the artistic merit of the composition. There is a similar want of unity in the 'Pastor Aristaeus' of Virgil, which was also composed in the manner of the Alexandrine Epyllion. The Alexandrians seem to have aimed rather at a combination of diverse effects than at a composition 'simplex et unum.' They cared much for the elaboration of details, little for the consistency of the whole. And the same tendency appears in their imitators. Neither can the poem be called a successful specimen of narrative. There is scarcely any story to tell in connexion with the marriage of Peleus. It is a succession of pictures, not a tale of passion or adventure. The romance of Theseus and Ariadne is told much less distinctly and simply than the myth of Orpheus and Eurydice in Virgil. There is dramatic power in the soliloquy of Ariadne, as in that of Attis, but the dramatic faculty in Catullus is rather a phase of his special lyrical gift, which enables him to identify himself with some single passionate situation, than the power of giving life to various types of character. The imaginative excellence of the poem is idyllic rather than epic or dramatic. There is a wonderful harmony of tone in his whole conception of the heroic age. He does not attempt to reproduce the picturesque life represented by Homer, nor the majestic passions imagined by the Attic tragedians, but he has his own vision of the stately and beautiful figures belonging to an ideal foretime,—

> O nimis optato saeclorum tempore nati
> Heroes, saluete, deum genus.

There is a sense of the freshness and brightness of the early morning in his conception of the time when the first ship, manned by the flower of Greek warriors, 'broke the silence of the seas'

> (Illa rudem cursu prima imbuit Amphitriten),

and when the Gods and Goddesses of Olympus, the mysterious Powers over-ruling mortal destiny, and the other beings, half-human, half-divine, whom Greek imagination so lavishly created, appeared in their bodily presence to do honour to the union of a mortal with an immortal. The poem abounds in pictures, or suggestions of pictures, taken from the world of divine and human life, and of outward Nature. Such are those of the Nereids gazing on the Argo—

> Emersere feri candenti e gurgite vultus
> Aequoreae monstrum Nereides admirantes,—

of Ariadne watching with pale and anxious face the perilous encounter of Theseus with the Minotaur—

> Quam tum saepe magis fulgore expalluit auri,—

and again, looking on the distant fleet—

> Saxea ut effigies bacchantis,—

of the advent of Bacchus—

> Cum thiaso Satyrorum et Nysigenis Silenis,—

a passage which has inspired one of the masterpieces of modern art,—of Prometheus—

> Extenuata gerens veteris vestigia poenae,—

of the aged Parcae—

> infirmo quatientes corpora motu—

spinning the thread of human destiny, as with clear-ringing voice they poured forth their truthful prophecy. So too the eye of an artist is shown in the description of the scenes in which the action takes place, and in the illustrative imagery with which the subject is adorned,—as in the pictures from mountain and sea scenery at lines 240 and 269; and in that image of a waste expanse of sea called up in the lines—

> Idomeneosne petam montes? a gurgite lato
> Discernens ponti truculentum ubi dividit aequor?

A genuine love of Nature, which his more personal poems only faintly suggest, appears in the lines describing the gifts which Chiron brought with him from the plains and vast mountain chains and river-banks of Thessaly—

> Nam quoscumque ferunt campi, quos Thessala magnis
> Montibus ora creat, quos propter fluminis undas
> Aura parit flores tepidi fecunda Favoni,
> Hos indistinctis plexos tulit ipse corollis,
> Quo permulsa domus iucundo risit odore[1];

and in the enumeration of the various trees which Peneus, quitting Tempe,—

> Tempe quae silvae cingunt super inpendentes,—

planted before the vestibule of the palace.

The diction and rhythm of the poem are characterised by excellences of a quite different sort from those of his other pieces. Both produce the impression of very careful study and labour. In no previous work of Latin genius was so much use made of an artificial poetical diction. Though this diction has not the naïveté or charm of his simpler pieces, yet it is very effective in its own way. It reveals new and unsuspected wealth in the ore of the Latin language. The old rhetorical artifices of alliteration, assonance, &c. are used more sparingly than in Lucretius, yet they do appear, as in the lines—

> Peliaco quondam prognatae vertice pinus,—
> Aut tereti tenues tinnitus aere ciebant,—
> Putridaque infirmis variabant pectora palmis,—etc., etc.

---

[1] 'Whate'er of loveliest decks the plain, whate'er
The giant mountains of Thessalia bear,
Whate'er beneath the west's warm breezes blow,
Where crystal streams by flowery margents flow,
These in festoons or coronals inwrought
Of undistinguishable blooms he brought,
Whose blending odours crept from room to room,
Till all the house was gladdened with perfume.'—Martin.

As in the Attis we find such word-formations as *sonipedibus, silvicultrix, nemorivagus,* so in this poem we have *fluentisono, raucisonos, clarisona, flexamino,* etc. We recognise his old partiality for diminutives, as in the

> Frigidulos udo singultus ore cientem,

and

> Languidulosque paret tecum coniungere somnos.

But there are many peculiarities of style which are scarcely, if at all, observable in his other poems. New artifices, such as those familiar to the Greek idyl, of the recurring chime of the same or similar words, are frequent, as in the lines—

> Vos ego saepe meo vos carmine compellabo ;—
>   Cui Iupiter ipse
> Ipse suos divom genitor concessit amores ; —
> Sicine me patriis avectam, perfide, ab oris,
> Perfide, deserto liquisti in litore Theseu ?
> Sicine discedens neglecto numine divom ;—
> Nulla fugae ra'io, nulla spes ; omnia muta
> Omnia sunt deserta, ostentant omnia mortem, etc.

The phrases are to a much greater extent cast in a Greek mould[1]. The words follow one another in a less natural order. Ornamental epithets, metaphorical phrases, and the substitution of abstract for concrete words, occur much more frequently. Latin poetry creates for itself an artificial diction by assimilating, to a much greater extent than in any earlier work of genius, the long-accumulated wealth of Greek poetry. This was a gain to its resources, opening up and giving expression to a new range of emotions, but a gain against which must be set off a considerable loss of freshness and naïveté.

The rhythm also is elaborately constructed after a Greek model,—the model, not of Homer, but of the later poets who wrote in his metre. It is much more carefully and correctly finished than the rhythm of Lucretius. Each

---

[1] E.g. 'Argivae robora pubis'—'decus innuptarum'—'funera nec funera,' etc., etc. Mr. Ellis's commentary largely illustrates the influence exercised by the phraseology of the Greek poets,—especially Homer, Euripides, Apollonius—on the poetical diction of Catullus in this poem.

separate line has a smoother cadence. The whole movement is more regular, more calm, and more stately. But with all the occasional roughness of Lucretius there is much more life and force in his general movement. It is much more capable of presenting a continuous thought or action to the mind. The lines of Catullus seem intended to be dwelt on separately, and each to bring out some point of detail. There is generally a pause in the sense at the end of each line, and thus the lines, when read continuously, produce an impression of monotony[1], which is increased by the frequent use of spondaic lines. The uniformity of his pauses, and the sameness of structure in a large number of his hexameters, enable us to appreciate the great improvement in rhythmical art which appeared some ten years later in the Bucolics of Virgil. Yet if Catullus does not, in this his most elaborate work, equal the natural force of language and rhythm displayed in his simpler pieces, the poem, as a whole, has a noble and stately movement, in unison with the noble and stately pictures of an ideal fore-time which it brings before the imagination.

The four longer elegiac pieces which follow add little to our impression of the art of Catullus. In the 'Epistle to Manlius'—perhaps owing to the trouble by which his mind was darkened at the time of its composition—he does not use the elegiac metre, as a vehicle of his personal feelings, with much force or clearness. There is much more than in his phalaecians and iambics the appearance of effort, and there is much greater uncertainty as to his meaning. The 67th poem keeps alive with some vivacity a scandalous story of his native province which might well have been allowed to sink into oblivion. In the 'Coma Berenices,' and the poem addressed to Allius, he again writes under the influence of his Alexandrian masters. He seems to have regarded the 'Carmina Battiadae' with the admiration which youthful genius, not yet sure of its own

---

[1] This monotony, as is pointed out by Mr. Ellis, is, in a great degree, the result of the coincidence of the accent and rhythmical ictus in the last three feet of the line.

powers, entertains for culture and established reputation,—the kind of admiration which led Burns to imagine that his own early inspiration might be of less value to the world than 'Shenstone's art.' Like Burns, too, Catullus is least happy when he gives up his own language, which he wields easily and powerfully, and the forms of art which came naturally to him, in deference to the standard of poetic taste recognised in his day. His selection of the 'Coma Berenices' as a task in translation, illustrates the attraction which the union of beauty and passion with truth and constancy of affection had for his imagination. The poem to Allius is the most artificially constructed of all his pieces. He endeavours to unite in it three distinct threads of interest,—that of his passion for Lesbia, that of the romance of Laodamia and Protesilaus, and that of his brother's death in the Troad. Although this triple combination is accomplished with much mechanical ingenuity[1], yet the effect of the poem as a whole is disappointing, and its motive,—gratitude for a service which no honourable man, according to our modern ideas of honour, would have rendered,—does not make amends for the want of simplicity in its structure. Yet as written in the heyday of his passion for Lesbia, and largely inspired by that passion, it has, along with an Alexandrian superfluity of ornament and illustration, many beauties of expression and feeling. The passionate devotion of Laodamia for Protesilaus is conceived with sympathetic power,—

> Quo tibi tum casu pulcherrima Laudamia,
>   Ereptum est vita dulcius atque anima
> Coniugium[2]—

There is an exquisite picture of his own stolen meetings with his 'candida diva'; and depth and sincerity of affection are purely and simply expressed in the two last lines—

[1] Westphal, pp. 73 83, has given an elaborate explanation of the principle on which the various parts of the poem are arranged and connected with one another.

[2] The lines immediately following these are in the worst style of learned Alexandrinism.

> Et longe ante omnes mihi quae me carior ipso'st
> Lux mea qua viva vivere dulce mihi'st.

In this poem too, although the application of the image is an incongruous adaptation of an old Homeric simile, we meet with a descriptive passage which, more perhaps than any other in his poems, shows that Catullus was a true lover and close observer of Nature,—

> Qualis in aerii perlucens vertice montis
> Rivos muscoso prosilit e lapide
> Qui cum de prona praeceps est valle volutus
> Per medium sensim transit iter populi,
> Dulce viatori lasso in sudore levamen,
> Cum gravis exustos aestus hiulcat agros.[1]

The perfection attained by Catullus in his best lyrical poetry, and the power displayed in his longer pieces, are so high and genuine that we are hardly surprised at the enthusiasm of those who have ranked him, in respect both of art and genius, foremost among Roman poets. If the pure essence of poetry could be separated from the whole spiritual and intellectual being of the poet, much might be said in favour of that estimate. Others, who think that the work accomplished by Lucretius, Virgil, and Horace is, both in quantity and quality, of more lasting value to the world, cannot forget that had they died at the same early age as Catullus, their names would have been unknown, or perhaps remembered as those of Cinna and Cornificius are now. From the exquisite skill with which Catullus has treated light and playful themes, he has been sometimes compared to modern poets who have no other claim to recognition than a similar facility. But if he is to be compared with any, it is not with the minor poets, ancient or modern, but with the greater, that he is to be ranked. The two eminent English scholars who have made a

---

[1] 'As some clear stream, from mossy stone that leaps,
    Far up among the hills, and, wimpling down
  By wood and vale, its onward current keeps
    To lonely hamlet and to stirring town,
  Cheering the wayworn traveller as it flows
    When all the fields with drought are parched and bare.'
                                                    Martin.

special study of this poet, and have done more than almost any others in recent times to elucidate his meaning and gain for him his just recognition, look upon him as the equal of Sappho and Alcaeus. Among modern poets he has been compared to one, most unlike him in all the outward conditions of his life, and in many of the conditions of his art,—the poet Burns[1]. In general intellectual power, in the breadth of his human sympathies, the modern poet is much the greater. He is, in all ways, the larger man. But in some endowments of heart and genius the ancient poet is far from being the inferior. He was more fortunate in his nearness to the greatest source of poetic culture, and in the use of a medium of expression, not of a local and limited influence, but one which brings him into immediate relation with educated men of all ages and countries. But in the passionate ardour of their temperament, and the robustness, too closely allied with coarseness, of their fibre; in their susceptibility to beautiful and tender emotions, and the mobility of nature with which they yielded to impulses the most opposite to these; in their large capacity of love and scorn, of pleasure and pain; in their genuine sincerity and firm hold on real life; in the keenness of their satire, and their shrewd observation of the world around them;—in their simple and direct force of feeling and expression; in the freshness of their love for the fairer objects in Nature with which they were most familiar,—they have much in common. The resemblance of the concluding lines of the 'Final renunciation of Lesbia' to the sentiment of the 'Daisy' has been already noticed. The scornful advice, conveyed in the words 'pete nobiles amicos' finds many an echo in the tones of the modern poet. The art of both is so inseparably associated with their lives, that our admiration of it can hardly help being enhanced or qualified by personal sympathy with, or dislike of their characters. In the case of Catullus it must be

[1] This parallel was first pointed out by the writer of an excellent article on Catullus in the North British Review, referred to by Mr. Munro in his 'Criticisms and Elucidations,' p. 234.

allowed that if a careless pursuit of pleasure, an apparent absence of all high aims in life, the too frequent indulgence in the coarsest language and the vilest imputations, could alienate our affections from a great poet, his art would be judged at a disadvantage. But his own frank revelations, from which we learn his faults, must equally be taken as the unintended evidence of his nobler and more generous nature. If his passions led him too far astray, he himself, so far as now appears, alone suffered from them. There is no trace in him of the selfish calculation, or the baser falsehood, which renders 'the life of pleasure,' as led by many men, detestable. There was in his case no 'hardening of all within' as its effect. The small volume bequeathed by him to the world is in itself a sufficient result of his few years. If he is in a great degree unreflective, if he does not consciously realise what are the ends of life, yet he does not look on life in a spirit of cynicism or frivolity. Whatever vein of reflection appears in him is not devoid of reverence and seriousness. His too frequent coarseness is to be explained by the manners of his age and race; and the imputations which he makes on his enemies were, in all probability, never meant to be taken seriously. Although unfortunate in his love, he has shown a capacity of ardent, self-forgetful, and constant devotion, that deserved a better object. He could care for another more than for his own life and happiness. And he had, in a degree rarely equalled, a virtue which devoted lovers often want, the truest, kindliest, most considerate and appreciative affection for many friends. His very dependence on their sympathy in all his joy and sorrow is a claim on the sympathy of the world. If to love warmly, constantly, and unselfishly be the best title to the love of others, few poets, in any age or country, deserve a kindlier place in the hearts of men than 'the young Catullus.'

www.ingramcontent.com/pod-product-compliance
Lightning Source LLC
Chambersburg PA
CBHW022114300426
44117CB00007B/702